Profiles in Polo

Also by Horace A. Laffaye
and from McFarland

The Polo Encyclopedia, 2d ed. (2015)
Polo in Argentina: A History (2014)
Polo in Britain: A History (2012)
Polo in the United States: A History (2011)
The Evolution of Polo (2009)

Profiles in Polo

The Players Who Changed the Game

Edited by Horace A. Laffaye

Foreword by
H.R.H. The Prince of Wales

McFarland & Company, Inc., Publishers
Jefferson, North Carolina

The present work is a reprint of the illustrated case bound edition of Profiles in Polo: The Players Who Changed the Game, *first published in 2007 by McFarland.*

LIBRARY OF CONGRESS CATALOGUING-IN-PUBLICATION DATA

Profiles in polo : the players who changed the game /
edited by Horace A. Laffaye ; foreword by H.R.H. the Prince of Wales
p. cm.
Includes bibliographical references and index.

ISBN 978-1-4766-6273-2 (softcover : acid free paper) ♾
ISBN 978-1-4766-0518-0 (ebook)

1. Polo players—Biography. I. Laffaye, Horace A., 1935– .
GV1010.3P77 2015 796.35'3092—dc22 2007018919

BRITISH LIBRARY CATALOGUING DATA ARE AVAILABLE

Front cover: *from top left*, Tommy Pope, age 54; Sinclair Hill, Ambersham ground, Cowdray Park, ca. 1960; Joe Barry and Alabama at the 1979 World Cup, Palm Beach; Juancarlitos Harriott, the best player ever in the opinion of many; polo game (© 2006 Ingram Publishing)

Printed in the United States of America

McFarland & Company, Inc., Publishers
Box 611, Jefferson, North Carolina 28640
www.mcfarlandpub.com

Acknowledgments

This book has been written thanks to Chris Ashton. It was his suggestion that persuaded me to call upon recognized experts to assemble this collection of profiles.

The contributors are all members of a dream team. Their individual biographical sketches appear at the end of the book; my personal gratitude to each one is recorded here at the beginning. They all lead busy lives and I am keenly aware of the demands I have made upon their time. Their unswerving commitment to a quality publication is deeply appreciated.

Nigel à Brassard wishes to thank a number of people, far too many to mention in full, but in particular: Gwen Rizzo, editor of *Polo Players Edition* magazine, for going through the magazine's archives to help him with his research; Robert ffrench-Blake, the Prince of Wales's polo manager, for all his helpful advice and suggestions; Lord Patrick Beresford, Alex Ebeid, Christopher Hanbury, Julian Hipwood, David Jamison, Alan Kent, Urs Schwarzenbach and Mark Vestey, for all the recollections and anecdotes about the game's great players that they shared with him; Memo Gracida, for all the time and patience he showed when Nigel interviewed him; David Woodd, chief executive of the Hurlingham Polo Association, for all the helpful suggestions and for allowing him unrestricted access to the H.P.A. records.

Dennis Amato would like to extend his sincerest thanks and heartfelt appreciation to the late Philip Iglehart, who between 1984 and 1992, through more than 150 letters, innumerable telephone conversations and several visits, provided him with a wealth of information on the history of American polo, particularly on Long Island during the interwar and immediate postwar years. Also, special recognition is owed to the late "Doc" Steve Roberts and the late Tommy Glynn for educating him on intercollegiate polo.

Sebastián Amaya wishes to express his gratitude for the opportunity to write a profile on Adolfo Cambiaso, and his thanks to Adolfo himself, whose trust and generous offer of biographical data are much appreciated. His thanks go also to Ernesto Trotz, who through his personal knowledge graciously shared his insights into Adolfo's personality traits and thought processes.

Chris Ashton is grateful to all those who assisted him in compiling the six profiles written for this book; in particular, to the late Bob Ashton, author of the unpublished memoir of the Ashton brothers' polo career, and to Chris's cousins James Ashton and Rosemary Foot, children of Jim Ashton; to Sinclair Hill, not only for the story of his own life, but for his memories and the pictures he supplied of Hanut Singh; to Jim Gilmore, Ellerston Polo Club manager, for his reflections on Kerry Packer; and to Glen Holden, former chairman of the Federation of International Polo, for his thoughts about his friend the late Bob Skene.

Yolanda Carslaw would like to thank the staff at the H.P.A., especially David Woodd and Millie Scott, and *Horse and Hound* magazine, for allowing her access to their archives; Claire Tomlinson's nephews, Will and James Lucas, and their mother Ann, for insights into the Lucas family; her father, Kay Carslaw, for fact checking and proofreading; Simon Tomlinson and Liz Bradshaw—Claire's P.A.—at Beaufort Polo Club, for providing graphic material and information; and Jorge MacDonough, David Morley, Peter Sidebottom, Milo Fernández Araujo, Luke Tomlinson, Lavinia Black, David Jamison and Paul Withers for offering much firsthand information and many anecdotes.

Roger Chatterton-Newman would like to thank the following for their enormous help and encouragement: Graham Dennis, of the celebrated Blacklock's Bookshop; Angela Tarnowski, of the 9th/12th Lancers Museum, Derby; John and Anthony Traill and the late Corona Norty, who not only created one of the finest gardens in Ireland but stimulated his interest in her kinsman, the "Great" John Watson.

Sarah Eakin would like to thank Julian Hipwood, a great friend, for sharing his life story with her. Terry Hanlon was also a willing subject and her thanks go to him as well as to her father, Bernard Dukes, as always, there to help when needed.

Susan Reeve wishes to thank Alex McDonald and the Chaplin family for sharing their reminiscences of Tommy Pope.

Peter J. Rizzo would like to thank John Oxley and his wife, Mary Oxley, and sons Tom and Jack Oxley, as well as the Oxley Foundation, for their contributions to the sport.

As editor, I wish to express my gratitude to H.R.H. Prince Charles, the Prince of Wales, for so graciously contributing the foreword to this book. It is an honor to recognize his involvement.

Francisco Dorignac, Juan Carlos Harriott, Alberto Pedro Heguy and Marcos Uranga gave generously of their time in helping complete their individual profiles. Tatiana Aguerre, Enrique Braun Estrugamou, Margie Brett, Gastón Dorignac, David Miles, Paul Pieres and Paul Withers offered firsthand insights on some of the featured personalities. Lewis Lacey's children, Ann, Nigel and Tony, examined their father's manuscript and corrected factual errors.

I am particularly indebted to George DuPont and Brenda Lynn, who have gone far in making me feel at home during my frequent visits to the Museum of Polo. The museum not only houses a comprehensive library, but also provides an atmosphere that exudes a fine feel for the game's history and traditions.

I also wish to thank Marge Hickey, who made the transition from editing surgical papers to polo matters without a blink of her eye. Her education at an Irish nuns' school has proved invaluable in "translating" into American profiles bearing shades of South African terms, Australian modisms, Queen's English and Spanglish lingo.

The continuing and valuable advice and counsel of Chris, Dennis, Nigel and Roger must be mentioned, because their contribution to the total project extended considerably beyond the individual essays that bear their names as author.

As always, my children, Patrick and Gisèle, provided support in many ways, including much needed help in computer matters. And, finally, my thanks go to my wife, Martha, whose support during the months it took me to compile this book is only the tip of the iceberg.

Table of Contents

PART V. THE GREAT CONTEMPORARIES

CLARENCE HOUSE

As someone who has enjoyed playing polo for over forty years, I am delighted to be able to contribute a foreword to this book of profiles of some of the great players who have changed or influenced the game.

My family seem to have been involved with polo since its introduction into Britain in the mid nineteenth century. My great great uncle, The Duke of Connaught, my great grandfather, King George V and his brother, The Duke of Clarence, were amongst some of the early players of the game in this country. My grandfather, King George VI and his three brothers were all devoted to polo. My father gave me one of his old ponies when I was a teenager and gave me much instruction at the start. And then my great uncle, Lord Mountbatten, took a great deal of interest in the improvement of my game. Being able to play with both my sons has given me more pleasure than I can say, even if they may not have paid a great deal of attention to my attempts at tuition!

During the years I was lucky enough to play polo I had the great pleasure and privilege of playing with, and learning from, many of those profiled in this book. The most memorable, I think, was Sinclair Hill whose energetic coaching inspired me enormously. His strictures on the importance of practicing on the wooden horse will never be forgotten – nor will those sessions with stick and ball when he had me going round and round executing one nearside backhander cut shot after another. But, above all, I shall always remember that familiar voice repeating over and over again – "the faster you go, the slower the swing!"

Polo today is certainly a changed game from when I first started. Nevertheless it remains the most unique and wonderful team game which has challenged and inspired so many players from around the world. I am sure this book will become compulsive reading for those aspiring to emulate the achievements of those great players profiled in this book.

Charles

Preface

We are proud to present a collection of polo player profiles. It is a book for enthusiasts of the game, whether they are well acquainted with its history and traditions or perhaps just venturing for the first time along an unknown trail. The intent is to depict the players as people, allowing as much emphasis on their family backgrounds as on their accomplishments and personal traits.

Great polo players seldom have been the subjects of biographical endeavors in the English language; Tommy Hitchcock, Hanut Singh and Cecil Smith are the exceptions. About 1930, Alphons Stock published a large volume containing one or two pages of individual sketches, accompanied by one formal photograph of each individual. As to autobiographies, Carlton Beal's *Into Polo*, Brigadier Jack Gannon's *Before the Colours Fade*, Foxhall Keene's *Full Tilt* and Colonel T.P. Melvill's *Ponies and Women* are the ones that come to mind. To that short list can be added the memoirs written by Seymour Knox Jr. and his son Northrup about their polo travels. It is to fill this great void in polo's literature that this collection of essays was created.

The selection criteria for the thirty-four subjects were primarily based upon the subjects' impact on the game, rather than their prowess as players. The history of polo counts more than ninety players—depending upon which list you consult—who reached the magical 10-goal handicap rating, while the nine- and eight-goal players number in the hundreds. Nevertheless, only a few significantly changed the way polo was played in their times.

The arrangement of the profiles presented some difficulty, but eventually it was found best to present the essays in chronological order, under the headings "The Pioneers," "Between the Wars," "The Superstars," "Shakers and Movers," and "The Great Contemporaries." Each of these parts is preceded by an introduction that should make the individual profiles more sequent and easier to place in the general scheme of the game's development. With ten writers contributing profiles, there was no question of trying to achieve consistency of style. Furthermore, the profiles are of uneven length, the reason being the widely different amount of time each subject dedicated to the game during his own life.

Among "The Pioneers," thank Captain Edward Hartopp and John Watson, who drafted the initial rules of the game; Francis Herbert, who was the founder of the first club in Britain; and Colonel Thomas St. Quintin, who carried the gospel far and wide. They, along with other founding fathers, initiated respect for an organized pastime, with laws, customs and traditions that have lasted into our days. Foxhall Keene was a multidimensional superstar, the first 10-goaler in the world. At the end of this epoch, Harry Payne Whitney brought into the game standards in preparation and organization probably dreamed of, but unknown till then.

The years spanning the two world wars have been characterized as the golden era of polo, thus, "Between the Wars." It was undoubtedly so in America. Devereux Milburn — a member of the immortal "Big Four" — is a prime exponent of the unquestionable American primacy in that period. Earl Mountbatten earned his place mainly as the author of *An Introduction to Polo*, a treatise still in print some seventy-five years after initial publication. Hanut Singh exemplified Indian polo at its best. Canadian-born Lewis Lacey, Irishman Johnny Traill, Tommy Pope from South Africa, and Australian James Ashton complete the selection for that time span, reflecting the increased development of the game in the British Commonwealth and in Argentina, sometimes referred to as the "sixth dominion" because of the tremendous English influence upon that country's economy.

Thomas Hitchcock and Cecil Smith also achieved fame and glory during the peacetime period. However, their superior qualities as players merit their inclusion within "The Superstars." The same qualifications can be said about Stewart Iglehart. The rise of Argentina as a polo power is best exemplified by the charismatic and at the same time egocentric personality of Carlos Menditeguy. Then we present Juan Carlos Harriott Jr., the aristocrat of polo because of his impeccable style and civility in playing superbly at home and abroad, in the eyes of many the greatest player ever to grace a polo ground. Fittingly, next to him is Francisco Dorignac. Franky and Juancarlitos skippered the legendary clubs Santa Ana and Coronel Suárez for more than twenty years, enduring terrific duels for supremacy at Tortugas, Hurlingham and Palermo. Two Australians fill out the rest of the slots. One is the celebrated Charles Robertson Skene, a 10-goal handicap wherever he played, and the other the gifted and controversial Sinclair Hill, the most influential player to emerge from the Antipodes and the best after Bob Skene.

"Shakers and Movers" are those individuals who by sheer dedication and strong personality made a remarkable impact upon the game. In the aftermath of the Second World War, Britain was exhausted and polo was no more than a distant glory. It was the unshakable faith and financial support of Lord Cowdray that allowed England to resume the game, even in precarious circumstances. Many helped, but without his personal commitment, polo in England might not have survived. The war also impacted the scope of polo in America; several years went by before the level of play reached pre-World War II standards. John Oxley, as a club proprietor and team sponsor, is a shining light in that era. More than most, South African Michael Rattray kept his country in the international picture, against heavy odds. Marcos Uranga was the prime mover behind the enterprise that crystallized the Federation of International Polo as a leadership entity, the "United Nations of polo." In Britain, Claire Tomlinson, perhaps the best female player ever, deserves a place because of her successful struggle to allow women their rightful place in the limelight of high-goal polo. We complete the section with an essay on the recently deceased Kerry Packer, whose largesse changed the game forever.

Lastly, we present "The Great Contemporaries." We open the scene with the Prince of Wales, who, besides achieving a respectable handicap in spite of overwhelming demands on his time, is the most recognizable figure in the world of polo. Then we have Alberto Heguy, who brought a new dimension to the most difficult position to excel at on the field, that of number 1. His grand adversary in international contests was Harold Barry, a figure of high repute on the American scene. We then introduce Gonzalo Pieres, who set a pattern of professionalism in polo, his own an attribute still unmatched in the overall scheme of the game. We include Julian Hipwood, England's captain for twenty years, as a way of redressing the great injustice committed in not awarding him the accolade of the maximum handicap. Mexican-born U.S. citizen Memo Gracida Jr. has dominated polo in America like no other contemporary player. And closing the list is Adolfo Cambiaso, still at the top of his game and facing such a promising future that no one can predict how high it may take him among this galaxy of players.

It has been my privilege to have met and gotten to know — some barely, others quite well — about half of the personalities depicted in the profiles. To my mind, the most prominent characteristics shared by all are pride of performance and total dedication to victory. Every one has been a fervent student and practitioner of the game of polo, from both individual and team angles, and they all achieved greatness in their chosen endeavor. We hope that most of the names mentioned in this book will open the floodgates of cherished memories.

As editor, I am aware of the controversies this selection will raise. Critics in the U.S. might question the absence of stalwarts such as Red Armour, Chico and Roy Barry, Alan Corey, Tim Gannon, John Goodman, Winston Guest, Henry Herbert, Glen Holden, Doc Linfoot, George Oliver, Eric Pedley, Pad Rumsey, Larry and Monty Waterbury, Tommy Wayman and Watson Webb.

Australians will express amazement that Glen Gilmore, the Manifold brothers, Ken Telford and Richard Walker were not included. Britons will raise eyebrows when noticing the omission of other members of the Royal Family, and legends such as Gerald Balding, Walter Buckmaster, Leslie Cheape, Howard Hipwood, the Miller brothers, Paul Withers and Lord Wodehouse, and the Irish contingent those of Rattle Barrett, the Beresfords, John Hardress Lloyd, Pat Roark and Austen Rotheram.

Indians will sigh after looking in vain for the hallowed names of the Maharajas of Bhopal and Jaipur, the 10-goal players Jagindar Singh and Jaswant Singh and, most notably, Shah Mirza Beg. Mexicans will clamor for the five Gracida Hoffman brothers, the brilliant Carlos, nephew and son, and Chamaco Herrera. New Zealanders might wonder at the unexplained omission of their own 10-goalers — Gould, Lyons, Mackenzie, Orbell and Peake — as well as those of Cody Forsyth, Peter Grace, Stuart Mackenzie, John Walker and Hamish Wilson. And South Africans will surely rue for Punch Barlow, Hugh Brown, Buddy Chaplin, the Goodman twins and the Watson brothers.

Argentines will scream aloud the names of the Alberdi brothers, Quito and Bebé; Manuel Andrada, Roberto Cavanagh, Gastón Dorignac, Luis and Heriberto Duggan, Daniel González, other members of the Heguy clan, the Merlos brothers, David and Juan Miles, Eduardo Moore, the Novillo Astradas, Alfonso, Facundo and Gonzalito Pieres, Jack Nelson, Hugh Scott Robson, Gonzalo Tanoira, Joe Traill and Ernesto Trotz.

Regrettably, some countries lack player representation in this book. Aficionados in Spain will moan when noticing the absence of their best player, Alvaro de Villabrágima, the rest of the Olympic silver medalists — Duque de Alba, his brother Duque de Peñaranda, and Conde de la Maza — the pioneer Escandón siblings, and recent figures such as the Domecqs, the Echevarrietas and the Moras. Belgium will miss that great supporter of the game, Alfred Grisar, and Baron Gastón de Peers, the only Belgian to have his name engraved on the Argentine Open Championship trophy. Their southern neighbors probably will fail to understand why Maurice Raoul-Duval, war hero and top player, is not mentioned. And what about Jean-Luc Chartier, Patrick Guerrand-Hermès, the Macaire family, Baron Jacques de Nervo, Hubert Perrodo, Baron Elie de Rothschild and Guy Wildenstein, all of whom did so much for French polo?

Other South Americans might find cause for gripe. Chile had a gentleman-player in the person of Alfonso Chadwick Errázuriz, and later stars such as Gabriel and José Donoso, Max Errázuriz, Jaime García Huidobro and José Antonio Iturrate, who travel the world showing the colors. Uruguay misses its own David Stirling, who played off 10-goals in his country, and Brazilians will lament the absence of Alcides Diniz, his nephews André and Fábio, the Junqueiras, Ronaldo Xavier de Lima, Silvio Novaes, the Souza Aranhas and the group of young players who have been so successful in F.I.P.'s World Championships.

And finally, north of us, Canadian supporters will rumble that gentlemen like Fred Mannix, Michael Sifton, Frank Vlahovic and Galen Weston, who have made enormous contributions to the game in their own country, were overlooked.

It is inevitable that admirers of other neglected players will criticize my choice of personalities selected for inclusion in this book. If it is any satisfaction, I am keenly aware of the lack of recognition to several worthy candidates. Innumerable times during the selection process, the thought came to mind: "How can I leave out _____?" (Fill-in the blank.) But in the final analysis, I asked myself the question: "Are there any individuals on this list who do not belong?" The answer is an emphatic *no*.

The contributors have been given a free rein to manifest their own opinions and if at times it may appear that they have taken the bit between their teeth, each essay is the result of long study and serious consideration of the available information, delivered in an objective, yet pleasant manner. In every instance the living players have been interviewed by each author and in many cases close relatives have been consulted regarding facts and personal reminiscences.

During the course of my research it became obvious that the road to develop and change the game was constructed by individuals rather than by institutions. Legends, icons, immortals, these thirty-three men and one woman changed polo as it was played in their time. Each one, in his or her own way, helped to improve the game. Many obstacles have marked the progress of the game of polo through war and peace, prosperity and recession, good breaks and bad luck. But always it was individuals propelling its progress that stood out. They surface, some from the past, others in the present, as remarkable people — often courageous, sometimes flawed, always fascinating — whose stories deserve to be told.

Horace A. Laffaye
Spring 2007

Part I

The Pioneers

Introduction

The development of modern polo began in Manipur, a remote mountain area tucked between India and Myanmar. Lt. Joseph Ford Sherer—called by some "Father of Modern Polo"—aide to the assistant commissioner in Silchar, district of Cachar, saw the game and, like countless others ever since, was smitten. Soon after, Silchar, the first polo club in the world, was formed at a meeting of tea planters at the bungalow of the assistant commissioner, Capt. Robert Stewart. The first written rules of the game were then drafted by an unknown hand and they make for amusing reading. The most illuminating is the ninth:

> *Any player may interpose his horse before his antagonist so as to prevent his antagonist from reaching the ball, whether in full career or at a slow pace; and this despite the immediate neighbourhood of the ball.*

One must wonder what had to have been the nature of the game's pace when players were allowed to place their mounts across an opponent's pony. The cardinal principle of the laws of polo is the "right of way," and, because of safety concerns for mount and man, players and umpires are admonished to strictly adhere to this rule.

Other unusual components included permission to catch the ball and then hit it unimpeded by the opposing players, a practice perhaps taken from the ancient Gaelic game of hurling. The prescient authors mandated that no dogs or cattle be allowed on the ground; a vivid picture remains of the chaos created by a runaway terrier during the finals of the 2006 U.S. Open Championship.

Like a contagious plague, polo spread around the Indian subcontinent, then to Britain, and in turn to the Americas, Australasia, Africa and continental Europe. It was the British who carried the flag: settlers in Argentina, retired officers in North America, vacationers to France, the Royal Navy to New Zealand, and the army—curiously enough the infantry—in South Africa. The newspaper tycoon James Gordon Bennett is credited with bringing the game to the United States, and one of the founding fathers, the rotund Col. Thomas St. Quintin, to Australia.

Rules of the game were unknown or nonexistent. A letter from Argentina to the editor of *The Field* in London asking for an explanation of the laws of "hockey on horseback" resulted in spirited discussion from readers as far away as India, because even in that country the ground's dimensions and the number of players showed significant variations. Local codes predominated; the Indian Polo Association eventually adopted the Bombay Code. Parenthetically, today there are four different codes: the Argentine, the United States Polo Association's, Hurlingham's, and that of the Federation of International Polo.

The number of players also varied; usually there were six-a-side — with one acting as goal-keeper — but eight was not uncommon. As the game progressed from scrimmage to gallop, the number of players decreased to five and finally to the current quartette. Polo being popular among the cavalry regiments in India, the commander-in-chief, Gen. Frederick Roberts, took special interest in the game and asked Capt. John Watson to draft a set of laws. The future Lord Roberts was also concerned about the increasing number of injuries— some fatal — among his officers, and he thereby mandated that all players must wear a protective helmet. This safety item's design is credited to Gerald Hardy, who achieved fame as a member of John Watson's Freebooters team. The story is told that Edward Bowen, a player on the Inniskilling Dragoons team, went to the manufacturer, Barnard's, to tell the proprietor he was wearing one of his helmets and had a fall that gave him a concussion. Mr. Walter Barnard asked for his account to be brought, and "gravely scratched out the charge for it. Thereupon Bowen, quite as gravely, said: 'Yes, and if I had not been wearing it I should have been killed.'"

The question of umpiring was also uncertain at times. Silchar's 1863 code mentions umpires, but it allowed bystanders to throw-in the ball. Doubtful points were sometimes decided by mutual agreement or reserved for decision by a friendly arbiter.

The backhand stroke pioneered by John Watson was considered illegal in America; at Newport, Rhode Island, any player guilty of such disloyal practice was liable to be dismissed from the field of play. At the first international match in 1886, Watson — John Watson again — demonstrated the tactical advantage of the backhander and the Americans promptly became converts.

The former colonists remained adamant in the matter of infringements as they relate to scoring. While the Hurlingham rules called for a free hit after a foul, in America, half-a-goal was deleted from the offending side's tally. Likewise, in the case of a defender hitting the ball behind his own back line, one-quarter goal was taken away in America; in England, the more lenient rule allowed the defending side to hit-in from the center of the goal line. All this came to end before the 1921 Westchester Cup series and some sense of uniformity became the norm.

An international set of rules was drafted in 1937 at Lord Mountbatten's urging, but World War II intervened and it came to naught, until the Federation of International Polo issued a pertinent booklet in 1988. Capt. Hartopp wrote the Rules of the Game without being aware of the Silchar code, and John Watson "found it [polo] a virtual free-for-all, and gave it pace, order and science," as so eloquently expressed by Roger Chatterton-Newman in his essay.

Hartopp and Watson were big men, physically and in their contributions to polo. Looking at his regimental group's photographs, Capt. Hartopp towers over his comrades-in-arms and looks disproportionate astride his pony. In the famous painting "The Hurlingham Team Mounted in Front of the Pavilion," by the hand of Henry Jamyn Brooks, which depicts some fifty polo players— of whom all but one have been identified — the undisputed main figure is John Watson on a chestnut pony.

Handicaps

The problem of how to allow teams of dissimilar ability to compete on even terms baffled officials and players during the game's formative years. Without any doubt, the concept goes back to the early days of thoroughbred racing, which allows the perceived slower horse some advantage, usually in the form of carrying lighter weight. The royal and ancient game of golf started the practice of giving strokes as far back as 1842.

The initial attempt at providing equality was provided by the pragmatic British settlers in Argentina, who in the first game at David Anderson's estancia Negrete, in 1876, allowed six players with little or no knowledge of the game to face five more experienced men.

In the early twentieth century the Hurlingham Polo Committee published the *Recent Form List*, an annual tabulation of the best players in the London season. No numerical value was assigned to each individual, but in some selected tournaments not more than two players on the list were allowed on the same team. Absolute credit for the current handicap system goes to Henry Lloyd Herbert, who as sole handicapper in 1888 assigned ratings from zero- to five-goals to active players. When the Polo Association of America was founded in 1890, Herbert expanded the range to 10-goals, and Foxie Keene became the first 10-goaler.

England lagged behind America in this matter, but in 1911 the Hurlingham Polo Committee issued the first handicap list on the British Isles and in April of the same year the Polo Association of the River Plate published its own ratings.

The issue of handicaps has raised more controversy than any other in the world of polo. Vested interests, individual egos and politics, all play a part in the decision making by handicap committees in what is really a subjective evaluation of individual prowess within a team sport. Heated discussions still take place among hero-worshipers as to who should have been a 10-goaler. Equally warm are the arguments put forward by aficionados regarding those players who reached such a lofty pedestal position only because of the confounded handicappers, who should have known better.

A Bumpy Main Street Becomes a Billiards Table–Like Surface

The village's main street or a suitable square was the common ground for a game of polo in Asia. This evolved into more appropriate venues, with clearly marked boundaries and goals. It is to be noted that—as played in Manipur—the entire length of the backlines was considered as the goal.

A glance at the correspondence generated in *The Field*, London's sporting publication, will shed light regarding the polo ground's dimensions at the dawn of modern polo. While reader "Bhal" tells the editor that the dimensions of Hazaribagh's polo grounds are 120 yards long by 50 yards wide, "Musafir" gives them as 400 by 120 yards. The first documented game in Argentina took place on a rectangular field marked by flags 300 by 200 yards apart. The reality was that available terrain dictated the ground's boundaries. One thing that has remained constant has been the width of the goals, eight yards. The stone goalposts on the main square in Isfahan, Iran, which date back to the seventeenth century, show that measurement. Fortunately, the Earl of Harrington came up with the idea of *papier-mâché* goalposts, which probably saved lives and limbs.

In order to prevent the ball to going out of play, wooden boards were designed. Thomas Hitchcock Sr. had low boards placed on the ground at Newport around 1886. The venerable Hurlingham Club in Fulham marked the ground's boundaries with a white wooden fence, an experiment that failed because of the ponies' propensity to jump over them. Guards, as the boards were called at the time, were then installed, it is said to compensate for the Number One ground's pear-like shape. The Argentine Hurlingham Club had its set installed, courtesy of Alexander Drysdale, in 1903.

Unquestionably, the biggest improvement has been in the science of turf management. From grounds on paddocks, racecourses, aerodromes, you name it, we currently enjoy the game on immaculate surfaces, some laser-measured and endowed with sophisticated irrigation systems that match those of the top golf courses.

From Ponies to Horses to Thoroughbreds

The six Manipuri pioneers that traveled to Calcutta in 1864 to participate in the first international game took with them ponies measuring some 11.2 hands (one hand equals four inches). Being quite handy, these ponies run circles around the larger and faster local mounts. The cagey Manipuris also began a tradition: after the matches, they sold their ponies to the locals, presumably for hefty prices.

Maximum height for ponies was established by the Hurlingham Polo Committee—precursor of the H.P.A.—enforced in Britain and India, and progressively raised until abolished before World War I. It was said that the rule was observed more in its breakage than in its compliance. America never subscribed to a height restriction.

Initially the polo pony was no more than a way to take the rider to the ball. But the lessons imparted by the Peat brothers and their Sussex team soon convinced the rest of the polo community that better mounts were not only desirable but essential. In this matter, the game's development has continued uninterruptedly. The Americans, led by Harry Payne Whitney, soon enough came to the conclusion that speed was paramount to achieving success. Speed, then and now, was expensive. Whitney led the way in disbursing great sums of money to purchase the best available mounts, overshadowing previous efforts by Sir Henry de Trafford and Walter Jones, owners of what were considered the best collections of polo ponies around the turn of the century.

From Cricket Ball to Plastic Compound

Edward Hartopp and his fellow 10th (The Prince of Wales's Own) Hussars officers had to do with a cricket ball in their postprandial game of hockey on horseback. The cricket ball, painted white for better visualization, competed with an India rubber ball and with a leather-covered cork ball. Both proved impracticable because they were too light; therefore, wood in the form of willow or bamboo root first, and several types of local trees later, reigned supreme for well over a century. At the regulation weight of 4.25 to 4.75 ounces (120–125 gm) and a diameter not to exceed 3.5 inches (80 mm), nothing is as good as the willow root ball.

Not that the wood ball is problem-free. Weight can be affected by climate: a rainy season may result in larger but lighter roots, which result in less weight and a propensity to change trajectory in mid-air, to the consternation of penalty-shooters.

With the explosion of plastic technology in the 1950s, an experimental plastic polo ball was tried, first gingerly, and with vociferous opposition from old timers. Lower costs, combined with better resistance to deformity, have made the current crop of plastic ball the favorite of polo clubs. Top polo players still show preference for the wooden ball, especially in penalty taking, because of its better flight characteristics.

In spite of some advances, polo-ball technology still lags in comparison to the tremendous improvements made to the golf ball.

International Contests

Morton is a calm and tranquil park near Newport's town center. Mothers keep a vigilant eye on their strollers; old men read their newspapers while basking in the sun; and youngsters cavort on the swings while the more athletically inclined kick a leather ball on the soccer field. Probably no one in the whole place even suspects that it was the venue for the first international polo match between American and British teams. The trophy itself, labeled the International Challenge Cup, later to be known as the Westchester Cup, is a work of art manufactured by Tiffany's. Frank Gray Griswold, who was charged with the task of obtaining an appropriate cup, wrote that he encountered some problems because he wished that the trophy be emblematic of the game, yet the designer had never seen a game of polo and there was no opportunity for him to do so. Examination of the polo players' figures represented on the cup leaves little doubt that they are Capt. John Brocklehurst — later Lord Rankborough — and "Tip" Herbert. They are depicted in the same attitudes as in George Earl's painting, mentioned in Herbert's essay.

British polo's dominance was confirmed time and time again in the few contests at international level. A match against a French team — actually French-American — at Dieppe followed, as well as contests for the Westchester Cup in England in 1900 and 1902. All ended with decisive British wins.

British players received their first lesson in the need for tightening up their game when the Big Four carried off the Westchester Cup in 1909, courtesy of the organizational ability and sound game tactics brought forth by Harry Payne Whitney. The American team successfully defended in 1911 and 1913, only to be beaten at Meadow Brook by the four captains led by the Scot, Leslie St. Clair Cheape, just before the clouds of war began to gather in Europe.

After the Somme, Verdun and Passchendaele, the world would never be the same.

Edward Hartopp: "This must be a good game"

by Roger Chatterton-Newman

Although John Watson has gone down in sporting history as the "father" of British polo, it was not actually he who introduced the game to England. The honors must go to Edward "Chicken" Hartopp, who initiated a scratch match of what was termed "hockey on horseback" in the summer of 1869.

Hartopp read an account of polo in a copy of *The Field* while under canvas with his regiment, the 10th Hussars, at Aldershot Camp in Hampshire.[1] It described a game at Calcutta Polo Club, where the game had been introduced from the little hill state of Manipur in 1863, and Hartopp was smitten.

"By Jove! This must be a good game," he said, reading the account to five or six fellow officers gathered in his tent. One of them, Tommy St. Quintin, a future major general and pioneer of Australian polo, recalled in later years in his memoirs how "We then and there sent for our chargers, and routed up some old heavy walking sticks and a cricket ball, and began to try to knock the ball about. A somewhat difficult thing to do ... on a tall horse with a short stick.... However, it appealed much to us, and resulted in us improvising a sort of long-handled mallet and having some wooden balls turned about the size of a cricket ball."[2]

It is amusing that one of the myths of modern polo is that those Aldershot pioneers used a billiard ball—obviously a task even more difficult than pursuing a cricket ball with conventional walking sticks. The truth, however, could have been discovered by anyone reading a copy of St. Quintin's highly enjoyable memoirs, published six years before his death. A further myth, that "polo" is derived from *pulu,* supposedly Tibetan for "willow," can also be dismissed. St. Quintin states categorically that the word comes from Tibetan for ball, coincidentally fashioned from willow root. Calcutta used bamboo root.

That scratch game at Aldershot means that the garrison town, the road signs of which proclaim it the "Home of the British Army," can lay claim to being the home, or at least the natal place, of British polo. Indeed, Aldershot Polo Club flourished from 1885 until the early 1960s, and the original polo field can still be seen, although it is uncertain if this was the exact site of Hartopp's tentative knockabout.

Although *The Field* correspondent provided a fair description of the game and its accoutrements, it must be remembered that neither Hartopp nor any of his friends had at the time seen a game in action. In due course, they were to be posted to India and to play polo, but for now it was a case of trial and error. Ironically, a detachment of the 10th Hussars are credited with the first game in Ireland, where it was known as "hurling on horseback," a year before Hartopp's experiment.

They had sailed from India directly to Ireland, where a match was got up between officers and locals at Rathbane, then a country district outside the city of Limerick, in the summer of 1868. Of this, Hartopp seems to have been unaware, although he was later to play a lively role in Irish polo. Having organized a public match in England against the 9th Lancers on Hounslow Heath—the year is, perversely, uncertain: it could have been later in 1869 or as late as 1871—he masterminded another on Gormanston Strand, County Meath, again between soldiers and civilians.

It was from Ireland, too, that Hartopp had acquired a string of ponies, army chargers having proved impracticable. He insisted on ponies under 14 hands—Calcutta Polo Club's average mount seems to have been 11.5 hands, unthinkable to today's players. Anything taller than 14 hands was prohibited until 1895, when the height was raised to 14.2, measurement finally being abolished after the Great War, in which so many polo ponies died.

The Hounslow Heath match, which saw a 3–2 victory for the 10th Hussars, lasted for ninety minutes, with a ten-minute break at halftime. There were eight players a side and, as St. Quintin recalled, the game soon degenerated into a regular scrimmage, only the two goalkeepers remaining in their respective places.

"We played without any rules—just think of it," said St. Quintin, which was understandable, as *The Field* had been vague on just how polo was regulated. It must have been very soon afterwards that Hartopp drew up a brief set of rules, on Mess notepaper. They were the first such rules in the western world, and formed a foundation on which John Watson was later to build:

- A game of polo is to consist of not more than twelve players, six on each side; a match not more than ten players, viz. five on each side.
- The goals to be 300 yards apart, when the ground will admit of such length, and the boundary flags from 150 to 200 yards apart.
- The goal posts to be eight yards apart.
- All sticks and balls to be approved by the committee.
- A ball to be thrown up in the centre of the ground, one player of either side galloping from a point agreed on.
- When the ball is hit out of bounds it must be thrown into the playing ground by an impartial person on foot.
- No player is allowed to hit an adversary's pony. It is permitted to crook an adversary's stick, but on no account is the player allowed to put his stick over the body of his adversary's pony.
- No player having gone through the bully [scrimmage] and lost possession of the ball, and finding himself between the bully and his adversary's ball, is permitted to hit the ball until he has at least one player, exclusive of the goalkeeper, between him and the hostile goal.
- In all matches, each side shall provide an umpire who, on detecting any irregularity or infringements of the rules, shall be empowered to suspend the game until the irregularity has been corrected.

Around 1873, Hartopp was a founding member of Royal Lillie Bridge Polo, which seems to have been a precursor of Hurlingham as London's first polo club.[3] Set off Brompton Road, Fulham, within a stone's throw of West Brompton Cemetery, the club did not have a long lifespan, perhaps because the ground was only two hundred yards long and was not in a particularly fashionable part of the capital.

An article on Hartopp appeared in *Baily's* magazine shortly before his death, recalling him as "an accomplished player, and that despite a height and weight that at first sight would not seem in his favour."[4]

> Yet those of us who have seen him play at the club at Lillie Bridge, which he established on his return from India with his friend Captain Macqueen, can bear testimony to his skill and the rapidity of his movements, though the sight of such a large man as "the Chicken" (a sobriquet he gained soon after he entered the service) on a small pony had something of the ludicrous. There was another tall man, however, and equally good player, to keep him company, the present Marquess of Worcester, and to see those two opponents in a brisk rally was exciting.

Edward Hartopp was born in 1845, the younger son of Edward Bouchier Hartopp M.P., of Little Dalby Hall, south of Melton Mowbray in Leicestershire. The Hartopps were an ancient Leicestershire family, the senior branch of which first received a baronetcy in 1619. Chicken's branch had been settled at Little Dalby Hall—still standing, although somewhat reduced in size since his day—from the 1580s.

Little Dalby was in Quorn country and from an early age Hartopp followed the Quorn and the neighboring Cottesmore. He was a fearless horseman; indeed his old friend, the Irish raconteur Derry, 5th Lord Rossmore, remembered him as a daring, all-round sportsman.[5] Hartopp was popular with the country people around Little Dalby, as a pugilist, singer of songs at village concerts and, rather more alarmingly, as a dynamiter. He was, it seems, forever "blowing up bits of Leicestershire," according to one contemporary. As *Baily's* recalled, after Hartopp's leaving the Army in 1876 he also devoted much of his leisure time to coaching, and for two seasons horsed and drove the Ranelagh coach to Hurlingham and Ranelagh clubs.[6]

The truly elegant Victorian polo player does not look at the camera. Perhaps Capt. Hartopp's facial features earned him the nickname "Chicken" from his fellow officers. Photograph taken circa 1880 (courtesy Museum of Polo and Hall of Fame).

Lord Rossmore's sister, Katherine, married Major Henry "Sugar" Candy of Somerby Grove, Rutland, in 1870. Candy was a great friend of Hartopp, and it was partly through this connection that Hartopp came to spend as much time as possible in Ireland, eventually owning nearly two and a half thousand acres in County Cork.[7]

Chicken was very fond of Ireland, recalled his friend, "and I think he used to pose as being Irish. He had a servant whose religious views were rather a mystery, and Chicken could never find out whether the man was a Protestant or a Catholic; all he knew was that his servant attended divine service somewhere. At last Chicken made up his mind to find out, so he applied aniseed to the soles of the man's boots, and put the hounds on his trail, with the result that they ran him to earth in the Roman Catholic chapel when Mass was in full swing.[8]

For several seasons, Hartopp had taken Kilkarne House, near Navan, where he entertained in lavish style. He hunted in Ireland with the Ward Union—the immortal "Staggers"—and the Meath, whose Master was John Watson, and in 1880 he accepted mastership of the Kilkenny Hounds, in a good ditch, bank and wall country first hunted by the Power family, of whiskey fame, in 1797.

His mastership coincided with the troubled Land League times in Ireland, when hunting was often disrupted, hounds poisoned and horses maimed. But Hartopp was as popular in Ireland as elsewhere and boycotting him would have been useless.

Alas, his reign was to be brief. He died, unmarried, at the Sackville Street Club, Dublin, on 7 September 1882, shortly before his thirty-seventh birthday. Lord Rossmore compared his sad and lonely end with that of "Sugar" Candy, also a keen polo player and, like Hartopp, kind-hearted and openhanded.

"They fared alike, as so many others of the same disposition do, for when all they had was gone, their so-called friends forgot them."

Hartopp was buried beneath an eight-foot cross in the churchyard of Little Dalby, where so many generations of his family are also at rest. His fair-weather friends may have forgotten him, but his memory has been revived in recent years at, most suitably, Rutland Polo Club, not far from his old home. In 2001, the club inaugurated the Hartopp Trophy as prize for an inter-hunt tournament in which the Quorn and Cottesmore are regular participants. Presentation is always made by Prudence, Lady Cradock-Hartopp, whose late husband was the penultimate holder of the family baronetcy.

What is unknown is the reason for his nickname, "Chicken," which he gained shortly after receiving his commission in 1864, but a final story about him is worth repeating.[8] A young English hunting man, visiting Ireland, was advised to go to a fair in order to find Hartopp, who wanted to sell a good hunter not quite up to his weight. When he arrived, the young man asked a horsey-looking bystander if he knew Captain Hartopp.

"Do I know him?" came the reply, "Why, murder man, doesn't all the world know him?" A suitable epitaph indeed.

Notes

1. *The Field,* 20 March 1869.
2. Colonel T.A. St. Quintin, *Chances of Sports of Sorts* (London: Blackwood, 1912).
3. "London's Forgotten Ground," in *PQ International,* Spring 1999. Sadly, all copies of the local newspaper, *West London Observer,* for the period have been lost.
4. *Baily's* 38 (1888): 311–312.
5. Lord Rossmore, *Things I Can Tell* (London: Eveleigh Nash, 1937).
6. *Baily's* 38 (1888): 311–312.
7. Rossmore. *Things I Can Tell.* Hartopp did have Irish blood, through his great-grandmother, the Hon. Juliana Evans, daughter of George, 3rd Lord Carbery of Castle Freke, Co. Cork. She married Edward Hartopp (later Hartopp-Wigley) in 1782. It was probably through this marriage that Hartopp's father eventually inherited property in Co. Limerick and Co. Kerry, although he seems never to have lived there.
8. Rossmore, *Things I Can Tell.*
9. *Ibid.*

Thomas St. Quintin: "A Great Polo Pioneer"

by Chris Ashton

In just twenty years polo changed from a free-for-all contested by any number of Himalayan tribesmen to four-a-side teams in set positions with rules against crossing the line of the ball. That transition was led by two countries, India and England.

British cavalry regiments throughout the Empire embraced polo to train and exercise men and horses for mounted warfare. Nowhere was this more conspicuous than on the Indian subcontinent, what are now the Republic of India, Pakistan and Bangladesh, and were then British India, three-quarters of the Indian landmass with the balance composed of princely states under British protection.

The Indian army and the British Army-in-India each boasted 20 cavalry regiments with the larger of the princely states adding a further 40 regiments, amounting in all to some 80,000 men and horses. Police and Indian Civil Service officers, tea-planters, British merchants and their like also adopted polo, far cheaper than anywhere else in the world.

Little wonder, then, that the three seminal figures in polo's metamorphosis from hill-tribe to Hurlingham were British cavalry officers—Edward "Chicken" Hartopp and Thomas St. Quintin, both 10th Hussars, and John Watson of the 13th Hussars.

Both by their prowess at polo and their role in drafting its rules, the names of Hartopp and Watson burn more brightly in English polo legend than does St. Quintin, but any audit of their contribution in pioneering polo to the world at large would rank St. Quintin shoulder-to-shoulder with his fellow officers.

His place in English polo folklore was secured as one of eight 10th Hussars officers, including Hartopp, in famously deploying walking sticks, cavalry mounts and a cricket ball in the first "game" of polo at Aldershot in 1869. Thereafter, again with Hartopp, he played for the 10th Hussars in England's first structured polo match, an eight-a-side contest against the 9th Lancers, played on Hounslow Heath. London society flocked to watch. St. Quintin recalled:

> After our match at Hounslow we got the Blues (Household Cavalry) and 1st Life Guards, both of which regiments were great pals of ours, to take up the game, and the following year we and the 9th combined played them a match—Heavy v. Light Cavalry. We played six-a-side and had drawn up some few rules which we tried to adhere to. The game took place at Richmond Park:

we had a most cheery game [and] all London came to see it.... From that time it took deep root and has never looked back since.[1]

What we know of St. Quintin stems largely, though not only, from his memoir, *Chances of Sports of Sorts.*[2] The author's preface declares his text will confine itself to personal recollections of field sports. Religion, politics and professional soldiering were off limits, as indeed were The Ladies. ("The chief factor in a man's life, and to man's pleasure and pain will always be. Never to be discussed.")

In nearly 450 pages no mention is made of his wife or children, and yet pages are devoted to each of his most beloved horses, whether in hunting, point-to-points, steeplechasing, flat-racing and, in India, pig-sticking. Comparable space is given to his favorite dogs, especially retrievers, for he was quite as besotted by stalking, whether on foot, horseback or elephant, and to shooting of every conceivable species of game, animal and bird. From bear and antelope in the Himalayas to tiger in India's jungles to lion in South Africa to kangaroo in Australia to English game bird of every stripe, no creature was spared his pleasure.

Caricature of Thomas St. Quintin by Marcel Pic, depicting two of his constant companions: his ever-present cigar and a pony (courtesy Museum of Polo and Hall of Fame).

Born in 1840 into a rural family sufficiently prosperous to enroll him to Eton but not to provide him with independent means, he grew up in Cambridgeshire near Hatley George. Apropos the dictum *give me the child of seven and I will give you the man,* his father gave him a pony for his eighth birthday, but forbad him a gun until he turned 14. "You may try and break your neck and the chances are you won't come to much grief," St. Quintin quotes his father as saying, "but one gun accident may be fatal."

His strong suit at Eton was not the classroom, but sport. He coxed crews and was a useful athlete and rugby fly-half. In regimental and inter-regimental contests he shone at racquets and billiards, while leading the regimental cricket and polo teams. With other junior officers he relieved the tedium of peacetime soldiering by gambling on cards, billiards and pigeon-shooting.

He recalls one night with other subalterns, summoning their mounts to the riding school, where they stripped off mess-jackets, donned basket-masks, and armed with staves slugged it out to the last man left on horseback. "No one was hurt. Fancy that in those days!" St. Quintin continues: "We should all have been cashiered or drafted into other regiments; and yet it did us good, not harm, and helped to teach us to hold our own and take the knocks in life without whimpering."

After being gazetted into the 10th Hussars in 1859, serving in England with frequent excursions into Ireland for its field sports, St. Quintin proved himself a consummate horseman, excelling at every equestrian sport, testimony to which was the swag of trophies he accumulated. But more than that, he won a reputation as a shrewd, knowledgeable judge in the breeding, training and care of horses.

When the 10th Hussars departed for India in the winter of 1872, St. Quintin had few regrets: "Barring the foxhounds, though it may sound ungracious and ungrateful, I felt that I had had my fill of the sports and pleasures of my native land and I was longing for fresh fields and pastures new."

India exceeded all expectations: "The sports of India are of the most varied nature and carried out under the most widely different conditions both as to ground, climate and scenery. But vast as the country is, even the uttermost parts have become accessible and the hospitality of the native rajahs and European residents are so unbounded that the whole country is really one huge personal estate, easily accessible to any keen sportsman, and he can with little trouble or expense merely for the asking, indulge in his particular kind of sport to his heart's content."

Stationed outside the city of Muttra in the northwest provinces, the army encouraged field sports to stave off boredom. "Tent life on the plains of India is certainly the greatest comfort and luxury if you are up to the ropes and have your servants properly trained," St. Quintin declared. "Servants in India quietly drop into your ways and know exactly what you wish done and how to do it. They have your tent up with its appointments—that is to say, beds, tables, chairs, baths, etc.—always ready. Your bearer knows exactly what kit, your *shikari* knows weapons you want and woe betide any *kutmutgar* if he does not have everything you may ask for in the way of eatables and drinkables. Your *syces* with your ponies understand their work and if you intend going out for ten or twenty miles to shoot or pig-stick, all you have to do is tell your bearer that you require your tent pitched at such and such a point at a given hour...."

In 1875 every British cavalry regiment in India gathered in Delhi for the durbar to welcome Edward, Prince of Wales, heir to the British throne. Scheduled to return to Delhi the following year for the Proclamation of Queen Victoria as Empress of India, regimental polo officials, St. Quintin included, committed themselves to developing a single code of rules for inter-regimental polo.

"I was elected Hon. Secretary and we drew up a set of rules and agreed to hold an annual regimental tournament," St. Quintin recalled. "I had previously sent round to all the polo teams asking them to subscribe to the rules and heights of ponies, which we fixed at 13.2, and all the native cavalry regiments and most of the other players who had started or were about to start the game agreed to do so...."

In March 1877 the army cantonment at Meerut in northwest India hosted the first inter-regimental tournament. The final saw the 10th Hussars against its old adversary, the 9th Lancers, the two having been pitted against one another in that first legendary polo match, eight-players-a-side, on Hounslow Heath several years before.

Playing number 4 for the 10th Hussars, St. Quintin would later recall the hostility toward the new rules in the early days of inter-regimental polo. One 9th Lancer, Tim Butson, cheerfully announced his determination to cross the line of the ball. Soon after play began, he challenged St. Quintin's right of way. St. Quintin called his bluff, causing their ponies to collide. "It was a foolish and wrong thing to do, no doubt, on the part of both of us, though I was in the right," St. Quintin recalled. "However, it brought him to his senses and showed him the danger of it and, gentleman that he was, at the first interval he came up and apologised, said he fully recognised how wrong he had been and the necessity of the rules, and that he would not attempt anything of the sort again."

Captain St. Quintin's appointment as honorary secretary of inter-regimental polo was not by chance. Word of his skill and knowledge of horses had reached the civil and military high command of British India. Two years after his arrival he was seconded to accompany the Indian Government Remount Agent, Col. James Thacker, on a six-month assignment in Australia. Meeting with breeders, dealers and shipping agents, their goal was to streamline the process of buying and shipping thousands of Australian horses, better suited than the English-bred to the Indian climate, for the use of military and civilian personnel.

Easy access and the modest financial outlay involved in hunting and shooting applied equally to polo. St. Quintin had figured prominently in English polo; in India he had become a driving force. When he departed with Col. Thacker for Australia in 1874, he took mallets and balls for the express purpose of introducing the game to a people who prized horses and horsemanship.

Australia at the time comprised six self-governing colonies, each under a British governor appointed by London to represent the Crown. Armed with letters of introduction from the Indian government, St. Quintin was hosted by successive governors, starting in Sydney with Sir Hercules Robinson (later Lord Rosemead). The New South Wales governor not only gave his blessing to polo but also conscripted his army aides-de-camp to play in the first match, staged in Moore Park on 24 July 1874. *The Town and Country Journal* reported how the team led by Sir Hercules began to pull ahead: "At about this time both men and horses were in need of a rest in which they indulged for some minutes; and it was found there had been great destruction of the sticks, though no horse accidents. The game had special interest being under the management of Captain St. Quintin who had marked the ground and who we believe was among the first to introduce the game to England." *The Journal* described him as "a fine, accomplished horseman who seldom gets into difficulties and when by accident his stick does fly out of his hand, he is very clever at regaining it."

St. Quintin was equally lavish in praise of Sir Hercules, "a very fine horseman, who did much to encourage not only the breeding and racing but also the care of horses in his colony. I have never seen a team or a coach better turned out than his was, nor a racing stable better thought out and kept. He at once recognised the merits of polo, and gave it his hearty support and before I had left we had started a large and influential club...."

From Sydney he journeyed hundreds of miles southwest to the lush, undulating grassland of Victoria's Western District to join his brothers, John and Henry, on their pastoral property, Dwarroon, near Cudgee, purchased two years before. A month after the first Sydney game, the *Warrnambool Standard* reported on Victoria's first polo match at nearby Jetty Flat, with teams combining the St. Quintin brothers with neighboring farmers. "From the Western District the game spread rapidly into South Australia, but curiously enough Melbourne and the neighbouring districts would not for a long time take it up," St. Quintin later reported. "I went there myself and stayed with the then governor of Victoria and tried hard to get him to support it, without avail."

Imagine therefore his pleasure at returning to Australia 25 years on in 1899, for two test matches, Australia versus England, hosted by Melbourne in Melbourne Cup Week ("which all

The English team that participated in the first matches against Australia, November 1898. Col. St. Quintin, the umpire, stands next to Bertie Hill. In front, left to right: George Bryan, Neil Haig and Thomas Brand (courtesy Museum of Polo and Hall of Fame).

Australia attends, as England does her Derby"). Cream on his cake was the fact that two on the England team were former fellow officers of the 10th Hussars. As St. Quintin tells it, England (Major Neil Haig, Tom Brand, later Lord Hampden, George Bryan, later Lord Bellow, and Bertie Hill) was poorly mounted against the Australian team, Ernest de Little and three Manifold brothers, Edward, James, and William, all from Victoria's Western District. Wrote St Quintin:

> I umpired for our team. All Australia was there to look on and our team was to receive a severe hiding for their presumption. It was a great fight.... The Australians were undoubtedly as fine players as you could wish to see, but fortunately for us, they did not understand the science of the game and playing together, and each man played his own game. They were also a very rough lot in their play and as they became more and more excited the element of danger was strong and the whistle more and more in demand. Our men under the most adverse circumstances, played like heroes and after a most protracted and hustling game Australia got the better of us by only seven goals to six. I shall never forget the roar that went up from the Australian crowd. It was agreed to play a return match which came off three days afterwards, and to the astonishment of the Australian team, who said they had learnt a lot from the first game and expected an easy win, we beat them six goals to five. But it was a most desperate struggle.[3]

St. Quintin's concern for the future of Australian polo echoed all human endeavor in that vast, thinly populated landmass: "The long distances between the various clubs in Australia and the difficulties of rival clubs meeting, except occasionally, have been much against the advance of really high-class polo in that country as it was impossible to get constant opportunities between the various clubs which the English teams in their more circumscribed country enjoy...."

He returned to India and in 1876 took leave from his regiment to travel by foot and horseback into the Great Himalayan Range, from Kashmir to Tibet and neighboring Ladakh, both inhabited by seminomadic tribesmen for whom the horse was pivotal to managing their sheep and goats. In Leh, capital of Ladakh, he played his only game of hill-tribe polo:

> We played in the High Street, in fact the only street, which was about 180 yards long and about 30 yards wide, with narrow water course running down one side of the street, which consisted of low, flat-roofed houses on the top of which were gathered the spectators—men and women in their quaint, multi-coloured garments, and with a band composed of tom-toms, horns and various other ear-breaking, hideous instruments. The players themselves with their picturesque dress, on diminutive saddles with large wooden stirrups, were worth looking at. When mounted, my feet almost touched the ground; my hardy little Tat (Tartar Pony) was so small.
>
> There were thirty-two of us—sixteen-a-side. But there appeared to be only a few who thought about the ball, a hard wooden one; the rest shouted, and jostled and brandished their sticks, which were about three-feet long with heavy curved hardwood heads. The populace yelled in chorus, drowning the unearthly music (?) of the bands. It was real pandemonium.[4]

St. Quintin's tutelage under Col. Thacker established his claim as his successor. In 1882 he was seconded from his regiment to serve five years as Indian Government Remount Agent, based in Calcutta. In 1887 he was promoted to command the 8th Hussars, first in Meerut after which he was recalled to Norwich. From 1892 he served five years with the British Army Remount Division, variously assigned to compiling a register, in case of war, of every horse affiliated with every hunt club in the British Isles, and for the same purpose conducting a survey of horse-breeding in Ireland. In 1900 and by now retired, he was recalled as a remount officer to South Africa to marshal horses required by the British army fighting the Boers.

Like other Britons who invested so much of their lives in India, he was enthralled with it ever after. His description of its landscape, peoples, and cultures, quite as much as the pleasure it afforded by its hunting and polo, are invested with an eye for detail and a passion that is largely absent, apart from his triumphs in field sports, from his recollections of his own country.

Forty years on from his glory days, starting with that first match on Hounslow Heath, he grieved at how polo had altered: its elegance blemished by the fad riding off the man rather than playing the ball; the decline of delicate stickwork once limit of the height of ponies was lifted; and the escalating cost, up to 80 pounds, for a "made" polo pony, putting polo beyond players of modest means.

He lived out his last years in London's Bath Club and died in 1918, the last year of the war that was supposed to end all wars. Death held no fears for him. "I'm inclined to think the East is the wisest, and has the best of it in its belief in *kismet*," he wrote, "and in not putting such high value on life as we do in the West." He was survived by a son, Captain Ernest Snowdon St. Quintin, late of the 19th Hussars. In *British Sports and Sportsman*, published in London in 1922, author Osgold Cross wrote in the polo section a profile of Thomas St. Quintin aptly entitled "A Great Polo Pioneer."[5]

Notes

1. T.A. St. Quintin, *Chances of Sports of Sorts* (London: Blackwood, 1912).
2. *Ibid.*
3. *Ibid.*
4. *Ibid.*
5. "The Sportsman," in *Polo and Coaching* (London: London & Counties, n.d.).

John Watson: The Founding Father

by Roger Chatterton-Newman

Known in his day, and for decades afterwards, as the "Father of British Polo," John Henry Watson, M.F.H. (1851–1908), did perhaps more than anyone to lay the foundations for the modern game.

Born at the Watson ancestral home of Ballydarton, near Leighlinbridge in County Carlow, he was the son of Robert Gray Watson, M.F.H. (1821–1906), a legend in his lifetime in the hunting field. Indeed, the Watsons generally had a long reputation as first-rate sportsmen, and Robert — the "Old Master," as he was known — was master of the Carlow and Island Hounds for thirty-five years. A younger brother of Robert, George Watson (1829–1906) was distinguished in Australian racing and hunting circles, and was known as the "Prince of Starters."[1]

According to brief details supplied for his entry in *Who's Who,* John Watson first played polo in 1870, which would suggest games on private grounds in County Carlow. The inaugural — scratch — match had been played at Rathbane, outside Limerick, two years earlier, and it was introduced to County Carlow by the Rochfort family of Clogrenane, friends and neighbors of the Watsons.

Horace Rochfort founded the Carlow Polo Club in 1872, followed a year later by the All Ireland Polo Club in the Phoenix Park, Dublin. The Carlow Club held what was possibly its inaugural match at Oak Park, the seat of Henry Bruen, in August 1872, Robert and John Watson being among the players.[2]

Two years later John Watson was gazetted into the 13th Hussars and sailed for India. He took part in the epic march from Kabul to Kandahar, when the Afghan expeditionary force, traveling single file over mountainous mule tracks, were lost to the outside world for twenty-one days. Drinking water out of cow tracks, they reemerged 331 miles later, routed the enemy at Rabat and relieved Kandahar.

In India, of course, Watson was able to see polo as it had been played for centuries. Such was his enthusiasm for the game that the commander-in-chief, General Frederick Roberts, V.C.,[3] decided that Watson was the man to draw up fundamental rules, which he did, although one can only hazard a guess at his fiery reaction to the plethora of rules inflicted on players

today. In Watson's heyday, the rules of the Hurlingham Polo Committee, of which he was a member from 1887 to 1903, totaled no more than thirty-nine.

He left the army as a captain and returned to Ireland in 1884. Polo was by then well-established in the Phoenix Park, and other clubs and grounds were appearing, notably in the Irish midlands. Watson's comparative youth and forceful personality—he did not suffer fools gladly—soon made him the most significant figure in the game.

His most significant, indeed revolutionary, introduction was the backhand shot, in the face of considerable opposition. Revolutionary, too, was his insistence on players combining and working together as a team. Although the year before Watson's return to Ireland the number of players had been reduced from five to four a side, teamwork was minimal, each player tending to capture the ball and keep on it as long as he could. If a defender found the ball too close to the goal, he took it around the field as far as he could, with no thought of passing it on.

Lt. Col. Edward Miller (1865–1930), no mean player, had known Watson well and recalled in his memoirs the difference that combination made to the game:

> Watson taught No. 1 to ride the opposing back and to leave the ball alone. The two other players were called No. 2 and half-back; they were taught to stick to their places vigorously, and the back remained purely a defender, and acted as a sort of long stop, simply serving the ball to his forwards. Polo was played on these lines for some years, and Watson's teaching went right through the Army, soldiers being almost the only players in those days.[4]

Watson's teaching certainly produced dividends. The 1884 season saw his Freebooters squad capture the All Ireland Cup, a trophy he went on to win no fewer than nine times. Then, in 1886, he captained the Hurlingham team that went to Newport, Rhode Island, for the inaugural International—soon to be known as the Westchester Cup—against the United States.

The visitors were all original members of the Freebooters, comprised initially of soldiers past and present, but eventually a scratch pack of the best players available. For the International, Watson—who invariably played at back—had recruited Captain Thomas Hone, 7th Hussars, at number 1, the Hon. Richard Lawley, 7th Hussars, at number 2, and Captain Malcolm Little, 9th Lancers, at pivot. They won by broad margins in two games, 10–4 and 14–2, and while Watson acknowledged that the Americans worked hard and hit the ball well, he felt they were at a disadvantage by riding mustang ponies of much dexterity but little speed.

Watson was to play at back again in the second International of 1900, when Britain retained the cup after a single game, with a score of 8–2. His many other triumphs included a hat trick in the final of the Champion Cup, then the premier British tournament, at Hurlingham, but the only time he actually played for Ireland was in the 1904 Patriotic Cup against England. Ireland lost 3–5, one of Watson's very few defeats.

All who knew Watson spoke of his charming personality—when off a horse. As master of the Meath Hounds from 1891 to 1908 and on the polo ground, his "tremendous language," as the poet and writer Lord Dunsany called it, awed the field and intimidated fellow players.[5] Hunting and polo anecdotes, few of them apocryphal, involving Watson are legion. His famous temper evaporated when he was out of the saddle, although his heavyweight appearance—he was about fourteen stone at his peak—could still be daunting to strangers. Indeed, one observer described him as an undoubted throwback to his freebooting ancestors on the Cumbrian border, who for generations defied English and Scottish law. There was certainly nothing about his character to remind one of his family's strong connections with the Quaker movement in Ireland during the late seventeenth and early eighteenth centuries. Although his contributions

Opposite: **John Watson on a pony. After Henry Jamyn Brooks' painting "The Hurlingham Team Mounted in front of the Pavilion, 1890" (courtesy Roger Chatterton-Newman, PQInternational).**

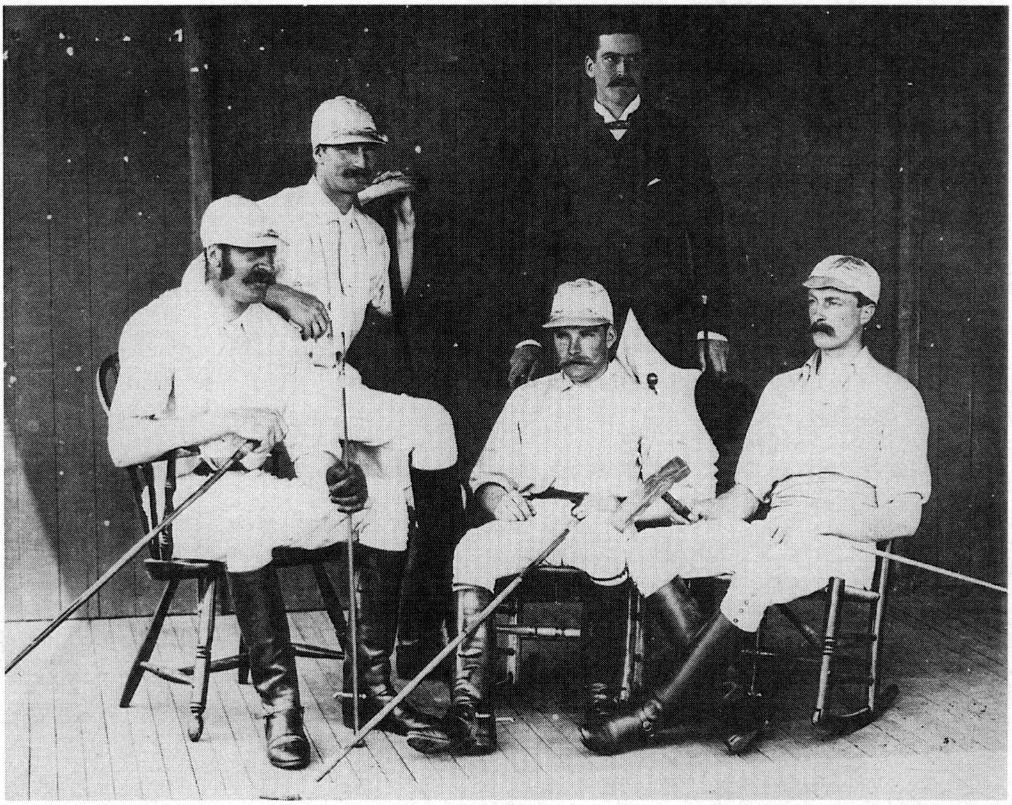

The first international match took place in Newport, Rhode Island, in 1886. This is the winning team from Britain. Left to right: John Watson, Thomas Hone, Malcolm Little and Richard Lawley. Standing: Charles Lambton, who officiated as umpire (courtesy Museum of Polo and Hall of Fame).

to polo and hunting—his reign as master established the Meath as "the Quorn of Ireland"—were undisputed,[5] he had a high opinion of his own brilliance, as one story will illustrate.

Playing one day at Hurlingham, he had Col. Willie Walker, afterwards Lord Wavertree and founder of the Irish National Stud, at number 2. Throughout the game Watson was abusing and shouting at Walker, who finally replied, with admirable restraint, "We forwards are going all right—you yourself are making a mess of it behind."

Watson, more furious than ever, replied, "You dare to speak to me, who is acknowledged to be the best back in the world?"

"*Not* by me," said Walker.

Watson bullied his old friends with impunity, and because they were so fond of him, they ignored his harsh words and temper. Towards the end of his polo career, however, there arose a new generation of players who refused to tolerate his outbursts. As a result, Watson became as charming in the saddle as he was out of it, although his tongue could remain blistering in the hunting field.

He particularly disliked women following hounds. "I wish they'd go home and do their knitting," he once remarked to a neighbor, although by coincidence one of the hardest-riding women of her day was Watson's sister Myra, wife first of a County Carlow neighbor, John McClintock Bunbury of Moyle, and then of Baron Maximilian de Tuyll, a Dutch nobleman.

She was known as one of the few women of the time to take her own line across country, and she certainly provided an excellent advertisement for the hunters bred and made by her brother, and sold on both sides of the Atlantic. Surprisingly, Lady Fingall, whose husband had been the previous master of the Meath, thought Watson "the cruelest man with a horse I had ever seen — he would always ride a horse until it dropped to get to his hounds." At the same time, however, an old groom would recall how Watson had only to come into sight, and to call them, "and tired horses were all leppin on their hind legs, like two year-olds."[7]

When Watson took on mastership of the Meath, he moved to Bective House, on the banks of the River Boyne, near Navan. Bective quickly became a polo and hunting mecca, with the Meath kennels relocated there and polo grounds laid out.

In 1905, during a polo match in the Phoenix Park, Watson suffered a heart attack. Ted Miller, playing on the other team, managed to catch him as he fell from the pony. Watson never played polo again, although he continued to hunt for another two full seasons.

Ill health returned at the start of the 1908 hunting season and, unwillingly, he resigned the horn of the Meath. He died at Bective House on 12 November, at the age of fifty-seven, having outlived his father by only two years. Sadly, Watson had no children by his marriage to the former Christine Booth, who was to survive him until 1925.

A final story is worth recalling. As Watson lay dying at Bective, a few miles away one of his oldest friends, Leonard Morrogh, was also on his deathbed. A mutual friend decided to pay them both a last visit, beginning with Morrogh.

As the visitor was turning to leave, he mentioned he was on his way to see Watson. "Give John my love," said Morrogh, "and tell him that I shall get there first, and that he will find me holding the gate open as I have often done before."

Watson's legacy to polo is immeasurable. He found it a virtual free-for-all, and gave it pace, order and science. An anonymous tribute in a Carlow newspaper after his death described him as "the life and soul of the game":

> The inclusion of his name on a team, whether insular or international, made the boldest of the opposition hold his breath. In the field of sport, he was born to rule, and he invariably asserted his birthright.[8]

Notes

1. *Baily's* 71 (March 1899): 157–160. See also *Racing through History* (published quarterly by the Australian Racing Museum) (Spring 2000): 9.
2. *Carlow Sentinel,* 24 August 1872.
3. The Victoria Cross (V.C.), Britain's highest service medal, was instituted in 1856 and is awarded for conspicuous bravery — the inscription on the medal reads "For Valour." Roberts (1832–1914) won the V.C. in 1858 during the Indian Mutiny. He became one of the most celebrated soldiers of the nineteenth century, serving as commander-in-chief of the Indian army from 1885 to 1893. Raised to the peerage as Lord Roberts of Kandahar and Waterford in 1892, he became field marshal and commander-in-chief, Ireland, in 1895. Elevated to an earldom in 1901, "Bobs" (as he was known to an adoring public) retired only in 1904. He died while visiting British troops in France at the start of the Great War.
4. Lt. Colonel E.D. Miller, *Fifty Years of Sport* (London: Hurst & Blackett, 1925).
5. Lord Dunsany, *My Ireland* (London: Jarrolds, 1937).
6. The Quorn is regarded as England's grandest pack of foxhounds. The country lies in Leicestershire and the founder is generally considered to have been Thomas Boothby of Tooley Park, known as "Old Tom of Tooley" who was master for a record fifty-five seasons from 1698 to 1753. The Meath, originally the Clongill Hunt, dates in its present form from around 1813. The Quorn and the Meath have always been popular with sporting visitors from the U.S.A.
7. Lady Elizabeth Fingall, *Seventy Years Young* (London: Collins, 1937).
8. *The Carlow Sentinel,* 14 November 1908.

Francis Herbert: "Killed a salmon, shot some grouse and played polo"

by Roger Chatterton-Newman

Aldershot Camp was the setting for the proto-game of polo, organized by Edward Hartopp in 1869. Appropriately, it was at Aldershot two years later that Captain Francis Joseph Alphonse Herbert, known always as "Tip," first took up polo while serving with the 9th Lancers.

Looking back on those early days, towards the end of his life, Herbert recalled polo as a decidedly dangerous activity, with sticks and balls of all descriptions in use:

> I particularly remember a special stick I had manufactured, so that it should not break. It was of ash, with a head of oak, and shod with iron and square heads. After considerable damage had been done to ponies and men by this stick, it was declared to be undesirable, and was relegated to my barrack rooms.[1]

As the favorite shot at the time was under the pony's neck, Herbert also tried to play with a golf club. The result was that it curled round, and after nearly braining himself several times, he exchanged it for a more conventional mallet.

It was fortunate that he escaped unscathed; otherwise his home county of Monmouthshire, on the border of England and Wales, may not have been the setting for the first polo club in the British Isles.

A member of an old landed family, first recorded in the Welsh Marches in the thirteenth century, Herbert was born on 6 February 1845, the younger son of William Herbert of Clytha Park, near Usk. Clytha was the home of Monmouthshire Polo Club, established by Herbert in 1872, a full two years before the game was played at Hurlingham, together with a group of friends and his brother, Reginald, later to take the surname of Herbert-Huddleston.

An early problem for the Monmouthshire players was finding good mounts, as players with any value balked at risking their legs in the rough and tumble of a game. Instead, they borrowed horses from local farmers who remained ignorant of the potential danger, and on one memorable occasion Herbert stopped a "drove of wild Welsh ponies" that happened to be passing the Clytha gate-lodge and struck a deal with the owner for the loan of a dozen for two hours:

> When we mounted, the fun began. The ponies were tractable enough until one raised one's stick, when — Hey! Presto! you were either on Mother Earth or being carried to the furthest limit of the ground.... I never saw ponies have such a rooted objection to going near a polo ball.[2]

Rules, of course, were virtually nonexistent. John Watson was still to formulate them in India, while those drawn up by "Chicken" Hartopp on Mess notepaper for the 1869 match were largely ignored. Herbert — who had played for the 9th Lancers in that match — recalled the only "understood" rule being that a player was off-side unless two of his opponents were between him and the goal. The game consisted of hooking each other's mallets more than anything else, and the lack of rules meant that hooking was carried on over, under, before and behind the pony. "The entanglements that ensued can be imagined, with sometimes eight-a-side."

Herbert founded the club after retiring from the army. The first recorded Monmouthshire match took place at Clytha on 23 September that year, somewhat late compared with the modern calendar, and was followed by an inaugural dinner at the Angel Hotel, Abergavenny. The club began with sixty members, each paying an annual subscription of ten shillings. Ponies were not to be over 13 hands. No spurs or rowels were allowed. The club livery consisted of a white flannel shirt, bearing its monogram in red, a red sash, tie and cap, white breeches and butcher's boots.

The first season lasted until early October but no away games were played — for the simple reason there were no other clubs. Radnorshire, Manchester, Staffordshire, Beaufort and Lillie Bridge were to follow shortly, but in 1872 Monmouthshire had to make up opposing teams from its own members.

Their first away match took place at Lillie Bridge — off the Old Brompton Road in London — on 9 June 1874, in front of a large crowd. The band of the Royal Horse Guards attended and play began at 4:30 P.M., with six players a side. Monmouthshire fielded Tip Herbert, Capt. Ferdinand Hanbury-Williams, Sir Charles Wolseley, Capt. Burchall Helme, James Mellor and Capt. William Henry Wheeley. Lillie Bridge had the upper hand from the beginning, with far better trained ponies, and won 3–0.

Four days later, Monmouthshire lost 0–2 to a 9th Lancers team at Hurlingham, but for the final game of the 1874 season — against Radnorshire and West Hereford Polo Club on Hereford Racecourse on 28 September — Herbert's team rode out the winners, 3–0.

A more notable score was recorded in September 1875, when Monmouthshire defeated Radnorshire 11–0 on Norton Racecourse, Presteign. The winners were afterwards entertained to dinner in the Shire Hall.

Herbert recalled that games were much longer in those days. The agreed time was two hours, with fifteen-minute intervals between each half-hour. "One had to play for half-an-hour at a stretch, and in one case play was kept up for forty minutes," he said.

Highlight of the early days was a Monmouthshire visit to Hurlingham on 12 July 1876 for a match in the presence of the Prince and Princess of Wales— afterwards King Edward VII and Queen Alexandra. Sir Bache Cunard, from the shipping family, scored first for Hurlingham but Herbert soon equalized and followed up with a second goal. Sir Charles Wolseley took the score to 3–1 and the final score was 5–2 in Monmouthshire's favor. As the *Morning Post* reported:

> The Hurlingham Committee have presented the Monmouthshire club with a handsome Silver Cup in recognition of the great form they displayed before the Prince and Princess of Wales ... a compliment the Monmouthshire Club richly deserve, as they are enthusiastic supporters of polo, good horsemen and generous-minded sportsmen.[3]

It was a splendid tribute and Herbert must have felt proud that his efforts had been so well acknowledged. Better was to come, however, for the 1877 season found the Monmouthshire players at the zenith of their glory.

Probably the earliest depiction of a polo match in the British Isles, painted by Capt. Ferdinand Hanbury-Williams in 1875. It shows a match on what is now Avergavenny Golf Course. Tip Herbert, mallet raised, is in center front. His brother, Reginald, sits on the far right. This painting hangs in a private collection (courtesy Roger Chatterton-Newman, PQInternational).

Having entered the Champion Cup—first played in 1876 and the precursor of the modern British Open—with seven other teams, Monmouthshire reached the final on 9 June. They faced the Tyro Club, captained by Bache Cunard, and again had the Prince and Princess of Wales as spectators.

The match was generally reckoned as being one of the hardest ever seen at Hurlingham. An hour-and-a-quarter was the agreed time but, as neither side managed to score, it went into an extra half-hour, still with no result. In the end, it was decided to declare a tie and both teams received a cup. The *Morning Post* reported some of the best and strongest hitting coming from Herbert and, despite the lack of goals, regarded Monmouthshire as undoubtedly having the best of the game. Monmouthshire took home the Champion Cup a year later, having beaten the 5th Lancers 3–2.

Although Clytha Park remained the headquarters of the club, many home matches were also played on Abergavenny Racecourse. The site was conveyed to Reginald Herbert, who had inherited Clytha from his father in 1885, by another player, Capt. Ferdinand Hanbury-Williams of neighboring Pontypool Park. It was apparently an ideal polo ground; being sandy, there was little danger of slipping, and Tip Herbert could never remember such a thing occurring.

From the first season of 1872 until 1896 polo flourished in Monmouthshire without a break. Monmouthshire Polo Club Week, every autumn, was a highlight of the social season, with house parties made up for the annual tournament and other matches. Teams from

Francis Herbert as a young man (courtesy Roger Chatterton-Newman, PQInternational).

several army regiments and from clubs such as Hurlingham, Ranelagh, Liverpool, Manchester, Ludlow, Warwickshire and Sussex all took part, and a polo ball, gymkhanas and pony races usually extended the week into a fortnight.

Herbert achieved something of a sporting record during the 1892 season, as his old friend Lt. Colonel Ted Miller, founder of Rugby and Roehampton polo clubs, recalled, "He killed a salmon, shot some grouse and played in the Abergavenny Polo Tournament all in the same day."[4]

Sadly, Monmouthshire Polo Club became moribund after 1896. Looking back, Herbert did not give a reason and was optimistic that he would live to see a revival by a new generation; but by then tournaments had started to concentrate themselves around the five or six London clubs, and incentive apparently departed from the Welsh Marches. Indeed, Herbert himself may have unintentionally encouraged the exodus to the capital when he became polo manager at Ranelagh.

He also played for other teams, including Derbyshire County, with which he won the County Cup in its third season, 1887. The Derbyshire squad was put together by Charles, 8th Earl of Harrington (1844–1917), and based on his Elvaston Castle estate in the British Peak District.

Harrington, nicknamed "Old Beardy" in consequence of his luxuriant facial hair, was a popular, if somewhat eccentric, figure on British polo fields. A keen inventor, he pioneered the idea of safety goal posts for the 1889 Inter-Regimental tournament at Hurlingham. The hollow *papier mâché* cylinders were revolutionary at the time, but modern players owe Lord Harrington an immense debt.

He was also a founding member of the Polo Pony Society, on which Herbert joined him and which published the first official pedigree register, *The Polo Pony Stud Book,* now long defunct, in 1894.

That same year Tip Herbert launched *Polo* magazine, now also long extinct, with himself as editor. Three years later he contributed the article on polo to the *Encyclopaedia of Sport*, edited by the 20th Earl of Suffolk and Frederick Aflalo.

Herbert died on 26 October 1922, and it was not until 2000 that Monmouthshire Polo Club reemerged, based this time at Ruperra Castle, near Newport, thanks to the enthusiasm of businessman Ashraf Barakat.

Tip Herbert married the Belgian Baroness Cecile d'Anethan in 1879 and settled at Ty-Gwyn, Raglan, not far from Clytha Park. They had no children, and when in due course Clytha was inherited by Reginald Herbert's daughter, the surname vanished from the list of players.

There are, however, two visible reminders of the high days of Herbert and his friends, both in the form of oil paintings. The first is a somewhat primitive but highly evocative work by Herbert's teammate Ferdy Hanbury-Williams, showing a game in progress on the old Llanfoist racecourse. It is dated 1875 and must be the earliest depiction of polo in the British Isles; certainly it is the first, and perhaps only, work executed by a pioneer player. Hanbury-Williams (1834–1891) included artistic, or perhaps filial, license in his painting: in the distance is Coldbrook Park, his father's house, which in reality is out of view.[5]

The second painting is by George Earl, showing Monmouthshire in action against the Royal Horse Guards at Hurlingham on 7 July 1877. Tip, mallet raised, is in the center of the painting and is about to strike the ball, while brother Reginald sits on his grey pony in front of the Monmouthshire goal.[6]

The game was timed to last an hour-and-a-quarter and it was twenty minutes before Hugh Owen, one of the five Monmouthshire players, made the first goal. In the end, Monmouthshire won 4–1, Herbert recalling "a very spirited match ... some capital Polo was witnessed." Both paintings are in private collections in England.

There is also in existence, in the collection of Herbert's great-nephew in Shropshire, a set of salt, pepper and mustard pots in a handsome leather case. An inscription on the case records the presentation of the set to "Reggie" (Reginald Herbert) by "Charley"—presumably Sir Charles Wolseley—in July 1877, with the motto "Long Live Polo."[7]

Traditionally, it commemorates the game against the Blues at Hurlingham.

Notes

1. *Polo Monthly*, June 1909.
2. *Ibid.*
3. *Morning Post*, 24 July 1876.
4. Lt. Colonel E.D. Miller, *Fifty Years of Sport* (London: Dutton & Co. 1925).
5. An illustration appears in *PQ International*, Summer 1998.
6. This is the date as recorded by Herbert. A plaque attached to the frame gives 7 July 1878, although it seems that Herbert was correct.
7. *PQ International*, Summer 1998.

Foxhall Keene: "A Life of Pure Delight"

by Dennis J. Amato

In the formative years of polo in America, perhaps no other individual embodied the game more than Foxhall Keene. His daring and dash on the polo field combined with his colorful personality off it, along with his substantial accomplishments in numerous other athletic pursuits, undoubtedly made him one of the country's most recognizable sportsmen in the Gilded Age. His guiding philosophy seemed to epitomize the concept of "living on the edge" several generations before the expression itself came into vogue.

Foxhall Parker Keene was born in San Francisco on 18 December 1869. His grandfather, who was a London merchant, emigrated in 1850 from England with his whole family, including his twelve-year-old son, James. After a brief stay in Virginia, the family eventually settled in California. With the Gold Rush in full swing at the time, it was somewhat natural that James, Foxhall's father, would be drawn to the mining sector, initially as a mine worker in nearby Nevada as well as in California and later as a highly successful speculator and trader in mining stocks. In fact, over time he would amass a reputed $6 million fortune.

While building his business career, James Robert Keene met and fell in love with a young woman, Sarah Jay Daingerfield, who was visiting from Virginia. Soon after James and Sarah were married, they departed from the small town of Shasta, California, for the big city of San Francisco. In addition to Foxhall, the Keenes had a daughter, Jesse. The elder Keene would also eventually gain additional prominence in the San Francisco business community beyond mining when he was named president of the local stock exchange as well as a governor of the Bank of California.

When Foxhall was just seven years old, the family pulled up stakes and moved east to Newport, Rhode Island, where they quickly ensconced themselves in a large residence on fashionable Bellevue Avenue. Shortly after their arrival, Foxhall was given his first pony, which ignited a lifetime attraction to and affection for all things that were horse related.

Also with the move east, James Keene started to take an interest in the turf. Over time the Keene stable of Castleton Farm in Kentucky would breed a succession of renowned thoroughbreds, including Commando, Colin, Pelt, Pan and Superman. As the *New York Times* remarked many years later, "For more than a quarter of a century, beginning in the late nineties,

Foxhall Keene, an outstanding polo player and one of the finest sportsmen in the Gilded Age (courtesy Museum of Polo and Hall of Fame).

the colors [white with blue spots] of James R. Keene and his son virtually dominated thoroughbred racing in the United States and England."[1]

It was also during his days in Newport that young Foxhall developed an interest in polo. As he described his initiation into the sport:

> I learned to play polo knocking a ball up and down the broad, tree-shaded length of Bellevue Avenue in Newport. There was a regular field there, but the boys of my age were never allowed to play on it. Occasionally they were permitted to practice on the edges of the field, but I disdained such a niggardly favor and did my practicing on the Avenue, once in a while scoring a "goal" between the wheels of a dowager's landau.[2]

Around 1884 these halcyon days in Rhode Island unfortunately came to an abrupt end, virtually forcing the Keene family to leave the state. In Foxhall's own words: "The reason we finally left Newport was twofold. Our house on Bellevue Avenue burned down, and father at the same time lost all his money."[3] The father's financial reverses came at the hands of his old nemesis, the notorious financier Jay Gould, who managed to outwit Keene when the latter tried to corner the wheat market. Gould had finally taken his revenge in a threat he had made many years before: "Keene came east in a private car. I'll send him back in a boxcar."[4]

The Keenes first moved to rented quarters in Babylon, Long Island, and as James Keene's fortunes slowly started to improve, they relocated next to Wavecrest and then finally in 1886 to Cedarhurst. In a case where calamity sometimes begets opportunity, the resettlement to Cedarhurst proved to be fortuitous. At the time of the Keenes' arrival, this quaint Long Island town had become "a colony of the carriage trade—Harrimans, Cowdins, Cheevers, the Whitelaw Reids, the Sidney Ripleys, the Lawrence Turnures...."[5] "Foxie," as Foxhall was affectionately called, provided this vivid description of Cedarhurst in its heyday: "It was a very sporting community.... Everyone rode, hunted, played polo, and fairly lived out of doors. Sunday mornings you would see thirty or forty men riding over the countryside...."[6]

When Foxie was only fourteen years old, he must have made quite an impression on his neighbors in terms of his equestrian skills, as they made him a member of the Rockaway Hunting Club. It was also at this time that Keene started to seriously engage in polo. While not actually playing, he would also devote a substantial amount of time to practicing his hitting. Further, Keene maintained a rigorous routine of physical training to keep his 140 pound frame in peak competitive form.

This attention to detail would continue over his playing lifetime in every aspect of the game. For example, Keene would have saddles specifically made for each pony so that he was always exactly the same distance above the ground. He would routinely visit Holbrow's in London each spring to order 50 to 60 custom-made mallets and then have the handles crafted elsewhere to fit his grip.[7] Of course, he maintained an outstanding stable of polo ponies and claimed that he "was the first player who ever used the big ponies in America."[8]

In 1886 a major event occurred that would propel Keene onto center stage of the polo world: the inauguration of the Westchester Cup. This special tournament between England and America had originated as a result of a somewhat casual remark by one of James Gordon Bennett's associates, Griswold Lorillard, while being entertained by his English hosts at the Hurlingham Club in London. The first contest for the Cup took place in Newport, Rhode Island, in late August of that year. The American team consisted of Foxhall Keene, Raymond Belmont, Thomas Hitchcock Sr. and William K. Thorn. The Americans were woefully unprepared for their British counterparts, Capt. Richard Lawley, Capt. Thomas Hone, Capt. Malcolm Little and John Watson, and were soundly trounced 10–4 and 14–2 in the two-game series.

In the fall of 1887, Keene matriculated at Harvard University but was soon suspended after hosting a raucous "punch" or drinking bout on Bloody Monday Night. Upon his return, Keene went out for football in the spring but his career was short-lived when he suffered a ruptured kidney the following fall in a game against Penn. He then tried his hand at boxing with the intent of going for the lightweight boxing championship at the university. However, here again misfortune struck as Keene was felled by a bad case of measles. As a result, "he concluded that there was something unlucky about Harvard, and at the end of the year he left for good,"[9] although he maintained a lot the friendships he had made while at the school.

However, during his Harvard days, Keene did achieve a major sporting success when he went over with his Rockaway team to Meadow Brook in nearby Westbury in 1888 to play for the Autumn Cups. The Rockaway quartet of Jack Cheever, John Cowdin, Foxhall Keene and Henry Herbert scored a surprise upset over the powerful Meadow Brook team of August

Belmont, Raymond Belmont, Oliver Bird and Elliott Roosevelt, and thus further fueled what would become a long and bitter rivalry between these two clubs which had first confronted each other in 1885. Of particular note was that John Cowdin in the number 2 position and Foxhall Keene in the number 3 position would constitute for almost 30 years the core of the Rockaway team.

By 1888 the players at Rockaway and Meadow Brook so outclassed other poloists that Henry L. Herbert, then president of the Brighton Polo Club, was asked to create a handicap system to equalize the game among participants of varying abilities.[10] The original scale was 0 to 5, with only two players among the forty-two initially listed being accorded top honors: Foxhall Keene and Thomas Hitchcock Sr.[11]

In 1890 when the Polo Association of America (as the U.S.P.A. was then called) was formed, the handicap system was immediately adopted but the scale was widened, from 0 to 5 to 0 to 10. However, only one player in 1890 merited the ultimate accolade of 10-goals: Foxhall Keene.

Keene would maintain this 10-goal rating until 1903, when the Polo Association decided to tighten standards in an unexpected move which resulted in Keene and Monty Waterbury, the only 10-goal players at the time, being cut to 9-and-8 goals respectively. After what was tantamount to a fourteen-year moratorium, the association in early 1917 finally raised 5 players, including Keene, back to 10-goals, mainly to put the U.S. rating system on a par with the one prevailing in England at the time.[12] Keene would maintain his 10-goal standing until 1920, when he retired from high goal competitive play. Not only was Keene the world's first 10-goal player but during his long career no one would ever be rated above him in America.

Foxhall Keene's polo activities were extensive over his playing career, as were his successes. For example, he reached the finals of the first Polo Championship (later renamed the Senior Championship) held in Prospect Park, Brooklyn, in 1895 but was unfortunately knocked unconscious for seventeen minutes in the seventh period. He was replaced by Albert Franks, who at that moment was having a drink at the bar but jumped onto a pony without changing attire to finish the game! However, the Rockaway team, which had been ahead by two goals prior to Keene's accident, ultimately lost to Myopia 4¾ to 2¾.

In 1896 Keene was able to avenge the prior year's loss when his Rockaway team defeated a strong Meadow Brook squad. Other Senior Championship titles followed in 1899 (Westchester), 1901 (Lakewood), 1907 (Rockaway) and 1912 (Meadow Brook).

There were numerous other notable as well as memorable victories in the U.S. One was for the Point Judith Cup in 1899, a contest the *New York Times* proclaimed as "probably the best polo game ever seen at the Point Judith Club"[13] with the "last two periods ... of breathless interest,"[14] where the Westchester team, which included Keene, defeated Meadow Brook.

Another was for the Ladies' Cup finals at Cedarhurst in 1907, which Keene vividly described as "the hardest polo match I ever played."[15] In this tournament held in 101-degree weather, Rockaway went up against Meadow Brook on the flat even though their opponent had a several goal advantage over them. The game was tied in the seventh period when it was suspended by darkness. Since Meadow Brook had another engagement the following day, they had to default the play-off. Keene noted that "that cup stands in the Rockaway Club, a monument to the unconquerable spirit of my teammates."[16]

In addition, other important American victories included the Polo Association Cups, the Government Cup, the Hitchcock Cups, the Myers Cups, the Meadow Brook Club Cups, the Westchester Club Cups, the Myopia Polo Cups, the Special Cups, the Westbury Challenge Cup and the Rockaway Hunting Cups.

On the international front, Keene was a frequent participant in English polo circles over the years during the so-called London season, as play among the Hurlingham, Ranelagh and Roehampton Clubs was known. He coveted winning the Champion Cup at Hurlingham as

The American team that contested the 1902 Westchester Cup. Left to right: Rodolphe Agassiz from Myopia, Foxie Keene, Monty Waterbury from Meadow Brook, John Cowdin from Rockaway and Larry Waterbury from Meadow Brook (courtesy Museum of Polo and Hall of Fame).

well as the Open Challenge Cup at Ranelagh but lamented that "ill luck has followed me when I tried.... Three or four times I have played in the finals but each time something happened."[17] One year a teammate was laid low by a "touch of jungle fever"[18] and another year Keene himself was knocked unconscious—yet again—but this time for thirty or forty minutes.

During his 1900 visit to England, Keene even pulled together an American team to challenge their English counterparts in a special match, but lost 8 to 2. However, this single-game encounter was not viewed as an official Westchester Cup event. Also while in Europe that summer Keene went over to Paris for the Olympic Games. The Foxhunters team, of which Keene was a member, took home the gold medal in polo.

In 1901 the Polo Association of America mounted a formal challenge for the Westchester Cup to be held in London in 1902. Keene was named captain, joined by Rodolphe Agassiz, John Elliott Cowdin and Larry Waterbury. In a stunning upset in the opening game, the Americans won 2 to 1, the first time they had ever beaten the English in international competition. According to Keene, "the original agreement with England was for one match, but meanwhile I had received a cable from William Hazard, secretary of the Polo Association, saying the English wanted to make it two out of three. To this I agreed."[19] The English then brought in some stronger players and went on to win the next two games and thus retain ownership of the cup. As a result of these Westchester series, Keene noted that "when we got back to America we were all put down one goal on our handicaps"[20] per the aforementioned 1903 ratings changes.

In 1909 the Polo Association turned to Harry Payne Whitney to organize the American effort for the Westchester Cup. Whitney responded by drawing together a powerful quartet of himself along with the Waterbury brothers, Larry and Monty, and Devereux Milburn. In addition to manpower, Whitney assembled a standout string of 28 ponies. The net result was not only a resounding two-game sweep of the Westchester Cup contest that year but also the introduction of a revolutionary manner of play that changed the game of polo forever.[21]

When the cup was similarly contested in 1911, the association once again turned to the "Big Four," as the 1909 combination became known, who quickly reprised their prior success with another two-game victory. In 1913, it was only logical that the association would once more defer to the Big Four to represent the U.S. in that year's encounter. However, the team played somewhat poorly in the practice matches, which included a notable loss to a team led by Foxhall Keene. As the *New York Times* then reported in a front-page story in early June 1913, "polo enthusiasts received a decided shock ... [when] a bomb exploded"[22] as a result of the association's decision to replace Whitney as captain with Keene as well as the Waterbury brothers by Louis Stoddard and Malcolm Stevenson. The only original member of the Big Four who was retained was Devereux Milburn, who was universally regarded at the time as the best player in America, if not the world.

Keene's new found glory at age 44 proved to be relatively fleeting, as he broke his collarbone on the first day of practice play. The Big Four were then called back in and were able to retain possession of the cup, although by relatively narrow margins in the two match series.

Thus, once more, Keene's long-held dream of winning the Westchester Cup was dashed at a point in his life that he was unlikely to be given another chance. The poignancy of the loss was made even greater by the strong rivalry between Keene and Whitney both on and off the playing field. Ironically, Harry Payne Whitney's father, William Collins Whitney, had largely replaced Jay Gould as James Keene's principal business rival. In addition, the Whitney and Keene stables were frequent competitors in the racing circuit. Furthermore, Foxie apparently did not approve of the "revolutionary" manner of polo play that Whitney had developed with Devereux Milburn (i.e., having team members play far apart from each other and making long hits rather than short ones in a tightly clustered format).[23]

Keene commented that "their style of play was bad for polo. As Harry could only hit on the offside of his pony, he played everything to pass to Dev and let him go down the field with the ball. Everyone imitated this method of attack, but few could get away with it. It depended upon the brilliance of one man."[24] He added, "There was a time when good team-play prevailed, but when Meadow Brook's big field [International Field] was built, it was so wide that it became the thing to carry the ball down to the boards, have a hell of a run with it, a wild shot for the goal. This tendency has persisted to the present day [1938]."[25]

While Keene excelled at polo, his sporting horizons were far broader. Besides his achievements in the breeding and racing of thoroughbreds mentioned earlier, he attained fame in steeplechase and foxhunting and became a champion jumper at horse shows. Moreover, he tried his hand in a wide variety of non-equine endeavors over his lifetime, with varying outcomes. In addition to his unlucky college forays into football and boxing, his athletic repertoire included pool; pigeon shooting; lawn tennis where he had the opportunity to play with Tom Slocum, the national champion, in the National Doubles Championship; court tennis, where he distinguished himself and even competed against Tommy Pettit, the world champion at the time; golf, where he played superbly and won several tournaments; sailing, including competitive yachting, although he nearly drowned in 1883 when his boat capsized in the waters off Newport; and motor racing, where he was often more avid than accomplished, crashing his car into a telegraph pole on one occasion and singeing his eyebrows and moustache on another when his vehicle caught fire! At one point in his life, when Keene had gained such an outstanding reputation as a sportsman, his father offered $10,000 for each of any 10 sports that anyone was willing to challenge his son in, but there were no takers.

Splendidly dressed, Foxie Keene (right) and the Maharaja of Rutlam (left) in 1924 (courtesy Museum of Polo and Hall of Fame).

Arguably, though, Keene left his deepest and most lasting legacy in the sport of polo. Newell Bent in *American Polo* wrote that "Mr. Keene was a very brilliant and finished No. 3 and his play in both England and America was so outstanding over so many years, that he was long considered above all other players in this country. An English writer in 1906 said of him; 'Mr. Keene is generally looked upon in England and America as the finest all round player of his country. The only man in England to be placed with him is Walter Buckmaster. Mr. Keene knows the game thoroughly, has brilliant command of the ball, works hard, and is an expert and dashing horseman.'"[26] The *New York Times* also noted in 1913, when Keene was asked to captain the American team for the Westchester Cup: "Keene ... was a member of the 1886 team, and was considered without a peer in the finesse of the game. In all of his work this Spring when lined up against the 'big four' he has been the one man to anticipate plays by the opposition."[27] Not surprisingly, as recognition of his exceptional polo career and his enormous contribution to the game, Keene was an early inductee into the Polo Hall of Fame in 1992.

Keene's extravagant lifestyle and somewhat reckless behavior ultimately took their toll on him both financially and physically. With deluxe travel, lavish parties for as many as 500 people, costly seasonal country home rentals, expensive automobiles (e.g., a $14,000 Mors in 1901) and other indulgences, Keene slowly but steadily depleted his inheritance. At times he also attracted unwanted publicity with newspaper reports about tradesmen going to court for back payment.[28]

Similarly, his many sporting accidents over his lifetime left their mark on his body. By his own account, his injuries included "one broken leg; one compound fracture of the ankle; nose broken twice; one ruptured kidney; one nearly fatal internal hemorrhage; brain concussion three times, lying senseless for 17 minutes, 30 minutes and 16 days; one broken neck, collarbone broken three times; one dislocated shoulder, three broken ribs; and six stitches in [the] eyelid after being hit by a polo ball."[29]

Around 1935, when he was virtually penniless, Keene, arriving with but one suitcase, was taken in by his sister, Jesse, at her estate in the village of Ayer's Cliff, Canada. He initially stayed in the main house but subsequently moved to a modest cottage on the property. During the winter, while his sister was to be away, she arranged for accommodations for him in the village. His health continued to deteriorate further and he died on 25 September 1941 at age seventy-one, "an old and tired man who had lived much too long."[30]

As was in character for this remarkable individual, no one better summarized Foxhall Keene's life than he himself in his now classic autobiography, *Full Tilt*, written with Alden Hatch: "Now I ride no more. My strength and skill, and even the fortune which enabled me to live so royally, are spent. But if I had it all to do again, I would follow exactly the same way. It was a life of pure delight."[31]

Notes

1. "Foxhall Keene, Famous Poloist," *The New York Times*, 26 September 1941, p. 23.
2. Alden Hatch and Foxhall Keene, *Full Tilt: The Sporting Memoirs of Foxhall Keene* (New York: The Derrydale Press, 1938), 127.
3. *Ibid.*, 63.
4. Finis Farr, "Part I: The Fabulous World of Foxhall Keene," *Sports Illustrated*, 16 February 1959, 66.
5. *Ibid.*
6. Hatch and Keene, 66.
7. Farr, 61.
8. Hatch and Keene, 133.
9. Farr, 69.
10. See in part Benjamin R. Allison, M.D., *The Rockaway Hunting Club* (Brattleboro, VT: Alan S. Browne, 1952), 118.
11. Horace A. Laffaye, *The Polo Encyclopedia* (Jefferson, NC and London: McFarland & Co., 2004), 156.
12. For further details on this handicap history, see footnote 2 of the author's profile on Devereux Milburn.
13. "Westchester Wins at Polo," *The New York Times*, 6 August 1899, p. 6.
14. *Ibid.*
15. Hatch and Keene, 137.
16. *Ibid.*

17. *Ibid.*, 138. In actuality, Keene played only in the finals of these two tournaments once (the 1900 Champion Cup at Hurlingham). However, he undoubtedly played for these two cups other times but bowed out before the finals such as in 1909 when his Beauchamp Hall team lost in the semifinals at Hurlingham as well as in the semifinals at Ranelagh. It was in this latter match against Meadow Brook that Keene was knocked unconscious.
18. *Ibid.*
19. *Ibid.*, 140.
20. *Ibid.*, 141.
21. See the profiles in this book on both Harry Payne Whitney and Devereux Milburn for more details.
22. "New Team Will Defend Cup," *The New York Times*, 5 June 1913, p. 1.
23. See also Whitney and Milburn profiles in this book for more details.
24. Hatch and Keene, 136.
25. *Ibid.*, 138.
26. Newell Bent, *American Polo* (New York: Macmillan, 1929, 344–345.
27. *New York Times*, 5 June 1913.
28. Finis Farr, "Part II: The Fabulous World of Foxhall Keene," *Sports Illustrated*, 23 February 1959, p. 64.
29. *Ibid.*, 57.
30. *Ibid.*, 64.
31. Hatch and Keene, 170. [Foxhall Keene married the widowed Mrs. Frank Worth White (Mary Lawrence Keene) in 1892, filed a petition of abandonment in 1905 and was divorced in 1909. They had no children. Keene was survived by his two nephews, Foxhall Parker Keene Taylor and James Robert Keene Taylor, who were his sister's children from her first marriage, to Talbot Taylor. When Keene's father, James, died in 1913, he left an estate estimated at $15 million to his wife, which upon her death went to her two children.]

Harry Payne Whitney: "Total Polo"

by Nigel à Brassard

"America's polo Napoleon" was how A.S.G., writing in *The Graphic* in June 1911, described Harry Payne Whitney (29 April 1872–26 October 1930).[1] Whitney was a lawyer and businessman, a 10-goal polo player, a thoroughbred horse-breeder, racing's leading owner-of-the-year in the United States on eight occasions, an America's Cup contender with his yacht *Vanitie,* and a scion of the Whitney family. His marriage in 1896 to the heiress Gertrude Vanderbilt united two of the most socially prominent and wealthy families in America. The reason for Whitney's inclusion in this collection of essays is that he, more than anyone else, can claim to be the person responsible for the introduction of "total polo." His impact was important to polo, both in England and America, because it signaled a sharp change in the way that polo was played. He introduced the form of polo that was a precursor to the game we know today. In the *Hickok Sports History,* Whitney's tactics are contrasted with the English team's: "short passes to work the ball slowly toward the opposition's goal," whereas, the Whitney style is described as "the equivalent of basketball's fast break."[2] It was polo that was free roaming, involving long passes among the players, and hard hitting down the field of play. Edward Miller said when writing in *Modern Polo,* "Whitney's American team which beat England in the Westchester Cup made the year 1909 marked with red letters in the American calendar, for in this year the Cup, which had been since 1886 in England, returned from whence it came. The effect of this has been largely to increase the interest taken in polo all over the States."[3]

Newell Bent wrote about Whitney in *American Polo* in 1929, "As years come and go, no matter what any other man accomplishes, his name will go down alone in American polo as the man who proved to us that the seemingly impossible was possible, and that the Westchester Cup could be brought back to America."[4] When Whitney was inducted into the Polo Hall of Fame in 1990, it was cited, that "it would be impossible to overestimate the debt that American polo owes this ten-goal player."[5]

As is well-documented elsewhere, the modern game of polo that we know is directly descended from the form of polo played in the 1850s in the extreme northeast of India, in Manipur and Assam. Having read an article about "Hockey on Pony Back" in *The Field* in

Whitney on his top pony, Cottontail, previously owned by Laurence McCreery. A bay gelding, and Irish-bred, Cottontail was Whitney's best pony. When Cottontail died, Whitney had an inkstand made out of one of his hooves, now in the Museum of Polo (courtesy Museum of Polo and Hall of Fame).

March 1869, a group of British cavalry officers played the first recorded game in England. James Gordon Bennett, the proprietor of the *New York Herald*, saw polo played in London and thought the game would appeal in America and in 1876 he returned to New York with a supply of sticks and balls. Polo proved very popular with Americans and soon a number of polo clubs were being founded on the east and west coasts.

In the spring of 1886 an American player, Griswold Lorillard, watched some polo at Hurlingham. That night at dinner Lorillard suggested to the British players that Hurlingham send a team to Newport to play a series of matches against the Westchester Polo Club. The challenge was accepted and in August the matches were played. The superiority of the British players resulted in Hurlingham winning both games easily. An American, Cochran Sanford, wrote, "We can never bring the cup back until we meet the Hurlingham players at their own system." The English magazine *The Field* remarked, "The American genius for assimilating knowledge may enable the Westchester polo players to correct their play, and learn how to turn defeat into victory." It was to be fourteen years after the English victory in Newport before a team of American players had a return game against a Hurlingham team. In 1900 only one game was played, in which the Americans were resoundingly beaten 8–2. In 1902 the Americans visited Hurlingham again and played a series of three matches. The first the Americans won and the English won the next two games easily.

Harry Payne Whitney spent the summer of 1908 at the Rugby Polo Club playing the English polo season. During the winter of 1908 he had the idea of taking a team of American players to England to take part in some of the major tournaments of the season, but as this idea developed he decided the team should also have a go at trying to win the Westchester Cup for America. In April 1909 he sent a challenge to the English that was accepted by the Hurlingham Club. Whitney held a high opinion of English polo and knew that for the Americans to stand a chance at success they were going to have to be very well mounted. Whitney approached the task with a sense of determination; *The Graphic* noted that he "must have made a solemn vow to bring back the cup." He knew the English had more good players, better ponies and had proven in the international contests that they understood team and position play. Whitney realized that to win the Westchester Cup and make America the world champions of polo would require a single-minded effort. First, he needed to assemble the strongest possible team of American players. Second, he needed to build the strongest stud of polo ponies ever brought together up to that time. Third, and perhaps most importantly, he had to build a team that through their tactics and speed would result in a style of polo never before seen. Whitney's approach can be best described as developing "total polo." Edwin Hoyt, in his book *The Whitneys: An Informal Portrait 1635–1975,* described Harry's impact thus "... and where before his advent polo was a gentleman's preoccupation, he made his polo players work and learn how to play the best polo in the world. He made a job of it."[6]

Whitney was first to assemble the best players in America at the time. He selected the young Devereux Milburn. Milburn learned the game of polo as a young boy, played at Oxford, and then as a student at Harvard. He has been called the greatest back the game has ever seen and in his prime he had no peer. Milburn changed the way the back position is played. Previously the English regarded the back's role as similar to a "goalie" in soccer, i.e., to stay by his goal and defend. Milburn, by nature an aggressive player, always wanted to be part of the melee and if he saw an opportunity would take the ball downfield and occasionally score a goal. The 1909 American team played as a cohesive force and as their teamwork improved their positions on the field became more fluid. If Milburn went on the attack, Whitney and the Waterbury brothers would rotate behind him, ready if they had to turn back to defense. Apart from his natural talent, Milburn was a great "gentleman-athlete"; he maintained himself in top physical fitness and trained every bit as hard as any other professional athlete. Larry Waterbury was a superb all-round athlete, a rough and daring rider able to play at any position on the field. Monty Waterbury lacked some of Larry's physical toughness, but was full of finesse and shot-making ability. Together with Harry Whitney they constituted a formidable team of talent and determination.

While in England in 1908 Whitney observed that the British had an advantage over the Americans insofar as their horses were far superior to those the Americans rode. Mainly from Texas, American polo ponies were small rugged cow ponies, but what they had in stamina and hardiness they lacked in speed. Whitney, sparing no expense, sent his agents all over the world to find horses suited to polo and also started to buy British mares and breed them to western stallions. Whitney introduced a thoroughbred into the mixture that added not only size to the American mounts but also speed. When Whitney started to assemble the stud of ponies to take to England in 1909 he was fortunate that many of America's leading polo players offered to lend their best ponies. August Belmont, Robert Beeckman, James Abercrombie Burden, Howard and Harold Phipps and Paul Rainey all contributed ponies to the final twenty-eight that were taken by the team to England. The stud included such famous ponies as Laurence McCreery's Cottontail, along with English ponies like Cinders played by Walter Buckmaster, Mallard played by

The Big Four, unbeaten in international play (left to right): Dev Milburn, Harry Payne Whitney and the Waterbury brothers. No other team in polo's history had more influence upon the game (courtesy Museum of Polo and Hall of Fame).

Captain Miller, Flora played by Sir Frederick Freake, and Cinderella played by Rivy Grenfell. Larry Fitzpatrick, Whitney's great trainer, had brought on a number of high class ponies including Cobnut, Grayling, Summer Lightning and Kitty. This was without doubt the finest lot of ponies ever assembled. Within a decade of starting his quest to improve American ponies, Whitney made the American pony the equal of any other, and probably had a claim to being the best in the world.

According to Devereux Milburn, Whitney was an inspiring captain. Whitney had made a careful study of how the English played polo. This style is best described by one of the English Peat brothers as "what I call good polo is when the number one and his opposing back are galloping hard together up the field, riding each other off for all they are worth, followed by another pair doing the same, and they in turn followed by two other pairs."[7] Whitney was a natural captain and he stepped naturally onto center stage to perform this role. Foxhall Keene described Whitney on the field: "He had a stentorian voice and not only the players but everyone for miles around knew just what he thought at all times."[8] He was in command always, never stopped talking during a game, and played the team as though it was a unit obedient to his brain. When he captained a team he worked at it. He kept strict tabs on his players, making sure they kept training rules, chasing the Waterburys and Milburn around London like a headmaster after schoolboys and making certain they got in at a reasonable hour each evening. While Whitney insisted on complete dedication and commitment to the game, he also insisted on maintaining the tradition of cordial and friendly relations between the American and English teams both on and off the field.

The famous British polo commentator, Thomas F. Dale, wrote in *Polo at Home and Abroad* about Harry Payne Whitney's 1909 team displaying a combination of skill with discipline.[9] He remarked upon the wide intervals between the players and the long passes that they made. He noted their hard and accurate hitting. In addition he felt their success was due to the condition of their ponies. Dale also pointed out that the Americans had taken great care in studying the playing style of their opposition and adapting their tactics accordingly. This was total polo and based on a desire to win. Dale felt that the impact of the Whitney team was dramatic. He thought it changed the way polo was played in a number of ways, not least of which was the English decision to suspend the "offside" rule. Under the terms of the Westchester Cup deed of gift it had been stipulated that the rules played would be those of the defending home team. In 1909 the American team had to play with the English "offside" rule and when the English team went to challenge America in 1911 they had to do so under the American rules that did not include an "offside" rule. In 1911 the English decided to abandon the "offside" rule in their domestic polo. Another impact was that the English decided to abandon the Recent Form List and adopt the same handicap system for players as used by the Americans. Dale also noted that the English players were made to realize the importance of the training and conditioning of ponies. The surprise defeat by the visiting American team was a wake-up call for British polo. Dale summarized his account of the 1909 invasion in this way: "All they [the Americans] wanted was the right man, and they found two—Mr. Harry Payne Whitney and Mr. Devereux Milburn—one the best polo captain of the day and the other one of the best backs who has ever been on a polo ground."

The two captains in the 1911 contest at Meadow Brook: Irishman John Hardress Lloyd for Britain and H.P. Whitney (left) for America. Both achieved a 10-goal rating (courtesy Museum of Polo and Hall of Fame).

The team of the Waterbury brothers, Larry and Monty, Harry Payne Whitney, and Devereux Milburn were known as the "Big Four" and followed up their 1909 Westchester Cup success with further wins of this cup in 1911 and 1913. The team was never beaten and it is immortalized in the sculpture of the team by Herbert Haseltine, arguably the greatest ever polo bronze. Gertrude Whitney was a sculptor and shared with Harry a great interest in the arts. Her collection was to form the basis of the renowned Whitney Museum of

America vs. England at Meadow Brook, 1911. Harry Payne Whitney about to hit an off-side forehand shot (courtesy Museum of Polo and Hall of Fame).

American Art in New York. After the matches in England in 1909 Harry visited the Paris studio of Haseltine. There he saw Haseltine's bronze sculpture *Riding Off*—two polo players in full action riding each other off. Whitney took a liking to the bronze and commissioned Haseltine to come to America and execute a group portrait of the champion polo team. At the Whitney estate on Long Island, Haseltine was to share a studio with Harry's wife, Gertrude. The bronze called *The Meadow Brook Team MCMIX* was completed in 1911 and has the four players astride their horses. Haseltine was later to regard this commission as a turning point in his career. This author believes that three bronzes were cast: one was presented by Whitney to the Hurlingham Club in London and is on display in the club's polo bar, one was kept by Whitney, and one by Haseltine. In the New York Tennis and Racquet Club there is a set of maquettes of the individual mounted figures.

Whitney's contribution to American polo specifically and the game more generally cannot be overestimated. As Newell Bent wrote, "American polo for the first time having been teaching instead of, as in the past, learning."[10] *The Graphic* described the 1909 American victory as "the Whitney invasion" and was in no doubt about the man responsible for it. It is Whitney "... to whom is due all the credit of making American polo the formidable game it is today."[11]

Notes

1. *The Graphic*, 1911.
2. "*Polo in the U.S.*," in *Hickcok Sports History*, HickokSports.com.
3. E.D. Miller, *Modern Polo* (London: Hurst & Blacket, 1911), 361.
4. Newell Bent, *American Polo* (New York: Macmillan, 1929), 350.
5. Museum of Polo and Hall of Fame, Citation (West Palm Beach, Florida), 1990.

6. Edwin Hoyt, *The Whitneys: An Informal Portrait 1635–1975* (New York: Weybright & Talley, 1976).
7. Bent, p. 180.
8. Aldin Hatch and Foxhall Keene, *Full Tilt* (New York: Derrydale Press, 1938), 142.
9. T.F. Dale, *Polo at Home and Abroad* (London: London & Counties, 1915), 17–19.
10. Bent.
11. *The Graphic.*

Part II

Between the Wars

Introduction

The impact of the Great War, as it was then called, was more severely felt in Great Britain than in the United States. A large number of polo players were felled in the trenches of Belgium and France; along with the flower of British manhood, half the English team for the 1914 Westchester Cup, Capt. Leslie St. Clair Cheape and Capt. Herbert Haydon Wilson, were killed. The interminable roll of honor includes Jack Atkinson; John Campbell; the Grenfell twins, Rivy and Francis; Lord Hugh Grosvenor; Nigel Livingstone-Learmonth and Sir Francis Waller, all of whom embodied the fundamentals of character that pre-conflict society prized so highly: devotion to family, friends, duty, honor and country. America also shed blood; Maj. Augustus Peabody "Gussie" Gardner, from the Myopia Hunt Club and a winner of the Senior Championship, was the most prominent polo player to pay the ultimate price.

This period began with a sigh of relief at the end of the war, followed by a prosperous and carefree period, the times of speakeasies and flappers in America and the "lost generation" in continental Europe. The Great Depression tinged the 1930s with an aura of hopelessness and a reality of mass unemployment. Then came a new war, even more global and sinister than the last one.

Foreign Tours and Pony Power

Inevitably, polo was swinging on the seat of the changing economic situation. The mighty Americans continued to delve into their pockets at private and public polo pony sales. John Sanford was prominent in this regard, purchasing for son Laddie the best horseflesh that came on the market. The record bid was set for Jupiter, Lewis Lacey's big chestnut, who after the 1928 Cup of the Americas was sold at Fred Post's auction barn for the then astronomical sum of $22,000. The total sum paid for the Argentine pony string—$276,100—was so unbelievable that when Jack Nelson was notified of the amount, he sent a cable from onboard ship requesting confirmation. It was a preview of modern times, when many bidders spend considerable money in buying ponies; but no one reached the heights set by Australian Kerry Packer.

It was the heyday of foreign tours, of polo-pony shows, of comprehensive specialized publications and public support, especially in Argentina and the United States. It was a time when the best polo players, many ponies, and the top teams became household words. Large crowds made their way to Long Island to watch the matches: 40,000 at a game in 1914; a total of 101,000 in the 1928 series versus Argentina; and 85,000 against Britain two years later.

The year 1922 rang a loud bell. It is true that long before the war the world of polo had been warned about players from Argentina. From 1896 on, teams from that country had traveled to England and had performed well. But in 1922 an unheralded Argentine team — John and David Miles, Jack Nelson and Lewis Lacey — made the long sea voyage to England and proceeded to shock the British establishment. Although successful visits from South America had occurred intermittently, none had achieved the success that the Argentine Polo Federation team left in its wake. Winners of the Hurlingham Champion Cup, among other prestigious London tournaments, the reputation they gained merited an invitation from the U.S.P.A. to cross the North Atlantic to compete in the United States Open. This they did, and added the American Open crown to their credit. Effectively, this campaign established Argentina as a polo power to be reckoned with.

The worldwide economic depression took its toll. In Australia and New Zealand many clubs closed their doors, some forever, others temporarily, hoping and waiting for better times. The Savile Cup, New Zealand's oldest sporting trophy, was cancelled between 1931 and 1934. The Australasian Gold Cup was not played in 1931, 1932 and 1935. The number of teams participating in the U.S. Open and in the London season decreased dramatically. In spite of the worldwide economic turmoil, it is nothing short of amazing that the Ashton brothers took a trip around the world playing polo. Lesser efforts included two trips by the Argentine club Santa Paula to California and Long Island. The collected rewards were substantial: the Pacific Coast Open and the U.S. Open, plus reasonable prices at the usual post-tour pony auctions.

Equally creditable was the 1933 South African tour to Argentina. Hampered by totally different field surfaces— softer and with taller grass compared to South Africa's firm grounds— and more significantly by inferior mounts, the Springboks did well to reach the finals of the Argentine Open. Our contributor Susan Reeve is on record stating that Tommy Pope, the South African captain, would turn in his grave if excuses were offered after a defeat; nevertheless, Alberto Laffaye, a good judge of horseflesh who was an eyewitness to the games, was adamant that the majority of the ponies allotted to the visitors were not up to international standards because, prior to the Springboks' arrival, buyers from the United States and England had already purchased the best available ponies. To place the South African team's accomplishment in perspective, in its 113 years of existence only three other foreign teams have reached the Argentine Open final game: the American army squad in 1930, Meadow Brook in 1932 and Bostwick Field in 1950.

The International Scene

Polo as an international sport reached its summit. Those were the years of glory for the Westchester Cup between Great Britain and America, the International Field at Meadow Brook and Hurlingham's Number One ground becoming the showcases for many great and nearly great players. It showed to great advantage the rise of Tommy Hitchcock and the twilight of the still grand Devereux Milburn; the classicism of Lewis Lacey and the power of Winston Guest; the style of Captain Pat Roark and the efficiency of dour James Watson Webb, the only left-hander to reach a 10-goal handicap.

America challenged Britain for the Westchester Cup, and in 1921 brought the cup home in a series— so vividly described by Nigel à Brassard in *A Glorious Victory, A Glorious Defeat*— at the Hurlingham Club in Fulham. Five subsequent challenges proved sterile for the British hopes.

This era also saw the beginning of the Cup of the Americas, created by Jack Nelson of Argentina when the up-and-coming South Americans were denied participation in the Westchester contests. The international seasons in the United States were mirrored in London with visits from Australian, Indian, Argentine and Uruguayan teams, plus the added attraction of a Westchester Cup challenge at Hurlingham in 1936.

Polo as an Olympic sport reached its zenith at Ostend and Paris, and, sadly, its end—it is to be hoped only temporary—in Berlin. While polo at the 1900 games in Paris was a lark and London 1908 a purely local affair, the first postwar event in Belgium had a truly international flavor. Great Britain took the gold medal; Spain, with four grandees wearing the crimson and gold, won the silver, and the United States, meagerly represented by a military team drawn from the army occupation of the Rhine, took the bronze. The Belgian host team earned the wooden spoon.

Paris 1924 was even bigger. Played at the aristocratic venues of Bagatelle—still going strong today—and St. Cloud, it witnessed Argentina taking its first ever gold medal. America, with only Tommy Hitchcock as a marquee player, lost the final by one goal; while Great Britain took third place. The French and the Spaniards were outmatched.

At the 1936 Games in Berlin it was different. By that time the gap between polo's haves and have nots was so wide that three nations, Argentina, Great Britain and Mexico, entered a round robin to crown the gold medalists, while Germany and Hungary played two games, the winner to face the last team in the round robin, to decide the third place position. Inexplicably, the United States did not compete. The full American team—Eric Pedley, Mike Phipps, Stewart Iglehart and Winston Guest—had successfully defended the Westchester Cup at Hurlingham in June in two close, desperately fought games. An American presence would have added much to the Games. Argentina, superbly mounted, routed Mexico and England in its two appearances at Maifeld, located next to the Olympic Stadium. England, once more represented by a team of four serving army officers, took the silver medal, a creditable performance taking into account that they only had their regimental horses to ride against the pick of Argentina's pony strength. The final result, 11–0, amply tells the story of what will happen when thoroughbreds or nearly thoroughbreds are matched against inferior ponies.

The Argentine team then crossed the pond to challenge for the Cup of the Americas. Leaving no stone unturned, fourteen more ponies were shipped from Buenos Aires to New York to reinforce an already powerful string. The U.S.P.A.'s rationale in the selection process for the national team should be questioned. Rather than follow the careful and laborious method so well-proven in the 1928 and 1932 defenses, it was decided that the winner of the U.S. Open Championship would face the Argentines. Perhaps it was thought that Templeton, Winston Guest's team that counted three of the players that had been so successful at Hurlingham, would come through in the Open. However, Tommy Hitchcock and friends had other ideas and, surprise—Jock Whitney's Greentree took the Open. Thus, Greentree, completed with Pete Bostwick and Gerald Balding, rode on Meadow Brook's field to uphold America's colors. It is notable that in an international contest, Balding, a 9-goal handicap—later rated at 10—Englishman, played for America in September, after representing his native country against the U.S. in June. None of the American players selected for the Westchester Cup defense were included; neither was Cecil Smith, or Ebby Gerry, nor Raymond Guest.

The first game shook the American public: Argentina won 21–8. Clamors went up to change the team, and most sportingly, Jock Whitney—a 5-goal handicap player—offered to step aside. No changes were made to the team, except their shirts. The red jerseys worn in the first game were replaced by Greentree's pink. It did not matter. In a dull game, Argentina took match and trophy with an 8–4 win. There had been some intrigue from the Argentine side between the games. Anxious to secure the cup, a telegram was sent from A.A. de Polo headquarters in Buenos Aires to the delegation president, Jack Nelson: "Try to have the Americans keep the same team." Nelson kept the cable in his pocket.

After the double conquest of the Olympic gold medal and the Cup of the Americas, Luis Duggan, Roberto Cavanagh, Andrés Gazzotti and Manuel Andrada became national heroes. Two large landholders, descendants from Irish immigrants, were joined by a small-tenant farmer and a gaucho to write a glorious page in the annals of Argentine sport. The cutting from a Black Forest oak given as a prize for the Olympic gold medal was planted with much ceremony between Palermo's two grounds. It is now a large tree, having survived an encounter with a cement-loaded truck. That year of 1936 started the primacy of Argentina in world polo. At full strength, its national team has not lost a series since 1932.

The summer of 1939 witnessed the last Westchester Cup challenge for nearly half-a-century and the further rise of Argentina as a polo power. But for Britain, September brought an end to peace when German panzers crossed the Polish border. Two years and three months later the United States experienced another sneak attack, in Pearl Harbor. Once more, polo players from both countries suddenly found themselves with more important matters to attend.

Johnny Traill: An Irishman from the Pampas

by Roger Chatterton-Newman

During the century-and-a-quarter in which polo has risen to the highest level in Argentina, players with Irish antecedents have long been preeminent. One thinks of the Cavanaghs, Garrahans, Donovans, O'Farrells, Duggans and Lalors, among others, many of them still progressing steadily in the Asociación Argentina de Polo handicap lists.

High on what might be termed the Hiberno-Argentine role of honor stands John Arthur Edward Traill, known always as Johnny. The first player to reach a 10-goal rating in his adopted country, he achieved an international reputation, not only as a sportsman but also as a pioneer in the breeding of top polo ponies. Many people still recall with gratitude his teaching abilities at Roehampton, his English home for some thirty years. Perhaps the most notable of his pupils was Pat Smythe, first lady of show jumping. Traill lived to see her become not only the first woman to enter her particular discipline in the Olympic Games but also the first woman medalist.

Although Argentina claims Johnny Traill as its own — in print he always appears as Juan Traill, a named used in his lifetime generally by those employed on his family's *estancia* — he had, in a sense, triple nationality: by descent, a member of an old Anglo-Irish landed family,[1] by upbringing Argentine, by birth English, born in the London suburb of Penge, while his parents were on home leave, on 8 December 1882. A greater contrast between his birthplace and the wide-open spaces of his childhood cannot be imagined.

Ireland and Argentina are alike in love of the horse, and heredity can be seen in Traill's early success as a horseman. Yet, judging from the opening paragraphs of his unpublished memoir, The Last Chukka, it seemed an inheritance of which he knew little and of which his father, Robert Walter Traill, spoke but rarely.

Robert and his younger brother, Edmund, had abandoned their studies at Trinity College, Dublin, to become ranchers in Argentina in 1868. They were sons of the Reverend Dr. Robert Traill, rector of the desolate parish of Schull in west County Cork, during the devastating years of the Irish Famine from 1845 to 1847. The rector spent most of his modest income attempting to alleviate the miseries of the starving people, and had died of typhus— the notorious "famine fever" — in the process.

Dr. Traill's wife and large family[2]—Robert Traill was age three at the time, Edmund a mere baby—moved to Dublin, living in reduced circumstances until such time as the boys could take up a profession. By the time they decided to go to Argentina, Robert was reading civil engineering at Trinity and Edmund was studying medicine, but one gathers from Johnny's memoirs that they were both high spirited and did not fit easily into the bleak Calvinistic atmosphere of their mother's house.

Argentina offered them adventure and the chance to make their fortunes, with the government offering vast tracts of untamed land at almost token prices. They purchased around 40,000 acres in North Santa Fe Province, creating the estancias Las Limpias and Chirú, and never looked back. By the time Johnny was born, his father was a wealthy landed proprietor on a scale he could never have been in an Ireland torn by agrarian troubles and political agitation.

When Johnny was about ten, however, Robert decided the time had come to settle down as a country squire in England and he took a lease on Long Stratton Manor, near Norwich in Norfolk. The house, which was to be demolished after the Great War, stood at the heart of an estate that was small in comparison to La Esterlina, the Traill estancia, but it nevertheless conferred a social cachet on its tenant.

The Traills' tenancy was brief—problems at home in Argentina forced a return after barely twelve months—and all Johnny was to recall from his Norfolk sojourn was the comfort of the brougham taking him and a sister to children's parties. It was in striking contrast to the less sophisticated transport on the pampas.

The return to La Esterlina also meant that Johnny was never sent to Eton—part of the wider Norfolk plan—and one gathers that he learned more that was of use from Sixto Martínez, the criollo who coached him in polo. Martínez was an ideal teacher, having won the Argentine Open with Las Petacas in 1895 and 1896; indeed Frank Balfour, who did so much to promote polo in late nineteenth century Argentina, called him the best player in the world.[3]

Johnny's older brothers, Bob and Ned, were already established players by the time he began to take an interest in polo. Their father never played, although he would have been still in his thirties when the first "official" match took place in Argentina in 1875. (One memory of Ireland of which Robert Traill obviously spoke was playing cricket against W.G. Grace, so the sporting gene was there. In Johnny, apart from polo, it was also to come out in golf, at which he became a scratch player).

The three siblings, together with their cousin Joe, honed their skills playing as the family team of North Santa Fe.[4] Ned and Bob had won the Argentine Open for the first time in 1898, with the Casuals, and in 1904 John and Joe joined them to recapture the title. Johnny was to win the Open a total of eleven times, eight of them between 1904 and 1917 with the family squad, with Las Rosas in 1910 and Hurlingham in 1918. Two other regular players for North Santa Fe were the brothers David and John Miles of the estancia La Porteña, who were taught their game by Johnny. The friendship was to be cemented years later, when John Miles' daughter, Yvonne, known as Nenia, married Johnny Traill's elder son, John Basil.

The Traills owed much of their success to their pioneering pony breeding, as *The Polo Monthly* was to record:

> They were the first breeders in the Argentine to play ponies bred by themselves for polo, and their ponies by their first stallion, Spring Jack, marked the change between the old-fashioned Argentine and the blood pony of today. Being very strong horsemen, they did a good deal of their own breaking in, and a number of the ponies they used to play would be considered only half-broken by many. In spite of this most of their ponies turned out very well and made a big name for themselves, but few men would have done as much with them as the Traills did when they were first entered to the game.[5]

Las Rosas team, 1923 Argentine Open champions. Left to right: Johnny Traill with his trademark sheepskin, David Miles, Joseph Edmund Traill and John Miles. Interestingly, Joe Traill's mallet is equipped with an obsolete square head (courtesy Museum of Polo and Hall of Fame).

The 1911 season was particularly memorable. Again playing for North Santa Fe, Johnny and Joe, with Geoffrey Francis and Leonard Lynch-Staunton, took part in thirteen matches, many of them on difficult grounds, and won every one, scoring a total of 175 goals to 11. Later that year, they went to Chile to play a series of internationals and, although the ponies had a long and difficult journey over the Andes, the Traills were again undefeated, scoring 60 goals to 7 in four matches. Johnny's wider polo success was phenomenal at a time when the "hired assassin," or Latin American professional, was unknown. His arrival in England, with cousin Joe, in 1912, caused a sensation. Playing for Harold Schwind's El Bagual team, they were the cynosure of British polo society:

> The sensation of the London season has been the fine play of Mr. H. Schwind's Wild Horse team, a South American combination which takes its name from his ranch in the Argentine Republic. Two members of the side, Mr. John Traill and his cousin, Mr. Joe Traill, are remarkably good strikers and really brilliant players, being at present under-handicapped at 7 and 6 points respectively....
>
> Representing the new Argentine Club, they won the Social Clubs Cup at Hurlingham. The following week the Wild Horse competed in the Whitney Cup Tournament, and gave a great display against the Eaton team [run by the 2nd Duke of Westminster, whose seat was Eaton Hall in Cheshire], who attempted to concede a start of no fewer than a dozen goals to the South Americans. This Eaton woefully failed to do, for the Wild Horse, well served by their Argentine ponies, practically held them all through, actually hitting ten goals to Eaton's twelve.[6]

Johnny's handicap rose to 9-goals after his Hurlingham debut—much to his annoyance. A cartoon appeared in *Polo Monthly* of September that year, showing him literally "handicapped" with an appropriately numbered ball and chain.

On 5 June 1912 Johnny and Joe rode to the defense of Ireland when the annual Patriotic Cup match against England was played at Hurlingham.[7] The game was nearly cancelled, due to wet weather and soft grounds, and it was only when the Traills were found to be of Irish parentage that they were dragooned into saving the day. As it happened, England won 10–4.

The following year, Johnny married Henrietta Roberts—known as Rita—from the estancia El Injerto, not far from Las Limpias. By now he was rated at 10-goals, *el primer jugador* of Argentina, and much in demand, as the 1914 season was to prove. Two years later, he had been selected to play for a visiting Argentine team but Lord Wimborne, nonplaying patron of the British team preparing for the annual Westchester Cup tournament against the U.S.A., demanded that Johnny join him.

Johnny was reluctant to let down Argentina, but Wimborne—wealthy and something of a bully—would not consider a refusal and threatened that the press would "be disappointed" should the offer be turned down. In the event, Johnny went to America for the tournament, although he was unwell at the time and, because of the short notice, had to make do with unsatisfactory ponies. The combination proved too much, and he withdrew his services. As it happened, Great Britain won, but for the last time until 1997.

In 1921, he stood in for the injured Lord Rocksavage in a preliminary Westchester game. Great Britain won that match but the cup returned to the U.S.A. In 1927 he again played against the Americans in a pre–Westchester invitation match. Once more, Great Britain won, only to lose the cup in the final. One wonders if Johnny's inclusion in the principal tournament would have reduced the long period during which Great Britain waited to regain the trophy.

Indifferent health saw Johnny make England his principal home during the 1920s, the management of La Esterlina being left in the capable hands of Tom Willans, who had married Bob Traill's daughter, Daphne. Once he was settled in Putney Lane, Roehampton, almost opposite the gates of the polo club, British teams sought Johnny eagerly. For example, he won the prestigious Roehampton Cup with Eastcott in 1921 and had a happy association with the Duke of Westminster's Etonians—ended only when the mercurial "Bendor" tired of polo. It was, in many ways, an ironic association: Traill had thrashed Eaton, supposedly the best-mounted team in the country, with El Bagual in 1912, but the Duke was quick to restock his stables with Traill-bred ponies.

As a player and coach at Roehampton, Traill soon became a legend on the polo field.[8] With his sons, Jim and Jack, he formed his own team, the white-shirted Traillers, and the 1930s saw them carry off a series of prizes, including the Ranelagh and Roehampton Handicap tournaments. He was also known for his fiery temper on the field—an Irish legacy, perhaps. On one memorable occasion, he cracked his whip to such effect that a woman spectator cried out in alarm: "My God! Now that man's shot his horse!"

The war years brought tragedy. Johnny's elder son, Jim, was killed at the age of twenty-one while serving in the Royal Air Force, as were two of Bob's sons and Joe's only surviving son, Anthony. Tom Willans, Johnny's manager in Argentina, was another family casualty. The future of postwar polo was also unsettling for Johnny, and while he was involved closely with Billy Walsh in reviving Ham Polo Club—today the sole club within the Greater London area—the end of polo at Roehampton in 1956 caused him great sadness.[9]

His memoirs, written shortly before his death in 1958, reveal a man of singular modesty; but the fact remains that Johnny Traill was, and remains, a polo legend. It is pleasing to know that the family polo tradition continues among his grandchildren and great-grandchildren, and that there is once more a John Traill of North Santa Fe in the handicap lists.

Notes

1. Descended from Orcadian Norse settlers, the family traces its immediate ancestry to the Scottish lairds of Blebo, in Fife. The Irish branch was founded in the 17th century by James Traill, a colonel in Cromwell's army, who settled in Co. Down. Of interest is the origin of the family motto, *Discrimine salus*—"Salvation in danger." In or about 1418, an ancestor was shipwrecked off the Scottish coast and was saved by clinging to a rock in the sea. A column, or pillar, set in the sea is the family crest. See *Burke's Landed Gentry of Ireland* (London, Burke's Peerage Ltd., 1958).

2. The eldest child, Kathleen married in 1858 a Dublin barrister, John Hatch Synge, and became the mother of the playwright John Millington Synge (1871–1909). See *My Uncle John — Edward Stephen's Life of J.M. Synge.* Edited by Andrew Carpenter (London, Oxford University Press, 1974)

3. Horace A. Laffaye, *The Polo Encyclopedia* (Jefferson, North Carolina & London, McFarland & Co., 2004)

4. Joseph Traill (1877–1955) was the eldest son of Edmund.

5. *The Polo Monthly,* September 1912, p. 21.

6. *The Polo Monthly,* June 1912, p. 248.

7. The Patriotic Cup was first played in 1903. The tournament continued until 1932, when a high-goal Irish team beat England 12–1, and was revived in 1999. See *PQ International,* Autumn 1999, pp. 84–86.

8. Elizabeth Hennessy, *A History of Roehampton Club 1901–1986* (London, private printing, 1986).

Devereux Milburn: A Back for the Ages

by Dennis J. Amato

While Devereux Milburn's life was relatively short, his polo career was long and his legacy enduring. Even today, almost 65 years after his passing, Milburn still ranks not only as one of the greatest polo players of all time but also as one of the most influential. Moreover, he was the very embodiment of the gentleman-athlete in the first golden age of the sport.

He was born on 19 September 1881 into the family of John George Milburn, a distinguished Buffalo lawyer, who had emigrated from England to America as a young boy. As the second of the Milburns' two sons, Devereux took up polo at the tender age of 10, initially playing on a bicycle, with a sawed-off mallet, and then advancing to Shetland ponies. It is not at all surprising that he would be drawn to the sport, as Buffalo was one of the earliest venues for polo in the United States, it having arrived in this upper northwestern area of New York State in 1877, a mere year after James Gordon Bennett imported the pastime from England into America.

Devereux Milburn's progress in the sport was quite rapid, if not meteoric. By the age of 12, he had even organized his own polo club which included among its members another great future poloist, Charles Cary Rumsey, as well as J. Newton Scatcherd and Hallam Movius. Also, since Milburn was such an advanced junior player, he was frequently invited to join teams of his elders.

Devereux Milburn might have remained primarily in Buffalo for most of his professional and sporting career had it not been for one of those sudden and unfortunate episodes of history which would not only have a profound impact on the man but also on the sport itself. In 1901 President McKinley visited Buffalo to attend the Pan-American Exposition, which John Milburn headed up. While in this upstate city, the president and his wife resided at the Milburn home. On the second day of his visit, the president was shot, by an anarchist, while attending the exposition. After being rushed to a somewhat makeshift infirmary on the fair grounds, McKinley was later returned to the Milburn home where he subsequently died. Following the extremely intense and totally unwanted, not to mention untoward, print media glare of the day as well as the accompanying sidewalk gawkers outside his home, John Milburn decided to flee Buffalo and take a position at a prominent law firm in relatively anonymous New York City around 1904.

During these years of the early 1900s, Devereux Milburn, after graduating from the Fox Hill School in Pottsdam, Pennsylvania, went to his father's native land to attend Oxford University. While a student there, he was an active member of the university's polo team and made his mark by contributing significantly to back-to-back wins over the school's archrival, Cambridge University, in 1902 and 1903. In fact, the margin of victory in both years was an astounding 14 goals (14 to 0 and 15 to 1). In addition to polo, Milburn was on the university's rowing and swimming teams—earning a "blue" in the former to boot. Later in life he would add a number of other sports to his stable of endeavors, including steeplechase, fox hunting, tennis and golf. From most accounts he excelled in all of these activities.

During the summer months at university, Milburn returned home to upstate New York where he played polo at the Buffalo Country Club. In his first year as a listed member of the club in 1900, he carried a 0 handicap but, as chronicled in the Polo Association yearbooks of the time, he catapulted to a 3-goal rating a year later and to 4-goals the following year.

From Oxford, Milburn returned to the United States to follow in his father's legal footsteps by attending Harvard Law School, from which he graduated in 1906. At Harvard he also enjoyed the rare distinction of being admitted to the Porcellian Club as a graduate student, which was further evidence of this individual's ability to accomplish the unusual in a variety of undertakings.[1]

During his years in law school, Milburn regularly played polo at the Myopia Hunt Club in nearby Hamilton, Massachusetts, and saw his handicap rise in unison with the year from a 4 in 1904 to a 5 in 1905 to a 6 in 1906. Undoubtedly the highlight of his polo career up to this point was winning his first major tournament, the Senior Championship, in August 1904. The Myopia quartet of Maxwell Norman, Robert G. Shaw II, Rodolphe L. Agassiz and Devereux Milburn handily defeated the Bryn Mawr team 14 to 1¼ in the final match, played at the Point Judith Country Club in Narragansett Pier, Rhode Island.

Devereux Milburn in his student days, already an outstanding player (courtesy Museum of Polo and Hall of Fame).

Following graduation from Harvard, Devereux Milburn moved to New York to begin his legal career at his father's law firm of Carter, Ledyard & Milburn. His polo pursuits continued apace but now at the famed Meadow Brook Club in Westbury, Long Island, which was the epicenter of the sport in America at the time and would remain so until the outbreak of the Second World War. In his first year as a listed member of Meadow Brook in 1908, Milburn's handicap was raised from a 6 to a 9, which by whatever standards—those of the day or even contemporary ones—was a fairly substantial leap in so short a period of time for a high-goal player.

However, the rating probably belied his true ranking as the handicap system in this era was capped at 9 in the United States in 1903 and would not be raised back to its former plateau of 10 until a virtual fourteen-year moratorium ended in 1917.[2] Milburn, who had carried a 9 goal rating since 1908, would, in a long overdue move, finally be raised to this new ultimate rating of 10 with the 1917 revision and would continue at that level until 1928 when he voluntarily relinquished it at the age of 47.

In the milieu of Meadow Brook at the time, Milburn was exposed to the best polo of its day, be it the quality of the matches, the high caliber of the players and teams, the seemingly endless strings of world-class ponies, or the unmatched facilities. With regard to the latter, Meadow Brook alone had three polo fields in 1908—besides outstanding stabling—which would later be expanded to eight grounds. Among them was the famous International Field with its trademark "robin's egg blue" grandstands that would be reserved for the most important events, including in later years the National Open, the Monty Waterbury Cup, and the major international matches.

Furthermore, the Island was honeycombed with scores of other polo clubs like the Rockaway Hunting Club and the Piping Rock Club as well as a large number of private fields. In fact, in the era in which Milburn played, Long Island would eventually sport close to 30 clubs and two dozen private fields for a total of some 60 outdoor playing fields of which close to 50 were in active use at one time or another at the game's zenith in the period between the two wars. So impressive were the playing facilities on the Island that *The Polo Monthly* noted somewhat ruefully: "The wealth of good polo grounds in America and especially on Long Island, is almost unbelievable, and accounts very largely for the high quality of the polo there."[3]

Small wonder that in this unique environment Milburn was able to thrive and to hone his already formidable polo skills even further. The resultant effects were abundantly apparent in Milburn's first season at Meadow Brook, where he played in a number of important high-goal events including the Hempstead Cups (runner-up), the Westbury Challenge Cup and the Meadow Brook Club Cups (winner). At the nearby Rockaway Hunting Club, Milburn was a member of the Meadow Brook squad that took home victories in both the Rockaway Hunting Club Cups and the Cedarhurst Challenge Cup, which were major events in their day. Similar Meadow Brook representation in Rhode Island in late summer brought wins in such important challenges as the Narragansett Cups and the Westchester Polo Club Cups. Among his teammates that year were W. Russell Grace, J. Peter Grace, John S. Phipps, Larry Waterbury, Monty Waterbury, and Harry Payne Whitney. Although Milburn generally stayed in the number 4 or back position, he occasionally played in the number 3 spot.

With the opening of the 1909 season, the major event looming on the horizon was the upcoming Westchester Cup series, which was a special polo tournament played between England and America that had been initiated in 1886 as a result of a somewhat casual remark by one of James Gordon Bennett's associates, Griswold Lorillard, while being entertained by his English hosts at the Hurlingham Club. In addition to its inaugural year, this Anglo-American rivalry had been revived in an informal but officially unrecognized single game match in 1900 as well as in a formal challenge in 1902. The English easily took honors on all three occasions. Moreover, they won all but one of the individual games.

In an era when England was clearly dominant in the sport, an attempt to win the Westchester Cup, or the "International Polo Cup" or the "International Polo Challenge Trophy," as it was alternatively referred to, was indeed a daunting one. However, the Polo Association selected an individual who ultimately proved to be well up to the task: the indomitable Harry Payne Whitney.

Although Whitney may have exuded outright confidence, he later conceded that he was pessimistic about the Americans' chances for success. Nevertheless, he persevered in his inimitable methodical fashion in assembling the finest selection of players and ponies available at the time. For team composition, his core group consisted of Larry and Monty Waterbury in

A mighty back on White Rock. Dev Milburn played for America in every Westchester Cup match from 1909 until 1927, an unbeatable 14-match record, all but six as captain (courtesy Museum of Polo and Hall of Fame).

the numbers 1 and 2 positions, himself in the number 3 slot as well as team captain, and Devereux Milburn as back. This combination would eventually gain the moniker of "The Big Four" and become legendary in polo lore. The spare player brought along was the rising star, Louis Stoddard. Each of the Big Four carried a 9-goal rating, which as previously mentioned was the highest Polo Association rating in 1909. Arguably, this combination was to all intents and purposes the world's first "40-goal" team.[4]

For the horseflesh, Whitney himself for a considerable period of time had been acquiring some of the best polo ponies that were available on the market for what was initially planned to be play during the "London season," as the polo circuit among Roehampton, Ranelagh and Hurlingham, England's top clubs, was called. Besides his personal stud, he was loaned a number of superb horses for the international series by several friends.

The net result of this carefully choreographed effort was an American dominance from start to finish during their English visit. They won all but one of the trial matches, including the prestigious Ranelagh Cup, and swept the two-game Westchester Cup challenge by hefty margins of 9 to 5 and 8 to 2 respectively. Yankee superiority was attributed to a combination of stronger horsepower and better play.

The play that London season, particularly during the international matches, in fact represented a major inflection point in the history of polo and in many respects ushered in the era of "modern polo" as we know it today. The importance of the event is vividly captured by Newell Bent in his classic work, *American Polo*:

> Team play, developed to an extent never reached before, was shown by our team, and the brilliant passing to each other by the Waterbury brothers ... was superb; the team with Mr. Milburn's long and accurate hitting and his long runs with the ball, made possible by the watchfulness and interchanging positions as taken care of by Mr. Whitney, revolutionized the conception of polo play of the day.[5]

These sentiments were echoed by Captain J. Hardress Lloyd, the British back in the second match, who commented: "Their play has been a revelation."[6]

This breakthrough manner of play was not at all accidental but quite deliberate. When Milburn joined Meadow Brook, he and Whitney realized that the American polo fields, which were typically hard and dry, would afford their ponies very secure footing. Consequently, they soon experimented and ultimately perfected a new style of play of riding at top speed to the boards and passing the ball great distances. As a result, instead of team members being tightly clustered together, they could spread out and hit the ball substantial lengths to each other. The dynamics of polo matches would thus be changed forever.

Milburn was also credited for transforming the role of back from what had previously been almost exclusively a defensive position to a somewhat interchangeable defensive/offensive one. As an English writer at the time stated, "The duty of the back is purely defensive and he should never leave his position, though Mr. Devereux Milburn, the American player, has on occasion gone on through the field and scored brilliantly."[7] Further enhancing the position of the back was Milburn's quantum advancement and refinement in the use of the backhand shot. If Milburn had not in fact invented the offside backhand, he perfected it as a potent weapon. Robert F. Kelley, a noted polo journalist years later remarked, "His development of the backhand, particularly the on-side [near side] backhand has revolutionized the theory of backplay."[8]

The *New York Times* added at the time of his death: "He was the first player whose backhand strokes were as long and accurate as forward hits."[9] All of this was reflected by numerous chroniclers of the 1909 matches who, in the parlance of the times, were "dazzled" by Milburn's awesome ability to hit the ball great distances backwards or forwards from either side of his pony. *The Polo Player's Diary* even went so far as to say,

"There is no stronger hitter in England than Mr. Devereux Milburn."[10]

The Big Four reprised their performance in both the 1911 and 1913 rematches of the Westchester Cup, although by substantially smaller margins of victory. In the final encounter before World War I in 1914, the Americans lost to the English squad due to an unfortunate convergence of factors, including the replacement of Harry Payne Whitney, who had retired from international play, by the 7-goaler René LaMontagne, as well as the strategic error in the first match of moving Devereux Milburn to the number 3 position from back.

In between these international matches, Milburn in 1913 married Nancy G. Steele, the daughter of a J.P. Morgan partner. In fitting fashion, Harry Payne Whitney gave his former teammate six polo ponies and a groom as a wedding gift! The couple later built a house in Old Westbury, Long Island. When the United States entered the First World War, Milburn joined the army and went on to serve with distinction as a major in the field artillery in France.

Following the war, Milburn also joined, as well as captained, the new American Westchester team combinations of 1921, 1924 and 1927 which included the constants of J. Watson Webb and Tommy Hitchcock along with Louis Stoddard (1921), Robert Strawbridge Jr. (1924)

The last international appearance for Milburn: the 1927 Westchester Cup at Meadow Brook, Long Island, against Army-in-India, representing Britain. Left to right: Devereux Milburn, Malcolm Stevenson, Tommy Hitchcock Jr., J. Watson Webb (courtesy Museum of Polo and Hall of Fame).

and Malcolm Stevenson (1924 and 1927). So broadly known and highly regarded had Milburn become beyond polo circles that he even merited a *Time* magazine cover story the week prior to the 1927 internationals.

As the British were severely depleted, both in terms of men and horses, by the war, the Americans rather easily defended their possession of the trophy in all three of these postwar encounters. Milburn noted that these challenges were not particularly exciting given the mismatch of resources. Notably, Milburn's participation in seven Westchester Cup teams established a record that is unlikely ever to be matched.

Interestingly, the Westchester Cup series in many respects served as a broader barometer of the leadership in American polo since its earliest days until the Second World War. Peter Vischer noted in *Polo* magazine that after the "formative years" following the game's introduction into America by James Gordon Bennett there ensued three distinct eras of American polo which were presided over by Harry Payne Whitney (1909–1913), Devereux Milburn (1914–1927) and Tommy Hitchcock (1928 to World War II).

In addition to his prominence in the Westchester Cup matches, Milburn won numerous other polo events over his playing career including the Open in 1916, 1919, 1920 and 1923 as well as the Monty Waterbury Cup in 1923, 1926 and even as late as 1931 after he had "retired" from most high goal events. Besides his previously mentioned victory in the 1904 Senior Championship, Milburn was also a member of the winning teams of 1909, 1910, 1911, 1915, and 1920. He was only excluded from participating in the Junior Championship because his handicap was too high!

In March 1928, Milburn had a major steeplechase accident in Aiken, South Carolina, in which he broke his collarbone and an arm in addition to injuring his right shoulder. Nevertheless, even as late as August of that year, he was still expected to play in the first Cup of the Americas match between Argentina and the U.S. However, his injuries proved to be so debilitating that Milburn not only withdrew from consideration for the American team but also took the more dramatic step of disengaging altogether from high-goal competitive polo, although he would continue to play the game off and on for the rest of his life and would even win a nine-goal tournament not too long before his passing. The legendary sportswriter Grantland Rice once quipped about the cumulative effects of Milburn's many accidents over his lifetime: "Dev Milburn, one of the all-time greats, in keeping his bones together, has used enough wire to encircle Long Island."[11]

Despite his pullback from major tournaments, Milburn's rating was still an impressive 6-goals in 1929, 7-goals from 1930 to 1937 and 6-goals from 1938–1942. His involvement in the sport further extended to the ongoing training and development of younger players, to participating in various advisory posts within the United States Polo Association and to serving as the chairman of the selection committee of the East team for the landmark East-West games in 1934, and to making his eighth and final Westchester Cup appearance in 1939, but this time as the referee.

While Milburn is universally regarded as probably the best back to have played the sport of polo with the possible exception of Lewis Lacey, his memory conjures up associations in a number of tangential areas. For example, several of his ponies, such as Tenby, Ralla, Flora, Beatrice, and Perico, have become legendary in the sport. Among all his ponies, the venerable Tenby was probably his favorite and when the horse died of natural causes on the return trip from the 1921 internationals his shipside sendoff was replete with full funerary honors.

In the art world, there are linkages as well. The renowned English painter Sir Alfred Munnings, on a six-month visit to United States in 1924, spent some time on Long Island to work on a number of society portrait compositions. Among them was the enduring one of Devereux Milburn as a polo player riding the piebald Gargantilla. In bronze, the incomparable Herbert Haseltine sculpted an extraordinary piece entitled "The Big Four," which was commissioned by Harry Payne Whitney. The bronze immortalized the famous four members of the American international team. In front is Devereux Milburn in an almost lyrical position, with his head cocked back and his mallet slung tightly in an upright position against his chest as the horse is also being pulled up. Haseltine's individual trophies presented to all the team members of the 1924 Westchester Cup have a variation of this figure, although the player is not specifically identified as Milburn.

Finally, turning to print, Milburn's monograph, *The Science of Hitting in Polo*, has been long considered a staple of polo literature. In this work the author opined upon an aspect of polo he was long noted for. Milburn also contributed the "Polo" chapter to Frank Wrench's well known 1937 book, *Horses in Sport*, as well as the foreword to Walter B. Devereux Jr.'s now standard work, *Position and Team Play in Polo.*

On 15 August 1942, just shy of his sixty-first birthday, Milburn died of a heart attack on the ninth tee of the Meadow Brook course where he had been playing a round of golf. According to *The New York Times*, "Seeming to be in good health, Mr. Milburn played a strenuous round of the course at the club here, of which he was president, just before he collapsed."[12] He left behind a widow, Nancy; two daughters, Katharyn and Nancy; and two sons, Devereux Jr. and John. His namesake would go on to become a noted polo player in his day, achieving a 5-

goal rating, as well as rise to senior partner status in the same law firm as his father and grandfather, and the chairmanship of the U.S.P.A. from 1950 to 1960.

On the day after his death, *The Times* obituary in one insightful sentence in particular succinctly summarized this individual's remarkable polo career:

> Mr. Milburn, one of the great figures in the history of American sport, was a magnetic and stirring leader as a consummate performer; a man of forceful, bold personality, quick to seeing new ways of doing old things; finding joy in every moment on the polo field and playing the game to the last whistle with every ounce of his strength and spirit.[13]

While Milburn's life had unfortunately cut short, it was nevertheless been a very full one. Perhaps the ultimate accolade accorded him came from Tommy Hitchcock, who, when in response to a query, indicated that his all-time best polo team would be "Milburn, Milburn, Milburn and Milburn," if there were four Milburns available.[14] Certainly the remark contained a lot of theatrical hyperbole but nevertheless reflected the high esteem Milburn was held by his contemporaries, a view that largely remains undiminished with the passage of time among current aficionados of the game.

Notes

1. Founded in 1791, the Porcellian Club is an exclusive all-male, so-called final club at Harvard University.

2. A somewhat obscure fact is that the American handicap system as ingeniously devised in 1888 was initially calibrated on a 0 to 10 basis but in May 1903, as the *New York Times* reported, the executive committee of the Polo Association "made changes of a more radical nature than usual" whereby "a higher standard for polo excellence has been shown by the reduction of several of the star players." (2a) This "tendency ... to make a severer test for the highest polo honors" resulted in two players (Foxhall Keene and Monty Waterbury) losing their 10-goal ratings. (2b) What then followed—and undoubtedly unintentionally—was tantamount to a fourteen year suspension on the top ranking which would not be reversed until February 1917 when the association raised five players to the highest level, "the object being to make the rating in this country uniform with abroad. The maximum rating in England has always been 10." (2c) This sea change was an event clearly welcomed in the pages of *The Polo Monthly* in its March issue, as England had steadfastly retained awarding the 10-goal rating since the adoption of the handicap system in 1910 by the Hurlingham Polo Committee, the official English governing body of the sport. In the magazine's words, "An innovation was introduced [in America] by the raising of the limit mark from 9 to 10 goals, the scale now being exactly the same as that at Hurlingham."

(2a) *New York Times*, 24 May 1903, p. 16.

(2b) *New York Times*, 14 February 1917, p. 6.

(2c) "Handicap Changes," *The Polo Monthly* 17, no. 1 (March 1917): 25.

3. "Polo Grounds in America," *The Polo Monthly*, 56, no. 1 (June, 1939): 18.

4. Further corroboration of this point is that all four players were rated at 10-goals by the Hurlingham Polo Committee in at least 1911 and 1913. See E.D. Miller, *Modern Polo* (London: Hurst and Blackett, 1911), third edition, 478–487; and L.V.L. Simmonds and Captain E. D. Miller, eds., *The Polo Annual for 1914* (London: The Field & Queen [Horace Cox] 1914), 229.

5. Newell Bent, *American Polo* (New York: Macmillan, 1929), 171.

6. "America Regains the Cup," *The Polo Monthly*, 1, no. 5 (July 1909): 337.

7. Bent, 171.

8. "Devereux Milburn Dies Playing Golf," *The New York Times*, 16 August 1942, p. 45.

9. *Ibid.*

10. *The Polo Player's Diary for 1910* (London: S.B. Vaughn, 1910), 39.

11. Grantland Rice, "The Last of the Grenadiers, "*England vs. America, 1939* (Program), New York: United States Polo Association, 1939, p. 41.

12. *New York Times*, 16 August 1942.

13. *Ibid.*

14. Thomas Hitchcock Jr., "All-American Polo Team," *Polo* 9, no. 1: (December, 1932) 17.

Lewis Lacey: Master of the Game

by Horace A. Laffaye

On a cool spring morning in 1889, a young couple and their three children alighted from the horse-drawn Lacroze tramway close to the entrance to the Hurlingham Club, on the outskirts of Buenos Aires.[1] William Lacey, his wife Martha Brook, with Charles, age three, Lewis, age two, and Leonard, just a baby in his mother's arms, were to begin a new life in faraway Argentina.

Mr. Lacey, a professional cricket player who had recently returned to England after a sojourn in Canada, had been contracted by the club as a general factotum. Founded just a year earlier, the club was a long way from what it was to be quite soon: the symbol of the British establishment in South America.[2] Therefore, when William Lacey took his first walk around the premises, he realized that everything had to be done. This he accomplished in a remarkable way. The racetrack, the cricket ground, the polo field, the landscaped park and the tennis courts were operational within a year. "The Magician" William Lacey, who also designed the initial nine holes of the golf course, became an institution within the club, which he also represented in cricket.[3] When the urgent need for polo equipment arose, William started selling mallets at the club, an endeavor that eventually led to Lacey & Sons, the premier supplier for polo players in Buenos Aires.[4]

William and Martha's second son, Lewis Lawrence Lacey, was born in Montreal, Canada, on 17 February 1887. As a child, he attended Buenos Aires English High School, that redoubtable institution founded by Alexander Watson Hutton, the Scot educator who was the father of Argentine soccer.[5] Lewis's polo career began early, when he began playing with his father and brothers, all polo players. Charles Frederick, the eldest sibling, and Eustace Leonard both took the Argentine Open; and Henry Cecil was a finalist in the U.S. Open. The youngest of the brothers, William George, flying with the Royal Air Force in World War I, was posted as missing just one week before the Armistice was signed in France in 1918. His memorial is located at Thivencelle churchyard.

Lewis's polo career was meteoric. The first documented polo match in which he participated was in 1903, while he was still a student.[6] By 1908 he had won the Anchorena Cup — now the Tortugas Open — had played in the Open Championship and taken the subsidiary Handicap Tournament. When the first list of handicaps in Argentina was published in 1911,[7] the name Lewis Lacey was at the very top, one of only four players handicapped at nine goals, the others being John Argentine Campbell, Hugh Scott Robson — both born in Argentina — and Joseph Edmund Traill, an Irishman from Santa Fe born in Dublin.[8]

Lacey reached the summit in 1915. That year he took his first Open Championship, playing off a 10-goal handicap, as a member of Palomar, an "Argentine" club in an era dominated by "English" teams. Then it was off to war for Lewis Lacey.[9] Like many other Anglo-Argentines, Lewis enlisted in the 1st King Edward's Horse (The King's Oversea Dominions Regiment). For his military training, he was posted to the Reserve Regiment in Dublin.

Tony Lacey writes: "The British Army in 1915 took over the Curragh Racecourse in Ireland where they held equitation courses for recruits who had not ridden too much. Father was sent on such a course and as they realized he could ride quite well, they gave him the job of acting as escort to the Colonel who could not ride at all! Father and another soldier would ride on either side of the Colonel when doing a jumping course or some other military exercise, and were there to see that the Colonel did not fall off his horse."[10]

From Ireland, Second Lieutenants Brakell and Lacey were posted to the K.E.H. on the front line in 1917, the year of Passchendaele, in which horrible battle they were engaged. On 31 July, Lt. J.F. Brakell was posted as missing. Luckily for him, he had been wounded and taken prisoner.

In spite of the miserable conditions of trench warfare, there were some opportunities for sports. To quote from Lt. Col. Lionel James's *History of The King Edward's Horse*:

> Gen. Sir A.E.A. Holland who commanded the 1st Corps was a keen polo player. He had a quite serviceable team in his H.Q. and it played several games against the "C" Squadron, King Edward's Horse, billeted near. With Lieutenant Lacy [sic] as No. 4 and Lieutenants Fannin, Murray and McCulloch playing forward the unit had quite a creditable team, but the regiment could not produce much in the way of ponies, and there was little time or opportunity to train them.[11]

Capt. Lewis Lacey was fortunate enough to survive the carnage relatively unscathed. Not so Lt. Frank Benitz, killed while flying; not so Lt. John Campbell, Inniskilling Dragoons, dead from wounds near Honnechy; the Cobbold brothers, Norman and Walter; Capt. William Cowper-Coles, Royal Flying Corps; Maj. Richard Cox, M.C., Devonshire Regiment; Frank Leared, also from King Edward's Horse; Dr. Anthony Traill, killed in France, and Lt. Nigel Grenville Wells, Welsh Guards, who died in Palestine. All were polo players from Argentina. And close to Lacey, were Lt. John Frend, Royal Field Artillery, a civil engineering student, son of Dr. and Mrs. John Alfred Frend from Rosario, whose sister Nora in due time would be Mrs. Lewis Lacey, and the already mentioned Capt. William Lacey, M.C., his youngest brother.[12]

After demobilization, Lewis Lacey returned to Argentina and his polo career began in earnest. Lacey joined forces with his lifelong friend Jack Nelson to anchor Hurlingham teams that took the Argentine Open in 1920, 1921, 1925, 1927, 1929 and 1937. His international career was most distinguished. It began with the historic tour of 1922, an enterprise that placed Argentina on the polo map of the world. Organized by Nelson, led by Lacey and financially supported by the Jockey Club, eight men traveled to England with the avowed goal of learning. They taught more than what they learned. At full strength, the team of John Miles at number 1, Jack Nelson at number 2, David Miles at number 3 and Lewis Lacey at back was unbeaten in England. The reserves, Louis Nelson, Eduardo Graham Paul, Alfredo Peña Unzué and Carlos Uranga, acquitted themselves quite nicely. At the end of the day, different teams had taken the premier British prize, the Hurlingham Champion Cup plus the Roehampton Open Cup, the Whitney Cup, the Ladies Nomination Cup and the Junior Championship.

The final match for the Coronation Cup gave an example of Lacey's sportsmanship. With the game in the balance, David Miles took a high shot that every player on the field thought was a clear goal, and so did the umpires. While the teams were galloping back to the center of the field, it was noticed that the flagman had not signaled a goal. The umpires overruled the flagman, but Lewis stated that he could not accept a goal under the circumstances. It was disallowed, and after a titanic struggle, the 17th/21st Lancers won the match in extra chukker.[13]

Canadian-born Lewis Lacey was one of the few to play international polo for two countries, Argentina and England (courtesy Museum of Polo and Hall of Fame).

The extraordinary performance of the Argentine team resulted in an invitation from the U.S. Polo Association to cross the Atlantic Ocean and compete in the U.S. Open Championship. Men and horses made the journey, which culminated in taking the United States Open at Rumson Country Club, defeating the Meadow Brook team with 10-goalers Tommy Hitchcock and Dev Milburn by a decisive 14 to 7 score. There was drama during the game, because David Miles injured his leg in a collision with Hitchcock. After some delay, David removed his boot, wrapped a polo bandage around the leg, put on a tennis shoe and finished the game. Not only did Miles continue playing, he also scored four goals after his injury, being the high scorer of the match. Devereux Milburn, no mean judge of the game, said afterwards, "If there is a better 10-goal player than David Miles, show me, because I don't see anyone."[14]

This tour of 1922 became the lore of Argentine polo. No other team has taken the open championships of England and the United States in the same year with identical players.

In 1923 Lacey crossed the Andes to play cricket in Chile. When the locals found out that Lewis was on tour, they promptly invited him to play a game of polo. Charles Crawford-Smith, Harry Wesley Smith and Willie Warde, all members of the cricket eleven, formed a team that defeated the Chilean national squad.

From then on, Lacey traveled to Britain every year. Trophies came his way: the Ranelagh Open Cup and the Coronation Cup completed his own quadruple crown of English polo. Considered at the time the premier back in the world, and perhaps the top player, he was invited to play for the best teams. The Spanish Duke of Peñaranda counted on him to spearhead his team, El Gordo, named after his Spanish estate; King Alfonso XIII invited Lewis to join him at Casa de Campo, near Madrid; Prince Georg Fugger requested his presence at his castle in Bannacker, Germany. Lacey also toured the United States every other year, playing in the Open Championship and representing both England in the Westchester Cup and Argentina in the

A picture-perfect swing: Lewis Lacey at the top of a forehand shot. Soft hands on the reins, exquisite balance, absolute control of mallet and pony. Palermo, 1932 (courtesy Museum of Polo and Hall of Fame).

Cup of the Americas. Incidentally, he was field captain on every occasion. His last competitive appearance in America was in 1931 with a Hurlingham team.

Both Britain and Argentina wanted Lacey—and also Johnny Traill—to represent them at the 1924 Olympic Games in Paris. Lacey was quoted as saying that he would play for England; nevertheless, he would not compete against the Argentine team.[15] Nationality requirements being more strict in those days, Lacey, Canadian-born, was not considered as eligible for the Argentine team. As it was, the South American team with Argentine-born players, three of them with British surnames, won the first ever gold medal in their country's history. Arturo Kenny, Juan Nelson, Juan Miles and Col. Enrique Padilla added another laurel to polo in that country.

Lewis Lacey kept on playing during the 1930s, finally retiring from competitive polo in 1941, with an 8-goal rating. His first Open win had been in 1915, the last one in 1937, twenty-two years apart. Juan Carlos Harriott Jr. equaled his record, winning the Open between 1957 and 1979; only Enrique Alberdi has surpassed that mark, for he took his first Open in 1934 and his last one in 1957.

By the mid–1920s Lewis was at his prime. While his friends thought he might become a lifelong bachelor, he wooed and won Nora Frend, daughter of a Rosario physician. They were married in 1926. The groom was thirty-seven, the bride twenty-three. Nora Amy Charlotte Frend was a beautiful woman. A photograph taken at Meadow Brook in 1928, when she presented the prizes after the U.S. Open Championship, shows a tall, elegantly dressed lady, with a friendly smile. Three children were born: Lewis Anthony, Ann Louise and Jeremy Nigel. A family man, Lacey spent most of his leisure time at his farm, La Bienvenida, located between Hurlingham and Morón and purchased with the earnings from his pony Jupiter's sale.

The January 1928 issue of the magazine *Polo & Equitación* carries a brief note announcing the birth of the Laceys' first son, Lewis Anthony. The unknown writer stated, "It is expected that the child of the prestigious polo player will inherit his abilities so he will become the pride of Argentine polo." Years later, in adulthood, Tony Lacey wryly noted, "My brother Nigel and I could never be near a horse, handle a mallet or even wear polo gear without someone saying, 'Of course, they will never be as good as their father.' At least, Nigel had father's blue eyes, while my sister and I had brown eyes."

Such is the burden of having a famous parent. Tony continues:

> My father was the best dressed man I ever saw and as time went by his frame remained the same. Gradually he acquired an impeccable collection of suits, all perfectly tailored. He wore a starched collar and gold cufflinks, occasionally the pair given to him by the Prince of Wales as a wedding present. Father was an early riser and before showering he polished his shoes very carefully. Such fastidiousness with his attire arose from his experiences as an officer in the First World War. When he met with some of his war comrades, they all would put their right foot forward to inspect and compare the shine on their shoes.
>
> My father did not smoke, drank quite moderately, and during weekends, when us youngsters were hoping to have tea at the Hurlingham Club, which offered a sumptuous chocolate cake, he would say, "Let's go home, it's tastier there."
>
> Quite frequently, he entertained us playing the ukulele after dinner. Sometimes, ladies of Mother's age would compliment him, starting with his perfect equitation, continuing with his light blue eyes, and finally, admiring his polo swing. Mother listened in silence, with a shy and passing smile.

The Laceys had a summer farm in Córdoba, halfway between Río Ceballos and La Falda. It was a remote and marvelous place. Picking up the mail and purchasing food required a 40-minute ride. It was also the site for spirited polo games. The players were Lewis, sons Tony and Nigel, daughter Ann and her husband, Willem, a Royal Dutch senior executive.

Nigel Lacey writes:

> We rode almost every morning on horses sent by rail from Buenos Aires. Among those were Tormenta, Mother's favorite, who was close to a mountain pony, so she felt quite secure while riding. Bosque was Father's pony, a beautiful zaino, but quite churlish. I know that very well because he threw me off a few times until my father schooled him and cured his vices forever. After those lessons, Bosque never gave me any trouble. When we played a game, it was preferable to play on Father's team because he always passed the ball in such a way that it was easy to hit at. If Ann played on his team, there were continuous shouts, such as "leave it, Daddy" and even a hoarse "dejála." If for any reason the match was slow, Father would slide to the sidelines to school his pony; once finished, he would return to the fray. I remember him doing the same thing when he umpired practice games at Hurlingham, because he thought there was no sense in blowing the whistle when the players were having fun.
>
> His unflagging courtesy, good manners and utmost consideration toward everyone made him loved by his daughters-in-law, nephews and grandchildren. Everybody seemed to want to greet him. Once he stopped the car and hurried to greet a man whose attire proclaimed straitened circumstances. Later he explained that he was an old neighbor at a time when there were only three houses in Hurlingham.
>
> His patience with animals was never-ending, whether schooling ponies or teaching Mother's Dachshunds to beg for food. He was a wonderful father; however, on the polo ground he was simply too fast for us to maintain his pace of play.[16]

Lacey's ponies were excellent and superbly trained. Mention must be made of Jupiter, a chestnut who was sold at auction in 1928 for $22,000, a sum unheard of at the time. He was purchased by John Sanford for his son Laddie. A difficult pony, Sanford could not handle him. He lent Jupiter to Dev Milburn, who broke his jaw. Jupiter ended his days pulling a cart at the Sanford farm in New Amsterdam, New York, a sad ending for a great pony. In 2005, Jupiter was the first foreign polo pony to be inducted into the Polo Hall of Fame's Horses to Remember category. Nigel and Molly Lacey flew in from Australia to receive the award in an emotional ceremony. A painting of Jupiter by Canadian artist Melinda Brewer was presented to the Lacey family; a copy hangs in the Museum of Polo.

The celebrated Tobiano was purchased by Lacey for Tommy Hitchcock and became a favorite of the New York crowd at Meadow Brook. Flick-A-Maroo and Royal Flush were awarded the Lady Susan Townley Cup for best pony in the Argentine Open. There were many others: Amy, Bayo, Pepe and Windsor joined Jupiter as the cream in the 1928 series for the Cup of the Americas.

Eduardo Rojas Lanusse gave his opinion of Lewis Lacey as a player: "A very particular player, gifted with great individualism when necessary, what a player.... At Palermo, I saw him score three goals from end-to-end, all alone, to win the match. What a fantastic player!"

Asked about Lewis's ponies, Eduardito reminisced: "I remember Jupiter, first owned by Bocha Rojas, it was bred by Estrugamou, an overwhelming chestnut. Another one was Tobiano, also owned by Rojas—it was given to him by his foreman; it was a cat made into a horse. They run a race at Matreros and with his unusual speed, Jupiter won. But on the polo field, Tobiano was the winner because of his quick reactions."[17]

Jupiter, Lacey's pony, was sold to John Sanford for $22,000 in 1928. Adjusted for inflation, it is still the top price for a polo pony at auction (courtesy Museum of Polo and Hall of Fame).

Lewis Lacey wrote thoughtfully on the game of polo. His best known essays are "The Judge's Task in Polo Pony Shows," "If the Umpires will Allow Me...," and "Equitation in Polo," which should be required reading for all polo players. He designed a head for the polo mallet, quite similar to the one being used today: larger and heavier than the one commonly utilized in his day, and with an oblique cut in the near end to facilitate shots taken away from the pony. It is still known as the 3-L head, after his initials.[18]

Following retirement from active play, Lacey remained an icon in polo circles. The author remembers him, vividly, umpiring games in the High School championships, sartorially elegant, polite and yet firm, a picture-perfect rider on a borrowed pony. Lacey's waning years were spent in the shade of the Hurlingham Club, mixing with his innumerable friends and playing the occasional game of billiards. Don Luis to most, Lewis to a few, Luiggi to his old friend Jack Nelson, he passed away on 1 November 1966 at his home in Hurlingham, just days before the start of a new series for the Cup of the Americas. He was mourned by all.

Lewis Lacey represented sportsmanship, fair play, advanced equitation and pure striking ability. He was the prime exponent of the correct seat on the saddle, of the proper training and selection of ponies, of team strategy and tremendous individual effort in pursuit of excellence on the polo field; an example to all. His presence on the field changed polo to a more fluid style, based upon speed, impeccable horsemanship and the tactical concept that the ball is faster than the mounted man.

Notes

1. The Lacroze tramway was drawn by horses, occasionally supplemented by mules, until it was electrified in 1903.
2. Founded in 1888 by William Dawson Campbell, Michael Fortune, John Ravenscroft, and Hugh Scott Robson, Hurlingham, named after the famous club in Fulham, became the most important sporting club in Argentina. Amenities include a golf course, cricket ground, clay and lawn tennis courts, swimming pools, squash courts, four polo fields and stables. The clubhouse has facilities for resident members.
3. Since the early days of the game, cricket allowed professionals to play on the same team with amateur players.
4. Lacey & Sons had premises in downtown Buenos Aires. Not only polo items were sold, but also high quality gentlemen's clothing as well. The business was carried on until 1958, by sons and grandsons of the founder. William Lacey returned to England in the 1920s.
5. The Buenos Aires English High School was founded in 1880, the second oldest British school in Buenos Aires after St. Andrew's Scots School. The soccer team formed by former pupils, named Alumni, supported by no fewer than five Brown brothers, was practically unbeatable in soccer's early days. Mr. Watson Hutton was the first president of the Argentine Football Association.
6. *Polo & Equitacion*, November 1925.
7. Published by the Polo Association of the River Plate on 24 March 1911.
8. John Argentine Campbell (1877–1917) was educated at Fettes College in Edinburgh, where he was school captain, and then went on to Cambridge, where he was a Blue in rugby, athletics and cricket. An exceptional athlete, he represented Scotland in international rugby and Argentina in cricket versus England. Campbell took the Open twice with his own team, Western Camps. Hugh Scott Robson (1856–1930) was the first great player in Argentina. He was ambidextrous, a heavy hitter who took seven Open Championships, and was listed in England's elite Recent Form List every year it was published. Joseph Edmund Traill (1887–1955) took the Argentine Open five times and represented Ireland in international play. He was an outstanding sportsman in several games, especially golf. Joe Traill, from estancia Chirú, was a cousin and teammate of John Arthur Edward Traill (qv) who became the first player in Argentina to reach a 10-goal handicap.
9. Letter from John Campbell to Lewis Lacey, courtesy of L.A. Lacey, Esq.:

> Aug. 5. 14
>
> Dear Lewis
>
> I have just heard that war is declared between England and Germany. Although possibly it may seem foolish, I would prefer not to play public polo while our people are at it over there; so I hope you will allow me to stand out. I feel that if one can go in for games at this time we shouldn't be here but should be on the way to the other side. What I do hope is that the Almighty, on whom that big German emperor is always calling, will give the Germans such a hiding that they wont rise up again for another 100 years!
>
> Yours,
> (Signed) J.A. Campbell
>
> Will you tell Casares and Holway I am very sorry not to play with them.

Anyway, the Open Championship was not played in 1914. Capt. Samuel Alfredo Casares (1888–1934) and Dr. Lindsay Rudolph Sillitoe Holway (d. 1962), a lawyer, took the Open the following year. Charles Lacey was the fourth member of the team.

10. Lewis Anthony Lacey, personal communication, 23 March 2006.

11. Lionel James, *The History of King Edward's Horse* (London: Sifton, Praed & Co., 1921), 341. Lt.-Gen. Sir Arthur Edward Aveling Holland (1862–1927) was Commandant, Royal Military Academy. His name was Butcher, which he changed later. Lt. Col. Edward Miller related that during the Anglo-Boer War Maj. Butcher, Royal Artillery, who was always ready to go anywhere or do anything, kept his horses in wonderful condition, and taught the yeomanry a lot in the way of foraging for extra supplies. In World War I, Miller asked him if he was as good at looting in France as he had been in South Africa. Holland replied, "Oh, no; it is now my job to see that no one does any of that sort of thing." E.D. Miller, *Fifty Years of Sport*. (New York: Dutton & Co., n.d.), 189.

12. Arthur L. Holder, ed., *Activities of the British Community in Argentina during the Great War 1914–1918* (Buenos Aires: *The Buenos Aires Herald*, 1920), 69–111.

13. Francisco Ceballos, *El polo en la Argentina* (Buenos Aires: Dirección General de Remonta, 1968), 110.

14. *Ibid.* 112.

15. *La Nación*, 12 June 1924, p. 2.

16. Letters from Anthony Lacey and Nigel Lacey to the author.

17. Interview in *PoloLine*. Eduardo Rojas Lanusse (1910–2005), a 6-goal handicap player, left his mark as a polo instructor in England. He played with Lewis Lacey on the Hurlingham team that took the 1937 Argentine Open.

18. Horace A. Laffaye, *Evolution of the Polo Mallet* (Wellington: Sidelines, 2001). Information provided by Santiago "Tato" Alvarez, expert mallet maker.

Rao Raja Hanut Singh: "There is only one tiger...."

by Chris Ashton

Though it barely rates a moment's thought in the polo world nowadays—it was so long ago—India was the very cradle of the game and the mould of its formative years. As to India's legacy to 20th-century polo, no star shone more brightly than Rao Raja Hanut Singh, in England as well as in India.

As a player, tactician, coach, talent-spotter, team-maker and horse-master, he was central to Indian polo from the 1920s to World War II and a larger-than-life presence in English polo from the early postwar years until 1970.

Those who knew him, whether as polo patrons, teammates or protégés, regardless of social rank, nationality or age, share strikingly consistent memories of the great Hanut. By common consent he was inspirational, charming, single-minded in his pursuit of excellence, didactic, egocentric and despotic.

There was his passion for the game and the importance he attached to honoring it and respecting its rules. England international Lt. Col. Alec Harper recalled Hanut's dismay at unseemly behavior seen from the sideline, when he exclaimed, "The game is for princes, not grooms!" Another time he declared, "There are men who enjoy the game, there are men who play it to shake up their liver, and there are men who play it for social reasons. I like men who play it for the sheer love of the game."[1]

Who was Hanut that he could establish the role he assumed for himself, first in India, then in English polo? In answer we must recall India's own role as the slender thread linking polo as played before, as the genesis of modern polo, through the fierce unruly contests of Himalayan tribesmen.

Starting in imperial Persia around 500 B.C., polo was taken up by the great empires of Central Asia to train men and horses for mounted warfare. By the 18th century those empires had collapsed or were in terminal decline. Only among the hill tribes of the Great Himalayan Range did polo persist. There it was discovered in the 1850s by British tea-planters and army subalterns who in turn introduced it to the plains of India.

Cavalry regiments embraced it, as did police, the Indian Civil Service, tea-planters and the ruling families of the princely states. British cavalry officers serving in India drafted the rules of modern polo and afterwards promoted it, not only to England, but to the world.

The contribution of cavalry regiments to the modern game was complemented and matched by the princely states. Britain by now ruled two-thirds of the Indian landmass and three-quarters of its people. The balance was an intricate maze of hundreds of principalities, ranging from a few square miles to the State of Hyderabad, half as big as France, and each protected by treaty with the British government protection.

Maharajas and their extended families, descended from warrior castes that prized horses, horsemanship and valor in battle, took to polo with gusto. Britain had pacified the Indian subcontinent, ending cherished traditions of warfare between tribes, castes and dynasties for power, wealth and land. Polo offered a ritual substitute for mounted warfare, a test of warrior skills, horses and horsemanship, tactics, teamwork, leadership, speed, danger and courage, in sum, the validation of manly virtues.

Nowhere was polo embraced more fervently than in Rajputana, the cluster of princely states in the northwest of India: an area of 343,000 square miles, a landscape of barren desert and mountain, hot and dry, complemented by forts and palaces, arts, crafts and religious festivals, legacy of successive Hindu and Moghul rulers, a sumptuous cultural heritage. One ancient saying had it that the Rajput disdains the plough; another, that the Rajput who reads a book will never ride a horse. From the beginning of the golden age of Indian polo, in 1880, one or another of the Rajput states dominated Indian polo. Jodhpur first held sway, followed by Alwar, which was then eclipsed by Patiala.

The chief architect of Jodhpur polo was Lieutenant-General Maharaja Sir Pratap Singh (1843–1922), brother of the Maharaja of Jodhpur, and for a time Jodhpur Regent. He founded and commanded the Jodhpur Lancers, introducing them to polo, and coached among others a young British subaltern stationed in Jodhpur, Winston Churchill. Of the Indian princes received at Buckingham Palace, Sir Pratap was apparently among Queen Victoria's favorites.

But his most durable legacy to polo was his son, Rao Raja Hanut Singh, born to him in 1900 by one of Sir Pratap's "unofficial" wives, or concubines, as distinct from his "official" wives, qualifying the child for the title Rao Raja, as distinct from Maharaja.

As successive generations of Hanut's protégés can attest, he was a consummate raconteur. His stories, recounted time and again, centered on himself, every one a polished jewel, an incident elevated into fable. Witness his account of his induction into polo. To mark the coronation of King Emperor George V and his consort, Queen Mary, Delhi hosted a durbar. For this a vast amphitheatre was built to stage mass events, including a polo match, the State of Alwar against a British cavalry regiment. Eleven years old and already, it seems, a skilled horseman, Hanut attended with his father:

> Imagine the scene. Nearly every maharaja with the whole panoply of their teams and retinues and hundreds of ponies, while around the King Emperor and Queen Empress, in the Royal box, the potentates and dignitaries sat with all the splendour of the India of the early 1900s, and over a quarter of a million people cheered the players, the highlights of the chukkas and above all, the victors. The Maharaja of the winning team, Alwar ... rode a highly decorated elephant across the ground to receive the cup; then, following the custom, he steered the beast through the streets of Delhi, tossing gold coins to the crowds.[2]

Here are childhood memories elevated to myth. Hanut tells how he begged his father to teach him polo. Sir Pratap consulted the 9-goal Maharaja of Alwar, who devised tests involving jungle creatures—a boar, a tiger and a partridge—to measure Hanut's courage, horsemanship and speed of eye. "Yes, he'll make a polo player," the Maharaja apparently declared. So swiftly did Hanut progress that he was soon practicing daily with high-goal players: in Hanut's words, "as many as ten practice chukkas a day, going at full tilt."

Following the outbreak of war in 1914 Sir Pratrap withdrew his son from Mayo College (founded to educate the sons of Indian princes), assigning him to his beloved Jodhpur Lancers. Lord Kitchener, then commander-in-chief in India, protested that Hanut was surely too young. Sir Pratap was apparently unbending: “It’s alright,” he responded, “because he’s a Rajput.”

At 14 Hanut was posted with the Lancers to France; at 15 he was made an officer. In 1917 the Jodhpur Lancers, part of the British imperial cavalry brigade under General Allenby, were posted to the Middle East. At 17 Hanut rode in the Indian Army’s last cavalry charge against the port city of Haifa. Some 1,350 prisoners under Turkish command were taken, together with artillery pieces and machine guns. To this day India’s 61st Cavalry Regiment, retaining its horses for state ceremonial occasions, celebrates Haifa Day, 23 September, with exhibition polo and other equestrian contests at its Jaipur barracks.

In 1919 the Lancers returned to India where Hanut alternated between the claims of polo and soldiering. At one point he led a mounted troop to hunt, and eventually kill in a shootout, a brigand looting and pillaging Jodhpur villages. All that ended with the 1921 Prince of Wales Cup, Delhi’s championship trophy. The final pitted two Rajput states against each other, Patiala and Jodhpur, with Hanut leading the Jodhpur team.

Attending the 1921 Prince of Wales final was the Prince himself (later the Duke of Windsor), the Viceroy, at least 50 Indian princes and a dozen generals, together with 150,000 other spectators. Hanut described the progress of the game:

> My father had set his heart on us winning this game and we had a string of 150 horses from which to choose. Patiala had ever greater resources, including a style of polo that I can only describe as a chess game, a wonderful control of the ball from all corners of the field. We knew the only way to beat them was with a game of speed, always playing the ball to an imaginary line straight down the centre of the field from one goal to the other.
>
> This is the way we played, but Patiala was still leading 4–0 in the third chukka. I finally scored just before the interval; and after that, we caught fire, drawing even with Patiala; and in the final minute of the battle, just passing them. The roars of the crowd were so deafening that none of us heard the final bugle. We knew the game was over only when thousands of spectators began pouring onto the field.... It was a scene I shall never forget, but what I remember most was the reaction of my father, who died later that year.
>
> Only one figure sat motionless. In front of the stands sat my father, Sir Pratap Singh, Regent of Jodhpur and grand old player. He was 78 years old and still sat his horse beautifully. All India knew that the Jodhpur team was the very apple of his eye; his darling and his pride; and he had coaxed and nursed them for this fight. Through all this game he had sat immobile, not a muscle, not an eyelid, not a finger moving. Not even that last demoniac minute when Jodhpur won its sixth goal and won. [Hanut scored the decisive goal.] My father was like a figure carved out of wood. Then, as the horn sounded, people from all sides broke, cheering and tumultuous, to congratulate him, the Prince among the first. And as the old man stood up, tears poured down his cheeks.[3]

As Hanut tells it, his father declared, “Now I can die happy.” To deter his son from any illusions of grandeur following his triumph, Sir Pratrap forbad him any polo for a month, allowing him only to help the grooms exercise the Jodhpur ponies. Thereafter Jodhpur Lancers gave way entirely to Hanut’s polo career. His polo handicap was raised at once to nine-goals. By his mid-20s Indian polo acknowledged him as a judge without peer of promising young players and ponies, allied to a gift for nurturing them to their full potential, and for forging players and ponies into winning teams.

As captain of Jodhpur in 1924 and Bhopal in 1927, Hanut won the Indian Polo Association Championship, triumphs reinforced in 1925 when he took the Jodhpur team to England for the English high-goal season, claiming a succession of victories culminating in the Hurlingham Champion Cup. Testimony of his gift for nurturing promising young players in winning combinations was his success with another Rajput team, Jaipur, and its patron, Man Singh, Maharaja of Jaipur, known to the polo world—in England as in India—as Jai.

Hanut first saw Jai play in the late 1920s after he returned from the British officer training school at Woolwich. With Jai playing back (a nine-goal handicap at his peak), Hanut (also 9-goals) at number 3, Hanut's half-brother Abhey Singh (8-goals) as number 2 and the Crown Prince of Baria, Prithi Singh (8-goals), at number 1, Jaipur State won the Indian Championship Cup from 1932–39. Invited to explain its success, Hanut responded with his customary aplomb: "We were the best strikers, we had the best ponies, we were the best horsemen. What could the others do?"

In 1933 Hanut led Jaipur to play the English season. With the team came 39 ponies, 59 grooms (splendid in flowing orange turbans), and a polo-stick maker. Under his captaincy Jaipur cut a wide swath through the English high-goal tournaments, culminating in the Hurlingham Championship Cup.

No one could doubt that Hanut was the mastermind to the Jaipur team, but to London society and the media its brightest star was the 22-year-old Maharaja. Under the heading *The Luckiest Young Man Alive*, a London tabloid itemized his assets as "his fortune of 100 million pounds, a 10-million pound palace, a room full of glittering gems, six million faithful subjects, two lovely wives, princesses in their own right. In addition, he has good looks and charm. This Prince, who might have stepped straight from the pages of the Arabian Nights, is a slim, broad-shouldered Adonis."

Jai, eleven years younger, was distantly related to Hanut through dynastic marriage between the Jodhpur and Jaipur families. In 1921 Hanut's father, then Regent of Jodhpur, negotiated the betrothal of two Jodhpur princesses (one 22 years old, the other, her niece, five years old, both kinswomen of the Crown Prince of Jodhpur) to Jai, who was then ten and recently anointed heir to the Jaipur throne.

In 1940 Jai married again, this time by his own choice, into the ruling family of a distant princely state, Cooch Behar. His third wife, Gayatri Devi, but known as Ayesha, recalled herself as a teenager in the 1930s and how her future husband (with whom she was already besotted, as was he by her) would arrive at the family home in Calcutta, the entire Jaipur team in tow: "Calcutta was very gay and social during the Christmas season. Every night there was a party. The players of the Jaipur team were young and attractive. Hanut would always be the first to bed and first up in the morning overseeing the work of the polo ponies and riding and practicing."

By the early 1920s England was also aware of Hanut's exceptional gifts. According to J.N.P. Watson, English polo commentators argued for his inclusion in the England squad for the 1921, 1924, 1927 and 1930 Westchester Cup series against the United States. "But the Hurlingham committee decided he was too small and light and would be too easily bumped and ridden off by the hefty Americans," wrote Watson. "Hanut did not agree. 'My ponies were so fast and handy I could have slipped them every time,' he said with his smiling shrug, 'and they would have been bumping air!' He was eventually invited to play for the 1936 Westchester matches, but injury prevented him taking part."[4]

India's demise as a force in world polo began in 1937 as cavalry regiments, British and Indian, were mechanized. Polo was suspended in India as elsewhere for the duration of World War II. Peace ushered in a British government determined to cede sovereignty in India immediately to a democratically elected government. In so doing it would effectively repudiate its treaties of protection with the princely states which, with the cavalry, had been central pillars of Indian polo.

The position of the Indian princes became untenable, leaving them no choice but to cede sovereignty to the government elected to power in what had been British-ruled India. Perceived by the left-leaning Congress Party government as obstacles to social and material progress, and as challenging their own authority, from 1947 successive Congress Party governments stripped the princes of their titles, privy purses and residual powers guaranteed under the Indian constitution.

From 1947 Indian polo became a shadow of its former self. That year coincided with the election of John Pearson, 3rd Viscount Cowdray, to the chairmanship of the Hurlingham Polo Association, signaling the revival of postwar English polo. Recognizing Hanut's gifts for nurturing young talent, Lord Cowdray became his most important benefactor.

That same year, 1947, saw a large farmhouse outside the village of Bepton, itself a few minutes' drive from Cowdray Park's principal polo fields, converted to a private guesthouse. Standing in eleven acres of garden, Park House Hotel looked out onto farmland and the South Downs of West Sussex.

The new owners, Major Mike and Ione O'Brien, had met and married in prewar British India. Both were passionate about polo. From the quality of its kitchen to the personal touch of the O'Briens and their commitment to polo, Park House became the hotel of choice for individual players and teams from abroad, together with their spouses, playing the English season courtesy of Cowdray Park.

Encouraged by Lord Cowdray, Hanut based himself at Park House for the English polo season, indeed, for 16 consecutive seasons. With him came his companion, English-born Beryl Hill, his principal adviser in all things polo, protector of his interests and herself a consum-

Hanut Singh's Ratanada team, winners of a low-goal tournament at Cowdray Park, 1954. Left to right, Robert de Pass (UK), Sinclair Hill, Hanut Singh and Peter Wilson (South Africa) (Chris Ashton, courtesy Sinclair Hill).

H.M. Queen Elizabeth presents Hanut Singh with the trophy for the inaugural Royal Windsor Cup, at Smith Lawn, 1955 (Chris Ashton, courtesy Sinclair Hill).

mate horsewoman. His retinue was completed by his bearer, Sawai. As one fellow guest recalled: "In those days there was only one bathroom in Park House and Sawai would sit cross-legged outside the door so that no other guest could use the bathroom before Hanut."

English patrons and teammates called at Park House to talk polo with Hanut at meal-times, complemented by foreign players enlisted by Hanut to play for his teams, lodging there as fellow guests. "I would sit in the Park House bar at the great man's feet listening by the hour," Sinclair Hill recalled.

Mollie Tatham, wife of Cowdray Park Polo Club manager Lt. Col. P.R. "Bolshie" Tatham, recalled Hanut holding court: "He taught polo at the breakfast table, using salt cellars, mustard and pepper pots as players, showing the younger players where to place themselves, where to attack and so on." Then there was the time he appeared for a Park House cricket match clad in a suit of armor, courtesy of Lord Cowdray.

Hanut's post-World War II English polo career is described nowhere more eloquently than by the late Sir Andrew Horsbrugh-Porter, former England international and London *Times* polo correspondent in the 1960s and '70s:

> It was always from No. 3 that organized his teams, seldom hitting goals himself, but with the unforgettable cut-shot from the sidelines, placing the ball twenty yards in front of the goal for his No. 1 to tap through.... Hanut thinks deeply about all aspects of polo and no one knows more about how to school and produce ponies and players. I think his finest achievement in later life was to win the Cowdray Gold Cup for Eric Moller's Jersey Lillies in 1964 and 1965.
>
> Hanut selected three unknown young players and collected and supervised the ponies. He

Top: **Hanut Singh pictured with Lt. Col. Peter Dollar in the 1960s.** ***Right:*** **Elegant in his attire, Hanut Singh at the Hurlingham Club, near Buenos Aires, for the 1966 Tri-Nation Series, hosted by Argentina (Both photographs from Chris Ashton, courtesy Sinclair Hill).**

> was himself then rated at 4 goals, but his brainpower was still equal to his old 9-goal handicap, and his meticulous management of the ponies was based on many years experience. He was quite the best judge of potential polo ponies of his generation.... You never saw Hanut having to put pressure on the reins—a delicate touch and the pony responded. Likewise he could suit ponies to players....[5]

The three young unknown players recruited by the 64-year old Hanut to play in the 1964 Gold Cup were Argentines Eduardo Moore and Ricardo Díaz and Rhodesian Patrick Kemple, all in their late teens or early 20s. To general astonishment the 17-goal Jersey Lillies defeated several 22-goal teams to claim the trophy.

The following year Hanut added a 19-year old English player, Julian Hipwood, to his protégés. Hanut having watched him with a low-goal Cirencester team, Hipwood was summoned as if by royal command: "You must give up that tiddlywinks polo at Cirencester and join me permanently."

Hipwood relocated to lodgings at Park House. For ponies and players alike the training regimen was martial in its routine and attention to detail. Hanut was sparing in praise, on one occasion telling Hipwood, "The day I stop shouting at you is the day I give up on you!"

Under his tutelage Hipwood's handicap rose from 0 to 5 goals. In a chance meeting in Calcutta in 1970 Hanut declared, "Now you're a real polo player!" to which the 6-goal Hipwood responded, "And you made me!" A 9-goal player at his peak, Hipwood's polo achievements included leading England to victory in six Coronation Cups, winning the 1980 U.S. Open championship together will all the high-goal English trophies at different times, and playing twice in the Argentine Open final.

Polo returned to India after independence, albeit as a poor cousin of what it was before the war. After each English season, Hanut would return to play there. Sponsored by the Indian Polo Association he led a team that won the Deauville Gold World Cup in 1957. With his family team, which included his son Rao Raja Hari Singh, he won the Indian Polo Association Championship Cup from 1957 to 1966. But as he freely acknowledged, Indian polo could no longer compare with what Cowdray Park offered.

No one else is more deeply embedded in postwar English polo folklore than Hanut Singh. Space does not permit more than a few token anecdotes conjured up by mention of his name. "He was a law unto himself," said England international Lord Patrick Beresford. "Everything revolved round him. He was a very egotistical man, very conceited and there are endless stories about him saying there is only one Hanut!" No other anecdote celebrating Hanut's famous vanity comes close to Sir Andrew Horsbrugh-Porter's contribution:

> Once when Hanut was playing holiday polo at a French resort behind a No. 1 who needed a bit of Dutch courage, he dosed him with brandy and they won the match, he reported. Afterwards the No. 1 said to him, "I saw two sticks, two polo balls, four ears on my pony and two Hanuts." At which the Rao Raja drew himself up to his full height and replied: "There is only one Hanut!"[6]

Brian Bethell, Lord Cowdray's Master of the Horse for twenty years, recalls Hanut as a creature of habit: "Procedure at half time—Dismount, No.1 attendant takes away pony. Remove hat—hand to attendant No. 2. Take clean white silk handkerchief from attendant No. 3. Wipe brow and throw handkerchief on ground. Sit down on chair and rest. Take back hat from attendant No.1. Take polo stick from attendant No. 4. Ride onto ground—complete!"[7]

Hanut set great store by his own physical fitness, and expected nothing less of teammates or teams under his management. "He was a great disciplinarian," recalled Lord Beresford, a member of the British team managed by Hanut in the 1966 Tri-Nation International, hosted by Argentina. "Some young players once arrived back from a night's revelry at 6am one morning and passed Hanut on his way out to exercise the horses, immaculately dressed. Hanut ordered the players to go straight in and get changed for the day's work."

He was an ascetic without sympathy for human frailty or indulgence. Of a maharaja who had fallen short of his early promise in polo, Hanut retorted curtly: "Too much curry and women!" In dress he was fastidious on and off the field. Sinclair Hill recalls that, though Hanut was by no means wealthy, he nonetheless bought his clothes from London's most fashionable shops: his suits and breeches and jodhpurs from Huntsman, his boots from Maxwell, his shirts and ties from Turnbull, his jewelry from Asprey.

As a raw Australian teenager, Hill remembers, he regarded Hanut with a mixture of affection and awe: "My entire life revolved round this elegant masterful and brilliant human being, both on and off the field. He was the most self-centered and opinionated man I ever met. And we loved him. We won every game we played together, except a match at Roehampton when Charlie Smith-Ryland was late.... At one point when Hanut thought I was getting too big for my boots he said, 'Sinclair, we have a rule in India—only one tiger in the cage. I am that tiger!'"

Hanut was still playing off a three-goal handicap when he retired from polo, at 72 years old, to settle permanently at the family seat, Ratanada. He died in Jodhpur in 1982.

Notes

1. I am indebted to J.N.P. Watson, former London *Times* polo correspondent, historian and author of *Hanut: Prince of Polo Players* (London: The Sportsman Press, 1995) and to John Tylor, former Hurlingham Polo Association chairman, for permission to draw extensively from Watson's biography of Hanut Singh.
2. *Ibid.*
3. Herbert Spencer, *Chakkar* (New York: Drake, 1971).
4. Watson.
5. A.M. Horsbrugh-Porter, *The Times*, London.
6. *Ibid.*
7. Derek Russell-Stoneham and Roger Chatterton-Newman, *Polo at Cowdray* (London: P.B.I., 1993).

Tommy Pope: The Horse Whisperer

by Susan Reeve

Edward Ernest Ecroyd Pope, always known by his nickname, "Tommy," is one of the most well-known and highly regarded polo players from the early years of South African polo. He attained a handicap of 9, still the highest of any South African, but, more importantly, his polo career spanned nearly 50 years, during which time nothing gave him greater pleasure than coaching younger players and sharing his knowledge of the game, especially in the schooling of ponies.

Tommy was born on 30 July 1895 in the small farming community of Matatiele in East Griqualand, which borders the southern Drakensberg mountains that run down the spine of South Africa. The name "Matatiele" comes from two Sesotho words, "matata" (pronounced ma-ta-ta) and "iele" (pronounced ee-yella). The first word means "duck" and the second means "over there." For anyone who knows this beautiful remote district it is very evocative of the V-formations of wild duck that fly low in the evening sky over the marshy, flat wetlands known in South Africa as "vleis" (pronounced flays).

His father, Dr. Charles Ernest Pope, at the age of 26 left his position as surgeon at the Worcester Infirmary and sailed from England to the Cape Colony on 2 April 1878. Initially he was based in the Eastern Cape but left for Matatiele after his wife and firstborn died in childbirth. He rode from King Williamstown to Matatiele, a journey of nearly 300 miles. Of his new hometown he noted wryly in a letter to his parents in Dorset: "I understand that it is a very healthy place—not a good prospect for a doctor!" He remarried in 1892.

Dr. Pope was the first physician in the district and he also served as a medical officer in the armed forces during both the Boer War and the First World War. He was elected Mayor of Matatiele and had the distinction of owning the very first car to be seen in the district, in 1911. It apparently looked like a spider cart, with the engine under the front seat, and, according to his daughter, Daisy, "Went well downhill but often needed pushing up!" Dr. Pope and his wife had two children—a daughter, Beatrice Mary, and Tommy. Their daughter was always known as Daisy and, as Tommy was never called by any of his three christened names, one can only conclude that their parents preferred nicknames. Family tradition holds that "Tommy" and "Daisy" were given by their nanny.

As a young boy Tommy displayed a talent for all sports, especially athletics, cricket and rugby, playing for many years in the E.G. Murray Cup rugby side. (The Murray Cup is a prestigious interclub rugby tournament, equivalent to polo's Beresford Cup.) As a youngster, Tommy won many trophies as an athlete. He was a keen fisherman, enjoyed tennis and was an excellent shot.

He went to school at St. Andrews College in Grahamstown and had just started his tertiary education in 1914 when war broke out. He was one of the first to volunteer and went through the Free State rebellion campaign, on through German West Africa (Namibia, as it is known today) and finally to England, where he joined the Royal Flying Corps. He was sent to France as a lieutenant and was soon a captain and flight commander of a squadron. Letters written to his parents during this period tell of lively "scraps" in the air against the renowned Red Baron and reveal much of his personality—nerves of steel, clear thinking and a sense of humor but, above all, the delight he took in a challenge.

On 4 January 1918 his plane came under heavy fire and his observer and great friend, Flt. Lt. Alfred Wylie Nasmyth, a Canadian, was killed. Tommy crash-landed behind enemy lines in Flanders and was taken prisoner. Nothing was heard from him and, on 24 January, an obituary was published in the *Matatiele Mail*: "Of the many announcements that have had to be made during the war, there is none more painful as regards this community than the report received this week of Capt. E.E.E. Pope being missing. He was taking part in the operation on the Flanders front and went missing on January 4th." The report continues as an obituary, referring to Tommy in the past tense.

Tommy may well have quoted Mark Twain, who had famously cabled Associated Press from Europe in 1892 to say, "The report of my death was an exaggeration!" Of several attempts to escape that were made, one involved tunneling in which many prisoners did manage to get away. Tommy, however, remained a P.O.W. for the last months of the war, returning to Rye in England, and was about to enlist with the White Russian army when a berth on a ship sailing to Cape Town became available in Southampton. The pull towards home proved strong enough to bring him on board and he spent the rest of his life in South Africa. He married Madalene Bruce on 21 August 1922 and they had two daughters, Marie Madalene and Anne. Madalene was his ideal life's companion because they shared many common interests, including polo and fishing. On one of their fishing trips into Basutoland she fell and broke her hip and Tommy brought her back strapped over her pony. She limped for the rest of her life and, sadly, she was to die at a relatively young age in 1959. Tommy outlived her by sixteen years, dying on 20 January 1975, but his life was never the same.

Despite his prowess at other sports, once Tommy had discovered polo there was no turning back. The demands for speed, teamwork, physical fitness and horsemanship all combined to convince him that this was the only sport he wanted to play for the rest of his life. And he did. At the age of 56 he was still representing his country's national side and, at 71, played for his province's B side in the Inter-provincial Tournament. He continued to play until his late 70s when emphysema finally forced him to leave his beloved East Griqualand and move to the coast. With a tall and spare frame, his friends described him as being held together by biltong[1] and piano wire.

Tommy started playing polo in his mid–20s after he had started farming in Matatiele. The local club was known as The Levels, named after the adjacent railway siding on the line between Swartberg and Cedarville. Some years later it moved to Martin Gilson's farm and changed its name to Matatiele Polo Club. Martin's grandson, Glynn Bodley, the current president of the South African Polo Association, now owns the farm.

Tommy played in most positions, but back suited his game best and he was renowned for the unerring accuracy of his long raking penalty shots. His quick hand-eye coordination and

The Springbok team that visited Argentina in 1933. Left to right, standing: Russell Burdon, Martin Henderson, G.D. Henderson, Allan Ross and Ian Gibson. Left to right, seated: Ernest Greene, Hugh Brown, Walter Shaw and Tommy Pope. Greene, Gibson, Burdon and Pope were one of only four foreign teams to reach the Argentine Open's final game (courtesy Museum of Polo and Hall of Fame).

riding skills saw a meteoric rise in handicap. East Griqualand had many outstanding players, and competition between the clubs was fierce.

The highlight of his polo career was undoubtedly the tour to Argentina in 1933. There were some great South African players on that side. Together with Tommy were Ian Gibson, Russell Burdon, Martin Henderson and Ernest Greene. Hugh Brown was the nonplaying captain of the side. Six teams entered the tournament that year — Santa Paula, Los Indios, Santa Inés, Hurlingham, Coronel Suárez and South Africa. After a postponement of days because of incessant rain the tournament opened on 4 November with a match between Santa Paula and Los Indios which was won by Santa Paula. The South Africans' first game was against Santa Inés, which they won 11–8. Hurlingham then swung into action and were narrowly defeated by Santa Paula 9–8. The other semifinal was just as exciting and aroused great passion among the crowd. Here was the homegrown side of Coronel Suárez struggling valiantly against invaders from abroad. The South Africans won 11–10 and Tommy used to reminisce about the umpires needing a police escort off the field to protect them from some very disappointed spectators.

The final was set for 18 November but the odds were always in favor of Santa Paula, as the three Reynals and Manuel Andrada were on top form. The South Africans could not quite match the speed or the force of their opponents and, in the end, it was a fairly one-sided affair, 12–3. However, the South Africans had made lots of friends in Argentina and, to this day, the Springbok Trophy that was donated that year by the S.A. Polo Association is contested.

For many years after this, Gibson from Mooi River, Burdon from Natal Estates and Pope, along with Raymond Gold from Underberg, Buddy Chaplin, also from Matatiele, and Allan Ross of Nottingham Road were the top players in the country playing for their respective provinces and, when the occasion arose, for their country.

The first time the coveted Beresford Cup, played for at the annual South African Polo Championships, was won by a club outside of the province of Natal was in 1949, when Matatiele took the trophy, beating Natal Estates in a nail-bitingly close final at Willowbridge. On the way to the final, Natal Estates eliminated the excellent Mooi River side under Ian Gibson, 9 goals to 4. Mooi River's team was Pip Davis at back, Ian Gibson at number 3, Keir Hall at number 2 and Michael Green at number 1. Together they would win many tournaments in the years to come. In the next round Natal Estates defeated Otto's Bluff, who, in turn, beat Inanda. Matatiele beat Underberg easily in the first round, 6–1, and then defeated Bedford Park 9–3, again a surprisingly easy victory over a side that included the famous Goodman twins, Allan and Derek.

A delighted Tommy Pope, captain of the Matatiele side, makes his victory speech on winning the Beresford Cup in 1949. It was the first time a team outside of Natal Province had won this prestigious trophy (courtesy Susan Reeve).

Matatiele's side was Tommy Pope, 8-goals at back, Buddy Chaplin, 5-goals at number 3, Alex McDonald, 4-goals at number 2 and Aubrey Stubbs, 6-goals at number 1. Natal Estates was Jack Martens, 4-goals at back, Russell Burdon, 7-goals at number 3, Craig Brown, 5-goals at number 2 and "Goondie" Francis, 3-goals at number 1.

The final was very fast, with tight marking all round and neither side getting many quick breaks from loose play before being ridden off hard by an opponent. The score went with the chukkers—1-all after the first, 2-all after the second all the way through to the 7th when it was 7-all. (Seven chukkers was the order of the day in those times.) Late in the game Russell, having been injured in a previous game, could not continue and was replaced by Raymond Gold on an Underberg pony. Tension was at a peak when, near the end of the first chukka of extra time, Alex McDonald managed to get in an offside neck shot that was blocked by Craig Brown but only after it had crossed the line by inches! Victory went to Matatiele, by the very narrowest of margins, with much celebration to follow.

Tommy also won the Lolo Ross Memorial (Natal Championship) and the Pirates Cup (East Griqualand Championship) but, frankly, for a player of his stature it is astonishing that his name does not appear on many more trophies. Therein lies Tommy's legacy to South African polo, which had nothing to do with victories on the field.... Far from it. Tommy took far greater pleasure in entering tournaments on teams with aspiring, keen players than with other high handicappers. In his later years, playing with three beginners, his team was thrashed 16–1. Afterwards, he was overheard to remark how much he had enjoyed the game because the youngsters had given everything they had for the full seven chukkers.

Buddy Chaplin's eldest son, Gavin, who has played for South Africa, coached the national side and manufactures polo sticks, has vivid memories of Tommy, especially with regard to the way he schooled horses:

> I can recall Tommy had a horse that tripped a lot, so he filled the school with rocks and cantered round. By the end the horse was stepping lively to say the least! Dad always raved about his horsemanship and how light his horse's mouths were. That had a great bearing on my polo and to this day I can't play a horse that is strong in the mouth. He also practiced what he preached. When my brothers and I were very young Tommy noticed that we were a little nervous of falling off. He proceeded to SHOW us how to fall at a really lively pace by doing it himself. He couldn't have been a young man at the time.
>
> He always had so much time on the field, but isn't that true of all the really greats, and he was certainly one of those. His man-focus on the field was amazing. I recall our groom, Solomon, recounting a story of a match against Transvaal where Tommy was marking one of the Goodman twins. The story goes that Tommy marked so successfully that a wail could be heard from the ground of: "Come on Tommy, let's just go and play polo, man."
>
> Of all the things I personally remember, his sportsmanship and manners stand out like a beacon. They have colored my life and I will be forever grateful for his example. I remember, while at university, my girlfriend Dorothy and I went to watch a Test match at Shongweni. Tommy must have been almost 80 years old, yet he still stood up when I introduced Dorothy and offered her his seat. What an example to a young man, but that was the way he lived. I remember him saying, "You can't tell people, you have to show them." I wonder how much that has influenced my coaching.
>
> I am delighted I have been asked to add my recollections to this tribute because I would love, now as a grown man, to be able to say "Thank you" to Tommy for everything he did to make such a positive difference in my life.[2]

More memories, from an older player, come from Alex McDonald, who was a neighboring farmer in the Matatiele district, and played on teams with Tommy on many occasions over several years:

> Tommy was a great tactician, captain and team leader. In many games, by the second chukka, he would change or reformulate his plans and, for sure, he was at his best if his team was down with a chukka or two to go. The way he spoke quietly to you and gave you your instructions made you realize that he had summed up the game, as well as your own difficulties, and in this way he inspired confidence in you. This did not mean that you got off scot-free after the game if you hadn't tried your best or if you'd been stupid—he told you so! He was a very forthright man and never afraid to make a point. He often said to me, too, how much better a lot of teams in South Africa would have been if they had only had the motto "A ship is greater than any member of her crew." He would far rather have a team that was happy and pulled together with great spirit, even if a better player, who did not think of the team first, had to be left out. Tommy was a great man in all walks of life.[3]

In recognition of his enormous contribution to the sport the South African Polo Association unanimously elected Tommy Honorary Life President in 1969, a position he held until his death.

Footnote from Tommy's Granddaughter

Tommy Pope's prowess on the polo field is well documented but I am sad to say that I have only dim memories of seeing him on the field, despite the fact that he was still an 8-goal player when I was born in 1949.

I am proud of the fact that winning trophies was not his main concern. The South African polo community remembers him with fondness as someone whose greatest delight lay in sharing his passion for the game with others.

What I remember most about my grandfather was his infinite patience and gentle but firm manner with polo ponies. The stables at his farm, "Chilfrome," were always filled with horses that had been sent to Tommy for schooling from players around the country. He had a unique way of communicating with these animals and it was a joy to watch him work them and ride with him. One, which I recall best, was a grey mare called Flavia who, Tommy was convinced, knew the game so well that she would kick the ball through the posts!

Tommy Pope's polo career spanned almost 50 years. He is seen here at age 54, about to play the game for which he had so much passion (courtesy Susan Reeve).

Riding on the farm with him, going on hair-raising fishing trips in his battered old Land Rover into neighboring Basutoland, being used as a beater on duck and guinea fowl shoots, along with my brother Bruce and Buddy Chaplin's three sons, on the freezing cold Matatiele vleis and, best of all, listening to his wonderful stories by the fire while he cut slices of biltong and we toasted bread on long forks—these are the happy memories I have of him. Outstanding polo player and superb horseman Tommy Pope may have been, but he was also the best grandfather a child could wish for.

Notes

1. Biltong is widely eaten in South Africa. It is made by drying strips of lean, salted meat, usually venison or beef, in the open air.
2. Personal communication from Gavin Chaplin.
3. Personal communication from Alex McDonald.

Earl Mountbatten of Burma: A Tangible Legacy

by Roger Chatterton-Newman

Accompanying his second cousin David, Prince of Wales, on a visit to India in 1921, Lord Louis Mountbatten fell in love with polo. He was not a natural rider, and an Army officer suggested, mischievously, that the correct way to mount a polo pony was to take a flying leap and vault over its tail into the saddle:

> Only when this had failed disastrously did Mountbatten manage to mount correctly. He said later that during this game he only succeeded in hitting the ball three or four times....[1]

But it sowed the seeds of a lifetime's passion. Mountbatten's extraordinary enthusiasm was to link his name indelibly with the game; and, by advising his nephew, the Duke of Edinburgh, and great-nephew, HRH Price Charles, the Prince of Wales, to take it up, he encouraged a widespread and lasting public interest in polo.

Born Prince Louis Francis Albert Victor Nicholas of Battenberg at Frogmore House, Windsor, on 25 June 1900, he was the younger son and fourth child of Prince Louis of Battenberg—later to become Admiral of the Fleet the 1st Marquess of Milford Haven—and his wife, Princess Victoria of Hesse and the Rhine.

His maternal grandmother was Princess Alice, second daughter of Queen Victoria and wife of Grand Duke Louis IV of Hesse and the Rhine. The Battenbergs were a cadet (or junior) branch of the Hesse royal house, the elder Prince Louis being the first of five children born to the morganatic marriage of Prince Alexander of Hesse and Countess Julia von Hauke.[2] The name came from the ancient castle of Battenberg in the upper Eder Valley of North Hesse.

In 1917, King George V changed the name of the British royal family from Saxe-Coburg and Gotha to Windsor; and, at the same time, asked those of the relatives who were British subjects but known by German surnames to relinquish them. As head of the House of Battenberg, Prince Louis adopted the anglicized version of Mountbatten and received a peerage. Now being the son of a marquess, the seventeen-year-old Louis Francis became known as Lord Louis Mountbatten, although to family and friends he was always known as Dickie.

He had entered the Royal Navy from the Royal Naval College at Dartmouth in 1913 and saw active service during the Great War. Between the wars, he pursued his naval career with a variety of postings and specialized in communications. In 1922 he married the Hon. Edwina

Ashley, daughter of the first and last Lord Mount Temple and heiress to the Broadlands estate at Romsey in Hampshire and to Classiebawn Castle in County Sligo, Ireland, which in due course became the Mountbatten's homes.

It was the most fashionable wedding of the year; the Prince of Wales stood as best man and crowds gathered to watch the couple leave St. Margaret's Church, Westminster.[3] A highly-publicized honeymoon tour in the U.S. included a visit to Hollywood, where Charlie Chaplin made a widely seen home movie, *Nice and Easy*, featuring the talents of Douglas Fairbanks Sr., his wife, Mary Pickford—and the Mountbattens.

Following their marriage, Lord and Lady Louis Mountbatten settled at Adsdean, in the West Sussex countryside not far from Cowdray Park Polo Club, epicenter of country house polo. Mountbatten's Adsdean team became a regular competitor there, and indeed in 1939 he ran Cowdray Park while Viscount Cowdray was in the U.S. for the Westchester Cup tour of that year. Photographs of Mountbatten's Sealyham terrier, Topsail, guarding his master's polo sticks appeared regularly in the national press.

His Royal Navy team, Bluejackets, also achieved prominence before the war, notably in high-goal tournaments at Hurlingham, Ranelagh and Roehampton. Victories included the Ranelagh Invitation Cup in 1930 and 1931, after which Mountbatten and his fellow players donated the Bluejackets Cup, to be presented to the winning team. He was also a prime mover for a set of international rules for the game, an excellent idea sidelined on the onset of the Second World War and still awaiting fruition.

In 1937 he had been promoted to captain, and when war broke out two years later, he commanded the 5th Destroyer Flotilla from HMS *Kelly*, seeing service in the North Sea, the Western Approaches and the Mediterranean. The sinking of the *Kelly* during the Battle of Crete in 1941 was featured in the film *In Which We Serve*, with Mountbatten played by Noël Coward.

That same year he was appointed commodore and became chief of Combined Operations and a member of the British Chiefs of Staff Committee. A major change of direction came in 1943, when he became Supreme Allied Commander, South-East Asia Command, with the rank of acting admiral. This culminated in Japanese forces being driven out of Burma and the surrender of the Japanese army of occupation in Malaya in 1945.

On 23 August 1946 he was raised to the peerage as Viscount Mountbatten of Burma, and advanced to an earldom[4] the following year, when he was appointed last Viceroy of India, a post which involved the unenviable task of overseeing independence and partition of the subcontinent. He stayed on as governor-general until June 1948.

The end of empire saw Mountbatten return to naval duties, including the posts of commander, 1st Cruiser Squadron, from 1948 to 1949, commander-in-chief, Mediterranean, from 1952 to 1954 and First Sea Lord, 1955 to 1959. This last appointment was of particular importance to Mountbatten because, in a sense, it was reparation for the injustice committed against his father, who had been forced to resign the post of professional head of the Royal Navy in 1914 because of his German birth.

In his early naval days, Mountbatten had played polo in Malta, as well as Gibraltar and China, and it is amusing to compare his comments on grooms in the three stations, as recorded in the pages of *An Introduction to Polo*,[5] which he wrote under the nom de plume of "Marco" in 1931.

In Malta, "the groom can be very good, as he is fond of horses and enthusiastic. But he is inclined to be lazy and unreliable, and is often noisy in the stable. On Gibraltar, generally speaking, grooms are not very good, even the best requiring a great deal of supervision; while in China the *mafoo* or groom needed constant supervision to prevent him from being definitely cruel to the ponies in his charge."

Mountbatten prepares for a game at Cowdray Park shortly before the war (courtesy Roger Chatterton-Newman, PQInternational).

The copyright for *An Introduction to Polo* was vested in the Royal Naval Polo Association (R.N.P.A.), of which Mountbatten was president. It was a typically generous act, for he was never particularly well-off in his own right.

The book was long regarded as the definitive work on the mechanics of the game. A great deal of thought went into it, and it is as applicable to today's players as it was to those of seventy years ago. Indeed, it was intended primarily as a guide for the complete beginner, someone who, as 10-goal player Lord Wodehouse said in his foreword, "knew no polo players to whom he could turn for advice, and who was living in the "unhorsey" atmosphere of ships. Its aims were to set down a certain amount of indispensable information, and to standardize, if possible, ideas among the polo players in the Service."

Wodehouse, who later inherited the family earldom of Kimberley and was killed during an air raid in London in 1941, felt the book to be the "most reasoned and progressive introduction to the game" he had ever read, and strongly advised the R.N.P.A. to put it on sale to a wider public. This they did, and between 1931 and 1982 it went into seven editions.

Malta had particularly close associations for Mountbatten. Not only had he served there as a midshipman, but it was where his father, Prince Louis, had taken up polo while also stationed in the Royal Navy in the 1870s. Indeed, it is a moot point as to whether Prince Louis or his cousin-by-marriage, the future King George V, was the first member of the royal family to play the game. Years later, the link was revived when Lord Mountbatten presented Malta Polo Club with the Prince Louis Cup, in memory of his father. It is still a coveted trophy every season on the Marsa, as the club's principal ground is known.

Mountbatten also presented Malta Polo Club with what is perhaps its most prized trophy, the handsome Cawnpore Cup, first played at Cawnpore Polo Club in India in 1901. He persuaded the club, dormant since 1939, to pass all its historic silverware to Malta after the last world war.

He is remembered in Malta today with great affection, as a recent article illustrated:

> He did everything he could to bring as many Maltese players as possible into the game, and during his spare time gave lessons to anyone he noticed was promising. He was known by all the Marsa stable lads and grooms as being firm and fair, but also generous and kind to them. They worshipped him![6]

The Duke of York — later King George VI — presents the Duke of York Cup to Lord Louis Mountbatten after the R.A.F. vs. Royal Navy match (courtesy Museum of Polo and Hall of Fame).

Of course, it was in Malta that Mountbatten introduced the Duke of Edinburgh — son of his sister, Princess Andrew of Greece and Denmark ... to polo. The Duke had first sat on a polo pony, and tried to hit the ball, at Adsdean, his uncle's Sussex house; but he did not take it up seriously until 1949, while serving in the Royal Navy in Malta, where Mountbatten commanded the 1st Cruiser Squadron.

The Duke's first team in England, Ancient Mariners, were to become as popular at Cowdray Park as Adsdean had been before the war, and crowds at games in those early post war years reflected the interest caused by royal participation.[7] The Mariners adopted white "sailor" shirts with blue borders, similar to those worn by naval ratings.

The interest increased after Mountbatten helped to bring the next generation, in the person of Prince Charles, into polo in the 1960s. His encouragement towards his young great-nephew was boundless.

Lord Mountbatten reached a 5-goal handicap at the height of his career — an achievement shared by the Duke of Edinburgh — and even after his playing days were over he maintained a close interest in the game. He was a familiar figure in the Royal Box at Guards Polo Club, especially on Queen's Cup and International Days, and was an active patron of the New Forest Polo Club, not far from his Broadlands home, and to whom he presented the Bluejackets Cup, a prewar prize at the long-defunct South Hants Club near Portsmouth, and played today as the New Forest's premier tournament.

In July 1979 he made what were to be his last appearances on the polo scene. He presented the Gold Cup to the winners of the British Open Championship, Songhai, at Cowdray Park and, a few days later, the Rundle Cup to the Prince of Wales and the Royal Navy team at Tidworth. On 27 August he was to fall victim to I.R.A. assassins while holidaying at his Irish home. A remote-controlled bomb exploded on Mountbatten's boat, and with him died one of his grandchildren, 14-year-old Nicholas Knatchbull, the boy's paternal grandmother, the 83-year-old Dowager Lady Brabourne and a local boy, 14-year-old Paul Maxwell.

Mountbatten's title was inherited by his elder daughter, Patricia, Lady Brabourne, who, with her husband, had been severely injured in the blast. Although unusual in the British peerage, Lady Brabourne's succession as Countess Mountbatten of Burma under a special remainder was not without precedent,[8] and certainly reflected the high regard in which "Uncle Dickie" was held by the royal family.

Mountbatten was buried at Romsey Abbey, not far from the gates of his beloved Broadlands, following a televised state funeral service in Westminster Abbey, a ceremony he had planned meticulously in every detail.

His memory is recalled today, in tangible fashion, through the Mountbatten Cup at Guards. It can also be seen in the distinctive oval-shaped head he devised to give "loft and length" to polo mallets. But his influence is felt most through the continuing participation of the British royal family in the galloping game, not least his great-nephew George, 4th Marquess of Milford Haven, who won the Queen's Cup, one of polo's most prestigious trophies, with Broncos in 1988, and reached the 2006 final; and two great-grandnephews, princes William and Harry of Wales.

Notes

1. Michael Clayton, *Prince Charles, Horseman* (London, Stanley Paul, 1987), pp. 21–22, *et seq.*
2. Philip Ziegler, *Mountbatten — The Official Biography* (London, Collins, 1985). A morganatic marriage was very much a concept confined to the royal and princely houses of pre-war Europe, and implied an alliance with a wife of non-royal or inferior status. For further information on the Hesse dynasty see *Almanach de Gotha* (London, 1999), pp. 129–136.
3. Lady Mountbatten died suddenly in 1960, while on tour in North Borneo as Superintendent-in-Chief, St John Ambulance Brigade.

4. *Burke's Peerage, Baronetage & Knightage*, Burke's Peerage Ltd., various editions 1948–1979.

5. Marco. *An Introduction to Polo* (London & New York, Country Life, 1931). He was also the author of *An Introduction to Umpiring* for the R.N.P.A., published in 1934. Although little-known, it is one of only two books devoted to the art of umpiring in polo.

6. Verité Reily Collins, *Very Tall Horses*, PQ International, Winter 2002.

7. Roger Chatterton-Newman, *Royal Memories*, PQ International, Autumn 1996.

8. Earlier examples were the daughters of military heroes Field Marshal Earl Roberts (1832–1914) and Field Marshal Viscount Wolseley (1833–1913) who, due to the absence of brothers, inherited their fathers' honors by special remainder.

Jim Ashton: Of the Brothers Four

by Chris Ashton

In the annals of Australian polo no team has dominated so completely in its own time as the Ashton brothers, Jim (born 1899), Bob (1900), Geoff (1904) and Phil (1906). Between 1929 and their retirement as a team ten years later they were never beaten in Australia in a scratch game. Australia has produced better players but no team is ever likely to equal their unbroken run of victories.

They were led by the eldest brother, Jim, who also managed Markdale, a 5,000-acre sheep station jointly owned by the brothers, some 60 miles from Goulburn, itself 170 miles southwest of Sydney.

Jim Ashton's impact on the wider canvas of Australian polo reflected the success of the team he led, always more significant than the sum of its parts. He was the manager of Markdale and captain-manager of the family polo team. He led his younger brothers on a consensus basis rather than by personal edict. Decisions emerged through a process of family discussion, sometimes spirited. Each brother was entitled to his say. In his unpublished memoir of the Ashton team's polo career, brother Bob wrote repeatedly of how "we," as distinct from "Jim," decided on one or another course of action.

Nothing in the brothers' upbringing pointed to a polo career. Their mother, Helen, was the only child of a widowed Anglican clergyman; their father, James, was an archetypal self-made late Victorian. He began work, at the age of ten, as a printer's boy, with a rural newspaper. Largely self-taught, he progressed from journalist, editor and newspaper proprietor to member of the New South Wales (N.S.W.) Parliament, serving variously as minister of lands and acting state premier before turning to the business world, where he served on boards of Sydney banking, insurance and pastoral companies.

Though his sons were keen and competitive at school sports, neither horses nor horsemanship featured in their upbringing in Sydney. As a member of parliament representing rural electorates and unstinting in his admiration of farming communities, he was resolved that his sons should follow that path. In 1920 he bought Markdale, appointing Jim, then 21, as manager with Bob his deputy, and the younger sons joining them as they left school.

The purchase of Markdale coincided with the opening of the Goulburn Polo Club. A World

The four Ashton brothers made history by touring round the globe playing polo. From left to right: Philip, Geoffrey, team captain James, and Robert, wearing Goulburn's red and blue (courtesy Museum of Polo and Hall of Fame).

War I artillery officer, Henry D.K. McCartney, conceived it as a way of persuading farmers' sons to enlist in the local citizen militia he commanded. Walking their horses from Markdale to Goulburn, Jim and Bob attended its first afternoon of practice chukkas. By 1926 the four brothers had become the Goulburn "A" team.

The first 50 years of Australian polo were characterized by hard riding and bustle, succinctly conjured up by Australia's most illustrious bush ballad poet, "Banjo" Paterson, in *The Geebung Polo Club*:

> Their style of playing polo was irregular and rash
> With mighty little science but a mighty lot of dash.

In 1928 the Australian tradition of so-called Geebung polo was challenged by another approach. At the invitation of the New South Wales Polo Association a British Army-in-India team, mounted by its hosts, played the N.S.W. tournament circuit for six weeks. Its manager, Colonel T.P. Melvill, wrote presciently:

> They're as keen as mustard and hard riders, hard hitters—ponies as good as anything in the world—but both need developing. The ponies play much more from the light of nature than anything else. A batch from a station is tried out. Those that show a natural aptitude are put straight into the game, the others are returned to grass or sent to India. If those showing natural aptitude could be bitted and carefully schooled, and if some of those young players whom I

Polo around the world: The exercise sand-yard on the vessel *Port Huon*'s forward deck (courtesy Museum of Polo and Hall of Fame).

> saw could be taken in hand and made to keep in their places there is no reason why a team should not be produced, and very shortly too, taking on everybody and anybody.[1]

From disciplined team play to rigorous analysis of tactics and strategy to the bitting ponies with curb rather than snaffle bits, the British Army-in-India team offered another possibility which was by no means welcomed by everyone. The Ashtons were the first to embrace and incorporate it into their own game.

On a sultry afternoon in January 1930 the 1500-ton cargo ship *Port Huon* slipped its moorings in Sydney Harbor, heading for open sea and the port of Hull on the other side of the world. Its cargo included 25 polo ponies, saddlery and six months' supply of lucerne, oats and chaff in case the English feed was too rich. With the ponies went four grooms and three Ashton brothers, excluding Bob, who, prone to seasickness, would follow with their parents on a passenger liner.

What followed established the Ashtons' claim to a place in polo folklore.

Nothing had been left to chance. Three years earlier, Geoff and Bob visited England and America to watch polo there and had returned convinced that Australia's best were the equal of either country. For two years, senior Australian and U.S. polo officials discussed proposals for a representative Australian team to play the American season, with all expenses paid and the promise of the sale of their ponies at the tour's end. To no avail.

Encouraged by the positive response of the Hurlingham Polo Committee to their overtures, the Ashtons decided by themselves to play the English season. They departed for England with the Australian Polo Association's blessing but with the understanding that they represented only the Goulburn Polo Club. They would travel at their own expense in the hope that by selling their ponies at the tour's end they would recover their costs. In his unpublished memoir of the Ashton team's polo career, Bob Ashton recalled:

> There was a ton of things which could go wrong—sickness of horses or men. Had we overestimated our playing ability? Or the quality of the horses? Would our horses recover quickly enough from their 48-day trip for the arduous London season? We were depending on our very good accommodation and exercise for this but there was no precedence for this and the experienced shippers were sure we were wrong. And how were the horse-boxes on open decks to stand up to violent storms? We were to find out.[2]

Horse traders exporting remounts to Indian cavalry regiments warned the ponies would need six months after the voyage to be match-fit rather than the five weeks the Ashtons had predicted. They were told their ponies must be stabled in narrow stalls to remain upright in high seas. The Ashtons instead built large stalls, 2.5 by 2 meters, fitted with coir matting to prevent ponies slipping, and a 9-meter by 5-meter railed sandpit for daily exercise.

From Melbourne to Perth the Australian Bight was too rough for exercise in the sandpit, but once in the Indian Ocean horses and riders settled into a steady if tedious routine. From Aden, Jim cabled that he expected the ponies to be match-fit within three weeks of arrival.

His optimism was shaken abruptly when the *Port Huon*, by now in the Mediterranean, sailed into a thunderstorm. All night waves crashed against its portside. A dozen ponies had to be moved aft. One mare, hindquarters wedged under the ship's railing, was almost swept overboard. Six stalls, lashed to deck railings with steel cables, were smashed, as was the sandpit. For the last 12 days a dozen ponies shared stalls, without space to lie down, and fought. Daily exercise was reduced to walking on the coir matting above deck.

Without further mishap they reached Hull. Ponies were unloaded and dispatched by rail to the Beaufort Polo Club, Gloucestershire, which would host the visiting team during the county tournaments that followed. Bob Ashton wrote that the brothers ever after recalled their safe arrival at Hull as the sweetest moment of their polo career.

For London journalists, the notion of four bachelor brothers with their ponies from Australia to challenge the might of British polo was newspaper fodder from heaven. In a dozen lines *Punch* magazine captured the public mood:

From a land so far below us
Where the fenceless fields lie wide
Here are four good men to show us
How the lean Australians ride.
Here's a tam distinct from others
With a unity made plain
By a lusty line of brothers
Linked in perfect chain.
Mr Punch, most proud to meet them
Boot and spur in England now
Though he hopes our best will beat them
Greets adventure with a bow.

The brothers were showered by invitations to balls, dinner parties and country house parties. Mindful that they had come to England to win whatever they could, Jim declined everything except those few that could not be refused without offense.

In English polo circles goodwill ran tandem with scepticism that the visitors had little to offer. Polo handicaps, long established in Britain, the U.S. and India, were yet unknown in Australia. Based on the performance of the 22-goal British Army-in-India during its 1928 N.S.W.

tour, the Ashtons ranked themselves as a 24-goal team. The British Army-in-India team manager, Colonel Melvill, for his part put it about — and was widely believed — that against English handicaps the visiting team was worth no more than 12-goals.

Melvill got it wrong. In the season that followed, Goulburn won 15 of its 21 games. Of its six losses, four were by one goal and three were to an Anglo-American team, the Hurricanes, which, after narrowly defeating Goulburn in the final of the Hurlingham Championship Cup, won the U.S. Open. Goulburn meantime won the Whitney, Ranelagh Handicap and Hargreaves Cups and the Indian Empire Shield. In a personal tribute the King of Spain, himself a polo devotee, presented a trophy to their father, who, with Helen Ashton, attended the entire English season.

In the officers mess of 17th/21st Lancers the commanding officer declared in a speech of welcome:

> When we heard you chaps were coming we said first of all, "they'll never start." When we heard you'd started, we said, "they'll never get here." And when you got here we said, "you'll never play your ponies for a year," and you played them in three weeks. We said, "you'll never win a match," and you've won almost every match.[3]

After a six-week four-day voyage, Jim Ashton lends a hand in debarkation at Hull (courtesy Museum of Polo and Hall of Fame).

But euphoria at their triumphs was tempered by the prospect of financial ruin. When they left home in January the Wall Street crash three months earlier had signified nothing. Australian wool prices had since collapsed, as had the price of polo ponies in England. On neither count could they hope to recover their costs. Their only hope was to continue on to New York to accept a standing invitation to play exhibition matches, followed by an auction of their ponies. Apparently polo pony prices in the U.S. were holding firm.

Seven months had passed since departing Sydney. The brothers and their ponies were exhausted. Bob Ashton remembers:

> It was a tremendous decision. The expenses were going to rise greatly because it meant a trip across the Atlantic with 25 ponies and

> spending several weeks on Long Island where the expenses were terrific. And if our ponies were to sell we had to play well.[4]

In New York as in London they were feted by the press, and were royally entertained by American polo's most illustrious players—Averell Harriman, Mike and Howard Phipps, the Hitchcocks, Jock Whitney, and Stewart Iglehart—whom they already knew from the English season. Of their seven exhibition games they won five, acquitting themselves better than they had dared hope, but well below their peak.

The auction of their 25 ponies which followed exceeded all expectations, netting 77,000 U.S. dollars. For exchange control reasons this money was held in New York until the following year, during which it rose by 60 percent against the Australian pound, which depreciated in the interval. The Ashtons more than recovered their costs, with sufficient remaining to buy Bob Ashton a sheep station.

Developing a new string of ponies from scratch, and forced to sell some of them to augment their depleted income from wool, the Great Depression brought the family back to earth. They played polo intermittently and always with an eye on costs. "We had very few games as a family team," Bob recalled:

> Most tournaments in Australia we were split, only getting one game a year together.... It may sound funny but lack of games together probably effects [sic] a team like ours which was largely dependent on good teamwork, more than a team of four experienced players who have not played a lot together.[5]

And yet they never discarded the idea of returning to England to claim its most coveted polo trophy, the Hurlingham Championship Cup. Though by now seasoned players they had three strikes against them: the lack of sustained team-play or high-goal competition since 1930; the lack of international-standard polo ponies, which they had sold to make ends meet; and the fact that both Jim and Geoff had married and had since become fathers. The proposed 1937 tour nearly foundered over whether wives and babies would also travel to England. The issue was resolved in favor of the wives accompanying their husbands, leaving their infant daughters with nurses in the care of doting Ashton grandparents.

Bob Ashton states:

> It was not the continuous thrill of the first trip. The first time it didn't matter how bad we were, anything we did was better than people expected of us. This time we were a known quantity and that though they were glad to see us, they were going to see that we didn't win too much.[6]

The county tournaments ended and the major metropolitan contests, Ranelagh, Roehampton and, finally, Hurlingham, approached. As an advance guard to relocating the Goulburn team to London, Geoff, Janet, Bob and Phil went ahead with the luggage, checked everyone and everything into a hotel, and were given access to the three double-rooms, one each for Jim and Irene, Geoff and Janet, and Phil and Bob. The three younger brothers allocated rooms to each couple and stowed the luggage accordingly. As the most recently married, Geoff and Janet were awarded the bridal suite.

Almost fifty years later, Janet Ashton recalled to the author a moment offering a vivid, fleeting insight of the discipline and hierarchy within the Ashton brotherhood. When Jim arrived with Irene some hours later his brothers showed him to the guestrooms, explaining the basis of their allocation. Quietly, calmly, Jim told them that he and Irene would occupy the bridal suite. There was no discussion. Each brother simply picked up his baggage, taking it to his new room. An only child, Janet Ashton told me of her fascination—not censure, but fascination—for the ground rules of the close-knit brotherhood into which she had married two years before, entirely different from her own experience of family life.

Split in early tournaments into opposing teams in the county tournaments, the Ashtons reached London below their peak form. As the Hurlingham Championship approached they faced a painful dilemma. They had brought with them as their reserve 23-year-old Bob Skene. As a guest player with English teams earlier in the season he had begun to show the brilliance that augured a future ten-goal player. For the first time in the Ashton camp, merit took precedence over ties of blood. Jim decided that Skene, on six-goals, would replace Phil, on five-goals, for Hurlingham.

In the final, Goulburn, 26-goals, faced the tournament favorite, Jaguars, 28-goals, comprising two Englishmen, Gerald Balding, Keith Rous, the American "Laddie" Sanford, and the Indian Rao Rajah Hanut Singh. Bob Ashton recalls the game as the toughest of their polo career. Chukker after chukker the scores drew level, with Goulburn edging ahead each time to win 9–7. Playing number one, Skene scored six goals for Goulburn.

Jim Ashton as seen by Austrian artist Carl Ferdinand Bauer (courtesy Museum of Polo and Hall of Fame).

At the season's end the Ashtons auctioned their ponies at Tattersall's. The prices did not compare to the 1930 Long Island auction but were enough to cover their costs. By now polo was no longer the consuming passion of the brothers, each of whom had acquired his own sheep station. Their career as a family team was drawing to its close.

For the Ashtons, as for the wider world, 1939 was a watershed year. Jim wanted to retire from polo to concentrate on business and pastoral interests. Reluctantly he acceded to the pleas of the N.S.W.P.A. to lead Goulburn one more time to contest the state championship, the Dudley Cup—a trophy which the Ashtons, or teams including Ashtons, had won every year they had played it since 1928.

The dream of every other team was to knock them off their pedestal. Trailing 3–5 at halftime in the final to the rising star of N.S.W. polo, Wirragulla, its club president imprudently declared in an interview broadcast over loudspeakers that a historic moment was at hand, the defeat of the Goulburn team. Smarting at the taunt, in the second half the Ashtons scored eight goals to Wirragulla's two to win their last game as a team, 11–7.

An era ended. Their father, James, died soon after, followed within weeks by their mother. Though the brothers were above the proscribed age limit, and as farmers working in a "protected" industry were not obliged to do so, they volunteered for active service at the outbreak of war. At Prime Minister Robert Menzies' request, Jim joined the board of the government's Commonwealth Bank and otherwise took charge of his brothers' families and sheep stations for the duration of their wartime service.

Following their demobilization at the war's end, Geoff and Phil, restored to their families and pastoral properties, returned to polo only briefly. Jim was long retired but Bob continued playing for another ten years and thereafter served as a commentator, umpire and coach. Early postwar players, Sinclair Hill among them, fondly recall his advice and encouragement. Bob died in 1974, three years after Jim. Phil and Geoff died within six months of one another in 1994.

No account of Jim Ashton's contribution to Australian polo would be complete without mention of his sons, James (born in 1941) and Wallace (1949). Like his father, James took up polo at 21. A four-goaler at his peak, he played in India and England and for several N.S.W. teams. That was, until he was infected with brucellosis, a debilitating blood disease contracted from cattle, which put his polo career on hold for 18 years.

With brother Wal, a three-goaler at his peak, James then played in the inaugural Federation of International Polo 14-goal World Polo Cup in 1987 and its successor in Berlin in 1989. Following the death of his son Jamie, himself a promising young player, in 1995 James founded Millamolong Polo Club. Since 1990 he has bred polo ponies from lines established by the Ashton brothers during their prime, selling into England and Southeast Asia as well as to local buyers.

In 1966 the Brothers Four, long retired from the game, donated a trophy named after them as the premier annual contest of the Goulburn Polo Club, whose colors they had worn onto hallowed polo grounds on the other side of the world. Playing that year for the Toompang Polo Club, Wal (18 years old) and James won the inaugural Ashton Cup. Playing later that same season for Toompang, James also won the N.S.W. championship, the Countess of Dudley Cup. Forty years on, the Millamolong team of James (now 65 years old) and Wal (58), supported by two five-goal professionals, again won the 2006 Ashton and Dudley Cups.

As the Millamolong team — named after the 8,000-acre sheep station inherited from his father, Jim, James and brother Wal have won most of Australia's most coveted trophies, while lending ponies to mount visiting teams. But James's most important contribution was as an administrator, president of the N.S.W. Polo Association (1994–98) and Australian Polo Council (1998–2002), mediating between the competing interests of the traditional clubs and polo patrons. In 2001 he led the Australian polo community in hosting the 6th World Polo Cup, after which he was elected treasurer of the Federation of International Polo. In 2005 Wal Ashton was elected president of the New South Wales Polo Association. They too are part of Jim Ashton's legacy to polo.

Notes

1. T.P. Melvill, *The Polo Monthly*
2. Bob Ashton, Unpublished memoirs.
3. *Ibid.*
4. *Ibid.*
5. *Ibid.*
6. *Ibid.*

Johnny Traill was the subject of this caricature when his handicap was raised to 9-goals in the midst of the London season (courtesy Nigel à Brassard).

Below: Always playing at back, Kerry Packer was a solid defender who earned his rating. Ellerston v. Labegorce in the 1995 Silver Jubilee Cup at Guards Polo Club. Alberto "Pepe" Heguy in the background (courtesy Mike Roberts).

Pimms at Cowdray Park. Left to right: Marcos Uranga, the Earl of Brecknock, the Queen of Bhutan, Alfredo Goti and John Tylor, who eventually would become the Hurlingham Polo Association's chairman (courtesy Marcos Uranga).

The most spectacular setting for a polo game — looking across the Lawns to the South Downs and ruins of Cowdray House (courtesy Roger Chatterton-Newman, PQInternational).

Half a century after the event, Marcos Uranga presents cuttings from the Olympic Oak to polo legends Roberto Cavanagh and Luis Duggan, gold medalists in the 1936 Berlin Olympic games. The setting is Palermo's number one ground (courtesy Marcos Uranga).

Another family team, La Picaza-Puerta Abierta. Left to right: Juan, Diego, Delfín and Mariano Uranga with their father Marcos and coach Alberto Pedro Heguy. The four brothers celebrate their success in the 2006 Metropolitano Handicap Championship. Their sister Paula is married to Alberto P. Heguy's son Pepe (courtesy Marcos Uranga).

Claire Tomlinson, who has done so much for the game as a player, sponsor, breeder, and coach. Mrs. Tomlinson irrevocably changed women's polo in Britain (courtesy Mike Roberts).

Wearing Tramontana's colors, Prince Charles at full speed. Cowdray Park's Gold Cup in the late 1980s (courtesy Mike Roberts).

Captain of England for 20 years, in his time Julian Hipwood personified the game of polo in Britain.

Prince Charles, the most recognized player in the polo world (both courtesy Mike Roberts).

Playing for England in the Coronation Cup, Julian Hipwood wearing his unmistakable blue helmet (courtesy Mike Roberts).

Poetry in motion: Adolfo Cambiaso taps the ball in the air, Marcos Heguy in the background (courtesy Museum of Polo and Hall of Fame).

Gonzalo in his White Birch days. *Polo* magazine once wrote, "As Gonzalo Pieres goes, so goes White Birch" (courtesy Museum of Polo and Hall of Fame).

La Espadaña was the dominant team in the 1980s, taking seven Argentine Open titles. Carlos Gracida, Alfonso and Gonzalo Pieres, Ernesto Trotz (courtesy Museum of Polo and Hall of Fame).

Dubai took the Queen's Cup at Guards. Left to right: Ryan Pemble, Alejandro Díaz Alberdi, Mr. Arnaud Bamberger, H.M. The Queen, Ali Albwardi, Adolfo Cambiaso (courtesy Museum of Polo and Hall of Fame).

Always in perfect balance, Guillermo Gracida Jr. prepares to hit a near-side backhander (courtesy Mike Roberts).

La Dolfina 2005 (left to right): Bartolomé Castagnola, Mariano Aguerre, Lucas Monteverde, Adolfo Cambiaso. They took the Argentine Open, shattering Ellerstina's dream of a Triple Crown (courtesy Museum of Polo and Hall of Fame).

Part III

The Superstars

Introduction

All games and sports, including the courageous, fascinating and incredibly alluring endeavor that is polo, generate idols. Juan Manuel Fangio in car racing, Dr. William Gilbert Grace in cricket, Rod Laver in tennis, Jack Nicklaus in golf, Pelé in soccer, Babe Ruth in baseball are just some examples that come to mind.

When the passage of time begins to remove polish from outstanding sporting careers, only those players at the very top remain as knights in shining armor. They are — to use an expression common in Argentina —*classic players.* A classic swing, a classic rider, these we instinctively know: a thing of beauty, a pleasure to watch, and a sense of fulfillment when performed well. But the term classic player when applied to polo implies something unique: an image that can quicken the heart and turn heads by just gliding down a polo ground.

The eight players presented in this section could form two all-time stars teams but for the particular that there are no number ones among them. It is true Bob Skene achieved fame initially at that position on Goulburn and British teams, but his real strength was in the middle of the game. So were all the rest, with the exception of Francisco Dorignac, a genuine back, and Carlos Menditeguy, who could play at back or at number three with identical facility. The explanation is simple: polo matches are won and lost down the middle. Even today in contemporary polo the question is where the weakest player should be: at number one, or at back? Opinions differ, but this is neither the place nor the time to enter into the argument, important as it may be.

The time span covered in this section extends for approximately 60 years, from Tommy Hitchcock's first Westchester Cup and its attendant personal reward of a 10-goal rating, to Franky Dorignac's last Argentine Open in 1982. There are other superstars featured in this collection of essays— John Watson and Adolfo Cambiaso stand at the extremes— and they are included in their respective epochs. There are also new champions— the Pieres brothers as an example — who have not yet reached the full stature of their game nor succeeded into their kingdom, the Argentine Open.

Certainly, there have been more stylish players than Tommy Hitchcock but no one with greater staying power or a temperament more ideally suited to the game of polo. However, he was the typical classic player in the sense that he embodied the ideals of honor, never-let-up, and unlimited determination to win. Cecil Smith was different. A much better horseman and a grand striker of the ball, he displayed coolness under pressure; poise is the word that surfaces. Stewart Iglehart's best polo years were cut in half by the war; but there were enough left for him to become the top American player until his retirement. Bob Skene was extraordinary: when both Carlos Menditeguy and Francisco Dorignac state that he was the best foreign player to play in Argentina, it tells that Skene was something unique. His compatriot Sinclair Hill endured a severe handicap: in all the high-goal teams on which he performed, he never had three teammates who could play at, or close to, his level. One can only speculate what his performance could have been with a really top team.

Charlie Menditeguy merits a separate paragraph. He was a rare mixture of two usually contrasting components: on the one hand, a casual, happy-go-lucky attitude tinged with supreme self-confidence; on the other, the artful preparation mind-set and the keen student of the game.

Along with these top of the cream players, others most distinguished were to arise, including two who were not only great poloists, but men of outstanding, forceful and remarkable character: Harriott and Dorignac.

With all respect to their contemporaries, it is safe to think that polo historians of the future will call their particular epoch, 1955–1980, that of Franky Dorignac and Juancarlitos Harriott.

These, then, are our superstars. Perhaps it is no surprise that oftentimes we ourselves dream we could also perform at polo with a touch of their style and a measure of their skill. In a game endowed with many great practitioners, they stand head and shoulders above most of the rest.

Thomas Hitchcock Jr.: "The best of America was in his veins"

by Nigel à Brassard

Tommy Hitchcock was the inspiration behind the description of polo as "a Persian invention, a British sport and an American profession."[1] Hitchcock has been called the "Babe Ruth of polo" and "polo's Tiger Woods." While it is tempting to try to identify the similarities between these sportsmen, neither sobriquet adequately sums up the genius which makes Tommy Hitchcock arguably America's greatest ever polo player. *Polo* magazine wrote about Hitchcock in the 1927 Westchester Cup matches: "There can never be a question about the amazing performance of Mr. Thomas Hitchcock Jr. in the Cup series of 1927. No one who has not seen a ten-goal player play fifteen-goal polo can imagine the stark power of this youth."[2] But Hitchcock earned his place in the history books not only as a polo player but also as a war hero, a successful investment banker with Lehman Brothers and a naturally talented all-round sportsman. When Hitchcock died on 19 April 1944, his death was reported on the front page of the *New York Times*: "He was intelligent, personable, humorous, of superb physical equipment and wholly devoid of pretense. The best of America was in his veins— not the nonsense of any social class, but the country's intellect and character." In the foreword to Nelson Aldrich's book, *Tommy Hitchcock: an American Hero,* Averell Harriman wrote:

> Tommy was a great athlete; one of the greatest athletes of my generation — by far the best polo player of our time. I don't know of anyone who could compare to him in every aspect of the game. He could not only hit the ball from every side of his pony, forward or back, but he had a great ability to block players. Tommy was also a great team player. He brought out the best in all of us, whether we were good, bad or indifferent. He never shouted at others as some polo players did, but he encouraged his team-mates in every way by his own excellence. Both as a player and a team player he had no rivals anywhere.[3]

Tommy was born into an American polo family on 11 February 1900. His father had captained the American polo team in the first international polo matches between England and America in 1886. Tommy's mother, Louise Eustis Hitchcock, is the only woman inductee in the Polo Hall of Fame. In the citation she is described as "a passionate poloist long before women became equal to men on the field ... a born leader and visionary. Her turf was the Aiken

Preparatory School and the Meadow Lark Club for Boys where she coached and inspired future polo stars."[4] One of the teams she coached was the Old Aiken team made up of under 21-year-olds Ebby Gerry, Jimmy Mills, Stewart Iglehart and Cocie Rathborne that reached the finals of the Monty Waterbury Cup in 1929. Under his parents' tutelage Tommy started his polo career at a very young age; they had imparted to the young Tommy their love of the game and knowledge of the finer points of polo horsemanship. At the age of 16 Tommy was a member of the polo teams that won the Junior—(Meadow Brook 3rd), and Senior (Great Neck), U.S. Polo Association Championships. He was an accomplished horseman and had developed an amazing ability with the polo mallet. He possessed all the physical and mental abilities that make a great athlete, such as superb hand-eye coordination, strength, toughness, sharp reflexes, and a highly competitive drive. But his polo success was not that just of a superb sportsman, he was also a keen student of the game. He continually analyzed angles of shots, the placement of players and speeds of attack. He was also one of those sportsmen who knew he had to practice hard and he spent hours on the wooden horse perfecting his stroke play and "stick and balling" his horses so that he knew their limits as well as his own. His attitude towards polo is best summed up in the special instructions he wrote to his teammates in his capacity as captain of the 1930 U.S. polo squad: "1. Try as hard as you can all the time. Do not let up for one second and do not stop until the referee blows his whistle." He also advised his teammates to "Play the man rather than the ball. The ball won't travel by itself if you eliminate the man. This is especially important when a man is trying to dribble the ball behind you. All you need do is check and bump into him hard and that will spoil his play." Some of his teammates noted that Tommy's intensity was almost to the point of fanaticism and remarked how difficult it was to relate to him on the day of a polo match. In addition, he had a habit of dismounting after the final whistle of a game and jumping into his car and disappearing, wishing to unwind on his own rather than socializing with his teammates and opponents. His approach to sport was in some ways more akin to that of a modern sportsman than the more gentlemanly amateurism of his time. He was passionate about his fitness; he tried to run at least one mile every day, was a nonsmoker and a modest drinker. Before breakfast he liked to have three fast rounds in the ring with a boxing trainer. He believed that boxing "brings a fellow to the point of exhaustion quicker than any other exercise." He also liked, and was extremely good at, squash, tennis, skeet shooting and skiing.

From his first Westchester Cup in 1921 to his last in 1939, Tommy Hitchcock was always in the picture (courtesy Museum of Polo and Hall of Fame).

Opposite top: Hitchcock established a standard of play that has never been surpassed. Here Tommy effectively blocks John Miles during the 1928 Cup of the Americas. Hitchcock is on his celebrated Tobiano; Miles rides Cascada. ***Opposite bottom:*** An American test team for the 1939 Westchester Cup (left to right): Mike Phipps, Cecil Smith, Tommy Hitchcock, Winston Guest.

Above: The fabulous Tommy Hitchcock's power at the top of the swing. Young Earle Hopping in the background. U.S. Open Championship, 1930 (all photographs courtesy Museum of Polo and Hall of Fame).

Hitchcock was attractive, handsome, well spoken, modest, and a dynamic presence on the polo field. He became the idol of a generation of young men entering the game. Hitchcock once said, "There is a fascination about the game of polo that is hard to describe to anyone who has never played. Once a man has had a taste of it, the task of curing him is rather hopeless. The intense mental excitement during the game and the physical and mental relaxation afterward are—well, as I said, it's hard to describe it unless you have had it yourself." On another occasion Tommy remarked, "Polo is exciting, but you can't compare it to flying in wartime. That's the best sport in the world. It's not a real sport unless the duck can shoot back." Newell Bent writing in *American Polo* repeated the description that Hitchcock was "the only man, with the exception of the late Captain Leslie Cheape, able to play any of the four positions on a polo team and be worth ten-goals in each of the four places."[5] More than anyone Tommy was the player that changed the number 3, long considered a defensive position, into an aggressive and offensive one. Pete Bostwick said about Tommy, "Sometimes he did things on the field that made you wonder." Another of his teammates, Jock Whitney, wrote, "My feelings for Hitchcock remained hero worship long after that kind of emotion is supposed to stop beating in a boyish breast."[6]

"Ten-Goal Tommy," as he was nicknamed, won a staggering number of polo's top honors during his playing career. Four times he was on the team that won the U.S. Open Championship: Meadow Brook 1923, Sands Point 1927, Greentree 1935 and 1936. When he won a silver medal in 1924 as captain of the American Olympic team in Paris, after the final, one of the Argentine players said to Hitchcock, "My God! You should be ranked at fifteen instead of ten, Tommy." He played against England in five contests for the Westchester Cup—the American team was victorious in all five—and played in the Cup of the Americas against Argentina in 1928 and 1936. In 1933 Hitchcock captained the East team in the celebrated East-West series.

Tommy first burst onto the international polo scene at the age of 21 when he was selected to play for America in the Westchester Cup matches at London's Hurlingham Club. His style of play was a revelation to the English players and spectators. He played an aggressive game, was a fearless rider and an accurate hitter of the ball. "Come the time come the man": the 1920s and 1930s in America were a time when the whole country had gone mad over the idea of spectator events. Americans in the thousands turned out to watch Babe Ruth, Jack Dempsey, Man O' War, and Tommy Hitchcock. This period was to be called the "Golden Age of American Sport" and it was the period that polo came into its own. In the 1930s crowds of over 40,000 watched the America versus Great Britain matches and the other major polo tournaments, and, as one newspaper remarked, the spectators came from all walks of life and the cheers from the crowd were from the "the throaty bravo of the Long Island debutante to the rebel yell of the cowboy." The games were on the front page of the American and British newspapers. It was noted that you could fill a copy of the social register with the mere introduction of "among those present were" and not be wrong, but the media was also realizing that polo was a major sport and not just a society happening. The 1930s match reports commented on the democratization of polo, "which is an accomplished fact along with its nationalization" and "although polo continues to be an expensive game, if a youth with no great fortune at his disposal shows promise, there are plenty to mount him, as it is within the rules to do so." America's domination of international polo at this time was a result of a number of factors. First, there was the constant introduction of fine young players into the game and these young men were welcomed enthusiastically. Louis Stoddard retired from international polo in 1924 and stated, "There has been a tendency in the past to use men against Great Britain who have been members of the team year after year ... I am withdrawing in order that this practice may be abolished." Second, polo was being played nationwide and all year round. When the northeast season came to an end in early fall, players moved on to play in California, South Carolina,

Texas and Florida. Thirdly, Americans such as Harry Whitney and Stephen "Laddie" Sanford had gone to great lengths to buy some of the best polo ponies in the world and devote themselves to breeding top polo ponies in the U.S. Fourthly, the Americans were revolutionizing the way the game was played and no one more than Hitchcock epitomized this innovative style. Ami Shinitzky in *The Endless Chukker* described the American style of play that was to influence the sport throughout the world: "Better-bred and faster ponies picked up the pace of the game, and this meant longer hitting rather than frequent dribbling of the ball. American polo enthusiasts were not content with the over politeness, controlled galloping and traditional defensive tactics of the British. Their game was wide open, slashing and always attacking."[7] In 1927 Robert Kelley, writing for *Polo* magazine, defined the American success at polo and noted, "No longer does the white ball roll properly along the deep green of the playing surface; it goes whistling through the air for all the world like a baseball drive."[8] Newell Bent in *American Polo* describes Mr. Hitchcock thus: "With his extremely long, accurate hitting, is now the greatest exponent of the fast, hard, modern game."[9]

As a result of his performance in the 1921 Westchester Cup series Tommy's handicap was increased from 9 to 10 goals. Tommy was the youngest player ever to be awarded a 10-goal handicap, a feat not bettered until the arrival on the polo scene of Adolfo Cambiaso. Hitchcock remained a 10-goal player until 1944 apart from one season, 1934, when he was dropped to 9-goals after a horrendous accident in the 1933 East v. West games.

Hitchcock is also remembered as an American military hero. While a seventeen-year-old at St. Paul's, Hitchcock tried to enlist with the U.S. Air Force but was rejected as being too young. With the help of family friend Theodore Roosevelt, he joined the Lafayette Escadrille—nicknamed "the cavalry of the air"—with which he saw active service. During a dogfight with a German plane Tommy's plane was hit and he was wounded. Tommy crash-landed his plane and was captured by the enemy and made a prisoner of war for four months in hospitals and prison camps. He made a dramatic escape from a train, walked his way to neutral Switzerland and was able to rejoin his unit. He was awarded the Croix de Guerre with three palms. In the Second World War, Hitchcock was thought to be too old for combat flying and was appointed assistant military attaché for air in the American Embassy in London. Subsequently he was made chief of a tactical research section in 9th Air Force fighter command. It was in this capacity that in April 1944 Hitchcock was to test a P-51 Mustang fighter plane that had developed a fault. Tommy took the plane up and it developed problems and crashed into Salisbury Plain, killing him. He was awarded posthumously the Legion of Merit, the Bronze Star and the Distinguished Flying Cross.

The novelist F. Scott Fitzgerald met Tommy Hitchcock in 1921 and they became firm friends. Fitzgerald was at once taken by Hitchcock as "a newspaper hero in his escape from Germany and the greatest polo player in the world." He admired Tommy's decision in 1918 to return from Europe and enter Harvard, "because he had the humility to ask himself 'do I know anything?' That combination is what forever will put him in my pantheon of heroes." Fitzgerald was subsequently to use Tommy as a model for Tom Buchanan in *The Great Gatsby*. In the novel Tom is described this way:

> He was a sturdy straw haired man of thirty with a rather hard mouth and a supercilious manner. Two shining arrogant eyes had established dominance over his face and gave him an appearance of always leaning aggressively forward. Not even the effeminate swank of his riding clothes could hide the enormous power of that body—he seemed to fill those glistening boots until he strained the top lacing, and you could see a great pack of muscle when his shoulder moved under his thin coat. It was a body capable of enormous leverage—a cruel body.[10]

A measure of the high profile of his prominence as a sporting personality is that Tommy was featured—seven years after his death—in a 1951 advertisement for PM Whiskey. The advertisement described Tommy as "one of the true immortals of the Golden Age of Sports" and suggested that his greatest triumph was playing against Argentina in 1928. The author of the description, the sportswriter Bob Considine, described Tommy as riding like "a reckless Indian. His brilliant mallet work kept a constant rain of drives pouring into Argentine territory, and on defense he completely baffled the visitors from the Pampas."

In July 1946 Tommy was featured in the lead story of a children's comic called *True Comics*. The story of *Ten Goal Tommy* is told over four pages and gives a description of his polo and military career. The comic strip includes pictures of what is described as "Tommy's greatest shot" and shows the dying minutes of the 1928 International game against Argentina when Tommy from midfield was able to turn rapidly and with time for only a quick shot make a hit so that "the ball flew 170 yards for a goal!" The author is not aware of any other polo player featured as a children's comic book hero.

Tommy Hitchcock's death was reported in newspapers across America and described him as "the greatest polo player of all time." The articles noted that Tommy was "the man who changed the international sport from tactics of slapping the ball around smartly amongst the players and gradually working it down towards the goal posts."[11] Tommy taught the art of smacking the ball a country mile and generally riding hell for leather in its pursuit. Tommy was a picturesque, daring figure on horseback, and he caught the crowd's fancy by the Ruthian power in his drives, many of them carrying a full 100 yards.

Notes

1. Tom O'Reilly in Allison Danzig and Peter Brandwein, eds., *Sports Golden Age* (New York: Harper Brothers, 1948).
2. Peter Vischer, ed., *Polo* (October 1927), 9.
3. Nelson W. Aldrich Jr., *Tommy Hitchcock: An American Hero* (Gaithersburgh: Fleet Corp., 1984). 5
4. Polo Museum and Hall of Fame citation, Lake Worth, Florida.
5. Newell Bent, *American Polo* (New York: Macmillan, 1929), 374.
6. E. J. Kahn, *Jock: The Life and Times of John Hay Whitney* (New York: Doubleday, 1981), 86.
7. Ami Shinitzki, and Don Follmer, *The Endless Chukker* (Gaithersburgh: Polo, 1978.)
8. Robert F. Kelly, *Polo* (October. 1927).
9. Bent, *American Polo*, 376.
10. F. Scott Fitzgerald, *The Great Gatsby* (New York: Scribner's, 1925).
11. *The New York Times*, 20 April 1944.

Cecil Smith: The Cowboy from Llano

by Horace A. Laffaye

In the aftermath of the 1933 East-West series, the American humorist Will Rogers wrote in his syndicated column:

> The hillbillies beat the dudes and took the polo championship of the world right out of the drawing room and into the bunkhouse.[1]

Credit Cecil Smith with the lion's share of wrestling away from the favored Easteners the unofficial crown of American polo. In so doing, Smith outplayed, out-horsed and outshone the immortal Tommy Hitchcock, the East's captain and anointed leader. The individual balance of power, as far as ratings go, was also tipped: eventually Hitchcock was lowered to 9-goals for the only time in his career and Cecil reached the 10-goal pinnacle for the first time in his life.

Born at the 30,000 acre Charles T. Moss ranch in Llano, Texas, on 14 February 1904, Cecil Calvert Smith was the only boy of Sidney Elmer Smith and Nettie Mae Ratliff's three children.[2] Sydney Smith would eventually become the ranch's foreman; nevertheless, Cecil grew up in what historian Samuel Marshall called "circumstances that have never been entirely favorable." There was no plumbing in the Smith house and electrical power had to wait until 1939 when the Rural Electrification Act was enacted, sponsored by a congressman from Texas named Lyndon Baines Johnson. In due time, LBJ would also rise to the top.

Cecil grew up on horseback: soon after he could walk, he started riding. By age 12, he was working and earning full wages at the Moss ranch. Continuing formal education was out of the question. Horsemanship, Smith would say years later, "is natural, it's something you inherit." Cecil also became adept at roping, required expertise for ranch hands. His ability in this task had an unexpected twist when the local sheriff recruited Cecil to help apprehend a mentally disturbed man who was waving a knife. "I just pitched the rope on him," said the young Smith, already showing the unflappable attitude that he would demonstrate on the polo grounds.

Cecil Smith's introduction to polo was delivered by horse dealer George Miller, who offered Cecil a job paying triple his ranch hand's wages. In 1925, the U.S.P.A. listed Cecil Smith at 0-goals, playing at Austin Polo Club. That same year, Miller and Smith went to Detroit to play polo and sell ponies. Smith's globetrotting days had begun. The third person in the show was Rube Williams, another cowboy from Texas, who would become a close friend.[3] They were an unusual pair, Cecil and Rube. Smith's demeanor was quiet, reserved, and stable; Williams was outgoing and temperamental. But the pair linked beautifully on the polo field. With Rube playing at back, Cecil could use at large his fast-improving hitting skills; as far as riding ability, there was very little room for improvement because Smith was considered the best.

By the 1930s and the onset of the Great Depression, Smith and Williams, now trading ponies on their own, settled into a routine of training horses, traveling and playing. In a certain sense, they were following the golden twins, money and the sun. Following the completion of the U.S. Open Championship, in those days always held at Meadow Brook Club in Long Island, they would come back home to Texas to purchase good prospects and begin the time-consuming job of training the mounts for polo. Smith much preferred to buy ponies aged five or six, because by then they were fully developed and could endure the fast riding and hard bumps characteristic of the style of play then prevalent in high goal polo. The fully loaded trailers would then head to Southern California in order to complete the spring season from Midwick to Del Monte. The long summer season saw Cecil play in Long Island, culminating with the jewel of American polo, the Open Championship, amidst the glorious foliage of late September.

This circle of travel, business and play remained a stable way of Smith's polo life. It was interrupted only by his trips to England in the late 1930s and the occasional big tournament in Chicago, such as the East-West series, and international play for the Avila Camacho Cup against Mexico. But the increased volume and quality of play in Florida in the 1950s lured Smith to forgo California and he began to spend more time near Boca Raton. Cecil Smith's dedication to the game of polo was total, interrupted only by hunting expeditions with friends such as Lea Aldwell, the Barry brothers, Sonny Noelke and, of course, Rube Williams.

Smith's rise in the polo hierarchy — read handicap ratings— was meteoric. From the very bottom rung in 1925 — 0 goals— he reached the magical 10-goal rating in 1934. Peter Vischer, editor of the authoritative *Polo* magazine, had this to say about the Texas cowboy:

> He rides easily, hits with force and touch, thinks quickly, and plays consistently a game characterized by response, quiet reserve and power. Smith might be described as a polo player's player; he has style.[4]

A classic player, indeed. A slightly different tack was described by Samuel Marshall, a strong critic of the eastern polo establishment, writing for the *Detroit News*:

> Hitchcock is wealthy; Smith hasn't a dime. Hitchcock is one of the game's keenest students; Smith was born with the technique of play in his brain and drive in his good right arm.[5]

Marshall's bias extended to the issue of selection of players to represent America in international play. In 1930, he wrote:

> Suppose the West should win. Would the East give way in the matter of International selection? You know very well they would not.[6]

Thomas Hitchcock Jr. proved Marshall wrong. As captain of the American squad, Hitchcock insisted that Cecil Smith — now rated at seven-goals— be invited to participate in the trials for the 1930 Westchester Cup, to be held on Long Island. Out of 16 players, Smith was selected as an alternate, and Eric Pedley, a Californian, played at number one in both matches, alongside young Earle Hopping, Winston Guest, and Tommy Hitchcock. As usual, when it came to assembling the best possible team, Tommy would not allow anything or anyone to stand in his way.

As a result of his performance in the International Trials, Cecil was asked by Harold

Talbott to play in the U.S. Open Championship on the Roslyn team, also based on Long Island. Englishman Gerald Balding and Smith's pal Rube Williams completed the squad, which lost by only one goal in the first match of the tournament. In those long-gone days, the Monty Waterbury Cup — now sadly relegated to a lower tier of U.S.P.A. competition — was played on handicap among the teams competing in the Open.[7] In a surprising result, the untried Roslyn team took the Waterbury Cup, defeating in the final match the mighty Greentree squad, led by no other than Tommy Hitchcock.

In 1932 the U.S. Open Championship was marred by the injury sustained by Cecil Smith while playing for Greentree, Jock Whitney's team. Cecil had to be replaced by Eric Tyrrell-Martin, the English 9-goal handicap player. The tournament was taken by Winston Guest's Templeton.

If there was a single event that propelled Cecil Smith into the public eye, unquestionably it was the 1933 East-West series. The question of how he would do against Hitchcock, who had been a 10-goal player for 12 straight seasons, was a popular argument. This East-West competition, dubbed by some as the World Series of Polo, was a special sports event connected with the Century of Progress exposition in Chicago.

Carleton Burke, the West's lonely selector and manager, called upon Aidan Roark, Elmer Boeseke Jr., Cecil Smith and, at back, the indefatigable Rube Williams, an aggregate of 31-goals. The East team was led by Tommy Hitchcock at number 2, Mike Phipps at number 1, and Phipps' cousins Winston and Raymond Guest as the defensive pair. Team rating was 32-goals. The East team was reckoned to be the better mounted, but in Carleton Burke the Westerners had a savvy judge of man and mount. A former winner of the U.S. Open in 1924 with a scratch team representing the Midwick Club, Burke had been in charge of the American pony string in successful efforts in both Westchester and Cup of the Americas competition. Horses were loaned, not only from western sources, but players like Jock Whitney and Harold Talbott also

The victorious 1933 West team at Onwentsia (left to right): Eric Pedley, Cecil Smith, Neil McCarthy, Elmer Boeseke Jr. and Aidan Roark. An injured Rube Williams holds the trophy. This East-West series changed the face of polo in America (courtesy Museum of Polo and Hall of Fame).

facilitated half a dozen mounts. In order to familiarize players and mounts, Burke assembled the team two weeks before the first game of the series.

Great publicity and speculation preceded the contest, perhaps the most intense coverage in the history of polo in America. When the ball was thrown-in on 13 August, the Onwentsia polo ground was filled with 15,000 onlookers. So many that at the conclusion of the game Maj. Frederic McLaughlin ordered more temporary stands to be build for Wednesday's game. Led by Smith, the West had conclusively defeated the highly favored East team by 15 goals to 11. Smith was top scorer with six tallies, five on penalty hits. A large number of fouls were called by the umpires, Earle Hopping Sr. and Capt. Wesley White. Ten fouls for the East and eight for the West was an unusually high number in those days. For comparison, in the Cup of the Americas at Meadow Brook in 1936 only three fouls were called.[8] By all accounts, it was a rough game. Rube Williams was stunned when he collided with a goal post. A bump by Raymond Guest sent Cecil Smith to the ground, where he lay flat for some 20 minutes. Regaining consciousness—but perhaps not common sense—Smith waved off both ambulance and manager Burke to resume play. Reported the *New York Times*, "The riding was so rough that only stout stirrups kept them in the saddle."[9] It was a historic victory.

The second match provided more of the same, if not worse. Team captain Hitchcock sat down Mike Phipps, placed Winston Guest at number one, and called on Earle Hopping Jr., who had a reputation not to become flustered when the going got heavy, to play number two. Within a couple of minutes, young Hopping unhorsed Boeseke, who sprained his ankle. Soon after, Hitchcock and Boeseke came together and Hitchcock hit the ground. His leg twisted under the pony's belly, Hitchcock had suffered a serious concussion that eventually probably cost him his 10-goal handicap. At the time of the accident, after a long delay, he courageously—and perhaps also foolishly—insisted on continuing playing and after the match he had amnesia regarding the final stages of the game. By the sixth period, the game was over for the West. To add injury to insult, Rube Williams, challenging both Hitchcock and Hopping, hit the dirt with a broken leg. The West's only reserve, Neil McCarthy, entered the fray at the number one position, Aidan Roark going to back. The final score was 12 to 8 in favor of the East squad.

Carleton Burke realized that his team could not beat the rejuvenated Easteners with a four-goal player in the lineup. Therefore, Californian Eric Pedley was called for and flew to Chicago in time for the third and decisive match.

Then a weird situation arose to add popular interest in the series. While having dinner with Maj. McLaughlin at a restaurant, Smith was served with a warrant charging him with criminal assault. Nurse Eugenie Rose, who had been tending to Rube Williams in the hospital, reported to police that Smith had offered her a ride home and had attacked her. A totally distraught Smith admitted that he had offered the woman a ride, but adamantly asserted that they had not stopped. The charges were dropped soon after without explanation. Rumors abounded. Apparently, there was heavy betting on the match, with the serious money behind the East team. It was thought that the charges would affect Smith's performance, for he had been the star of the series so far. The polo community was unequivocally behind Cecil. The committee representing the U.S.P.A. published a document stating that the charges were groundless. And the East team issued a statement saying that "We are convinced there is no word of truth in this foul accusation against his good name."[10]

Played in front of a crowd numbering 25,000—good thing that Maj. McLaughlin had arranged for extra stands—the decisive match showed Cecil Smith at the top of his game. The score was 6–4 at halftime, in favor of the West. By the time the final bell sounded, Smith and his cohorts had taken both game and series. Cecil was again the high scorer, with six tallies. Four fouls had been called on the West, while umpires Capt. White and Capt. Chandler Wilkinson had penalized the East team 11 times, seven of those against Tommy Hitchcock.

It had been a rough series, which prompted some changes in the rules of the game, most notably to prevent the situation involving Hitchcock, Hopping and Williams. From then on, when two players were together, the third one had to give the right of way.[11]

The press waxed lyrical over the cowboys' triumph. Were they really all cowboys? Apart from Smith and Williams, true Texans, Aidan Roark was an Irishman who had been selected to play for Britain in the 1930 Westchester Cup Series. Elmer Jules Boeseke Jr., silver medalist in the 1924 Paris Olympic Games, had been playing polo since an early age and was the son of a prosperous physician and polo player from Santa Barbara. Alternates Neil McCarthy and Eric Pedley were both well-off. McCarthy was a Los Angeles attorney and Pedley was the son of a British army officer. So much for the bunkhouse myth popularized by Will Rogers.

As expected, the Easteners had a different perspective. Writing for *Country Life*, Arthur W. Little Jr. had this to say:

> One of the most unpleasant repercussions from the East-West rivalry, from the official viewpoint, was the publicity given to the lusty mayhem committed on the field at Onwentsia Country Club, Chicago, where the bold Westerners spared neither themselves, their mounts, nor the opposition in proving that polo is a game not always distantly removed from the rodeo. The second East-West series, played at Meadow Brook a year later, was considerably tamer and resulted in no such procession of bumps and injuries as marred the Chicago interlude, when we saw Cecil Smith, who was stretched out cold on the ground for twenty minutes, arise and wave off an ambulance away.[12]

Blair Calvert relates that among the thousands listening to the radio was a pretty girl from Wading Valley, Long Island. About one month before, Mary Miller had met Cecil at a dinner at her uncle Thomas Mather's home; Tom was a polo player from Texas and occasional teammate of Smith. They married in October 1934 and eventually had two boys. Sidney, the eldest, became an architect, and Charles William, an aeronautical engineer. In spite of playing polo only part-time, Charles Smith reached a 7-goal handicap, took the U.S. Open Championship five times and represented America in both the Cup of the Americas and the Avila Camacho Cup. He was also inducted into the Polo Hall of Fame in 2003.

Cecil Smith never had a string of his own until 1946. Whenever he and Rube Williams found and trained an exceptionally good horse, Miller sold it. After they went into business for themselves, they found they often had to sell the good ones. Smith managed to get Badger, one of his favorite horses, which he found on a ranch in Sonora, Texas, and rode for 12 years. He found his most famous mount, Bonnie J, at a ranch near Brady, not far from his old home in Llano. Bonnie J, a dun mare, had started badly, but he stayed with her. "Her bones and muscles had set and she had worked around cattle," Smith said. "These were good signs, but she wouldn't stick and ball. She'd fight the stick and she'd shy at the ball, even paw at it. But once she was running with other horses, she never took time to worry about the ball or the stick. I just touched her to point her where I wanted her to go." When the Old Westbury team was assembling horses for the 1937 Open, Sonny Whitney made Cecil an offer. "You can't afford to keep that horse," he said. "I'll buy her and you can play her in the Open." Later, after Old Westbury emerged victorious, Whitney gave the mare back to Cecil.

He played her for another year, and then in the last game of the 1938 Open, he turned on her as he had so many times before. This time, though, it was different. She did not feel right. He kept playing, taking her down the field to the end line. As he dismounted, she had her foot up. It was broken up in the hock; there was no choice but to put her down.

Smith wrote an essay, "Man and Horse," for the book *Chakkar* edited by Herbert Spencer. In it he asserted his belief that horses account for 75 percent to 80 percent of the game: "You can't hit the ball if your horse can't get you to it."[13]

But it was Smith's uncanny ability as a horseman that gained the admiration of his con-

Cecil Smith's smooth, almost lyrical swing. Marked by Edward O'Brien, Smith is about to hit a near-side backhander. Long Island, late 1940s (courtesy Museum of Polo and Hall of Fame).

temporaries. As described by his biographer, Blair Calvert, "Cecil had an innate dignity that enabled him to fit in at the fanciest dinner party. But it was more than dignity or manners that enabled him to win the respect of his Long Island friends: it was his ability as a horseman."[14]

In 1936, the Westchester Cup was played in England at the Hurlingham Club. Cecil Smith was not on the team. Neither was Tommy Hitchcock. Mike Phipps, Eric Pedley, Stewart Iglehart and Winston Guest, with Elbridge Gerry and James Mills as alternates, composed the American squad. America almost paid the price of missing its two best players. In the closest games played between the two countries, the visitors squeaked by with scores of 10 to 9 and 8 to 6. But Cecil went to England as part of oilman Charles Wrightsman's Texas Rangers team. They won some tournaments, including the Whitney Cup, but lost the coveted Coronation Cup to Winston Guest's Templeton team.

The Texas Rangers returned two years later and made a clean sweep of the major London tournaments, with Aidan Roark and Eric Tyrrell-Martin in the lineup.

Oddly enough, Smith was dropped to 8-goals, while in England he was rated at 10. "I don't think I ever played better than I did in 1936, the year I was dropped to 8 goals. They did this because I didn't have good horses. I sold all my good horses. That's what I used to do. I'd sell off my good ponies and just play with what was left." Cecil was returned to a 10-goal rating in 1938.[15]

Back in the States, in the U.S. Open Smith became part of Cornelius Vanderbilt "Sonny" Whitney's Old Westbury team.

Top: **Old Westbury took the 1938 U.S. Open: C.V. "Sonny" Whitney offers the traditional champagne to Stewart Iglehart under the gaze of the presenter, Mrs. Robert Strawbridge, and teammates Cecil Smith and Michael Phipps. *Right:* Serious conversation between two superstars. Cecil Smith and Bob Skene in Beverly Hills, California, early 1950s (both photographs courtesy Museum of Polo and Hall of Fame).**

According to *Country Life*:

> Old Westbury is still the champion. No question about that. When the smoke of battle finally cleared—before 37,000 enthusiastic spectators, as large a crowd as packed the historic old robin's egg blue stands of Meadow Brook's International Field in many a day—Sonny Whitney's great team (Michael Phipps, Cecil Smith, Stewart Iglehart, and Whitney) which is one of the smoothest working combinations of all time, once rode triumphantly off

the field of honor with their mallets at rest and the national U.S. Open Championship tucked safely away in their celebrated treasure chest for the second year in succession.[16]

After their double victory, the U.S.P.A. changed the Open's format, which since inception had been "open to the world," to a 28 handicap limit. The Old Westbury team had to be dissolved, to Stewart Iglehart's enduring chagrin.

Then World War II came and polo in America, along many other good things of life, became impossible or quite difficult to sustain. In 1946 the U.S. Open was again played for at its old abode, Long Island's Meadow Brook Club. The decline of American polo was marked by the winning ways of the Mexican team of the four Gracida brothers and the fact that their opponents in the final match, Los Amigos, included two other players from south of the Rio Grande, Alberto Ramos Sesma and Antonio Nava Castillo, who joined Stewart Iglehart and Michael Phipps.

In 1942, Cecil Smith was rated at 9-goals by the U.S.P.A. This should end another myth about Cecil Smith's life: the notion that he was a 10-goaler for 25 consecutive years. There has been heated controversy about this issue, with spirited letter-writing in *Polo Players Edition* magazine, which included demands for an apology to the Smith family. The year by year changes in Cecil Smith's handicap were succinctly elaborated by Mrs. Sherry Browne, executive secretary of the U.S.P.A.[17]

After the war, Smith remained at the very top of polo in America. He led Stephen Sanford's Hurricanes to back to back championships in the Open in 1948 and 1949 and in 1960 with Paul Butler's Oak Brook. Cecil savored again the champagne in the East-West series, revived in 1951, but like many things in that decade, it was not the same feeling. He enjoyed helping his son Charles climb the ladder of high-goal polo, mostly in Chicago, while he himself represented the United States in the Avila Camacho Cup against Mexico.

In retirement, Cecil Smith was mostly interested in finding the horses required for high goal polo. Cecil traveled far and wide in search of prospects, continuing a lifelong endeavor. He found his son Charles's best horse, Sweet Bea, in Nebraska. Fly-fishing in Montana and shooting at the Armstrong ranch in Texas were his only recreations, besides enjoying country music. Smith lived a happy existence with Mary and their children, basking in the appreciation of friends and aficionados alike, who respected a true gentleman-player.

"Cecil has the most even temperament of any athlete I've ever known. That temperament, plus his cool approach to any kind of competition, kept him at the top. His greatest contributions have been the training of horses and proving that nice guys don't always finish last." This was the opinion of fellow Texan John Armstrong, a good judge of men.[18]

Roberto Cavanagh, the Argentine 10-goaler who was Smith's teammate in the 1949 Hurricanes squad that took the U.S. Open, and who had played against him in the International Series at Beverly Hills that same year, was emphatic in his assertion: "Cecil Smith is the best American player I've ever seen."[19]

Appropriately, Cecil Smith was one of the six initial inductees into the Polo Hall of Fame in 1990. He died in 1999, mourned by all who knew him as a gentleman, superb player and exquisite horseman.

Notes

1. Will Rogers, syndicated weekly article, 24 September 1933.

2 Blair Calvert, *Cecil Smith: Mr. Polo* (Midland, Texas: Prentis Publishing 1990), 4.

3. Hubert Winfield Williams was an 8-goal handicap player who usually was listed as Rube or H.W. in polo programs. As a practical joke, Rube once told an inquisitive reporter that his middle name was Windshield. At least one journalist took the bait and the bogus story was repeated many years later by Robert Cantwell in "The Cowboy Who Showed 'Em" in *Sports Illustrated*. pp. 68–80, 7 May 1977.

4. Peter Vischer, "The Cowboy from Texas." in *Polo*, September 1934.

5. Samuel Marshall, *Detroit News*, 1934.

6. *Ibid.* Brig. Gen. Samuel Lyman Atwood Marshall (1900–1977) made his fame by stating that only 25 percent of American infantrymen fired their weapons in World War II action. "Marshall was not a serious historian. His books should be enjoyed for the considerable insight they contain. But as a source, they must be used with caution.... Respect but suspect" (Melvin E. Matthews Jr.: *History News Network*, George Mason University, 21 April 2003).

7. The Monty Waterbury Cup was established in 1922 in memory of James Montgomery Waterbury Jr. (1876–1920), a 10-goal handicap player and a member of the immortal "Big Four," unbeaten in international play.

8. Interview with Stewart Iglehart, one of the umpires in that series, January 1986, which agrees with a report in *Polo y Campo*, Buenos Aires, November 1936.

9. Robert F. Kelly, *New York Times*, 14 August 1933.

10. Calvert, 103.

11. *U.S.P.A. Yearbook,* New York, 1935. When 8-goal player Ray Harrington asked Rube Williams why he did not give way, the Texan simply answered, "They could've given way just as easily as I could" (Calvert, *op. cit.*), 100.

12. Arthur W. Little Jr., "Polo from the Near-Side," *Country Life* (October 1938), 57.

13. Herbert Spencer, ed., *Chakkar: Polo Around the World* (Zurich: A.G. Drucker, 1971).

14. Calvert, 54.

15. *U.S.P.A. Yearbook*, New York, 1939.

16. *Country Life*, October 1936, p. 105.

17. Letter to the Editor, *Polo Players' Edition* (April 2002), 53: "Cecil Smith's record of membership with the USPA, as taken from old Blue Books is as follows: 1925, 0; 1926, 2; 1927, 4; 1928, 5; 1929, 6; 1930, 7; 1931–32, 8, 1933, 9; 1934, 10; 1935, 9; 1936, 8; 1937, 9; 1938–41, 10; 1942, 9; 1949–62, 10; and declining from there until his last listing, at 6-goals, in 1988. (Signed) Sherry T. Browne, U.S.P.A. Executive Secretary."

18. Robert Cantwell, "The Cowboy Who Showed 'em," p. 80.

19. Interview with Roberto Cavanagh, October 1954.

Stewart Iglehart: "Best backhander in the game"

by Dennis J. Amato

The Iglehart name resonated widely throughout the polo community during a good portion of the twentieth century. The patriarch of the family, David Stewart Iglehart, started playing polo in 1900 and for more than thirty years pursued the sport all over the United States, England, Spain and South America. He would carry a 2-goal rating for some seventeen years (1917–1934). He was also an active member of the renowned Meadow Brook Club on Long Island, serving as a steward, a member of the polo committee, governor and president. In 1930 Tommy Hitchcock named him to the Defense Committee of the United States Polo Association in conjunction with the upcoming Westchester Cup matches and, between 1938 and 1941, he also served on the U.S.P.A.'s Tournament Committee.

His love for the sport of polo was passed on to his two sons, D. Stewart B. Iglehart and Philip Lawrence Birrell Iglehart. The former would go on to become one of the most outstanding players in an era that spanned the interwar and immediate postwar years, while the latter would also become an accomplished player in his own right during a somewhat overlapping time span, as well as one of the driving forces in the 1980s and 1990s for the eventual creation and the initial operation of the Museum of Polo and Hall of Fame.

David Stewart Birrell Iglehart was born on 22 February 1910 in Valparaiso, Chile. At the time, his father had been seconded as an executive for one of the Grace companies and he would eventually rise to the presidency of both the Grace Line and W. R. Grace & Company. Stewart's mother, Aida Birrell, came from a prominent Anglo-Chilean family and her maiden name became her son's second middle one.

The family returned to the United States in 1915 and eventually settled on Westbury, Long Island, in an estate known as La Granja (country place). Here the elder Mr. Iglehart maintained an exceptional stable of American and Chilean born horses as well as having an active role in their training. His home also showcased an extensive art collection that included the works of a number of Latin American and Spanish painters.

Stewart took up polo in 1924 at the age of 14 and adapted to it quite quickly. Besides his father, one of his other major mentors at the time was the redoubtable Mrs. Thomas (Louise) Hitchcock Sr., who had organized the Meadow Lark Club to develop young players. During the mild-weather months, including parts of the scholastic year when Stewart studied at the Lawrence Academy on the South Shore of Long Island, the Meadow Lark Club typically played polo three times a week on either the Hitchcock or Phipps fields in the Westbury area. In the winter, Mrs. Hitchcock also organized a similar polo program at the Aiken Preparatory School in Aiken, South Carolina, which was attended by a number of the Meadow Larks, including Stewart.

It was during his period of apprenticeship with the Meadow Larks that Stewart played in his first major tournament, the 1926 Hempstead Cups, as a member of the Old Westbury team (Stewart Iglehart, Robert Young, Francis "Skiddy" von Stade and David Dows). With Stewart in the number 1 position, with a zero-goal rating that year, the quartet defeated the Meadow Larks and Great Neck teams in the sixth and ninth preliminary matches, respectively, only to fall to Camden 11 to 4 in the finals.

After the Meadow Larks were disbanded, a team composed of Ebbie Gerry, Cocie Rathborne, Jimmy Mills and Stewart Iglehart, with the Old Aiken namesake, would go on to play with great success for a number of years. During the period 1927–1931, this very young squad had an extraordinary run racking up 11 major tournament successes at a time that Stewart was still completing his secondary schooling at St. Paul's and undertaking his university studies at Yale. Among their important triumphs were the Thorn Memorial Cup in 1927, the Hempstead Cups in 1928 and the prestigious Junior Championship in 1929. However, their greatest achievements occurred in 1930 with a win over what was to become the legendary Goulburn team of the four Ashton brothers from Australia and in 1931 with a victory in two out of the three matches in the Chicago International Challenge Series against the mighty Santa Paula team from Argentina that eventually would go on to win the Open that same year.

While Iglehart was mainly known for his Old Aiken affiliation in these years, he also played on several other teams during the Long Island polo season, including Sands Point (1928 Monty Waterbury Cup winner), Halcyon Days (1929), the Camels (1929 Twelve-Goal Tournament winner) and the Aiken Knights (1930 Meadow Brook Club Cups winner). In addition, he participated in the test matches to qualify the American team for both the 1928 Cup of the Americas tournament between Argentina and America and the 1930 Westchester Cup matches between England and America. In 1932 Iglehart's budding international career was broadened still further when he was selected as a reserve player to accompany the U.S. team to Argentina for the Cup of the Americas rematch.

During the academic year at Yale, Stewart Iglehart actively took part in the indoor season during the winter months under the aegis of the Indoor Polo Association of America (I.P.A.). In 1932 his team, the Optimists, took honors in the Class A Championship as well as the Open Championship. Iglehart would continue as a member of the Optimists following his university studies playing from 1932 until the war; in fact, the trio would reprise their winning Open performance in 1933. After the war he would continue as an outdoor arena player in Florida and achieve his highest indoor rating of 9 in 1947. Moreover, during the postwar period he would serve as a delegate to the I.P.A. as well as a member of its Executive Committee.

Also during his college days, Iglehart returned to the outdoor fields in the autumn for practice and in the spring for competitive play as a member of the Yale Polo Association. In 1930 an outstanding Yale combination played at the 21- and 22-goal level (Hardie Scott/Mike Phipps, Jimmy Mills, Stewart Iglehart and Cocie Rathborne) and so decimated the competition on the way to the Intercollegiate Championship that the Intercollegiate Polo Association converted to a handicap basis the following year. In 1931 Yale, which had strongly opposed the move away from scratch play, fielded a somewhat weaker team — Iglehart "was asked to stay on the sidelines"[1] and Phipps did not play — and promptly lost in the first round on handicap. However, in 1932 Yale took its revenge by returning with a 23-goal squad (Mike Phipps, Jimmy Mills, Stewart Iglehart and Dunbar Bostwick), which the *U.S.P.A. Yearbook* described as being "a team of Open Championship calibre [*sic*]."[2] In the finals against Harvard, "displaying devastating power, Yale overcame the seven-goal handicap it spotted the Crimson" to win the Intercollegiate Championship 13 to 9 (or 13 to 2 on the flat).[3]

It was also during this pivotal year of 1932 that Stewart burnished his polo credentials still further. In September the Templeton foursome of Mike Phipps, Winston Guest, Stewart Iglehart and Raymond Guest had a resounding win over Aurora of 13 to 6 in the semifinals of the Open and still better results in the finals where they vanquished Greentree 16 to 3. This same Templeton team would repeat their performance in 1934 as well. To these two Open Championships, Stewart would gain three more during his career as a member of the Old Westbury team (1937, 1938 and 1947).

It was also during these prewar years that Iglehart would add three more Monty Waterbury Cup victories to the aforementioned won in 1928: 1936 (Templeton), 1937 (Old Westbury) and 1940 (Great Neck).

As the 1930s drew to a close, Iglehart's successes in domestic competition would soon be matched by similar results on the international front. He was a member of the American team that went to Hurlingham in London in June 1936 for a renewed challenge for the Westchester Cup. Here, he and his teammates defended the Americans' possession of the coveted trophy in a relatively tightly fought two-game series (10 to 9 and 8 to 6). When the English came to Meadow Brook on Long Island three years later, Iglehart was once again a critical component of the American effort, which yielded another two-match sweep (11 to 7 and 9 to 4).

A young Stewart Iglehart in Old Aiken colors, holding a pony, circa 1929 (courtesy Museum of Polo and Hall of Fame).

Following the Westchester Cup contest, a special single-game exhibition event was arranged which pitted the visiting British team against a formidable 40-goal American "Dream Team" of Mike Phipps, Cecil Smith, Tommy Hitchcock and Stewart Iglehart. In a six-chukker handicap match which the 1940 *U.S.P.A. Yearbook* described as "some of the most exciting polo of the year" and in particular "the last three periods of this match were as great as polo has seen anywhere"[4] the English won 16 (earned 6, handicap 10) to 14 (earned 14).

In 1937 Stewart was elevated to polo's ultimate pinnacle, a 10-goal rating. With the exception of one year (1951 at 9), he would retain that ranking continuously until 1956 when he voluntarily relinquished it and retired from high goal competitive play. Iglehart's long tenure as a 10-goal player has only been surpassed by two others, Cecil Smith and Memo Gracida. As one observer aptly noted after the war: "He is another ten-goaler and by many is rated as worth more than that.... His great resemblance to Hitchcock's play lies in the fact of his almost uncanny anticipation.... No higher praise can be heaped on the likeable, popular and all-powerful Stewart Iglehart than to say he resembles Hitchcock's play, perhaps more than any other man today in both attack and defense."[5] Another commentator provided this insight on both his rating as well as his invariable role in the number 3 position or that of the team captain: "Iglehart, of course, retained his rating purely through his great work as a field general. He is regarded by many as the best backhand shot in the game...."[6]

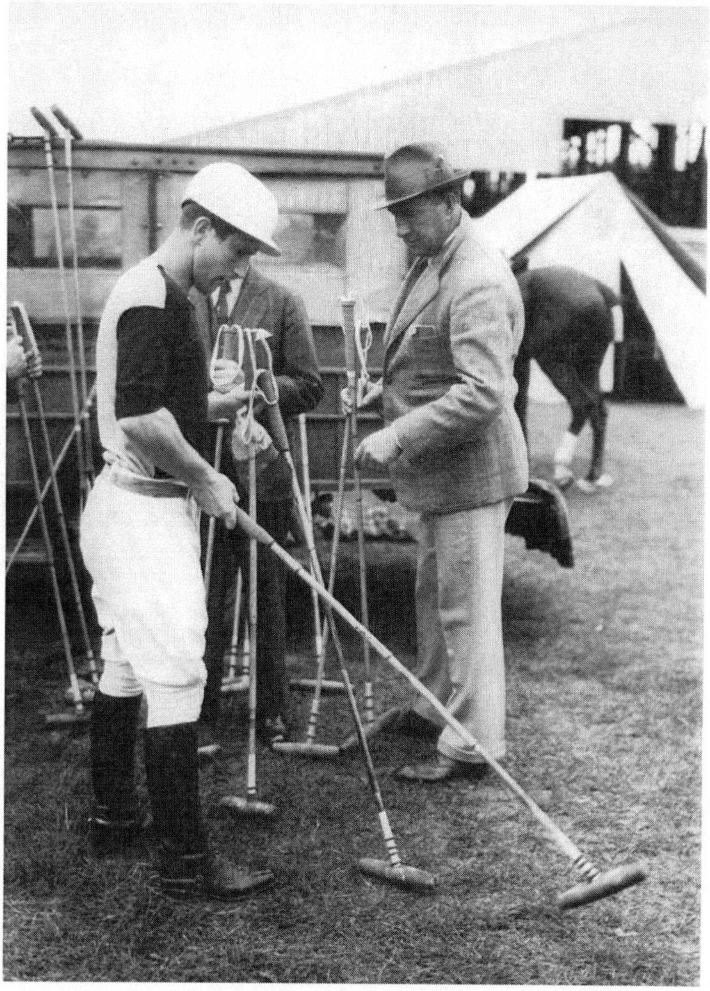

Now playing for Winston Guest's Templeton, Iglehart tests a mallet before the game (courtesy Museum of Polo and Hall of Fame).

In 1938 Stewart married Marjorie Le Boutillier whose substantial athletic interests and formidable skills somewhat mirrored his own. In polo, she ultimately would be rated at 8-goals by the United States Women's Polo Association and with the possible exception of Frances (Mrs. William) Wood was probably regarded as the finest distaff player of her generation. In addition, Le Boutillier was an exceptional hockey player, a champion in squash and a 6 handicap golfer. The Iglehart-Le Boutillier union produced one child, Stewart B. Iglehart, but ended in divorce in 1946.

Pearl Harbor sadly brought American polo to an abrupt end. Efforts to revive the sport after the Second World War proved to be both slow and challenging. Among those who were in the forefront of the postwar recovery was Stewart Iglehart.

In the immediate postwar years, Iglehart continued his polo pursuits at Meadow Brook on Long Island. He also played at the Blind Brook Turf and Polo Club in Purchase, New York, when he and Mike Phipps through a company they formed, Equine Sports, Inc., leased the club's polo facilities in the spring of 1947 and put managerial responsibilities into the hands of George Oliver. The threesome's goal, which was met with substantial success, "was to bring back to Westchester, not merely polo—but high goal polo."[7]

Also in this period Stewart Iglehart added two more major international titles to his litany of wins by helping the American squad retain the Camacho Cup against Mexico's famed Gracida brothers in both the September and November 1946 series. Furthermore, in 1947 he was a member of the East team that narrowly lost to the West 9 to 7.

Stewart Iglehart (dark helmet) riding off the field with Princeton's product William Post II, an underrated back at 8-goals (courtesy Museum of Polo and Hall of Fame).

In the late 1940s Iglehart increasingly started to focus a substantial amount of his polo interests—both on the playing field and on the promotional front—in South Florida. For example, in the winter of 1946–1947, the Phipps-Iglehart-Oliver combination helped to rejuvenate polo at the Gulf Stream Polo Club in Delray Beach, Florida, where the game had been introduced by the Phipps family some twenty years earlier.

However, a more novel approach in restarting polo emerged when the Equine Sports group of Phipps, Iglehart and Oliver decided to introduce an outdoor arena version of the game at Miami's Orange Bowl, in an effort not only to encourage play but also to develop a new audience. One contemporary account noted: "They wanted to bring the game where the public could watch it and to develop young players who could step into their shoes."[8]

From the many programs that exist from the era, the format was a relatively simple one but yet proved to be effective. Orange Bowl polo was typically held on Friday evenings with the games getting under way between 8:00 P.M. and 8:30 P.M. Two matches, or a "double header," were generally scheduled: initially two high goal events which over time evolved into a low goal contest, often of college teams, followed by a high-goal encounter among such well known players as Del Carroll, Al Parsells, Jack Ivory and Buddy Combs, in addition to the participation of Phipps, Iglehart and Oliver. While the Orange Bowl experiment was short-lived (January 1947 to March 1950), it nevertheless accomplished its primary mission in helping with polo's postwar revitalization.

Iglehart also took a special interest in helping develop players at the University of Miami that was not surprising given his experiences of being tutored by his elders a generation before. As U.S.P.A. Arena Polo Committee Chairman Dan Colhoun Jr. observed firsthand, "He had charisma, particularly with young people, not only in his playing days but later."[9] His efforts with the University of Miami were quite fruitful as evidenced by the school capturing the Intercollegiate Championship for four consecutive years (1948–1951).

Also in these postwar years, Stewart expanded his business interests in Florida. Together with his brother, Philip, they developed a successful cattle ranch and orange grove in Okeechobee which they continued to operate for the rest of their lives.

Stewart Iglehart was justifiably highly regarded for his skills as a polo player; however, his aptitude as an umpire is often overlooked. He brought the same passion and excellence to overseeing the play of others as to playing himself.

In a related vein, while Iglehart is now known primarily for his polo achievements, he was also an outstanding hockey player, so much so that he regarded it as his best sport. In addition to college play, he also starred on amateur hockey teams after graduation, including the U.S. National Hockey Team, the Brooklyn Crescents and the New York Rovers. As some measure of his skills (from the only statistics apparently extant), he ranked sixth in scoring among the 20 players during his second season. In 1933 he earned the additional distinction of playing on the world amateur hockey team. He was also asked to join both the 1932 and 1936 American Olympic hockey squads but had to decline. Further recognition of his standing came when he was offered a contract to play professionally with the New York Rangers, which he similarly turned down. However, the ultimate honors occurred years later when he was inducted into both the American and Canadian Hockey Halls of Fame.

Over his long polo career, Stewart Iglehart was particularly noted for the grace, the finesse and the fluidity of his play between offense and defense that in the newspaper and magazine columnists routinely opined on. For example, the well known polo journalist Robert F. Kelley remarked, "Iglehart was certainly a magnificent player of what is, in a great many respects, the most difficult position [No. 3] on a team."[10] Peter Vischer, the publisher of *Polo* magazine, commented on his 1932 win with Templeton, "Stewart Iglehart played a heady No. 3,"[11] and on other occasions wrote about his "dogged defensive work at No. 3"[12] and "present[ing] a defense that [the opponent] could hardly even see through."[13]

However, perhaps one of the most incisive critiques of his playing skills appeared in the 1941 U.S. Open program notes on the Westbury team: "Iglehart, of course is the dominant figure in this combination, as he is apt to be whenever he takes mallet to hand. Rated at 10 goals since 1937, he has been an Internationalist on several occasions and is a master at team strategy as well as one of the great shot makers the game has seen, both in the deftness of his stroking, when dribbling is called for and in power when that is needed."[14]

Visually, one can obtain a further appreciation for the quality of his play by viewing some

The off-side backhand. It became Stewart's trademark and a most effective weapon. The instructions read: "To gain momentum enough to get distance on the backhand shot, Iglehart raises his mallet over his head at arm's length. This gives the player his arc for a long easy swing. Notice that the height of the swing is reached when the pony's front leg reaches the willow" (courtesy Museum of Polo and Hall of Fame).

of the rare but nevertheless extensive movie footage that exists of the 1939 Dream Team match at Meadow Brook, as well as the numerous photographs from the era, particularly those by the noted "polo photographer," Freudy. However, in some ways the marvelous equestrian illustrator Paul Brown probably captured the essence of Iglehart's movements best in his many pencil sketches as well as in at least one limited edition color print.

Iglehart made a notable contribution to the world of polo literature when he wrote the introductory section in Warren T. Halpern's 1938 book *Hoofbeats.* Special mention should also be made of an important article he wrote for *Polo* magazine in September 1993 entitled "The U.S. Open: A Better Way" in which he repeated his long-standing criticism of the U.S.P.A.'s 1939 handicap limit on teams playing in the Open tournament. In this piece he made the strong case for truly open polo as "a real testing ground in which younger players can match their skills against the best"[15] and noted that "I would never have been a 10-goal player if I hadn't been given the opportunity to play with the best at Meadow Brook."[16]

As recognition of his substantial achievements in the sport, Stewart Iglehart was selected as one of the inaugural 1990 inductees into the Polo Hall of Fame in a ceremony in Palm Beach.

Part of the presentation citation succinctly summarized his contribution to the game: "He was a brilliant ten goal player who was always known for his tactical finesse, great anticipation and teamwork. At the #3 position he had the uncanny ability to turn the play and stay one stride ahead of the opposition. By his own play, he could inspire teammates to perform beyond their usual capabilities."[17]

On 19 December 1993 Iglehart died at the age of 83 in Delray Beach, Florida, and was survived by his third wife Sally and his son Stewart.

Notes

1. "Intercollegiate Polo," *Polo*, July 1931, p. 33.
2. U.S.P.A. *Yearbook, 1933*, New York: Privately Printed, 1933, p. 23.
3. "Yale Tops Harvard to Take Polo Crown," *The New York Times*, 18 June 1932, p. S1.
4. USPA *Yearbook, 1940*, New York: Privately Printed, 1940, p. 25.
5. Loc. cit.
6. Meadow Brook, Tournament Team Line-Ups, *Polo Championships, 1947* Program, New York: U.S.P.A. and the Meadow Brook Club, 1947, pp.17–18.
7. *Polo* [Program], Fairfield County Hunt Club Polo Association, Vol. 1, Summer Season, 1947, p. 25.
8. "The Blind Brook Turf and Polo Club," *Polo Championships, 1947, op. cit.*, p. 37.
9. Whitney Kelley, "Answer to Phipps-Iglehart Dream," *International Polo* (Program), 28 February 1947, Miami: Orange Bowl Polo Association, p. 12.
10. "Legends Lost, Two Hall of Famers Remembered, *Polo*, March 1994, p. 41.
11. Robert F. Kelley, "All-American Polo Selection," *The Sportsman*, November 1935, Vol. XXVIII, No. 5, p. 31.
12. Peter Vischer, "The Polo Season," *Polo*, October 1932, p. 28.
13. Peter Vischer, "The Open Championship," *Polo*, October 1935, p. 15.
14. Peter Vischer, "Greentree Wins the Open," *Horse & Horseman*, October 1936, Vol. XVI, No. 5, p. 19.
15. "Westbury" *Open Championship, September 1941* (Program), New York: The United States Polo Association and Meadow Brook Club, 1941, p. 17.
16. Stewart B. Iglehart, "The U.S. Open: A Better Way," *Polo*, September 1993, p. 6.
17. *Ibid.*, p. 7.
18. The National Polo Museum and Hall of Fame Website.

Bob Skene: "Hurricane Bob"

by Chris Ashton

Bob Skene is honored in three countries, each of which, at different times in his long polo career, has claimed him as its own.

Australia claims him because his father was Australian and though Bob was born in India he returned at age 11 to live in Australia; and because it was in Australia in late adolescence and early manhood, that he revealed the promise of a great player in the making. His citation in the Confederation of the Australian Sports Hall of Fame describes him simply as the single greatest player in the history of Australian polo.

England also claims him, albeit fleetingly, from 1937, when he accompanied the Ashton brothers' team as their reserve in their bid for the Hurlingham Championship trophy. Such an impression did he make on the England selectors that he was recruited into the 1939 British bid to regain the Westchester Cup from the United States.

In 1992 the Hurlingham Polo Association honored Skene as the sole surviving member of the 1939 team, flying him and his wife, Elizabeth, from California to England. He was guest of honor to the Westchester Cup, a single match hosted by Guards Club at Smith Lawn, Windsor Park, where they were received by Queen Elizabeth II. The United States defeated England by a single goal in extra time.

Like the English polo selectors in 1937, American polo was much impressed with the young Skene in 1939, prompting invitations to play the United States polo circuit. At the season's end he was raised to nine-goals, on which handicap he continued until he left the U.S. in late 1940. After an absence of ten years he returned to U.S. polo, and within a year was ranked at ten-goals, the handicap he retained until his retirement from high-goal polo in 1968.

In 1990 the U.S. Polo Hall of Fame invoked the names of just six players for their contribution to polo "in an extraordinary and honorable manner, whether by their dedication to the sport, or by ability and record as a player." Five were Americans by birth — Harry Payne Whitney, Devereux Milburn, Thomas Hitchcock Jr., Stewart Iglehart and Cecil Smith. All five had played for the United States and three — Whitney, Milburn and Hitchcock — led the U.S. for the Westchester Cup against England, played as a test series at irregular intervals since 1886. The other player was Bob Skene, a naturalized American and the only one to play the Westchester Cup *against* the U.S.

His citation lists three victories in the U.S. Open, four in the Pacific Coast Open, in the case of both trophies in the 1950s and '60s, two victories in the Monty Waterbury Cup, one National 20-Goal championship, and two Argentine Opens. The citation continues:

> Over the past four decades he has proved himself a tremendous asset to the game of polo as a role model of player, teacher and coach. He has always been known as a superb horseman, for great anticipation and ball control. Polo can be justly proud of his outstanding accomplishments and he stands in the top rank.

Born an Australian, played for England, matured in America. His opponents came to believe that Bob Skene's smile was that of a tiger (courtesy Museum of Polo and Hall of Fame).

But the final arbiter of any player is the Argentine Open. Playing for El Trébol, Skene won it in 1954 and again in 1956, a feat unmatched by any other nonresident foreign player before or since. Buenos Aires's leading sports magazine, *El Gráfico,* wrote in 1954:

> Personally we cannot remember there having been on the No. 1 ground such an exhibition of complete mastery of the stick, such as we saw this sensational player perform last Saturday. Skene belongs to that very small nucleus of unusual players who shine not so much for what they do on their own as for what they do to help their team-mates who are better placed, and when one asks him he leaves the ball with absolute discipline, riding like a bullet to take his man, sure that whoever spoke has all the right in the world to enter play, whatever the differences in their respective handicaps.... To cap all these virtues he was hitting his shots not so much with strength as with timing equal, if not greater, than our own Roberto Cavanagh.

Skene's ascent to the very pinnacle of U.S. polo, at times during his long career as its only

El Trébol, Argentine Open Champions in 1956. Left to right: Eduardo Bullrich, Julio Menditeguy, Bob Skene, Carlos Menditeguy. This was Skene's second win in the Open and assured his 10-goal rating and a place as one of the game's immortals (courtesy Museum of Polo and Hall of Fame).

ten-goaler in the country, exemplifies the adage that fortune is preparation meeting opportunity. Central to his good fortune was his father.

Curtis Skene was born in 1880 in Hamilton, in the Western District of what was then the Colony of Victoria. The large landholdings of his forebears were long gone, offering him a future working the small family dairy farm. He instead chose India, where he was employed as a tea-estate manager in the province of Assam, the very cradle of modern polo. Every district in the province boasted its own polo club. Skene embraced the game with gusto, was the best in the province, and played in Calcutta each year in December in the All-India championship tournaments.

For the sake of their children's education, in 1925 Curtis, his British-born wife, Margaret (neé Jessop), their son Robert, born in 1914, and daughter, Phyllis (1916), returned to live in Australia. Skene bought a sheep station in southwest New South Wales and founded a polo club in nearby Wagga Wagga. Playing with his own team, the Assamanders, which won all the most coveted trophies, Skene swiftly established his claim as arguably the foremost player in New South Wales.

In 1929 he assembled 48 polo ponies and with two modestly competent players, Australian Fred Beveridge and Stewart Pearson, a former British army captain whom he had known in India, sailed for Hawaii. There they were joined by an American six-goaler, Arthur Dillingham, and continued to California where they played as a team in the West Coast tournaments. Skene's performance earned him an eight-goal handicap from the U.S. Polo Association. He then auctioned his entire string of ponies, each one selling for between one and two thousand dollars.

Curtis Skene's first foray into exporting polo ponies was at once eclipsed by plummeting wool prices following the Wall Street crash. He was forced to sell his sheep station and in its place bought a small farm, Killbride, just west of Sydney, to start a new business: he would buy stock horses, train them for polo and export them to India.

Each year he made several journeys by car to country towns within a 300-mile radius of Sydney. By prior arrangement, dealers would assemble horses for his inspection, according to his exacting specifications: 15 to 15.3 hands, intelligent, with a calm temperament and preferably with some thoroughbred lineage. He would ride each of them for a few minutes and for those he liked pay between 20 and 30 pounds—on occasion as little as 10 pounds.

From their mid-teens Bob and Phyllis, who was judged to be worth a two-goal handicap though she was never ranked, assisted their father and his employees, riders with polo experience, in working his horses. As "made" polo ponies they were inducted into the game with practice chukkers and tournaments at the nearby club, Cobbity, before going further afield.

In the weekly magazine *The Australian Sporting and Dramatic News*, a regular contributor, Dr. Robert Crookston, described Curtis Skene:

> ... an artist in his job and a wizard with horses. How else, despite a system of training as logical as tomorrow's sunrise, could the transformation of 60 snaffle-mouthed Australian horses, chosen from all courses, the paddock, the race-track, the discarded failures of other polo men and a few from the stockyard, but all in the rough and completely untrained, be made in about three months into 60 polo ponies bitted up to the most exacting polo country in the world?

In August or September each year they were dispatched by train to the New South Wales port of Newcastle. From there they were loaded onto a cargo ship, whose coalhole was fitted with loose boxes and a sandpit allowing the horses to roll. Forty went to Calcutta in the first shipment in 1931, rising to 85 in the last voyage in 1937. Bob accompanied them each time, a task he recalled afterwards as sheer hard slog.

From all over India came players, from 8-goal maharajas to novices newly arrived from Britain, to buy ponies before the December tournaments. Central to the legacy Curtis bequeathed his son to introduce him to the Calcutta polo season, the two of them played with and against the best of India, including Rao Raja Hanut Singh, a role model to the teenage Bob for the supple wrist action of his stickwork and flowing style. Curtis Skene died in 1961, hugely proud of his son's achievement, though he never saw him play at his peak.

Another element of Curtis Skene's legacy to his son was the quality of mounts he supplied when Bob Skene accompanied the Ashton brothers to England in 1937. After the triumph of the Australian team in the Hurlingham Championship final, with Skene at number 1 position scoring six of his team's nine goals, at the auction of their ponies which followed—the Maharaja of Kashmir paid 1,700 guineas, the top price, for a Curtis Skene pony called Maitland.

Skene returned to Australia by way of India, where he played for the Maharaja of Kashmir's team in the Western Indian championship. When the Maharaja of Jaipur was sidelined by a flying accident, Skene took his place in the Jaipur team with Rao Raja Hanut Singh, Kunwar Amar Singh and Maharaja Prithi Singh to win the Prince of Wales Championship Cup in New Delhi.

To determine whether he merited selection for the British squad to challenge the United States for the Westchester Cup in 1939, the selectors invited Skene to return to play the 1938

English season, providing him with funds to buy for himself a string of outstanding polo ponies, six of which he bought from his father. His performance in the 1938 season secured his place in the British squad. In London at the season's end he married Elizabeth, neé Wheatley, to whom he had been attracted as a teenager growing up on neighboring farms west of Sydney.

The planning and resources assigned to the British Westchester Cup bid were worthy of a military campaign. Lord Cowdray was appointed to manage the tour with a budget of 100,000 pounds. Money was assigned to buy 60 of the best available polo ponies anywhere in the world, while to prepare players and their horses the squad was allotted four months of tournaments and exhibition matches on America's West Coast before the test series in New York.

Not everything went as planned. One member of the squad, Pat Roark, was killed in a polo accident in California. The captain, Gerald Balding, was sidelined for a time with a broken pelvis, though he recovered in time to lead his team for the Westchester Cup. In the event, the 31-goal British team (Skene, Aidan Roark, Balding and Eric Tyrrell-Martin) was no match for the 37-goal Americans (Mike Phipps, Tommy Hitchcock Jr., Stewart Iglehart, and Winston Guest). The Americans won the first two games comfortably, with British pride salvaged from total humiliation by its triumph in an exhibition match which followed.

Throughout the English squad's U.S. tour, as with the Ashton brothers' English tour two years earlier, Skene's performance kindled excitement. The elder statesman of U.S. polo, Earle W. Hopping, judged him the best British number 1 since World War I. "Skene is a rough, tough young fellow who loves the pace and loves to mix it," he declared. "You can't bluff him off the ball and if he's not scoring goals he's sitting on the back's lap."

The U.S. media tagged him "Hurricane Bob." When the British team arrived in New York for the test matches, newspaper banners screamed, *Hurricane Hits New York!* "Bob, there's going to be a hurricane," Elizabeth Skene exclaimed. "That's me they're talking about," was the laconic reply.

The nine-goal American player Eric Pedley, who had played against Curtis Skene in California ten years earlier, forecast Bob would become the greatest player of his generation. It took longer than Pedley or, indeed, anyone could have foreseen. September 1939 saw the start of World War II. First at the British Consulate in New York, then at the Los Angeles Consulate, Skene volunteered for the British armed forces, his offer declined each time with the explanation that the numbers volunteering far outstripped the armed forces' capacity to absorb them. In California he was hired to manage a polo club for an oil tycoon, Russell Havenstrite, and for much of 1940 found himself playing exhibition polo, with the proceeds going to a charity, Bundles for Britain, supporting the war effort.

Finally Skene could endure his civilian status no longer. Both his brothers-in-law, Elizabeth's brother and Phyllis's husband, were serving with Australian troops in the Eighth Division in North Africa. Through the polo community he learned that officers were in short supply for Indian regiments. Returning with Elizabeth to Sydney, he went on to India, and after officer training was posted in September 1941 with the 2nd King Edward's 7th Own Gurkha Rifles to Malaya. From Ipoh his regiment was suddenly dispatched to the Thai border to await the Japanese invasion.

"From December 16th to January 28th our battalion was in the front line without relief while the Japs threw fresh troops at us every 48 hours," he recalled. "When you're at it all the time, firing or being fired at for two months, fear is paramount. The Gurkhas couldn't understand why we were retreating. They weren't used to going backwards. We had to explain to them that we were very vulnerable. It was a relief to surrender."

The mental toughness which Earle Hopping saw on Long Island in 1939 served Skene well in the 3½ years that followed. As one of 50,000 prisoners-of-war (POWs) consigned from

Dutch and British imperial forces to Singapore's Changi prison camp, he read voraciously and gave lectures to patients at the prison hospital, recalling his impressions of the United States before the war. He never doubted the Allies would triumph, nor that he would resume his polo career. Equally convinced that Argentina would dominate postwar polo, he enrolled in classes teaching conversational Spanish, one of scores of programs organized by senior ranks for Changi POWs He also resolved to keep fit. Though officers were not obliged to work, he volunteered for P.O.W. gangs to gather wood, felled and chopped on nearby plantations, for the camp

A young Roy Barry and Bob Skene have a laugh at Oak Brook, Illinois (courtesy Museum of Polo and Hall of Fame).

kitchens. "I was very fit when the war ended," he recalled, "only ten pounds lighter than I am today."

Changi was liberated in September 1945. Skene returned to India, to Dehra Dun, regimental headquarters of 7th Gurkha Rifles, there to rehabilitate surviving troops who had suffered grievously from their Japanese captors. He was joined by Elizabeth, who, since departing California in 1940, had lived in Sydney, knowing nothing of Bob's fate until the war's end.

The early postwar years offered no prospect of resuming his polo career. Following his demobilization in December 1946, the Skenes departed India for Malaya where British expatriates Skene had befriended in Changi found him a job with the Straits Racing Association as a steward, officiating at race meetings in Kuala Lumpur, Singapore, Penang and Ipoh.

The trumpet summoning him to return to polo was sounded in September 1949, a cable from Lord Cowdray inviting him to join a British team to play in Argentina. He flew at once to Buenos Aires. As with his British teammates, their polo careers similarly suspended by the war, his handicap was initially fixed at six-goals. Though he had played only occasional low-goal club polo in Kuala Lumpur, within a month he was raised to eight-goals, and but for his strenuous protest would have been raised to his 1940 ranking of nine-goals.

His return to high-goal polo in 1950 was as swift as his departure ten years before. Oil tycoon Russell Havenstrite invited him to return to manage the Beverly Hills Polo Club, and within a year he had joined the former Texas cowboy, Cecil Smith, and Stewart Iglehart as America's only ten-goal players, a handicap he retained for 17 years. At the invitation of his friend Walt Disney, in 1952 he and a polo pony "starred" in a children's film called *Stormy*, inspired by one of Skene's own polo ponies, a failed racehorse which becomes a champion in polo.

After his playing days were over, Bob Skene toured the world teaching the game (courtesy Museum of Polo and Hall of Fame).

He managed the Beverly Hills Polo Club for three years, after which he traveled all over the country holding polo clinics sponsored by the U.S. Polo Association. In the course of his long polo career he joined Baron Rothschild's team in England for a season. In the course of his postwar polo career he also played for other patrons or clubs in Canada, Mexico, Guatemala, the Dominican Republic, Chile, Peru, France, India, Pakistan, Singapore, Jamaica, Egypt and New Zealand. He twice led Santa Barbara teams to Australia. Returning on a six-goal handicap to medium-goal polo in the 1970s, he played three seasons in the Philippines.

For twenty years, and for successive owners, he was involved, much of the time as manager, with the Santa Barbara Polo Club. As a veteran player of the first rank, he is remembered for his willingness to coach promising young players and, on request, to offer advice to more experienced players, recently elevated to high-goal handicaps, on everything from strategy and hitting techniques. Power struggles over the future of the club took their toll. According to a profile of Skene, written as an introduction to the Club's Robert Skene Trophy:

> Though it is hard to believe today in the early 1970s the Club did not have enough members or revenue to operate properly. Its very survival was continually at stake as property developers besieged the Santa Barbara County Supervisors with plans for redeveloping the polo fields. With the interest in polo waning nationally and property developers eager to purchase and redevelop the polo fields, Bob constantly put his personal reputation on the line....
>
> With lack of funding for properly maintaining the club and fields, and also without proper remuneration, he tirelessly organized volunteers to haul hoses, fix water mains, repair the stables and maintain the Club's aged maintenance equipment. Many times he personally marked the lengthy fields, organised the teams and then mounted his pony to play the game himself. When at one point the Club was on the point of losing its lease on the property without meeting payment immediately, he stepped in with personal funds to meet the debt and keep the Club alive. Gradually there was a rallying of interest, new patrons appeared and, thanks as well to their courageous efforts, the Club was saved.

The financial uncertainty of a professional polo career, which continues to this day, was compounded in Skene's case, playing as he was before the advent of performance fees. Precursors of today's patrons employed him as a coach or to manage their clubs, employment he far preferred to the alternative to which other polo professionals turned, trading in polo ponies. Mindful of potential conflicts of interest he would face as a professional player, he resolved never to follow his father into "making" and dealing in polo ponies.

From 1960 he and Elizabeth settled in Santa Barbara, living in a succession of homes requiring payment of rent or the servicing of a mortgage. There were times when they wondered how they would ever pay their way. As insurance against sole dependence upon polo for his income, Skene enrolled in a real estate course, qualified and thereafter combined a one-man business in real estate, pleasurably and profitably, with his principal commitment to polo.

He lived in the United States for more than half his life, mostly in California. He adopted U.S. citizenship but remained ambivalent towards the high honors and rhetoric U.S. polo heaped upon him. Pride at his achievement, on and off the field, ran tandem with memories, bemused rather than bitter, of the jealousies and intrigues of polo politics, of doors which remained closed to him. In the course of our interview in 1992, I read aloud his U.S. Polo Hall of Fame citation. He responded at once with a spare, blunt expletive, quintessentially Australian, to the effect that it was not worth the paper it was written on.

In dismissing the Hall of Fame citation he sells himself short. Forty years before and from the other side of the world, Jim Ashton, captain of the family team which enlisted him as its reserve for its 1937 assault on the Hurlingham Championship Cup, wrote to congratulate him at the news of his promotion to a 10-goal handicap:

> I told people in 1936 that I thought you would reach the top in polo if you had a reasonable chance but I never thought it would be 1951 before you got there, or that you would spend three years in a prison camp in the meantime. I appreciate that you consider that we brought you into big polo, but I think you only have to thank us for getting you there about one season earlier than would have been the case. On balance I think we were luckier to have you with us in 1937 than you were to be in the team, as I have told dozens of people.

Bob Skene died in 1997 and was survived by his wife, Elizabeth, and son, Curtis.

Carlos Menditeguy: "To be the best was effortless"

by Horace A. Laffaye

Carlos Menditeguy was, without a doubt, one of the greatest sportsmen the world has ever known. How many players have reached the magical 10-goal handicap in polo? How many racing car drivers have participated in Formula One competitions? What percentage of amateur golfers were scratch players? Charlie Menditeguy accomplished all that and more. In partnership with his older brother Julio, they were ranked nationally in the top five in tennis; in singles, Charlie was seventh. He excelled at other racket games, such as squash and pelota a paleta, a game related to jai alai that is very competitive in South America. You had to be very good at billiards, otherwise Charlie would give you a hiding. He played soccer well enough to win the High School Championship, playing the center-forward position; today he would be the striker prototype. In the hurly-burly ambience of Argentine open road racing, Menditeguy mixed with the very best, hallowed names like five-time world champion Juan Manuel Fangio, the brothers Gálvez, Oscar and Juan, who combined for an unbeaten record number of Grand Prix and national championship wins, and other stars of the first magnitude like Marcos Ciani, Rodolfo de Alzaga, and Dante Emiliozzi.

The magazine *El Gráfico* wrote:

> As a polo player, sublime: 10-goal handicap; as a race car driver on tracks and the open road, as good as the best, as fast as the fastest; as a golfer, soccer player, pelotari or tennis player, in all those and more Carlos Menditeguy is the complete sportsman. He was born this way, multiply-endowed for everything, and so to be the best was effortless. It was his destiny: a born champion, he need not try to be so.[1]

In reviewing the annals of sport, very few athletes have really excelled at more than two sports. Perhaps the earliest complete sportsman was George Osbaldeston (1787–1866), the Squire of England, who excelled in cricket and all the rural sports of his time. Another 10-goal American polo player, Foxhall Parker Keene, was also multitalented. Foxie Keene was successful in automobile racing, tennis, shooting, foxhunting, sailing, steeplechasing and golf. John Argentine Campbell, a 9-goal player, played cricket at international level for Argentina and represented Scotland in rugby. Northrup "Norty" Knox reached 8-goals in polo and took several national titles in court tennis. South African Charles Sydney "Punch" Barlow, 7-goals in polo, played county cricket for Somerset and as a rugby player captained both Cambridge University and Natal Province, and played in the Springboks trial matches. Devereux Milburn, playing polo off 10-goals, rowed for Oxford, and was an accomplished golfer and tennis player. Outside of polo, Jim Thorpe shone in athletics, American football and baseball. These are some of the most distinguished talents in several sports. Looking at the list, it seems clear that Menditeguy is in a class by himself.

Carlos Alberto Menditeguy was born in Buenos Aires on 10 August 1914, one year after his brother, Julio Alejandro. Both their grandfather and father were members of the Jockey Club and proprietors of the stud farm El Turf, which was established in 1903. The thoroughbred Chopp, bred at El Turf, took the Argentine Triple Crown in 1908. Julio and Carlos revived the stud farm in 1942, achieving great success. Indian Chief, Practicante and Uruguayo carried the salmon-colored silks to the winner's circle in the Argentine Derby, in addition to many other stakes.

Born with the proverbial silver spoon at his disposal, Carlos graduated from Colegio Carmen Arriola de Marín, a Marist institution located in the trendy suburb of San Isidro, half-an-hour north of Buenos Aires. It was at Colegio Marín that Carlos won his first sporting laurel: the High School soccer championship. By the early 1930s, the tennis doubles team of Julio and Carlos Menditeguy was nationally ranked in the top five. Then, they found polo, nothing unusual considering that they had grown up among thoroughbred race horses. Both were rated at 1-goal in their first year of competition, 1933. Charlie was raised to 10-goals at the end of the 1943 season, together with his teammate Luis Duggan and Enrique Alberdi, Venado Tuerto's captain. The trio were the first 10-goal handicap players in Argentina since the legendary Lewis Lacey had achieved such distinction in 1915. The following year, Julio followed his brother in reaching polo's pinnacle. He was joined by Juan Carlos "Bebé" Alberdi, Enrique's younger brother. At the time, Venado Tuerto (One-eye Deer) and El Trébol (The Clover) were at the beginning of their rivalry as the top teams in the world. A friendly match was organized mixing players from both teams. The team Basques, the Alberdi and Menditeguy brothers, played against cousins Juan and Roberto Cavanagh, and brothers Luis and Heriberto Duggan, the Irish element. In the event, the Basques won handily.

The Menditeguys began play at Los Pingüinos, the Braun Menéndez family club. In 1938, there appeared on the polo scene the most formidable polo combination seen on Argentine grounds up to that date: El Trébol, with Luis Duggan at number 1, Julio Menditeguy at number 2, Heriberto "Pepe" Duggan at number 3 and Carlos Menditeguy at back. Mauricio Kenny, polo-playing secretary of El Trébol Polo Club, watched the new team practice at San José, the Duggan's estancia in Capitán Sarmiento, and rang the magazine *Polo & Campo* in awe: "Stop the presses and take note: Luis and Pepe Duggan, Julio and Carlos Menditeguy. There you have it, the Argentine champion team for the next several years. Remember this well. I'm giving you the scoop; publish it and you'll be in clover."[2]

Cautiously, *Polo & Campo* published a watered-down story. Later, when El Trébol was on top of the heap, Luis Patricio "Paddy" O'Farrell, another one of the band of Irishmen who owned land near Capitán Sarmiento, every time he met Antonio Zea, *Polo & Campo's* editor, reminded him: "Well, do you now believe what Mauro Kenny told you? Yes? Now you start looking for a team that can tie the jingle to the cat's tail. You have your work cut out for you."

Years later Venado Tuerto, a club from that town populated by a large Irish contingent, finally defeated the unbeaten El Trébol. Then Rodolfo Hearne, a Venado Tuerto supporter, told editor Zea, "Now you can tell Paddy, 'There is the jingle, Dr. O'Farrell.'"[3]

To resume El Trébol's story, in that year of 1938 the new team won events at both Capitán Sarmiento and Venado Tuerto, by bulky scores. Then they took the Hurlingham Open and became the favorites to win the Argentine Open at Palermo. Alas, La Concepción, a medium-handicap team, defeated El Trébol in the first round, paving the way for Los Indios, a scratch side, to take the Open. This was the last time El Trébol lost a game until 1944.

The unexpected hiccup resulted in a temporary split within the team. In 1939, the Menditeguys made up their own team, while the Duggans enlisted Enrique, another of the seven polo-playing brothers. To fill in the back position, the brothers three called upon Manuel Andrada, a former 9-goal player with several Argentine Open championships, the U.S. Open, the Cup of the Americas and the Olympic Gold medal to his credit. The team easily won the

Carlos Menditeguy in a 1949 photograph. Charlie always lent an air of enterprise and adventure to the game (courtesy Museum of Polo and Hall of Fame).

Argentine Open. Next year, Carlos and Julio returned to the fold. From 1940 until 1944, El Trébol's style of play elicited wonderment among the polo cognoscenti. Polished play, superb ponies, exquisite team work, lightning speed, and good chemistry among the four players made it an invincible combination. Luis Duggan, number one on the Olympic Gold medalist team that also had taken the Cup of the Americas at Meadow Brook, was mounted on ponies that ran like oversized greyhounds. Julio Menditeguy was everywhere, with his keen positional instinct; handling very long mallets, he was able to secure the ball and feed his number one. Pepe Duggan, with Lewis Lacey, the best rider in Argentine polo, was the ideal number three, always in control, now feeding his forwards, now covering his roaming back, Carlos Menditeguy. If Pepe Duggan was El Trébol's brain, Charlie was its heart and soul. Endowed with superb eye-hand coordination, he thought nothing of picking a ball in the air and sending it 150 yards to his hotspur forwards. He took the penalty shots, the knock-ins and pushed the team forward, always at full speed. When he dribbled the ball, it was not at the slow pace of today's players. Carlos was a hurricane, an offensive player from the team's rearguard, with total disregard for the opposing number 1. They were four stars, reaching an aggregate handicap of 39-goals in 1944, but one was of the first magnitude: someone who an unknown scribe called "Le Grand Charles." His brother Julio once said, "If we were worth ten goals, Charles was worth eleven."[4]

Nothing was left to chance. They studied Cameron Forbes' *As to Polo*—translated into Spanish by Carlos Rodríguez Egaña as *Manual de Polo*—and developed set plays on a billiards table, utilizing four red and four black poker cards, plus a small chip as the ball. They were four serious students of the game who carefully prepared themselves prior to each game, spending a considerable amount of time going over the list of ponies, making sure that in no single chukker two players would play their weakest mounts. They held meetings after every game, going over the mistakes, striving to always improve an already exquisite game.

The great base for the team's success was the pony string. The Duggan family had a well-earned reputation for breeding formidable horses, because of the continuing selection and improvement of the pedigree. The stallion Morfeo, by Craganour out of Sleeping Sickness, was the principal sire in their stud farm.[5] The Menditeguy brothers, on their part, were recognized experts and in 1941 purchased from the Duggans thirty-one mares and seven yearlings, plus the great Morfeo, at the time the preeminent polo stallion in Argentina. Thus the entire string showed complete harmony, being on a clearly superior level compared to the rest of the high-goal teams. Some of the ponies, which were always identified with numbers on their mattresses, became household names: Bélgica and La Española, owned by Heriberto Duggan; Ruby, Corazón, Paloma and Calabrés, of Luis Duggan; Uriburu, Sillón and Perilla, of Julio Menditeguy, and Sombrilla and Paddy, played by Carlos Menditeguy. Of Paddy, Carlos said, "the best pony I ever played in my life."

To the remembrance of the ponies follows that of the *petiseros,* or grooms. Julio had only one in his entire 30-year polo career, Dineto Buffagna. Heriberto and Charlie had Guillermo Bertolini, Adán Caminos, Pablo Martínez, and Juan Rodríguez, who stayed in the United States and reached a 7-goal handicap. Luis Duggan's petisero was Hipólito Ramírez, who accompanied him to the Berlin Olympic Games and then to Meadow Brook for the Cup of the Americas. The American artist Paul Brown depicted a few of the petiseros on the night before the ponies' auction at Fred Post's in Westbury, Long Island. Brown was able to capture the sadness in those devoted helpers about to be separated from their charges at the completion of a glorious campaign.

Polo writers got tired of typing compliments and praises; they ran out of adjectives. "Never seen before at Palermo," "El Trébol superiority took away whatever little doubt remained as to the final score," "Invincible El Trébol," "We are witness to a situation in which there is no team that can realistically stretch this foursome," were some of the comments, year after year. In future times, only Venado Tuerto and Coronel Suárez received similar accolades.

Years later, all four players acknowledged Lewis Lacey as their great teacher, especially his emphasis on perfect equitation and his credo that the ball travels faster than the players. When asked about the best players ever, Julio Menditeguy quietly and cogently pointed out his brother Carlos. Heriberto Duggan said, "In his day, Charlie; now, Juancarlitos [Harriott]." As to Charlie himself, he categorically singled out Bob Skene.[6]

The self-confident champion's smile. Charlie Menditeguy, circa 1950 (courtesy Museum of Polo and Hall of Fame).

The days of wine and roses came to an end in November 1944. Heriberto Duggan was unable to play in the final game because of an abscess; therefore, El Trébol once more called upon the old warrior, 54-year-old Manuel Andrada. Nevertheless, Pepe Duggan's forced absence was too much of a handicap. The clover really needed all four leaves. With two chukkers to go, the defending champions were ahead 7–3. Then they ran out of steam; the final score of 10–8 marked the first championship for Venado Tuerto, who took the Open from 1946 until 1950 before retiring temporarily as a team.

In the vintage year of 1954, Venado Tuerto vanquished El Trébol 18–8 in the Hurlingham Open. But a month later at Palermo, El Trébol, this time with Bob Skene in Pepe Duggan's slot, won the Argentine Open in one of the several games dubbed "the match of the century" by sporting reporters.[7] Leading 12–6 at the start of the eight and final chukker, El Trébol went into a defensive mode, giving up three goals but hanging on for the win. At the sound of the final bell, fans rushed onto the field while the players were still congratulating each other; Carlos Menditeguy and Bob Skene were taken to receive their prizes on their partisans' shoulders, while the rest chanted "El Trébol, El Trébol," releasing the pent up emotions accumulated during eleven years without an Open Championship.

The next year was Venado Tuerto's farewell, closing their brilliant trajectory with yet another triumph over La Alicia, who surprised El Trébol in the semifinals. In 1956, once more with Skene's services, El Trébol regained the title against weaker opposition. Their last Open title was in 1960, when they inflicted upon the up-and-coming Coronel Suárez one of their rare defeats.

The story of El Trébol is inevitably linked to Charlie Menditeguy's story because he was at the beginning, and was the only one at the end. The Duggans essentially retired from high-goal polo in 1956; Julio soldiered on until 1960. That year, Charlie once more led El Trébol to its last Argentine Open Championship. Because of an injury to Julio during an early round,

Unbeaten for five consecutive years, this El Trébol team set a new standard for excellence. Left to right: Luis Duggan, Julio Menditeguy, Heriberto Duggan and Carlos Menditeguy in 1943 (courtesy Museum of Polo and Hall of Fame).

his teammates bore new names: Horacio Castilla, Teófilo Bordeu and Carlos de la Serna. The last hurrah was against Coronel Suárez, which would eventually become the best foursome ever. But on that warm November afternoon at Palermo, Carlos Menditeguy dazzled the crowd just as he had done for 20 years. Superb equitation, incredible timing in his swing, advanced tactical thinking. The polo star, the "superdotado," finished his career on a high note.

Carlos never had the opportunity to wear the light blue and white national shirt of Argentina. There was not much international competition after the war and when it presented itself the full Venado Tuerto team exchanged their chocolate colors for the national jersey. But then, in 1966, the United States challenged Argentina for the Cup of the Americas. In preparation for the series, Norty Knox, the American captain, asked the Argentine Polo Association to arrange practice games with high-goal teams. Charlie Menditeguy, six years away from competitive polo and age 52, played in a couple of games. In his memoirs Knox noted, "It was fun playing against Charlie — the last time I saw him play was in 1950 — Venado Tuerto vs. El Trébol — the greatest polo game of this century in my opinion. Charlie has not played Open polo in several years but has not forgotten how to play!" At the time, Menditeguy carried a 9-goal handicap.[8]

Juan Manuel Fangio, quintuple world champion in Formula One car racing, and a good friend and mentor, was Menditeguy's idol. "El Chueco" Fangio was the only individual that Charlie truly believed he could not beat.[9] Menditeguy, a born talent, had the champion's exalted faith in himself, with an ego to match. After polo, Charlie's passion was car racing; for a while, it even surpassed the game of kings. As an example of this dichotomy, the final game of the 1953 Argentine Open Championship was held at Palermo on a Saturday afternoon; that morning the first stage of the Gran Premio Nacional started from Buenos Aires' Autodrome; Charlie was at the wheel of his Ford stock car. He led the stage on open roads, reminiscent of Italy's Mille Miglia, most of the way, until his car slowed down. Next day, the engine gave up in a cloud of smoke. In the meantime, on Saturday afternoon, El Trébol lost the championship game to Coronel Suárez.

Menditeguy's debut as a racer was in 1950 in a sports car event in Mar del Plata, a summer resort town that every year hosted the equivalent of a Formula One race. As a curtain raiser, a motley collection of sports cars assembled for a short event. Driving a 2-liter Ferrari, clearly the best car in the field, Charlie ran away from the opposition.[10]

Next year Menditeguy silenced those who were saying, "With that Ferrari, anybody can win." In 1951, the Temporada highlighted three Mercedes Benz machines for Fangio, Hermann Lang and Karl Kling. Surprisingly, local ace José Froilán González, in a Ferrari, defeated the superior German cars in both races. But equally surprising was Carlos Menditeguy's performance. In the season's second race, driving a 1938 Alfa Romeo, a dinosaur by racing standards, Charlie held the second position for a long time, until his car gave up in the final laps. Ahead of the three Mercedes, ahead of Oscar Gálvez; Charlie accomplished such a feat driving an obsolete machine and only in his second race. Talk about natural talent.[11]

Menditeguy went on to be a member of the Maserati Formula One official team, as well as one of the top drivers in the series for the Sports Car World Championship. Charlie won races in circuits and on the open road, driving sports cars and stock cars, such was his ability to adapt to widely different machines and road conditions. A significant win was in 1956 at the Buenos Aires 1000 Kilometers race, in which he shared a 3-liter Maserati with Stirling Moss. Then he won the 1962 Mar y Sierras—813 kilometers at an average speed of 191.5 km per hour on the open road and a new speed record for the event. A serious accident on the airport track in Sebring, Florida, put an end to his international career. He continued racing successfully in Argentina, where he was poised to win the 1964 National Grand Prix when his engine gave up just 17 kilometers from the checkered flag. Seventeen kilometers–about 10 miles—after five days and almost 4,000 kilometers on the road. It was Charlie's most painful defeat.

His driving style was quite simple: foot to the floor from the start. If the car held up, he won by a country mile; if not, the broken machine would be left by the road side along with Charlie's command to his crew: "Burn it." Sometimes he would offer the mechanic a cigarette lighter to reinforce his request.

The royal and ancient game of golf was another of Charlie's pursuits. A good player, one day a casual conversation led to a bet: for—it is rumored—1,000 dollars he wagered that he would be a scratch player one year from that date. Once Carlos took up something, he committed himself to the enterprise with a vengeance. In this case, he hired professional Enrique Bertolini and took daily lessons.[12] He won the bet with time to spare. Then he entered the Campeonato del Sur held at the Mar del Plata Golf Club, one of the top four golf tournaments in South America, and took the amateur division with a score of two over par for 72 holes.[13]

Carlos Menditeguy's ego was legendary. Stories abound regarding this facet of his personality. One year his polo play did not display its usual brilliancy and his handicap was lowered to 8-goals. Playing at Palermo alongside Charlie was Mariano "Pepino" Gutiérrez Achával, a very good back also rated at 8-goals. Mariano was tapping the ball ahead of Charlie, who got impatient. "Leave it, leave it," said Charlie. More tapping. Then the scream, "Leave it Pepino! Your eight and mine are not equal!"

But at least one time he was outsmarted. During a match at Guardia del Monte, Charlie crossed the right of way a few times—as was his habit—and umpire Alvaro Pieres blew the whistle every time. Charlie, accustomed to more lenient umpiring, took exception and asked Bary Pieres, "Do you have something personal against me?" A deadpan Pieres—father of the four famous brothers—replied, "Personal? I don't even know your name." A chastened Menditeguy toed the line for the rest of the game.[14]

Outside of Argentina, Charlie played polo in North America and Europe. His irresistible smile wrought havoc among the fair gender at home and abroad, sometimes to the detriment of his play. His long time adversary, Juan Carlos Alberdi, regaled his friends with the story of Charlie taking the ball near the boards at Palermo, and upon hearing a feminine shout of encouragement, checking his pony and turning his gaze looking for the admirer. When Charlie tried to find the ball, Alberdi was long gone.[15]

Charlie's attire and demeanor were invariably elegant. Whether driving his street blue Ferrari along the tree-lined boulevards of Buenos Aires, sipping coffee at the trendy La Biela, or walking along a fashionable street, his figure commanded immediate attention. His arrival to watch a Saturday night boxing bout at the Luna Park or for any match at Hurlingham, Palermo or San Isidro received more attention than any other player, before or since. The urchins would fight each other for the privilege of carrying his mallets to the pony lines. Charlie had the common touch, and within seconds of chatting with onlookers, he had every one, young and old, in the palm of his hand.

Sadly, the man endowed with uncanny timing developed Parkinson's disease, an affliction characterized by muscular rigidity and tremors. His heart finally gave up on 27 April 1973. A multitude accompanied his remains to Recoleta cemetery. Manuel Caramelo Gómez wrote in *Centauros*: "Carlos Menditeguy, a man who is already a legend."[16]

Notes

1. *El Gráfico*, January 1956.
2. *Polo y Campo*, September 1938.
3. *El Gráfico*, November 1943.
4. Luis Ignacio San Román, "*El Trébol ... treinta años después!*" *Centauros* (Jan.–Feb. 1968): 20–27.
5. Craganour was the unjustly disqualified winner of the 1913 Derby at Epson. Purchased by Miguel Martínez de Hoz for his stud "Chapadmalal," Craganour had a large and successful racing progeny in Argentina.
6. Interview with Heriberto Duggan, October 1979.
7. Some examples are the final game of the 1944 Open, won by Venado Tuerto 10–8; the 1950 semifinal also won by Venado Tuerto 11–9, the final in 1954 won by El Trébol 12–9 and the first-ever 80-goal match at Palermo in 1976. Appropriately enough, the teams were labeled El Trébol and Venado Tuerto.
8. Northrup R. Knox, *To B.A. and Back ... Again* (Buffalo: private printing, 1967), 39.
9. Juan Manuel Fangio (1911–1995) was nicknamed "Chueco" because of his bow-legs.
10. Ricardo Lorenzo, *Medio siglo de automovilismo argentino* (Buenos Aires: Editorial Atlántida, 1953.), 196.
11. Alfredo Parga, *Historia deportiva del automovilismo argentino* (Buenos Aires: La Nación, 1995), 527–528.
12. Xavier A. Verstraten, *Golf Courses and Links of Argentina* (Buenos Aires: Verstraten Editores, 1998), 86.
13. *El Golfer Argentino*, December 1955. Mar del Plata Golf Club's course was initially designed by Juan Dentone, one of Argentina's early professional players. Dr. Alister MacKenzie, one of golf's great architects, extensively redesigned the course to its present configuration in 1930.
14. Interview with Alvaro Pieres Sr., November 2005.
15. *Centauros* 103 (1973), 52.
16. *Ibid.*, 8–12.

Sinclair Hill: "I'll give you fancy pants!"

by Chris Ashton

After the Almighty made Sinclair, He surely broke the mold. Sinclair's chutzpah and showmanship was to polo in England and Australia in the 1960s and early '70s what Muhammad Ali was to boxing or John McEnroe to tennis. He exuded a passion and intensity, a will to win and commitment to his teammates that extended them far beyond their ordinary capacities. In his audacity, his bravado and occasional bloody-mindedness, he either enthralled or enraged spectators, eliciting cheering and booing on three continents.

Australian polo had seen nothing like him before nor, it can safely be said, will ever see his like again. No one in the Australian polo community speaks of Hill; quite simply, there was only one Sinclair. He personified all the vices and virtues of humankind, but written larger and in brighter colors. By his example, his force of personality and encouragement of others, he left an indelible mark on Australian polo, mostly to its benefit.

Throughout his polo career he conducted polo clinics all over Australia. More recently he has emerged as a trenchant critic of patron polo for what it has done to polo as a spectator sport—but more of that anon.

He was born in 1934 into a prosperous pastoral family, part of what was then the upper echelon of Australian society. On his father's side he is sixth-generation Australian-born, descended from Noel Hill, who established the family fortune in the early twentieth century. On his mother's side he is descended from the Arnott family, whose name is synonymous with the Australian biscuit dynasty. His family owned pastoral properties of many thousands of hectares breeding sheep, cattle and stock horses. On the principal family sheep station, Terlings, near Moree in northern New South Wales (N.S.W.), his mother Jean was supreme arbiter of the social order. Her son recalls her dressing for dinner each night in an evening gown.

As to his father, Leslie Hill, Sinclair regarded him with awe and admiration: a graduate of Oxford University with a blue in tennis; a pillar of the Anglican Church; in sum, an Australian gentleman in the English mold—moderate in all things, restrained, unfailingly courteous; in a word, the very antithesis of his tearaway son.

From the security of a close, supportive family, at the age of ten Hill was sent to Church of England boarding schools. From a small preparatory school in the N.S.W. Southern Highlands, Tudor House, at 13 he went to the Kings School in Sydney, with its proud martial traditions, a rite of passage followed by generations of sons born into N.S.W. pastoral families. Like his father had before him, he captained the Kings' tennis team but, unlike his father, he suffered from dyslexia, a motor learning disorder then unrecognized that relegated him to the bottom of his class, a shame he suffered keenly.

For three months, after completing his schooling, he returned to Terlings, where he played polo on a rough ground nearby at the center of the local racecourse, and groomed for other local players. Custom among some Anglophile Australian pastoral families persisted that sons complete their education at one of England's ancient universities, as had Leslie Hill. Sinclair was dispatched instead to the Royal Agricultural College, Cirencester.

There, as a raw, gangling 19-year-old, he was selected for the college polo team. Playing well above his scratch handicap, he was spotted and inducted into the charmed circle of English polo by the likes of Gerald Balding, the former 10-goaler who had captained England before the war, and by the Indian 9-goaler Rao Raja Hanut Singh. First with Hanut Singh, with whom he won the 12-goal Silver Cup at Deauville, then with Balding, Hill became a more willing student of polo than was ever known to the Kings School or the Royal Agricultural College, Cirencester.

Following the 1954 English polo season the Argentine 8-goaler Tito Lalor invited him to Buenos Aires. Here the brash young Australian, mounted, as he recalls, on very ordinary horses, insisted on practicing with Argentina's most illustrious players on the grounds of the prestigious Hurlingham Club. As their suspicion of him thawed he was accepted and eventually was invited into a team to contest a low-goal tournament for beginners, the Copa Estímulo, which it won.

He tried to master the rudiments of Spanish without success, and instead courted his language coach, Vally (Valeria) Babacci, daughter of a hydrological engineer. Returning to England they were married in the garden of Park House Hotel in West Sussex, a guesthouse favored by foreign players for the English polo season. Rising to speak at the wedding reception, the enormity of the moment reduced the 20-year-old bridegroom to tears.

His second English season, playing in medium- and high-goal tournaments, confirmed his early promise. As Hill tells it, he wrote to the Royal Agricultural College advising that he was abandoning his agricultural studies to concentrate on his polo studies. By the season's end Australia beckoned. The Hills broke their journey home with a month in India, as the guest of Hanut Singh, who made it his mission to improve Sinclair's horsemanship, after which the pupil played for his mentor in the annual Calcutta tournaments. The Hills reached Sydney in January 1955, Hill a four-goal player, 21 years old.

The Hills settled into married life on successive family sheep stations. Hill played polo with local clubs on weekends, but without the option to take time off to play the tournament circuit elsewhere. From 1958 and playing off five-goals, he lived and worked on a family property called Berwicks, from where, for the rest of his polo career, he played for Quirindi Polo Club. With Hill playing in the number 3 position and a local farmer, Peter Cudmore, playing number 4, Quirindi was virtually unbeatable. Cudmore, who played off seven-goals at his peak, was judged Australia's best number 4 since World War II. He was also the solid anchor to his captain's excitability, which sometimes unsettled the team. Within the Australian polo community it was widely believed that Hill might be beaten with another number 4, but never with Cudmore.

That same year he was selected for a national team to tour New Zealand, together with Ken Mackay (six-goals), Jim Maple-Brown (five-goals), Ian Murray and reserve Dick Doolin (both four-goals). For New Zealanders, with a population one-fifth the size of Australia, patriotism is never more fervent than in sporting contests, especially rugby union or cricket but

With Quirindi teammates (left to right) Bruce McDonald, Theo Hill (no relation) and Peter Cudmore, winners of the 1964 New South Wales championship, the Dudley Cup (Chris Ashton, courtesy Sinclair Hill).

also in polo, against its giant neighbor across the Tasman Sea. Spectators flocked by the thousand to watch the Australians take on their best. In one game Hill borrowed a pair of leotards to wear over breeches that had split at the seam, and for his pains was dubbed "Fancy Pants." Goaded by spectators he eventually shouted, "I'll give you fancy pants!" and from a standing position hit a 60-yard penalty goal.

Hill's considerable achievement was to scale the very summit of polo while playing most of his career with Australian sheep farmers for whom polo was only ever a weekend recreation. "The wooden horse enabled me to achieve the ultimate in polo, though I wasn't able to play every day because I had to work my farm," he recalls:

> I built a wooden horse which was well away from the house. When I'd finished work for the day I'd take the car over to it and turn the headlights on because there wasn't enough power to light it after dark. I'd have music playing from the car radio because polo is musical and the beat helped the rhythm of my shots. You've got to remember that polo is really ballet.
>
> I think I'm the only ten-goal wooden horse player. Paul Withers used it, which is why he was such a magnificent striker. There are problems, of course. You've got to get the ball to roll off the wall at the right angle to simulate being on a live horse. If you spend 20 minutes on a wooden horse every day, that's a long time; if you spend an hour a day on a wooden horse, that's a very long time.

Sinclair in action, a stylish backhander on the Ambersham ground, Cowdray Park, in the 1960s (Chris Ashton, courtesy Sinclair Hill).

At intervals he returned to the international polo circuit. Funded by Lord Cowdray, in 1963 he led a 22-goal Commonwealth team to the United States that won successive test matches. *The London Times* waxed lyrical: "Let the flags fly high at Midhurst tonight and bells ring out at Willow Tree, N.S.W., for this week Australian Sinclair Hill and his team have written the name of Cowdray Park into American polo history. They have played and defeated two of the best 25-goal teams in the U.S. and in the manner of their victory have earned a new respect for British polo overseas."

Three years later and with a nine-goal handicap, Hill led another Commonwealth team to Buenos Aires, supported by two English players, Paul Withers (seven-goals) and Major Ronnie Ferguson (five), Rhodesian Patrick Kemple (seven), with Hanut Singh managing the team. In a three-cornered test series of 30-goal teams, the Commonwealth defeated the U.S. and was routed by Argentina.

Aside from epic contests in Australia which pitted Hill leading N.S.W. teams against the seven-goaler Ken Telford leading Queensland, Hill's finest hour was arguably his second New Zealand tour in 1972. With Sandy Tait and Richard Walker (N.S.W) and Hugh MacLachlan (South Australia), and their respective wives, 20 ponies and four tons of baggage, they billed themselves the Emus. Now, as in 1958, media interest was insatiable and, as before, Hill stamped his personality on the tour, on and off the field, most conspicuously in challenging New Zealand umpires' rulings.

In the final test, he blocked a shot in full volley and with three further strikes took the ball 200 meters up the field to score. In the month-long tour the Emus lost the first test, won the second and third — Australia's first victory against New Zealand in a test series in 34 years— and all ten games against club teams. "He was a wonderful captain," MacLachlan recalls. "He always encouraged and seldom criticized. He operated on the basis of building confidence in his team members. It was the finest polo I ever saw him play."

At the end of the season the N.S.W. Polo Association handicapping committee debated whether Hill should be elevated to ten-goals. His critics on the committee, citing instances of conduct unbecoming a ten-goaler, were virtually level-pegged with his supporters. The motion supporting his promotion was narrowly approved. Hill had joined a select list, one of five ten-goal players at the time and the only non–Argentine. Since the advent of handicapping, from 1890 in the United States, and from 1911 in Argentina and England, just 40 players had reached the pinnacle of polo.

No foreign player is accepted in Argentine polo as worthy of a handicap awarded elsewhere until he has been tested in Argentine high-goal polo. In the 1972 Open, Hill showed his mettle when he led the 32-goal Los Pingüinos to victory against 35-goal Mar del Plata. But against Santa Ana, led by Francisco Dorignac, now the president of the Argentine Polo Association, his team met his match. His Argentine peers nonetheless acknowledged him worthy of his ten-goal handicap.

Playing in Buenos Aires two years later, a head-on collision with Juan José Alberdi dislocated Hill's left shoulder, ending his high-goal career. He accepted this stoically. "I was 40-years-old and I'd played much of my best polo before I reached ten-goals," he recalls. "It took me three years to recover the use of my shoulder."

In his personal life the years that followed were quite as much a time of adjustment. From polo he had developed what golfers call *yips*, a muscular seizure caused by excessive practice and tension. In 1976 he and Vally, who had given him five children, dissolved their marriage. Sinclair subsequently married Wendy Burbank of Melbourne.

Following recovery from his injuries, he played the English season for four years with such patrons as Peter Palumbo and Ronnie Driver. At the Duke of Edinburgh's request he also coached the Prince of Wales in polo. He ruefully recalls offering to demonstrate a shot from the pony Prince Charles was riding, an invitation declined because, as the Prince explained, his mother had expressly commanded that on no account was Hill to ride "that particular horse."

The demonic passion which Hill brought to polo before his accident subsided, but his enthusiasm in teaching and promoting polo was undiminished. He traveled the length of Aus-

Sinclair Hill leads a polo clinic at Canberra Polo Club, circa 1960 (Chris Ashton, courtesy Sinclair Hill).

tralia to lead coaching clinics at rural polo clubs and gave or lent his own mares and stallions to improve breeding lines elsewhere. Convinced that outstanding eyeball coordination could translate from other ball sports to polo, he recruited to polo champions from other sports like John Goold from Australian Rules football and Hugh MacLachlan from cricket. In practice it fell short of theory, but within the polo community players everywhere recall him for raising their sights beyond raw bush polo.

Ted Hammersley, a six-goaler at his peak and founder-captain of Walkaway Polo Club, recalls, "He was the most dynamic lecturer I ever heard. He would start lecturing at 9 a.m., you'd think you'd been listening for 20 minutes and he'd say, "Gentleman, it's one o'clock. We'll adjourn for lunch." We'd been listening to him for four hours! He had everyone electrified. They'd go home and talk about nothing else but polo for months afterwards. One thing I remember him saying was, 'Even if you're not a great polo player, try to look like one.' I've never forgotten that and I always say to young players, 'Polish yourself up.'

But the admiration Hill inspired in his heyday is qualified. No one in Australian polo would dispute his standing as its most influential figure since World War II. But he is remembered also for consistently challenging umpires' rulings (never mind that he was better versed than most of them in the rules of polo) and for his determination to follow the line of the ball regardless of injury to players or ponies—a charge, it should be added, that he vehemently rejects.

Some of his protégés would concede in hindsight their failure to distinguish between his brilliance as a player and his temperamental flaws. Hugh MacLachlan, to this day a close friend and admirer, recalls, "He told me that the best way to play polo was to simulate the roughest game of rugby I could imagine. That was the first instruction I received from Australia's premier polo player! I'm sure Sinclair would admit his own views have changed."

Since his retirement from polo, Hill's formidable energy has focused on a multitude of causes and projects. With dormant investment-partners in southeastern Queensland he bought half-a-million hectares in marginal pastoral properties supporting scores of thousands of sheep and cattle. Flying 50,000 kilometres a year in his own light plane from one property to the next, through improved management he converted them to viable businesses.

Once, he was nominated for a seat in the Australian Senate, representing something called the Workers Party. Never mind the proletarian connotations conjured up by its name, it was actually committed to laissez-faire capitalism. So few votes did he win that he lost his deposit. More recently he worked to advance the socially and economically deprived Aboriginal community in the town of Moree, near the family seat, of Terlings. He played a pivotal role in acquiring a 19th-century bank building to house an Aboriginal commercial art gallery, and supported the local Aboriginal football team.

From 1986, when Kerry Packer decided to take up polo, for two years Hill devoted considerable time and energy to coaching him in the game. He persuaded Packer to join him in promoting the beef industry against the growing popularity of white meats and their supposed benefits to health compared to red meats. He also championed, in vain, the cause of retaining the century-old Sydney Showground, close to the city center, for the annual Royal Easter Show, since relocated to Sydney's western perimeter.

In interviews with U.S., British and Australian polo magazines, he has become a trenchant critic of patron polo for its impact on his beloved game. Echoed by other veteran players, by polo commentators and spectators, his sentiments, most recently voiced in *Polo Times* (U.K.) magazine in 2005, deserve to be quoted at length:

> Patron polo has changed the game. What you see are three players a side and a payer. There's no doubt patrons have improved the quality of horseflesh, but it means most tournaments are played nowadays on handicap. Patrons can't play off the stick, so the game has to take account of their standard.
>
> It's a free country and they can do what they want but club loyalties have disappeared with club polo. In the old days we had the spectators bellowing from the sidelines. They either loved you or they hated you, but there's very little loyalty left and no tension and that's sad. No one wants to watch patrons playing. You may watch them for who they are but not for how they play polo.
>
> I don't think the patrons, God bless them, really understand what sort of an influence they've had on the game. It's all very well galloping about on a polo pony at 40 mph—there's no greater thrill—but if the game is controlled by hugely wealthy and powerful men scattered all over the world, it isn't exciting to watch anymore. The patrons play it badly and don't know the rules. It's a tragedy.
>
> I don't want to deny that professional players have done a lot to keep the game going. They're probably better than we were, but there are 30 times more players than when I was playing. There are more tournaments, the horses are better and for whatever reason, more money is invested in the game. I played my first game in England nine years after the war. It was a time of austerity with food rationing coming to an end. It would be amazing if polo hadn't improved since then, but it's boring. I don't watch much polo nowadays, although I love the game more than people could ever imagine.[1]

Like so many other warriors since the dawn of time, he recalls his own era as the golden age compared with which those who now aspire to the pinnacle of polo fall short because they have it too easy: "People are less prepared to sacrifice themselves for success in polo nowadays and that disappoints me. A lot of people are terribly keen to succeed but they're not willing to suffer for it. What is lacking is dedication, application and the willingness to sacrifice to succeed at a higher level."[2]

Notes

1. Chris Ashton, *Polo Times* (Oct. 2005), 31.
2. *Ibid.*, 32.

Juan Carlos Harriott Jr.: "The aristocrat of polo"

by Horace A. Laffaye

The town of Coronel Suárez lies on the southwestern area of the vast Pampas, some 550 miles from Buenos Aires. It is a flat, rich soil, ideal for the agricultural and grazing pursuits that made Argentina the largest exporter of beef and wheat in its long-ago heyday. The town's original name was Sauce Corto (Small Willow) which was changed to honor an obscure warrior of the War of Independence from Spain, Colonel Manuel Isidoro Suárez.[1]

This sleepy, quiet town has been called at different times "the cradle of polo players" and, perhaps more ostentatiously, "the world capital of polo." There is some validity to such claims. The Coronel Suárez Polo Club was founded on 29 May 1929; but the first match had taken place in 1927 at estancia La María, the property of Doña María Alberdi de Garrós, two surnames that are part and parcel of the club's history. The first match almost did not take place. In preparation for the big event, Lacey & Sons had been requested to ship eight mallets and one ball. Prior to the game, Ricardo Garrós devoted some time to hitting the only ball, with the result that the match was played with an object less than perfectly spherical.[2]

Scanning the list of the club's founding members, it is astounding to find so many familiar names in Argentine polo: Alberdi, Amadeo y Videla, Andrada, Boudou, Grant, Garrós, Jencquel, Maitland, just to mention a few who achieved respectable handicaps.[3]

Within one year of being affiliated with the Argentine Polo Association, Coronel Suárez took the National Handicap Tournament. Since that year, 1930, the club has won this important tournament no fewer than 14 times, more than any other club. The Argentine Open was taken 25 times; again, a better record than any other team. It is an outstanding achievement.

Among the winners of the National Handicap Tournament and the Copa Cámara de Diputados in 1934 appears the name Juan Carlos Harriott at back, a position that he continued to play during his entire career.[4] And what a career! Eight Argentine Open Championships, eight Hurlingham Opens and a 9-goal handicap rating, along with many other tournaments.

This National Handicap Tournament for the Copa República Argentina is one of the most difficult tournaments to win. It is open to any club in the country, from 0 to 40-goal handicaps. It is not unusual for some clubs to enlist several teams under their colors, and at times more than 100 teams have participated. The final rounds among the Circuit winners are always played at Palermo.

It was a cold afternoon in August 1953 when the 9-goal Coronel Suárez team, once more winners of the Circuito Sud, rode onto the field to play against the military team San Jorge. Alongside Rodolfo Panelo, Guillermo Carrique and Eduardo Erize, there was a 17-year-old, one-goal handicap player. The tournament program stated: "No. 3 Juan C. Harriott (h.)." It was quite unusual for the lowest handicapped player to appear in the most important position on the team, but very quickly the spectators realized that they were witnessing the debut of a remarkable polo player. As for the team, it was not an auspicious performance. When the two-week play came to a close, both El Rincón and Chapaleufú were ahead of Coronel Suárez, Chapaleufú taking the prized Copa República Argentina.[5]

Immediately following the tournament, Juancarlitos—as he was already called—went up to a 3-goal handicap. He reached the top in 1961, the first 10-goaler in Argentina in seven years, and was to maintain this lofty level without interruption until 1981, when—at his own request—he was lowered to 9-goals. Juancarlitos had recently retired from high-goal polo following the successful defense of the Cup of the Americas at San Antonio, Texas.[6]

Juan Carlos Harriott Jr. was born on 28 October 1936, the eldest son of Juan Carlos Harriott and Elvira de Lusarreta. Like hundreds of polo players, Juancarlitos grew up at an estancia, in his case the family's property in Coronel Suárez. And, just like thousands of Argentine children, he was placed on a saddle and taught how to ride at the same time as he was learning to walk. His sister Elvira married polo player Guillermo Carrique, who became president of Coronel Suárez Polo Club. His younger brother Alfredo, born in 1945, would follow in his steps, eventually reaching a handicap of 10-goals and succeeding Juancarlitos as captain of a Coronel Suárez Open Champion team. Both children had the advantage of being nurtured by magnificent mentors in the ambience of high-goal polo. These mentors included his father, Juan Carlos, and uncle, Eduardo Harriott, who were polo pony breeders of note; neighbors Enrique and Juan Carlos Alberdi, both 10-goalers and the backbone of the celebrated Coronel Suarez and Venado Tuerto teams; and another set of brothers, Eduardo and Ricardo Garrós—winners of the Campeonato Abierto—who owned land nearby.

His most outstanding mentor was Enrique Alberdi, a 10-goaler who skippered Coronel Suárez, Venado Tuerto and Argentine teams to victory in 12 Argentine Opens, the World Championship, the Cup of the Americas and the gold medal in the Pan-American games.[7]

Juancarlitos Harriott on Enrique Alberdi:

> You had to see him on a bad day. If you want to analyze so and so as a polo player, you have to watch him on a bad day. Then I'll tell you his worth. The guy whose ponies don't go for him or is badly mounted, and still wins, he put everything into it, he's worth a lot. Quito Alberdi was like that. The first Open we won, I played at number 2 and he played at number 3. Hell, he was all over me. He could not conceive that you could ever let up. There is going to be a moment in which your opponent is going to be distracted, and then is when you beat him.[8]

Starting with the 1954 high-goal season, and for 26 consecutive years, Juancarlitos took his ponies to Buenos Aires and proceeded to set an unprecedented—and still unbeaten—record in the annals of the Argentine Open Championship. His first win was in 1957, playing on a team with his lifelong friend Bertil Andino Grahn, Enrique Alberdi, and his father Juan Carlos. The next year, another close friend, Horacio Heguy, joined the team. To complete the squad, Horacio's father, Antonio Heguy, playing off 5-goals, rounded out the team of the two fathers and the two sons. They won again, the only time in history that a major championship has been taken by a team so composed. At the end of the season, Antonio Heguy, his major ambition fulfilled, retired from high-goal polo. Therefore, Luis Lalor, from La Alicia—his own family club—was recruited for the team to obtain its third consecutive victory. In 1960, El Trébol, led by the legendary Carlos Menditeguy, stopped Coronel Suárez's winning ways.

The 1957 Open Championship saw the beginning of a winning stretch perhaps unparalleled in the history of sport. From that year until 1984, Coronel Suárez took the Argentine Open every year except 1960, 1971, 1973 and 1982. Twenty-three out of 27 championships is a record that will take some time to be surpassed.

Juan Carlos Harriott Jr. was on every winning team until he retired after taking the Cup of the Americas in May 1980. The team underwent some changes through the years. The 1961 team of Horacio Heguy, Daniel González and the two Harriotts lasted for two years, until 1963 when Alberto Pedro Heguy, Horacio's younger brother, took Gonzalez's place. The following year, two falls suffered by Harriott Senior in the course of the final Open match necessitated his replacement by Carlos Torres Zavaleta, so Daniel González returned as a starter. In 1966, also during the final match, Alberto Heguy sustained a broken wrist and was replaced by the American player Dr. William Linfoot. Finally, in 1967 Alfredo Harriott joined the team as planned. The two sets of brothers embarked on a record of their own. In the next 13 years they took the Argentine Open 11 times, the Hurlingham Open seven times and added to their mantelpiece two Cups of the Americas, one at Palermo and another at Retama in San Antonio, Texas.

Juancarlitos Harriott. Wonderful in every sense of the word. In the opinion of many, the best player ever (courtesy Museum of Polo and Hall of Fame).

Following the North American campaign, Horacio Heguy and Juancarlitos Harriott decided to retire from high-goal polo. A new Coronel Suárez took the field at Palermo. Young Benjamín Araya took the number one slot and Alfredo Harriott moved to number 3, his place at back being taken by Celestino Garrós. Fate provided a last hurrah for Horacio Heguy. In the second chukker, Celestino broke his collarbone and Horacio had to come down from the stands at Palermo and finish the game. It was his twentieth Open victory. Coronel Suárez went on to win two more championships, the last one with, once more, Daniel González, Benjamín's close friend Juan Badiola, and at back, his father, Horacio Araya.

The brilliance of Coronel Suárez during those years prevented another superior team — Santa Ana — from obtaining the recognition it deserved. Started in 1937 by, among others, Gastón Dorignac Sr., and the Jaeschke brothers, this club in Villa Valeria, Córdoba Province, had a distinguished history. Several times winner of the National Handicap Championship, it catapulted to the first rank of high-goal teams when the future superstars Francisco and Gastón Dorignac Jr. came of age and joined Olympic cham-

Coronel Suárez, the 40-goal polo machine. Alberto Pedro and Horacio Heguy, Juancarlitos and Alfredo Harriott took eleven Argentine Open Championships, six Hurlingham Club Championships and the Cup of the Americas twice. Playing in the Open at Palermo, they lost only one game in 12 years (courtesy Museum of Polo and Hall of Fame).

pion and Venado Tuerto stalwart, Roberto Cavanagh, to form the nucleus of a great team. Santa Ana provided in their struggles with Coronel Suárez a rivalry in Argentine polo similar to the ones previously offered by El Trébol and Venado Tuerto. In his efforts to break Coronel Suárez's monopoly, team captain Franky Dorignac called upon the top talent available: 10-goalers Daniel González, his brother Gastón and Memo Gracida, nine-goaler Héctor Merlos and quality players such as his own younger brother Marcelo, Teófilo Bordeu and Luis Lalor. Their efforts were rewarded in 1971, 1973 and 1982 when they took the Campeonato Abierto Argentino, popularly known simply as the "Abierto de Palermo." During those years, several deciding final matches between these outstanding teams were won and lost by just one goal. It was that close. There was one exception: In 1976, Coronel Suárez gave one of its most overwhelming displays of faultlessness and beat Santa Ana 20–6.

What made Coronel Suárez the greatest team in polo's history? The answer is a combination of factors; paramount was the personality and overall playing brilliancy of their captain and undisputed leader, Juancarlitos Harriott. Coronel Suárez made a cult of playing at full speed. The team played as if they were trailing by a single goal, with one minute to go. The attitude was, "We have to score a goal, if not we'll lose the game. Find a way to score a goal." The other basic component in Harriott's philosophy: Force the opposing number three to play facing his own goal. Sometimes, he had to face his own goal, but the intention always was to face the adversary's goalposts.

Harriott did not often travel overseas, at least not on the scale of many of his contemporaries, who undertook the long journey to European countries, mainly England, France, Spain and Italy, where all expenses were paid and high prices guaranteed for their ponies. It was the dawn of professionalism.

In 1966, the Argentine Polo Association organized the most ambitious international season since 1950. The season's highlight was the fifth series for the Cup of the Americas, tied at two-all. An additional international tournament for 30-goal teams included American and British squads. The Americans came out in force, led by Northrup Knox, whose father, Seymour, had been a member of the successful 1932 visiting team. This squad included Roy and Harold "Chico" Barry, and Dr. William Linfoot, a veterinarian and great horseman. As reserves, and candidates to complete the 30-goal team, Robert Beveridge, Jack Murphy, Allan Scherer and Lewis Smith — the only survivor of the 1950 national team — joined the delegation. The British squad included the Marquess of Waterford, his younger brother Lord Patrick Beresford, Maj. Ronald Ferguson and Paul Withers. Rhodesian Patrick Kemple and Sinclair Hill from Australia were welcome reinforcements. As coach, Rao Rajah Hanut Singh brought his experience of many decades as a 9-goal player.

The Argentines took the challenge seriously. Luis Duggan, Juan and Roberto Cavanagh — a total of 29-goals in their prime, and seven Abierto's titles each one — were appointed selectors. For the 30-goal team, Alfredo Harriott, Gastón Dorignac, Juancarlitos Harriott and Gonzalo Tanoira were the anointed. For the "big" team, it was Alberto Pedro and Horacio Heguy, Juan Carlos Harriott, and, at back, Francisco Dorignac.

In preparation for the Copa Sesquicentenario— the 30-goal tournament to honor the 150th anniversary of Argentina's independence — the "little" team participated in Hurlingham's open championship. In the final match they defeated, by only one goal, Windsor Park, with the Heguy brothers, Daniel González and Prince Philip of Edinburgh. As to the tournament proper, England and America opened the scene in a rough match that the British team won 13–6. Kemple, Hill, Withers and Ferguson then faced Argentina on Number 2 field at Palermo. In one of the most lopsided ever encounters the young Argentines beat the combined British-Commonwealth team 24–2, and then went on to defeat the Americans. At the end of the season, many observers were of the opinion that the 30-goal team was better than the national selection.[9]

The Argentine Open followed, and once more Coronel Suárez defeated Santa Ana in a very good match. Misfortune befell Alberto Heguy, when shortly after the beginning of the game he broke his wrist. Heguy's bad luck became Gastón Dorignac's good fortune. Although he had not been selected as an alternate, his performance during the season so much impressed the trio of selectors that they set aside the nominated alternates and placed Gastón in the number 1 position. Argentina won both games for the Cup of the Americas, 10–6 and 14–10. For the United States, Knox, Linfoot, Roy and Chico Barry played well, but Juan Carlos Harriott stole the show. The oft repeated comment, "He should be a 12-goal handicap," was heard again.

Three years later, Norty Knox mounted another challenge for the "Copa." He called upon a young Bennie Gutierrez and an experienced Ray Harrington to join veterans Chico Barry and Doc Linfoot. The result was the same, if not worse; Argentina won 12–6 and 18–6, featuring the same four players. Argentina's position as the top nation in polo was unquestioned, and its captain's brilliancy made him the undisputed number one player in the world.

A decade later, America tried again, this time as a home and away series. In the first game at Palermo, Charles Smith, Tommy Wayman, Lester "Red" Armour and Joe Barry faced the full Coronel Suárez foursome, the brothers Heguy and Harriott, winners of the last six Argentine Open Championships. A daunting project. A score of 18 to 6 reflected the power of the

Harriott battling it out with Red Armour in the 1979 Cup of the Americas (courtesy Museum of Polo and Hall of Fame).

best team in the game's history. The second game was one-sided as well, 16–6. The visitors had juggled their players, replacing Smith with Roy Barry at back; Armour went to the forward position and Joe Barry to pivot. It really made no difference.

It was a different story the following year in San Antonio, Texas. America recruited the up-and-coming Guillermo "Memo" Gracida to fill the number one slot, while Wayman, Armour and Joe Barry completed the team. The Argentines, coached by Roberto Cavanagh, presented the same team — no need to make changes— and sent Gonzalo Tanoira, his Mar del Plata team mate, Alfredo Goti, and Héctor Merlos as reserves. But in the eyes of the Argentines, the true hero was Dr. Alvaro Pieres, the team's veterinarian. Bad luck followed the pony string from the start. One of the ponies loaned by Jorge Torres Zavaleta — at the time the incumbent president of the A.A. de Polo and a noted breeder — died during the airplane flight. After quarantine, the entire complement of horses developed a cough, an epidemic so severe that the first game had to be postponed. One of the top ponies, the celebrated Purita, was bitten by a snake. Through all this, Alvaro Pieres— older brother of the famous Alfonso and Gonzalo— worked day and night at the stables. Old hands could remember a similar situation in 1928, when the Argentine string was taken ill just before the inaugural edition of the Cup of the Americas at Meadow Brook.

So it was that a depleted — pony-wise — Argentine team took the field at Retama. In a very close game that could have gone either way, the visitors emerged the winners 11–8. Juan Carlos Harriott remembers the players' shirts and pants being covered with blood from the horses' coughing in the course of the game.[10] But the rejuvenated American squad gave as good as it took. It was one of the most difficult victories by the Argentines in their long history in international play. The ponies were so exhausted after the game that the Argentine team considered giving a walk-over for the second match, allowing the ponies a week's rest, and then contesting the third and final game. Anyway, the ponies began to recover, and the second game was on. It was, once more, a closely fought match, Argentina winning 10–6.

Following completion of their fourth consecutive winning series for the "Copa," Juan Carlos Harriott Jr. and his close friend Horacio Heguy announced their retirement. In a sense, an unforgettable era had come to an end. For almost a quarter of a century, the two pals—Juancarlitos once said, "We never had an argument"—had delighted the crowds with their individual and team displays of virtuosity. But the number 3 reigned supreme. His sense of anticipation was unmatched; his striking ability unbelievable. Once, during a final at Palermo, Juancarlitos missed the ball. The "Oohs" from the spectators could be heard. His penalty-shot taking was awesome, his riding beyond reproach. He was an undisputed captain, organizer, and leader. An unidentified reporter called him "the aristocrat of polo" because of his impeccable style, his manners on and off the field, his respect for his adversaries and his loyalty to friends. Gonzalo Tanoira, who as a player was considered second only to Juancarlitos, once said of him, "*Juancarlitos' superiority is so obvious that it defies all comparisons, because he truly played a level much above any of his contemporaries.*"[11]

And yet, when Sebastián Amaya asked him how it felt to be the best player in the world, he answered, "That's a shot in the air!"[12]

Self-effacing, quiet, polite almost to a fault, Harriott enjoyed practice games more than did most players. On the field, he was all business, with no smiles. A gentleman, he never injured a player. With his ponies, it was slightly different. His opinion was that the horse was like a soldier in battle; sometimes you have to accept casualties in order to win. This is unusual, because he has acknowledged that sometimes he only had four or five top ponies, and had to "double-up" most of them. Burra was his best pony, which he played for eleven seasons and which then became a broodmare. Team preparation was precise. In the days prior to an important event, the team, if invited to a party, would eat at home so they would not touch any food that might upset their stomach. Practice games were serious stuff. After losing two slow-practice games, he admonished his teammates, "We better watch out, we are getting used to losing."

Juancarlitos married Susana Cavanagh, Roberto's daughter. They have two married girls, Marina and Lucrecia, so the expected male superstar—father and grandfather 10-goals, the other grandfather 9-goals—did not materialize.

Juan Carlos Harriott Jr. played polo during a period in history that could be called the age of the amateur. In comparing his career to more recent superstars, it is necessary to remember that the amateur code was the dominant polo ideology in his time. The central component of this code was the ideal of playing sports for fun. It also included other aspects such as fair play, voluntary adherence to rules, and non-pecuniary rewards.

Nowadays, Juancarlitos tends to his estancia in Coronel Suárez, enjoying the countryside's relative tranquility. Sometimes he ventures to Buenos Aires to watch games at Palermo, or to receive some award or another. Among these, he was the recipient of the 1976 Gold Olimpia Award for the Most Outstanding Sportsman in Argentina. Other winners of the Gold Olimpia include sporting legends golfer Roberto de Vicenzo, racer Juan Manuel Fangio, soccer player Diego Maradona, tennis players Gabriela Sabatini and Guillermo Vilas. The Silver Olimpia, awarded to the best in many different sports, was created only in 1970 for polo, the Gold dating back to 1954. Juancarlitos was given the Silver Olimpia in 1970 and from 1975 to 1978.

Why is he not playing? "One day I looked at the calendar and said, enough!" What about Alberto Pedro Heguy and Horacio Araya, both still playing: "Yes ... they are crazy. I told Horacio, I don't know whether I should admire or tell you that you're crazy."[13]

He is an avid hunter — Susan Reeve relates in Mike Rattray's profile how Juancarlitos was lured to South Africa — joined in his expeditions by Andino Grahn and Celestino Garrós, both distinguished polo players.

Juancarlitos is no longer directly involved in the game. Occasionally, he will watch his nephews Sebastián and Juan, Alfredo's children, play in an important game. The polo ground at the 3,000-hectare estancia La Felisa is overgrown, just a memory of the 30-plus-goal practice games held decades ago. For a while he bred racehorses, mostly as a hobby and with small financial success. At nearby Coronel Suárez Polo Club he is accorded the reverence usually reserved for the high and the mighty, which he cheerfully brushes aside. A credit to the game of polo and to the human race, Juan Carlos Harriott Jr. glides through life with the same easy style that was the hallmark of his polo career — a classic polo player, if ever there was one.

Harriott, together with Horacio Heguy, is the only four-time winner of the Cup of the Americas. The sole international trophy with no handicap limits rests on display in a closely guarded cabinet in the Argentine Polo Association's office at Palermo. Sadly, there are no immediate prospects for its resumption as the most important international polo competition.

Notes

1. Col. Suárez (1799–1846) fought in Chile and Peru under Gen. José de San Martín, Argentina's national hero. It is said of Col. Suárez that he refused all the decorations offered to him, stating "I only want to take back my scars to the Motherland." Eduardo Bautista Pondé, *La Argentina Perdedora* (Buenos Aires: Editorial Legasa, 1995).
2. Personal communication from Celestino Garrós, Ricardo's nephew.
3. Asociación Argentina de Polo, *Libro Anual* (Buenos Aires: private printing, 1930 —1980).
4. The Copa Cámara de Diputados (House of Representatives Cup) was established in 1924 in honor of Juan and David Miles, Jack Nelson and Lewis Lacey, who had taken the Hurlingham Champion Cup and the U.S. Open. The winner earns the right to enter the Argentine Open.
5. Asociación Argentina de Polo, *Programa — Copa República Argentina, 1953.*
6. *Centauros*, 1981.
7. Enrique Alberdi (1910–1959) was also president of the Argentine Polo Association. One of the best ever Argentine players, he was killed in foul weather while piloting his own aircraft.
8. *PoloLine*, 21 January 2002.
9. *Centauros*, December 1966.
10. Interview with Juan Carlos Harriott Jr., December 2005.
11. *Centauros*, April 1983.
12. *PoloLine*, 21 January 2002.
13. *Ibid.*

Francisco Dorignac: The Chieftain

by Horace A. Laffaye

Bagnères-de-Bigorre is a sleepy spa town located in the High Pyrenees in southern France. Its claim to fame resides in the fact that it was the birthplace of Field Marshal Viscount Alanbrooke, Chief of the Imperial General Staff during the Second World War.[1] The street where he was born near the center of town was named Rue du Maréchal Alanbrooke, in his memory. It was from here that, in 1890, Francisco Dorignac joined millions of European immigrants in the long sea voyage to Argentina. The Dorignacs settled in Villa Valeria, situated in the southern part of Córdoba Province, and prospered by virtue of plain hard work.

Francisco had three children: Gastón; Emilio, tragically killed in an automobile accident; and Marta, who would marry Enrique "Quito" Alberdi, one of the greatest Argentine polo players and also a capable administrator of the game.[2]

Gastón Francisco Dorignac—the immigrant's son—and the Jaeschke brothers were the founders of the Santa Ana Polo Club, which affiliated with the Argentine Polo Association in 1937. However, Gastón had been playing polo since 1930 at Tortugas Country Club, a large institution established in 1926 at Antonio Maura y Gamazo's villa, some 40 kilometers from Buenos Aires.[3]

Santa Ana and Gastón Dorignac came into national prominence in 1947, when the blue and white team took the Copa República Argentina at Palermo after three extra chukkers. Carlos, Héctor and Rodolfo Jaeschke completed the winning squad. Santa Ana took this tournament again in 1956, this time calling upon some members of the new generation: Franky and his brother Gastón joined Juan González and previous winner Héctor Jaeschke. Gastón Dorignac *pére*, who had an engineering degree, went on to win many tournaments in his long career. Undoubtedly, his most satisfying win was taking the Copa Campaña del Desierto—Argentina's Gold Cup—on a team that included his children. Within months, Dorignac perished as the result of a motor vehicle accident.

His progenitor's early demise placed a huge burden and responsibility on 22-year-old Franky's shoulders. To his everlasting credit, he challenged grief and adversity with enough inner strength to face misfortune and keep on going, now as head of the family.

Francisco Emilio Dorignac was born in Buenos Aires on 22 September 1938, the eldest son of Gastón and Lía Pietranera de Dorignac. The couple had four other children: Gastón Raimundo, Marcelo Eduardo, Juan Carlos and Carola, of whom Gastón and Marcelo developed into high-goal handicap players.

In turn, Franky married María Marta Danuzzo. They have four children, Valeria, Francisco, Agustín and Emilio. The boys are all polo players. There is another noteworthy Dorignac who plays polo around the world: Michel, Juan Carlos' son. Juan Carlos never played the game.

Like many other Argentine polo stars, Franky was educated at Colegio Champagnat, a Marist school in Buenos Aires. His fellow alumni bore names famous in polo circles: Crotto, Heguy, Hunter, Lottero, and also Dorignac, because all three brothers have their names engraved on the Copa Santa Paula.[4]

A fine back who fought gallantly to the end of every match, Franky Dorignac prepares for a game (courtesy Museum of Polo and Hall of Fame).

Franky was catapulted into the public eye in 1953, when his father, once more winner of the Circuito Noroeste, was participating in the finals of the Copa República Argentina on the Number Two ground at Palermo. The elder Dorignac suffered a concussion after a fall and Franky, a 14-year-old schoolboy at the time, donned boots and blue jeans to finish the game. Onlookers immediately realized that they were witnessing a budding superstar's debut.

The onlookers were absolutely right. Nurtured by his father, coached by his 10-goal uncle, Quito Alberdi, his natural skill polished by another 10-goaler in the person of Roberto Cavanagh, Franky Dorignac soon was playing with and against the high and the mighty in the top tournaments. Characteristically, Franky gives credit to those three mentors as the architects of his success in the game of polo.

Franky's first win in a major championship occurred in 1956 when he took Hurlingham's Open with a Tortugas team that included Andino Grahn, Horacio Baibiene and Carlos Torres Zavaleta. He would go on to win the tournament again in 1960, with his two brothers and Roberto Cavanagh; in 1967 with Teófilo Bordeu in Cavanagh's place; in 1969 as a member of the Argentine national team; and in 1973, the year of Santa Ana's Triple Crown.

The late 1950s saw two strong teams carrying the Tortugas orange banner. The three Torres Zavaleta brothers—Carlos and the twins, Jorge and José María—had represented the club for several years, completing the squad with different players: Horacio Baibiene, Bernardo Cavanagh, Andino Grahn, Ernesto Lalor and Nicolás Ruiz Guiñazú, as well as Franky and his brother Gastón. A new Tortugas was formed by Franky, his younger sibling Gastón, Roberto Cavanagh, and Franky's uncle, Enrique Alberdi. Once more, fate hit the Dorignac family

One of the very best teams ever, Santa Ana took the Triple Crown in 1973. Left to right: Francisco Dorignac, Daniel González, Héctor Merlos and Gastón Dorignac represented the club from Villa Valeria (courtesy Museum of Polo and Hall of Fame).

hard when Quito Alberdi was killed in a plane crash in the same month as the 1959 Argentine Open.

By then, at the age of 19, Franky was already a magnificent player, a great striker of the ball, though not as great a player of matches as he would become later. Enter Roberto Cavanagh. Roberto, the giant from Venado Tuerto and the team's senior statesman, became Franky's next mentor in his ascent to the polo world's summit. Roberto expressed the thought that it would take three years for the team to gel. It took just one year. Marcelo Dorignac, the youngest of the polo-playing brothers, had joined the team. With the younger brothers up front, Roberto at pivot and Franky in his customary back position, Santa Ana — as the team was now called — was leading eventual Open champions El Trébol when Marcelo had a spill and was unable to continue. Regrettably, no adequate substitute being available, Santa Ana had to default.

Roberto Cavanagh retired after the 1961 high-goal season, just at the dawn of the longest rivalry in Argentine polo. Coronel Suárez and Santa Ana, or Santa Ana and Coronel Suarez (to keep everyone happy), shared the leading role on Argentina's polo stage for the next twenty-plus years. There would be the occasional interloper, such as the Lalors' La Alicia, Eduardo Moore's Nueva Escocia, and most notably, Mar del Plata, led by the classy Gonzalo Tanoira, with his brother Jorge, Alfredo "Negro" Goti and Juan José Alberdi. In their struggle to remain competitive, Mar del Plata also called upon Alfonso and Gonzalo Pieres, Alberto Goti and Julian Hipwood at different times. Los Pingüinos, the Braun Menéndez family team, presented at times Sinclair Hill to reinforce their own band of Braun Cantilos, Braun Estrugamous and Braun Lasalas, all to little or no avail. The two "monsters" were just too much, as the British Commonwealth team discovered in 1966 and the American international squad found out in 1969.

Dorignac's international polo travel began very early in his career, in 1954. Taking his own ponies most of the time, Franky has played at Deauville and Bagatelle in France, winning, among other trophies, the 1960 Deauville Coupe d'Or. He did likewise in Spain, winning the Copa de Oro at Sotogrande. Other countries where he has shown his skill include Peru, Colombia, Chile, Brazil and Mexico. In the United States, Franky participated in the World Cup at Oak Brook, near Chicago, as a member of the Mexican Olazábal family's team Rancho Portales.

In 1963, Francisco Dorignac was raised to 10-goal handicap. He joined Juan Carlos Harriott as the only two ten-goalers in Argentina and one of only four in the world, together with Bob Skene and Cecil Smith. Rarified atmosphere, to say the least.

A new edition of the Cup of the Americas was held in 1966. Argentine selectors picked Franky to play at back, with the Heguy brothers and Juancarlitos Harriott completing the team. As related in his profile, Alberto Pedro Heguy sustained a fractured wrist and his number 1 spot was taken by Gastón Dorignac. It was an evenly contested series. The American squad, led by Norty Knox and completed by Dr. Billy Linfoot, Roy and Chico Barry, fought tooth and nail in the first match; leading the game at times, it eventually went down 10–6. For the sec-

Trophy presentation of the 1969 Cup of the Americas at Palermo (left to right): Franky Dorignac, Gastón Dorignac, Juancarlitos Harriott and Horacio Heguy collect the spoils of victory (courtesy Museum of Polo and Hall of Fame).

ond game, Argentina reversed Gastón Dorignac's and Horacio Heguy's positions. The final goal differential was the same, 14–10. For the American team, it was the same story, to be repeated years later: An even match-up, except for one or at most two chukkers in the game, when the Argentines would unleash a seemingly unstoppable barrage of goals.

Only recently, Francisco Dorignac was asked to compare the 1966 and 1969 series. His answer was unequivocally that the 1966 competition had been, by far, the most difficult.[5]

That great sportsman, the late Northrup Knox, tried once more three years later.[6] This time the American team presented the young star Bennie Gutierrez at number 1, Knox at number 2, Dr. Linfoot at pivot and Chico Barry at back. Argentina enlisted the victorious 1966 team, keeping Gastón Dorignac at number 2. The first game's final score, 12–6, reflects the Argentine team's power.

There were no changes for the second match; however, in the third chukker, Chico Barry injured his thumb in such a way that he was unable to continue. The Americans were forced to juggle their lineup. Ray Harrington was called in as a substitute, taking Gutierrez's place, Bennie moving to the back position. Chico Barry's absence—the Argentine press called him "a back with many carats"—plus the forced positional changes were too much for the team to absorb.[7] The game became one-sided, with the local representation ending up the winners, scoring 18 goals against six for the visitors.

The rivalry between Santa Ana and Coronel Suárez has become legendary in the annals of polo in Argentina. Starting in 1961, and until 1982, those two clubs met in the Argentine Open final game, or in the decisive match when the round-robin format was the norm, every year except 1978, when Santa Ana did not participate in the high-goal season.

In 1971, Santa Ana achieved its ultimate goal by winning the Argentine Open Championship. Teófilo "Toti" Bordeu, Gastón Dorignac, Daniel González and Francisco Dorignac formed the team that won all four matches in the round-robin at Palermo. They defeated La Alicia (Carlos Jáuregui, Héctor Merlos, replaced by Alfredo Lalor, Luis Lalor and Eduardo Moore) 12–4; Magdala (Jorge Marín Moreno, Ricardo Díaz Dale, Julian Hipwood and Juan José Díaz Alberdi) 11–3; and in the final match, Coronel Suárez (Juan José Alberdi, Alberto Heguy, Juan Carlos and Alfredo Harriott) by just one goal, 10–9.

Their second Open title was in 1973, when they beat the full Coronel Suárez team 8–6. Gastón Dorignac, Héctor "Cacho" Merlos, Daniel Gónzález and Francisco Dorignac also took the so-called Triple Crown, taking the Tortugas and Hurlingham championships as well.

The third and last Abierto crown obtained by Santa Ana was in 1982, when Memo Gracida joined the team in González's place at number 3. Once more, they faced Coronel Suárez in the decisive match; it was, however, a new Coronel Suárez. Because of Horacio Heguy's and Juancarlitos Harriott's retirement, Luis Eduardo Lalor, Alberto Heguy, Alfredo Harriott and Celestino Garrós wore the triangular blue and red. The final score was 16–13. And so ended Santa Ana's trajectory in high-goal polo's firmament, in a blaze of glory, and rightly so. A superb team, they were unlucky to be contemporaries with the best polo machine ever seen. It speaks a lot for Santa Ana that for two decades they were able to face Coronel Suárez on equal terms, losing several finals by the whisker of one or two goals. It was that close, year in, year out. How many teams would have shown Santa Ana's resilience during that long span? It was a glorious epoch in Argentine polo.

Credit must be given to Franky Dorignac, Santa Ana's undisputed leader, for his pluck and never-say-die attitude. The winner was the public, who filled Palermo to the rafters to enjoy, support, and commiserate or exult, in a true celebration of the game of polo at its best.

Francisco Dorignac showed early in life his aptitude for leadership. Those who know him well profess to have noticed the symptoms which showed the flames leaping up within.[8] Not in vain has he always been considered a *cacique*—chieftain would be the closest translation.

Franky became a director of Tortugas Country Club in 1964, and president in 1980, a position he still holds. There are no other likely candidates visible on the horizon. When Franky took office, the club was located on 70 hectares; under his leadership it has expanded to 270 hectares, further development being hindered by natural boundaries. However, he is quick to give credit to his supporting staff.

In 1989, Dorignac was elected, without opposition, president of the Argentine Polo Association. He had overall support from the polo clubs. He considers his greatest accomplishment at the association's helm the nutriment of the game in the country's interior regions, which culminated with the creation of a national tournament, the Campeonato del Interior, held by rotation at different clubs in the hinterland. It proved to be an unquestionable success.

When asked about the best foreign players he ever saw, Franky does not hesitate in his response: "Bob Skene, Doc Linfoot and Memo Gracida." With fraternal affection, he mentions his brother Gastón as a super player: "The best number 2 there was."

Regarding polo ponies, he expresses a preference for mares, but mentions that he had three great geldings. His best ever pony was La Delicia, bred by Dowling. Franky recalls that he played her in the finals at Hurlingham and Palermo three full chukkers (first, fourth and eighth): "Really, she played on her own. She was perfect. I can tell you that her qualities of a soft mouth, her speed and her timing, were second to none."[9]

Along his extended career, Franky never modified his seat, the stirrup leathers' length, the mallet characteristics, or the head's shape or weight. Known for years as one of the few top players who did not wear knee guards—Joe Barry is another example—he finally relented after an accident and began to use them.

Always the impeccable sportsman, Dorignac describes the rivalry between Santa Ana and Coronel Suárez as "a competition between gentlemen, the last one in amateur polo."

In 2005 an unusual situation developed prior to what had been a routine rite of passage: the filling of the post for the presidency of the Argentine Polo Association. For more than half-a-century the continuity of leadership was guaranteed by a consensus between the outgoing council and the clubs. The last election had been contested in 1949, between Juan José "Silvestre" Blaquier and Enrique Alberdi, the latter being the winner. Two candidates, Guillermo Alvarez Fourcade and Ramón Franco, made known their intention to run early in the game. Neither received overwhelming support. When Franky was asked about running again, he demurred. Eventually, it became a three-horse race, won by Dorignac with the support of a clear majority of the polo clubs.

Francisco Dorignac in his prime, playing in the United States. The 1977 World Cup at Oak Brook, near Chicago (courtesy Museum of Polo and Hall of Fame).

After the results were made public,

in a show of statesmanship, Dorignac offered posts in the new council to his erstwhile opponents. With that generous offer, peace and tranquility returned to the high echelons of Argentine polo. The old warrior had mellowed, and, coincidentally, gained political stature. Asked to compare his first and second terms, Franky says, "They are totally different. Other times, new organization. There have occurred significant changes. The growth of professionalism. The quantitative and qualitative rise in the level of play, both at the national and international level. It's a whole new challenge."[9]

Dorignac sees as the main problem facing the game in Argentina the increased demands on the organizational framework to cope with the continuing requests posed by the explosive growth of the game, including during the autumn season. Always the pragmatist, Franky tackles each problem seriously and without delay, with the support of what he calls "a deluxe team at the Asociación Argentina de Polo."

Franky does not contemplate an early resumption of the series for the Cup of the Americas. Wryly, he states, "It is safely well-kept in a trophy cabinet at the Asociación Argentina de Polo."

The man Guillermo Gracida Jr. referred to as "one of the most admired and respected players of all time" is still going full-blast, his incredible energy harnessed with the perspective of many years' experience in the higher councils of the game, as well as his knowledge of the game as played at top level. Like rugby football, the game of polo is well-served by administrators that have been active players, preferably good players. Franky Dorignac is a prime example of a player—a superstar in his case—who unselfishly gives back of his experience for the good of the game.

The gentleman who was awarded three Silver Olimpias for polo—the top sporting award in Argentina—for the best player of the year, continues to strive for the betterment of the game in his country.

When asked about his best remembrances about the game, Franky simply answered "The friends I made and the help they gave me during difficult moments."[10]

Notes

1. Field Marshal Alan Francis Brooke, 1st Viscount Alanbrooke of Brookeborough (1883–1963), an artilleryman, had a distinguished military career, rising to become the professional head of the British Army during World War II.

2. Enrique "Quito" Alberdi (1949–1952), captain and number 3 on Coronel Suárez and Venado Tuerto teams, took 12 Argentine Open Championships between 1934 and 1957, reached a 10-goal handicap in 1943, was an alternate in the 1936 Olympic Gold Medal team when a throat infection prevented him from playing. He also skippered international teams in the World Series at Beverly Hills in 1949, the World Championship in that same year at Palermo, the 1950 Cup of the Americas and the Pan American Games in 1951. Known for his "never give up attitude," Quito Alberdi took countless tournaments. His celebrated mare Marionette was a three-time winner of the Lady Susan Townley Cup. Alberdi was president of the Argentine Polo Association from 1949–1952. He was killed near Saladillo, Buenos Aires Province, while flying his own aircraft in foul weather. It is interesting that Quito Alberdi was a mentor of both Juancarlitos Harriott and Franky Dorignac.

3. The founders were señor Maura y Gamazo and Baron de Güell, two Spanish gentlemen. Tortugas started in the 1930s the concept of a country club, offering a beautiful clubhouse, chapel, golf course, swimming pool, equitation ring, stables and several polo grounds. The club's name, initially Las Tortugas (The Turtles), was suggested by Mrs. Maura y Gamazo, because while watching the initial games she felt the players were moving like turtles. A Tortugas team took the Argentine Open in 1935.

4. The High School polo championship was first played at Tortugas in 1936, Colegio Champagnat being the first winner. The Copa Santa Paula was presented in 1951 by the three Reynal brothers, José, Juan and Martín, in memory of their mother, Paula Llauró de Reynal. Their team, Santa Paula, took three Argentine Open Championships, and the 1930 Pacific Coast Open and the U.S. Open in 1931.

5. Interview with Francisco Dorignac, 14 July 2006.

6. Northrup R. Knox (1928–1998), an 8-goal handicap player, was a finalist in the U.S. Open and took the 20-goal Championship and the Butler Handicap. His ponies Rotallen and Raggamuffin were awarded the Hartman Trophy; Ragamuffin was Best Playing Pony in the 1969 Cup of the Americas. Knox was U.S.P.A. Chairman in 1966–1970 and was inducted into the Polo Hall of Fame in 1994.

7. *Centauros*, December 1969.

8. Interview with Dr. Enrique Braun Estrugamou, 12 December 2005.

9. Interview with Francisco Dorignac, July 2006.

10. *Ibid.*

Part IV

Shakers and Movers

Introduction

This part presents widely divergent personalities who nevertheless had enormous influence on the game in their day. We have Lord Cowdray, without doubt the savior of polo in England in the dismal economic climate during the immediate period after 1945, the year the war was won. Also in Britain, a polo player's daughter, Claire Tomlinson, challenged the establishment and won, earning for herself the everlasting endearment of the distaff side and the grudging admiration of her opponents in the mighty struggle for gender equality on the polo field.

In America, John T. Oxley was the prototype of the responsible sponsor: a respectable player, financially solvent, fair in his dealings, certain in his objectives, and always putting the game's best interest ahead of the rest. A born winner, his expedition to England was rewarded with Cowdray Park's Gold Cup. His team, Boca Raton, is one of only two American teams—Hap Sharp's Greenhill is the other—to take home Britain's top polo prize.

South Africa's political isolation for many years had a devastating effect upon many of its sporting endeavors. Mike Rattray was able to adjust to change and maintain a semblance of international relationships with other countries. He served well both his country and the game. Kerry Packer changed the face of polo on three continents like no one else had done. Australia, his home country, Britain, Argentina, and to a lesser extent, the United States, were the recipients of his influx of money, and, at times, of his bulldozing tactics in the pursuit of winning.

Argentine Marcos Uranga closes this section. His splendid vision of a functioning international body regulating the sport became reality, confounding the skeptics and comforting those who aspired to see a unified code of rules.

In many ways, these half-dozen personalities represent a true mix of what has happened to the world of polo in the last sixty years.

The International Scene After World War II

May, 1940. The British Expeditionary Force is slowly retreating towards the French port of Dunkirk, to be evacuated to English soil by the Royal Navy and a motley collection of civilian vessels. Among the 300,000 soldiers there is a captain in the Sussex Yeomanry at the wheel of a scout car. He is temporarily relieving his exhausted driver, who rests in the passenger seat. A German shell hits the vehicle, killing the soldier and inflicting severe wounds to the officer's left arm. The gods of war have chosen that John Cowdray should live.

Fast forward to October 1949. The Argentine Polo Association has organized its most ambitious international season ever. Invited teams from Chile, England, Mexico and the United States gathered for a two-month, high-goal polo festival. The inaugural match on number one field at Palermo features Chile and England; the red rose wins the game. This was the first post-war international victory for England. The man who made the journey a reality was John Cowdray.

The orange-shirted Cowdray Park also entered the Argentine Open, Peter Dollar taking Traill's place at number 1. Maj. Dollar, a long-standing Cowdray Park member and, in his own words, "an unashamed individualist," gave his German captors a hard time, eventually ending up in Colditz Castle, a prison reserved for the most recalcitrant P.O.W.s. Sadly, Cowdray Park went down to Los Indios in an early round.

The Chilean team was also defeated, but La Herradura, presenting four Gracida brothers, made it to the semifinals, where they lost to the eventual winners, Venado Tuerto. Meadow Brook (Pete Bostwick, Peter Perkins, Alan Corey and Devereux Milburn Jr.) easily disposed of the Argentine military team in its debut, only to fall down to an inspired La Concepción team, the "giant killers."

After the Open and a 30-goal Inter-American series between Argentina and the U.S., the grand finale was the first, and so far the only, World Championship with no handicap limit. Argentina, Mexico and the United States participated in a round-robin. Bob Skene played for the U.S., replacing Milburn. The American team defeated the Mexicans, but went down to Venado Tuerto, representing the host country, in the final match.

Once more the Americans visited Palermo, the following year. Carrying the Bostwick Field banner, they reached the Open's final game, but were defeated in the fourth edition of the Cup of the Americas. This most prestigious international competition was held again in 1966 and 1969 in Argentina, when Norty Knox brought over American teams.

The American team for the 1979 edition was sponsored by Steve Gose, only to go on to defeat. And the same thing happened the following May, when Gose hosted the tournament at his Retama polo complex in San Antonio.

The Westchester Cup, dating back to 1886, was revived only in 1988, albeit in a haphazard way. Unable to reach an agreement with the Hurlingham Polo Association, the U.S.P.A. elected to invite an Australasian team to dispute the historic trophy. A two-match series took place in Lexington, Kentucky, the outcome being decided on aggregate goals. In the event, the United States took the trophy by just one goal, 10–6 and 6–9.

The true Westchester revival was in 1992, when the United States (John Gobin, Adam Snow, Owen Rinehart, Rob Walton) defeated England at Guards Polo Club. Five years later, Britain took its revenge at the same venue, winning the Westchester Cup for the first time since 1914. William Lucas, New Zealander Cody Forsyth, Howard Hipwood and Andrew Hine were the day's heroes.

These are some examples of the generosity exhibited by polo players in support of the game. Without the support of the Knox family and Steve Gose, there would have not been a Cup of the Americas after 1950.

Patron Polo

"Patron polo" is a fact of life in the current game. In reality, it has been around for over a century. The Maharaja of Patiala, the subject of a well-known *Vanity Fair* caricature, was an early exponent of the genre. As far back as 1899 his two teams, Patiala I and Patiala II, reached the finals of the Indian Open Championship. In an exhibition of raw power by the patron, the final match did not take place because the maharaja wished that both teams have their names engraved on the trophy.

Another patron was a Frenchman, Count Jean de Madré. His Tigers team played tournament polo in America, England, India and continental Europe. One of his teams was good enough to take the 1923 Coronation Cup. From the gold-embroidered silk jerseys to the impeccable turnout of his pony string, every detail had to be perfect. The good Count Jean insisted that in each chukker the players be mounted on ponies with identical colors, such as bays in the first, chestnuts in the second and grays in the third.

Laddie Sanford indulged himself in high-goal polo for close to thirty years. His Hurricanes team took the U.S. Open in the 1920s, 1930s and 1940s, and Deauville's Gold Cup in 1952, a longevity seldom achieved by a patron's team. Laddie was able to recruit top players, most notably Irish-born Capt. Pat Roark, a 10-goal handicap player. Sanford's pony string was reckoned to be the best because he never hesitated to pay top price for the top available ponies.

The Maharaja of Patiala was handicapped by his enormous weight; on the other hand, both Laddie Sanford and Johnny de Madré were good players, the Frenchman playing off 5-goals and the American reaching 7-goals in his prime.

After World War II, other enthusiasts followed Lord Cowdray's lead in supporting the game in England. The list is long: Alfie Boyd-Gibbins with Silver Leys; Maj. Archie David's Friar Park at Henley; Arthur Lucas at Woolmers Park; Eric Moller and his Jersey Lilies; Sir Evelyn de Rothschild's Centaurs; Polo Cottage, Mike Holden White's own, and Ronnie Driver's San Flamingo.

As the level of play improved, new names appeared, notably the Vestey's Stowell Park and Foxcote; Lord Brecknock's Pimms (the first touch of commercialism); Alexandre Ebeid's Falcons; Galen Weston's Roundwood Park and Maple Leafs, and the successful Tramontana, five-time Gold Cup winner under the aegis of Anthony Embiricos. These sponsors were all big hitters, but they pale in comparison with, once more, Kerry Packer.

The 1990s witnessed the Australian invasion: The price of anything polo went up in a giant kangaroo leap. Few teams could muster the horsepower needed to keep up with Ellerston, either Black or White. Nevertheless, Urs Schwarzenbach's Black Bears, John Manconi's Alcatel, Brook Johnson's C.S. Brooks and Hubert Perrodo's Labegorce made the decade interesting and competitive.

As the millennium turned, another Australian made his mark: Rick Stowe, with his appropriately named Geebung. He was joined by Ali Albwardi's Dubai, which seems to have the edge at present. However, the competition is tough. There is a new Ellerston; Black Bears remain strong—they took the 2006 Gold Cup; and a 20-team entry at Cowdray Park all speak wonders for the current state of the game in the United Kingdom. In addition, a new all-professional tournament, the British Polo Championship at Coworth Park, is breaking new ground and may become the matrix for the future of high-goal polo.

In America, Carlton Beal, Peter Brant, the Busch brothers, Tim Gannon, John Goodman, Steve Gose, Glen Holden, S.K. Johnston, Fred Mannix, Russ McCall, the Oxley family, Hap Sharp and Mickey Tarnopol have made tremendous contributions to the sport's growth.

Florida has become the epicenter of American polo during the winter season. Palm Beach's beautiful people, including models, polo enthusiasts and movie stars, gather every Sunday with the regular crowd of players, patrons and sponsors, coaches, grooms, reporters, family, friends, administrators, photographers and club staff.

The magnificent Isla Carroll complex built by John Goodman is unrivalled as a club in the world. No other private institution can match its combination of a comfortable stadium, number of top tournaments held—including the U.S. Open—and privileged location. Isla Carroll's next door neighbor, Outback, owned by Tim Gannon, nicely complements John Goodman's facilities.

The number of private grounds close by is astounding; only Long Island in the 1920s and

Pilar in Argentina, currently, bear comparison. Gillian Johnston's Bendabout, Neil Hirsch's Black Watch, Skeeter Johnston's Everglades/Skeeterville, Erich Koch's Jedi, Memo Gracida's La Herradura, Steve Van Andel's Orchard Hill, Bob Daniels' Pony Express, Tommy Lee Jones' San Saba, the Escobars' Santa Clara and Peter Brant's White Birch are some of the most noteworthy. And last, but certainly not least, Venezuelan Víctor Vargas's La Lechuza, which offers what most players consider the best polo grounds in the Palm Beaches.

Regrettably, Palm Beach Polo Club is just a shadow of what it was only a few years ago, and Gulfstream, which dates back to 1936, has fallen prey to developers and will host its final season in 2008.

In the rest of the United States, polo continues to grow unabatedly. Southern California, the Houston area, Chicago's suburbs, Wyoming, Saratoga, the New England states, Long Island and Lexington, Kentucky, the U.S.P.A.'s home, continue to provide a full schedule during the summer months. Aiken has undergone a welcome revival, and in Calgary, Fred Mannix continues to brilliantly support Canadian polo. The game in North America continues to thrive, thanks to its patrons.

The scenario has remained the same; the only change is that playing the game has become much more expensive. "Patron polo" will remain in America for the foreseeable future. With some notable exceptions—Peter Brant at 7-goals, the Orthwein twins, Peter and Steve, at five- and six-goals—most patrons hover around a one-handicap rating. The net result is that, outside of Argentina, a high-goal team is usually made up of three top players and the sponsor. This is an economic reality that will persist until corporations see the light and realize that the best polo is played by teams composed by four superior players. And while some elements in the ticket-paying polo crowd attend matches with the main objective being to see and be seen, the great majority still wish to watch the game, preferably a good one. The best games are provided by the best players. The gulf between play at the top Open Championships in Argentina, namely Tortugas, Hurlingham, the Abierto at Palermo, and the U.S. Open and Cowdray Park's Gold Cup—the most prestigious tournaments elsewhere—is so wide it defies description.

The origins of "patron games" can be traced to the game of cricket. While football frowned upon the idea of professionals and amateurs playing on the same grounds, the leisurely game of cricket encouraged participation by professional players. Association football—soccer—quickly developed into a professional sport at the top level, because the best amateur teams such as Corinthians, were out-played by the established clubs.

Rugby football—rugger—was different. The issue was not individual or team proficiency, but the thorny reimbursement for "broken time." Eventually, it led to the split between the Northern clubs, which formed the professional Rugby League, and the public schools' old boys Rugby Union. It took years for the by then supposedly amateur Rugby Union to bow to the realities of modern sport and go professional at the top level.

Cricket went its own way. In many cases, it was sponsored by members of the aristocracy and gentry who enlisted players, nominally their household employees, for their matches against similarly formed elevens. Patrons obtained peer recognition and personal satisfaction out of their support of, and active participation in, cricket matches. They had the leisure time needed to improve their skills; therefore, they were able to participate meaningfully in teams composed mainly of professionals. It is interesting that contemporary cricket felt Kerry Packer's impact when he established World Series cricket. That revolution turned the ancient game upside down.

Money and Polo

We might wonder what John Watson would have made of the Stanford Financial U.S. Open or the Movistar Argentine Open Championships, or, for that matter, of the emergence of an entity known as the Polo Tour as a force to reckoned with by the Argentine Polo Association in deciding what polo will be in Argentina.

There is no way of knowing how Watson would have reacted to big money polo. One-hundred years later, John Watson would likely struggle to recognize polo, with its high-profile characters and plush corporate images. It is also likely that he would have scorned and then ignored it. But it is also possible he might have opted, like many others, to take a comfortable ride on its economic chariot. The past, after all, is another planet, a place where things were done differently. His day, his era, was very different from the modern one. What would he have thought of Kerry Packer threatening to take to court the successor to his own Hurlingham Polo Committee?

Some years ago, the amateur code of polo, a world of pleasure combined with danger, funded by private means, crossed an invisible line, making the change from sport to business, from friendly competition to winning no matter what. That day, something about high-goal polo changed forever.

Gender Equality on the Polo Ground

For many years after the introduction of the modern game any thoughts of women's participation were delayed by female attire, Victorian and Edwardian unspoken codes of propriety and gentlemen's skepticism regarding ladies' talent to play polo. Their ability to ride was not questioned; it was the capability to hit the ball and withstand the hurly-burly nature typical of early matches. On the other hand, feminine presence at field-side was, and still is, a welcome attraction. The stalwart polo-player wife was expected to cheer on her husband's team, commiserate or celebrate after the game was over, and cut a radiant image if chosen to preside at the postgame ritual of presenting the trophies.

With the passage of time, charming ladies were not entirely satisfied just cheering and giving silver cups; they had trophy-winning intentions for themselves. The Roaring Twenties provided the background for the initial efforts by women to obtain their place on the polo grounds. Eleanor Sears had been a pioneer in New England. Then appeared the formidable sportswoman Marion Hollis, America's amateur golf champion, who was considered the best all-around woman athlete of the 1920s. She played on men's teams in Aiken, Long Island and California. Very wealthy, she was responsible for the creation of two of the world's best golf courses: Pasatiempo and Cypress Point. Another good player on the West Coast was Canadian-born Doreen Ashburnham, the only player to have received the George Cross, Britain's second highest decoration.

In England, Lady Priscilla Willoughby was reckoned to be the best player in the 1930s. Marjorie Lancaster toured England in 1936, playing with her husband, Oliver, on the Sayago team from Uruguay. Their path was followed after the war by Mrs. Philip Fleming, also known as Celia Johnson, D.B.E., who had a long career on the stage and the screen and took Cowdray Park's Challenge Cup; and Judy Forwood, from the Rugby polo family, who started playing in the 1930s and won the Warwickshire Cup. Another player of note is Lavinia Roberts Black, now playing at Cirencester, whose father, Sq. Leader Alan Roberts, had his own team, Maidensgrove.

Argentina saw its first all-female match in 1927 at Los Pingüinos; it was a family affair, where everyone, including the umpires, referee and timekeeper, were ladies related to the Braun Menéndez family. The best Argentine player was Pamela Greenshields, later Mrs. Sandy Storey, who was the first woman in the association's list of players in 1937; she later moved to Rhodesia. It is said that she was so strong that she could bend a horseshoe with her hands.

Progress towards equality was slow because men were mostly amused about what they thought were feeble attempts to imitate them. Although some good women players were known, the world of polo was still strongly masculine and mainly skeptical.

In the United States it was just plain difficult for women to play polo. Pansey Elisabeth Ireland used her initials P.E. to obtain a U.S.P.A. handicap rating; when this ruse was discovered, her name was promptly erased from the handicap list. Sue Sally Hale, a much better player than many men, had to hide her hair before matches for fear that someone would tell. Her daughter Sunny was the first woman to take the U.S. Open with Tim Gannon's Outback in 2000. Sunny's handicap was raised to 5-goals after the event, no chance to be a ringer. Canadian Julie Roenisch had been the first female to participate in the event, in 1992, and Gillian Johnston became the first patron to win the Open in 2002.

In England, while Claire Tomlinson was perfecting her skill in Argentina and Gloucestershire, great events were brewing. Peter Grace immigrated to Britain from New Zealand and started the Rangitiki Club, now Ascot Park, in Berkshire. His four polo-playing daughters quickly caught the public's eye and became recognized as good players. Pippa Grace is now the chairperson and prime mover of the International Women's Polo Association and her younger sister Victoria is one of England's top female players.

Mrs. Tomlinson's struggles to obtain the recognition that she richly deserved are described in her profile. When Carina Vestey became the first woman to win the Cowdray Park Gold Cup in 2003, Claire Tomlinson was vindicated.

Lord Cowdray: He Saved the Day for England

by Roger Chatterton-Newman

There can be no doubt that John Cowdray deserves the accolade of "father of the postwar renaissance of polo in the British Isles." There were, of course, others who contributed much—but Cowdray, the man and his club, became synonymous with the revival and subsequent development of the game.

Indeed, it is fair to say that, without his enthusiasm, guiding hand and unstinting generosity, polo would not have returned to the British playing fields as quickly as it did in those years of postwar austerity and retrenchment; neither would it have reached so high a level in so short a period of time.

Weetman John Churchill Pearson, subsequently 3rd Viscount Cowdray, was born on 27 February 1910 at Capron House, Midhurst,[1] a mellow old Jacobean building in the main street of the Sussex market town. A twin with his sister, Angela, he was the only son of the Hon. Harold Pearson and his wife, Beryl, a granddaughter of the 6th Duke of Marlborough. Through his mother, John was cousin to another celebrated polo player, Winston Churchill.

The year 1910 was important in Pearson family history. John's grandfather, the distinguished civil engineer Sir Weetman Pearson, Bt., who had bought the Cowdray estate two years earlier, was raised to the peerage as Baron Cowdray.[2] That summer, too, his eldest son and heir, Harold, founded Cowdray Park Polo Club. The original home team was known as Capron House, and the first ground to be laid out was the House Ground, in front of Cowdray House, followed quickly by the River and the now-famous Lawns grounds.

Harold Pearson (1882–1933) was the first member of his family to take up the galloping game, while a student at Oxford in 1900. He was a member of the university team in 1903, 1904 and, as captain, 1905. A Liberal Member of Parliament for Eye, Suffolk, from 1906 to 1918—at one time he and his father sat in the House of Commons together—Harold Pearson represented the Commons against a House of Lords team in the Harrington Cup at Ranelagh three times.

In those days, of course, the hub of British polo was London, with the principal tournaments taking place at Hurlingham, Ranelagh and Roehampton. Coinciding with the London social season, tournaments attracted thousands of fashionable spectators and, at one stage,

A Cowdray Park team in the early 1950s (left to right): John Lakin, John Cowdray, Daphne Lakin—Lord Cowdray's sister—and Maj. Geoffrey Phipps-Hornby, after winning the Tyro Cup in 1950 (courtesy Roger Chatterton-Newman, PQInternational).

about ten thousand polo ponies were said to be stabled in the capital. The Cowdray ponies would go up by rail, in special horse boxes, to Barnes Station, and from there grooms would lead them through the London traffic to their stables.

Only in August would ponies and players return to the country, hence Harold Pearson inaugurated the Goodwood Week tournaments at Cowdray Park as a sequel to the London season. Goodwood Week remains a popular fixture at the club.

The young John first played polo at the age of seventeen, in 1927, while staying at Westbury House on Long Island with Michael Phipps, an old family friend and one of the leading American players of his day. Having progressed from Eton to Christ Church, Oxford, he started to play in earnest, emulating his father in captaining the university team and also equaling Harold's feat of winning the Oxford University Steeplechase three years running. In 1932, his final year at Oxford, he won the Tyro Cup, then of course a Hurlingham tournament.[3]

Harold Pearson succeeded his father as 2nd Viscount Cowdray in 1927, after taking over the running of the estate eight years before. In 1931, to mark the coming-of-age of John, a polo match on the River Ground was part of the celebrations, and that same season father and son played together in a match at Hurlingham—the team name Cowdray Park had by now replaced that of Capron House. The following year they led the orange shirts to a narrow 5–41/2 victory over the 7th Hussars in the Bordon Tournament.[4]

Sadly, they were not to play together for long. In 1933, Harold Cowdray died after a short illness at the tragically young age of fifty-one. John succeeded to the title and estate, and soon proved himself an able administrator—and a good polo player.

Before the war, John kept about a dozen ponies in the Victorian stables at Cowdray House, including several owned by John Lakin, his future brother-in-law:

> Really, six were enough for me then [he recalled in later life], and I remember one season in London when we had to play seven match games in six days. We won them all and I still had only six ponies! I played a chukka on each and I must say that I didn't care which one I rode: they were all good. There used to be weekly auctions of polo ponies at Tattersall's in London before the war, but I think the highest price I ever paid in those days was £500—that was from a horse coper near Midhurst and I considered it to be expensive. At Oxford I used to buy from Jackman, a coper who would charge around £350 for a pony that was not quite finished. If it was no good, Jackman was always happy to take it back, which a lot of dealers would never do.[5]

In the spring of 1939, John Cowdray, newly elected to the council of the Hurlingham Polo Committee, went to the U.S.A. as nonplaying captain of the British team hoping to recapture the Westchester Cup—last won in 1914. Tragedy dogged the visit. In a railway accident in Nebraska, Cowdray's pony Queen's Decision was the sole fatality out of twenty-eight mounts, but worse was to follow.

During the opening game at Midwick, Pasadena, on 19 February, Captain Pat Roark, the stylish young Irish-born player who was playing on an American team, suffered a fall that was to cost him his life a few days later. His tired pony stumbled a minute-and-a-half after the bell rang, supposedly to end the chukka, and his death certainly overshadowed the rest of the tour, which ended with a comfortable American victory.

Back home, storm clouds were gathering. At the outbreak of war with Germany, John Cowdray—who had been a territorial officer in the Royal Artillery—was called up as a reservist and was commissioned in the Sussex Yeomanry. Cowdray House was taken over by the 506th Royal Army Service Corps, later to be replaced by a commando unit. The Fleet Air Arm moved onto what, after the war, would become polo fields at Ambersham, and Cowdray Park was ploughed as part of the war effort, possibly the first time in history that the turf had been turned there.

The summer of 1940 brought the evacuation of Dunkirk, where John Cowdray was severely wounded. He reached the beaches and, after waiting two days, was rescued, but his left arm was damaged so badly that it was amputated on his return to England. The story that his first words after the operation were "Thank God I won't have to play golf anymore," may well be apocryphal, although they sum up the dry wit for which he became well-known.

Despite the loss, he continued to play his part in the war as commander of the local Home Guard and later, when polo was resumed, he was to play up to medium goal, and then umpire, with the help of an artificial arm. His "contraption," as he termed it, was made with the help of the Roehampton Limb-Fitting Centre and his gun-makers, Purdey, and an integral part was a spring for which the correct deadweight was 75 pounds. This meant that John Cowdray had to maintain his correct weight but nothing was going to prevent him from playing polo again; although when peace came in 1945 the future of the game in Britain was far bleaker than it had been at the end of the Great War.

Polo in London was over for good, although Roehampton managed to retain one ground until 1955. The future, if indeed one existed, lay with the prewar country clubs of which Rugby in Warwickshire had been preeminent. Indeed, Rugby and Cowdray Park were among a handful of clubs to revive a polo calendar for the 1947 season, although it was to be Rugby's last for over half a century.

That 1947 season saw John Cowdray organizing three-a-side teams, initially for practice matches, and at the beginning of August a local newspaper was able to report a tournament for the first time since the war:

Teams competing in the American tournament are Cowdray, Henley, Friar Park, and Cotswold. On Tuesday night an exciting match between Cowdray and Friar Park resulted in a narrow win for the latter by 6 goals to 5.[6]

By enlisting three of his five sisters, and brothers-in-law John Lakin and Alistair Gibb, as regular players, John Cowdray ensured that Cowdray Park was back in business. He still had ten or more ponies after the war and brought in the near-legendary Harold Freeborn as Master of Horse. Cameron, the head gardener, somehow returned the polo grounds to their former glory and for Goodwood Week 1948 no less than seven teams competed for the Cowdray Park Challenge Cup, at that time the premier tournament.

Among the spectators were Argentine players Jack Nelson and Lewis Lacey, and so impressed were they by the standard achieved, in many ways from scratch, that they invited John Cowdray to make up a team to compete in Buenos Aires the following season.

The visit marked a major step in the recovery of British polo. Of course, the team, under John Cowdray's nonplaying captaincy, had a difficult task ahead and it was decided to keep the individual handicap of players at 6-goals, making a 24-goal aggregate. Even then, it should be noted, it was higher than any contemporary national squad. Those selected were Bob Skene, soon to become a 10-goaler in his adopted U.S.A., Eric Tyrrell-Martin and Humphrey Guinness, two of the great prewar performers, and John Lakin. Tyrrell-Martin, a British Airways Oversea Company official in Cairo, broke his ankle on the day he was due to fly out to join the team, and his place was taken by John Traill.

Lord Cowdray and his Land Rover — for long a familiar sight in Midhurst (courtesy Roger Chatterton-Newman, PQInternational).

The tour was a tremendous success, and although Argentina ran out the ultimate winners, the British defeated Chile 12–9 in the inaugural match, a victory that shook the Chileans considerably. It was proof indeed that the British revival was well under way.

John Cowdray suggested a medium goal return visit for 1951 and Argentina was represented at Cowdray Park for the first time that year. The visitors, La Espadaña, were beaten in three matches by a team called Hurlingham — a landmark in polo history.

No matter how amateur some of those postwar matches may have seemed, John Cowdray was determined to build up a good team. He had brought fifty ponies over from Argentina to augment the stock surviving from before the war and, with Freeborn's expertise, a first-class string gradually emerged from the Cowdray stables.

By 1953, Cowdray Park was becoming the epicenter of British polo, and that season hosted the Coronation Cup, celebrating the coronation of Queen Elizabeth II, attracting a crowd of around 15,000. Writing in *The Field* the following season, Brigadier Jack Gannon, a formidable player in his day, was optimistic about the future:

> In Goodwood Week at Cowdray Park, the Holden White Cup for low-goal teams had 17 entries, and looking through the list I make out that 38 of the players never had a stick in their hands before the war.[7]

Fears that mechanization of the cavalry—prewar, the nursery for British polo—would see a serious reduction in players proved groundless. John Cowdray welcomed and encouraged anyone who was a proficient horseman to take up the game, hiring out ponies from his stables for £1 per chukker. He also attracted some of the world's leading players to make Cowdray Park their base during the season, notably the great Rao Rajah Hanut Singh, whose coaching was to prove inspirational for a new generation.

The icing on the cake was the inauguration, in 1956, of the Cowdray Park Gold Cup, later to develop into the British Open Championship, and today one of the world's top three polo trophies. It was, in effect, the successor to the prewar Hurlingham Open for the Champion Cup, and although the orange-shirted home team lost 9–4 to an Argentine squad led by Jorge Marín Moreno, the tournament proved beyond doubt that British players were back on form.

Rated at 4-goals in his heyday, John Cowdray was generous with his advice and with his time. He was a steward of the Hurlingham Polo Association—successor of the prewar polo committee—for fifty-five years until his retirement in 1992. He also served as chairman from 1947 to 1967 and chaired most of the H.P.A. committees during that time; and when he retired as steward, the post of president was created specially for him. In addition, played an instrumental role in helping the Duke of Edinburgh and Lord Mountbatten to set up the Household Brigade Club, now Guards, in Windsor Great Park.

Youngsters were not forgotten. The annual visit of the Pony Club to Cowdray Park, culminating every August with the National Pony Club Polo Championships, is very much a legacy of John Cowdray's willingness to encourage young people from varied backgrounds into the game.

Cowdray Park has always been known for its happy, country house atmosphere. It was, and remains, an atmosphere tempered with some of the best competitive polo in the world. That is John Cowdray's memorial.

Notes

1. According to various editions of *Debrett's Peerage*, he was born in London. However, Lord Cowdray himself told the author that his birthplace was Capron House.
2. Weetman Pearson (1856–1927) was created a Baronet in 1894 at the opening of the Blackwall Tunnel, one of his many engineering projects. He bought Cowdray from the Earl of Egmont in 1908, was created a baron in 1910 and advanced to viscount in 1917, for his work as president of the Air Board during the Great War.

3 Roger Chatterton-Newman and Derek Russell-Stoneham, *Polo at Cowdray* (London: Polo Information Bureau, 1992).

4. Bordon Polo Club was based at the military encampment of that name in Hampshire. It was not revived after the last war.
5. Chatterton-Newman and Russell-Stoneham.
6. *Southern Weekly News*, 2 August 1947.
7. *The Field*, 12 August 1954.

John Oxley: Patron and Benefactor

by Peter J. Rizzo

The following account is about the life and times of a remarkable man by the name of John Thurman Oxley (1909–1996). I knew John for more than twenty years, until a heart attack ended his life. He taught me some things about polo, much about business and a great deal about living life.

Polo dominated John T. Oxley's thoughts just about every moment of his life. He loved every aspect of the game and appreciated and admired those who had the courage to play one of the most dangerous games ever devised. From 1959 until his death in 1996 Oxley revived, designed, subsidized and managed one of the world's largest polo facilities. During that time he developed better ways to clean horse stalls, to irrigate and drain polo fields and to design and manufacture a safer polo helmet. When it came to playing a polo match, his attitude was: Ignore a seemingly unimportant detail, and the game will be lost. Reasoning that the better mounted team usually won the match, he raised and trained his own thoroughbred ponies. He played to win, and he worked hard to play hard.

Playing and winning major polo events until the age of 83 is a difficult feat—so unique an accomplishment that few players could possess the staying power or the dogged determination to challenge this longevity record. He pushed the age envelope for all polo players, confirming the notion that you can play the sport virtually, as he would say, "Until death you and polo part." His life, and inevitable demise, was testimony to one of his most frequently opined beliefs: There are only two ways to get out of polo, either you go broke or you die. His persistence and sheer willpower made it virtually impossible for him to go broke, so he was taken by the only thing with the power to do so, his own mortality. The final horn sounded for him, ending his struggle to defeat Father Time. He is sorely missed and because of so many he helped and motivated he will be long remembered.

Oxley's life and times personify the American workingman's dream. He was a pioneer in the liquefied natural gas industry, and his insight and hard work made him a wealthy man. Born in 1909 on a ranch near Bromide, Oklahoma, he was one of five children, all of whom had to work long hours to assist the family's hardscrabble livelihood. At age 16, he left the ranch for Tulsa, where he attended night school. For $100 a month, he was given the opportunity to work for Amerada Petroleum, putting in seven 13-hours days a week. While working for Amerada, he took a second job as an assistant to a photographer, in whose employ he later met his wife, Mary.

In 1935, Oxley joined Warren Petroleum, working his way up from a staff clerk to secretary of the company. His diligence, experience and successful track record paid off, and in 1948 he launched his own company, called Texas Natural Gasoline Corporation. Business was not good in those early years; overcoming $60 million of debt is a challenge for any man. For Oxley, however, it was the beginning of one success after another. His aggressive leadership facilitated a merger between Texas Natural Gasoline and Union Oil of Louisiana that resulted in Union Texas Petroleum. Oxley sold Union Texas to Allied Chemical in 1961, turning down an offer to become president of Allied. Instead, he and his son Jack formed Oxley Petroleum Company, which continues to be active in the oil and gas exploration business.

Leaving Jack to manage the business, Oxley, now in his forties, had ample time to pursue his polo passion. Only months before 1960, he rescued the financially ailing Royal Palm Sports Club in Boca Raton, eventually leasing and managing and substantially underwriting South Florida's only major polo center. The club's name, "Royal Palm," originated because the polo club was situated on the grounds of the Royal Palm Yacht Club. Oxley, along with his wife, Mary, and sons Tom and Jack, relocated the facility to its present location in 1978 and committed his body, mind and soul to the resuscitation and perpetuation of polo, especially the high-goal variety that he liked to play.

Oxley loved high-goal polo because he said it demanded more attention and ability from both horse and player. Unfortunately, few American high-goal players existed during the 1960s and early 1970s, and those few were scattered across the country. Oxley quickly developed

The 1966 National Twelve-Goal champions (left to right): Joe Casey, Tom Oxley, Mrs. Robert Beveridge presenting the prizes, the legendary Cecil Smith, Mrs. John (Mary) Oxley, John and Jack Oxley (courtesy Museum of Polo and Hall of Fame).

Royal Palm Polo into what he trademarked as "The Winter Polo Capital of the World" by encouraging and subsidizing young American talent as well as importing the best talent from Argentina, Mexico, England and New Zealand. In 1978, when Oxley invited Juan Carlos Harriott to play for his Boca Raton team, it signaled a new era of importing top foreign talent.

Oxley's polo fields became a nexus for world class polo in this country and for nearly two decades, the best polo players in the world made their winter homes near Oxley's club. Those players included 10-goal stars such as Memo Gracida, Gonzalo Pieres and Ernesto Trotz, and they all agreed that Oxley's ponies allowed them to reach their fullest potential. Gracida said, "John Oxley taught me the value of top ponies and proper organization. Without horses and planning you will be able to compete, but you will rarely win."

Oxley enjoyed the company of the polo players and polo pony trainers, as he got his start with player and horse trainer Kay Colee. Colee's grandson, Joey Casey, grew up to play professionally for the Oxley family and eventually Casey became the manager of Royal Palm Polo. Even after Oxley's playing days were behind him he continued to sponsor his Boca Raton team that competed in the club's Sunshine League, America's longest running high-goal league. When they were having a particularly bad afternoon, his halftime chat at the players tent allowed him a measure of vicarious interaction with his men on the field.

Oxley's commitment to polo was not limited to players, ponies and club facilities. He was the first to study the ways and means to make a safer polo helmet and manufactured the Oxley Polo Helmet, the first hard-shelled helmet with a face mask. To improve polo operations, he innovated new ways to irrigate and drain the polo fields using underground pipes that could pull water down to percolate and dry the fields, pumping water back into those pipes to water the turf roots. One of his not-too-successful innovations was a way to mechanize the cleaning of the box stalls. As he later conceded, this job basically required a pitchfork, wheelbarrow and someone paid to muck out the stalls.

For many years, his material contributions ensured the wellbeing of several Polo Training Foundation efforts such as the U.S.P.A. Professional Umpire Program and the matching fund to finance the head training umpire position. Royal Palm Polo was the initial test site for the training of the newly formed professional umpire corps and was the first club to employ their services. Oxley encouraged and supported numerous training publications such as *Linfoot on Polo*, and financed the U.S.P.A. Marketing Committee's filming of the Gold Cup for ESPN television. According to past P.T.F. chairman Dan Colhoun, Oxley was "the most generous supporter ever of the Polo Training Foundation, especially for our youth and new players."

The dream of a Museum of Polo and Hall of Fame was made a reality when John Oxley turned over the first shovel of sand at the Museum's Lake Worth location. Oxley friend Philip Iglehart's generous gift of the museum's site almost came to naught when funding for the museum slowed to a near standstill. Another friend, Carlton Beal, and Oxley matched endowment funding that allowed completion of the facility that is located in Lake Worth, Florida. Oxley was inducted into that Hall of Fame on 17 March 1994, and the following is displayed on his induction inscription:

> At the age when some players consider hanging up their mallets, John T. Oxley only picked his up for the first time. He has been a marvel ever since, playing high-goal polo well into his 80s and contributing immeasurably to the sport.
>
> During polo's lean years he stepped to the helm at Royal Palm Polo Club in Florida and nurtured the U.S.A.'s best polo, drawing on both American and foreign stars, pleasing throngs of fans while heralding the new era for the sport.
>
> The early safety helmet, the arena at Cornell University, American-bred polo ponies, generous support of polo causes, and opportunities for young players are part of John's illustrious record along with two U.S. Open Championships, the USPA Rolex Gold Cup, the Silver Cup

and Monty Waterbury titles, countless Sunshine League victories, and 27 medium-goal championships.

Leverett Miller, the first Polo Museum board chairman, said, "When John Oxley joined the Board of the National Museum of Polo, he instantly became immersed in all aspects. With his amazing youthful sense of adventure, he challenged us all to strive for a better museum, and he gave generously as an example to all in the polo community. He put us in position to begin construction and was innovative and supportive to the end."

Ten years after his death, the charitable organization founded by John T. Oxley, the Oxley Foundation, issued the Oxley matching challenge fund of one million dollars to raise two million dollars and has underwritten the major portion of building an expansion to the Museum to house the headquarters of the United States Polo Association.

Even beyond the seeming finality of death, Oxley continues to inspire others to contribute time, money and efforts to better and to preserve the sport of polo. Indeed, all who play this game can be grateful to John T. Oxley for his dedication, and we all miss his infectious enthusiasm for the sport.

Epilogue

Flying back home to Florida from John Thurman Oxley's funeral in Tulsa allowed me some moments for reflection about the man who had become my mentor. Oxley stressed simple, fundamental keys for achieving success. Set a goal, plan steps to achieve that goal and remember three important ingredients—persistence, persistence and persistence. Polo was, he believed,

John and Mary Oxley with the celebrated Best Playing Polo Pony, Cat-a-Joy (courtesy Museum of Polo and Hall of Fame).

the best way not only to keep the body strong but the mind alert. He credited his continued business success to his desire to play competitive polo well past his eightieth birthday. John made many business deals by handshake, even when that behavior became passé and downright foolhardy. He expected others to live up to the same standards he imposed on himself, whether it was closing a million-dollar deal or winning a polo tournament.

John Oxley played competitive polo well into his eighties (courtesy Gwen Rizzo, Polo Players Edition).

John Oxley and this writer had many things in common, most of all a love and respect for the game. John believed there was a difference between loving polo and respecting the sport. Just about everyone who takes up the game of polo loves to play, but for those who respect the game it means giving something back to the sport, be it time or money. John gave great measures of both, respecting everyone playing the game, and truly understanding and honoring the relationship between man and horse, especially a good horse.

Jack Oxley was right when he eulogized his father by saying, "Always a winner and accepting nothing less, he motivated many to perform at their very best. Firm opinion, he looked at issues as either black or white, and one found it reassuring to know exactly where he stood when agreeing or disagreeing."

It was comforting to have John as my friend, which reminds me of one of his favorite jokes:

Once there were two friends, Bob and Jim, who loved playing polo. One day Bob died. Several weeks later, his soul came back to earth to visit Jim. Bob said he had some good news and some bad news about heaven. The good news was, there was not only polo, but it was even better than on earth. Jim said, "Gee, Bob, that's great. But what's the bad news?" Bob said, "They have you scheduled to play in two weeks."

John T. Oxley may have played his last chukker here on earth; but there is little doubt he is now stabled in polo heaven, playing his great ponies such as Burrito and Cat-a-Joy. Knowing John, he may be expressing to the management, in no uncertain terms, his eternal concern for the care and maintenance of those fields and for the horses and people who play upon them.

Kerry Packer: Winning Whatever the Cost

by Chris Ashton

No one, least of all Kerry Francis Bullmore Packer—to the polo world, "KP"—would argue that as a player he had any lasting impact on the game. Mindful of his age when he started, 48, and physical condition at the time, his progress as a player was impressive. But two-goalers, as he was at his peak, do not change the way the game is played.

Jim Gilmore, manager since 1987 of KP's Australian polo complex, Ellerston, recalled:

> When KP came into the game he thought he could master it, but like the rest of us, he found that he couldn't. There are some things you don't master and polo is one of them. But he certainly tried. He could analyze the game; he loved it more than anyone else I know and everything about it—its horses, the way it's played, the people who played it, his desire to do better. And he made new friends. Polo brought him into contact with the sort of people who built this country and he respected them.
>
> He practiced long hours on the wooden horse. He always played No. 4 and had a good defensive backhand on both sides of the horse. He was difficult to get past. His strengths were his willingness to learn and his application to technique in hitting the ball. He rode well, and though he came down with a horse, he never fell off. He was always restricted by his fitness, especially his heart.

Packer's enduring legacy to polo was rather as a patron, a billionaire with the instincts of a high-stake gambler, a shrewd entrepreneur, a fervent devotee to all sporting contests, and with a gift for choosing able, loyal lieutenants to do his bidding, who in turn were generously rewarded.

In the polo complexes he developed in Australia, England and Argentina, he established new benchmarks of excellence in the quality of polo fields, breeding programs and horse management. He employed consecutively two of Argentina's leading ten-goal players, Gonzalo Tanoira followed by Gonzalo Pieres, who forged teams which enabled him and his son Jamie, playing with Ellerston White and Black respectively, to contest Australian and English medium- and high-goal tournaments from 1989 to 1999.

His glory days were the 1990s. In April each year he would hire a dozen of the world's best players and assign them to Australian teams, who mounted their guest players, to contest the high-goal Ellerston tournaments. In May he and Jamie would relocate to his West Sussex polo complex, Fyning Hill, for the three-month English season. One or other Ellerston team won the British Open Cowdray Gold Cup in 1994, 1995 and 1998; the Queens Cup in 1991, 1992, 1996, 1998 and 1999, and the Warwickshire Cup in 1990, 1993 and 1996.

In 1992, in partnership with Gonzalo Pieres, he founded Ellerston's Argentine counterpart, Ellerstina. In 1994, with Carlos Gracida, Mariano Aguerre and Adolfo Cambiaso, Pieres led Ellerstina to win the Triple Crown, the high-goal Tortugas, Hurlingham and Open trophies, and with Lolo Castagnola replacing Gracida, won the 1997 and 1998 Opens. The 2005 Argentine high-goal season saw generational change. Coached by Memo Gracida, Pieres's sons, Facundo and Gonzalito, 19 and 22, coupled with two youthful MacDonough brothers, represented Ellerstina, winning the Tortugas and Hurlingham trophies, but losing the Open by a single goal in extra time. KP chartered a Boeing 747 to watch the final, returning home two weeks before his death.

Whether he was bidding for rival media dynasties or television broadcasting rights for major sporting events, or lobbying Australian governments for special consideration for his own business interests, he attracted controversy. The same applied to his impact on polo. He was of a new generation of patrons unencumbered by custom or tradition, and rich enough to buy his way into the top of the game. English polo had always looked to patrons—the late Lord Cowdray comes to mind—as custodians of the sport. But the legacy of those who joined in the 1980s and 1990s altered radically the tactics of the high-goal game. Balanced teams of well-matched players gave way to teams typically comprising one low-goal patron, an under-handicapped English youngster and two high-goal Argentine professionals.

Kerry Packer changed the game's economics like no other individual in the history of polo. Photograph taken at Palermo, Buenos Aires (courtesy Mike Roberts).

The open, flowing, four-a-side team-game gave way to two-a-side contests of high-goal professionals on each team vying for possession of the ball while manipulating the right-of-way rule to entrap inexperienced opponents to commit fouls. Polo as a spectator sport has paid dearly. Ellerston teams embraced the new approach to their advantage but only as one of a legion of teams. Had KP never taken to polo, the new fashion would be no less powerfully entrenched.

No one can doubt KP's resolve to win, regardless of price or principle. Testimony to this was his response to an affray during the 1993 Queen's Cup. Ellerston captain Gonzalo Pieres, enraged after earlier brushes with an opposing player, fellow Argentine ten-goaler Sebastián Merlos, rode into his horse broadside. Heated abuse and blows followed. The incident occurred far from play, unseen by the umpires, but in full view of the grandstand.

The Hurlingham Polo Association appointed a stewards' committee that suspended Pieres for the rest of the season. KP thereupon instructed his lawyers to sue the H.P.A., with a promise to pursue the issue all the way to the House of Lords if need be, for interfering in his contract with an employee. A prominent English polo identity who volunteered to testify for the H.P.A. against Pieres then withdrew his support, coincidentally selling a horse to Ellerston. Strapped for cash to meet legal costs, the H.P.A. beat a retreat. Pieres's penalty was reduced to suspension until after the first game of the British Open Gold Cup, following which he resumed the captaincy of Ellerston. The dispute cost the H.P.A. several thousand pounds.

KP defied the ancient dictum for the ebb and flow of family fortunes, *Three generations shirtsleeves to shirtsleeves.* He was the second son of the third generation of a media dynasty founded by his grandfather, Robert, a journalist-turned-magazine manager and editor. Robert bequeathed to his son, Frank, the management skills and ambition to build a media empire, Australian Consolidated Press (ACP). From a national women's magazine launched in 1933 it added two tabloid newspapers, radio stations and in 1956 Australia's first television network, Channel Nine.

In his own era Frank Packer—later Sir Frank—kindled the public fascination and controversy that would one day be KP's lot. He was a media baron of the old school who directed senior editorial staff to define the great issues of the day to reflect his own perceptions of the national interest.

Sport and sporting contests were a shared passion with his second son. At age 24, Frank Packer was state amateur heavyweight boxing champion. From his father, Robert, he learned a love of sailing. On a scale comparable in its day with KP's financial commitment to polo, in 1962 and '70 he mounted unsuccessful challenges against the New York Yacht Club for the most prestigious of all yachting contests, the America Cup.

For 12 years before World War II he also played polo, a three-goaler at his peak. As with KP 60 years later, his height and weight required bigger, stronger mounts than for other players. One contemporary recalled his horsemanship as brave rather than brilliant; another likened the sight of Frank Packer in full gallop to a charging elephant—and about as dangerous.

Another passion that he bequeathed to KP was horse racing. Father and son enjoyed thoroughbred racing and won trophies at major metropolitan meetings, and gambling, whether on horses or cards, though it must be added that Sir Frank's bets were mere flutters compared with KP's betting sprees at racetracks and casinos.

KP's childhood years were privileged and miserable. He suffered ill health—polio, rheumatic fever and dyslexia, then unrecognized as a learning disorder—which consigned him to the bottom of the class. Following the one-night attack on Sydney Harbor by Japanese midget submarines in 1942, for his safety he was sent to successive rural boarding schools. His father inspired fear and awe rather than love. Having returned to Sydney from a boarding school more than 1,000 kilometers away, KP discovered he had forgotten his cricket bat and his father ordered him to return at once to collect it.

His unhappiness was exacerbated by his position as the second son. Much was expected of his older brother, Clyde. Little was expected of Kerry. Following his schooling, he joined ACP—as had Clyde—and was shunted from one department to the next to learn the family business from the bottom up.

His position suddenly changed after Clyde, CEO-in-waiting, quarrelled with his father, resigned, sold his shareholding and departed to live for the rest of his life in Los Angeles. All at once KP was heir apparent. Following his father's death he inherited Australian Consolidated Press.

To the astonishment of friends and family, he began to blossom, displaying hitherto unsuspected gifts for leadership and investment. Like his father, he surrounded himself with capable managers whose loyalty to him was handsomely reciprocated. But where Sir Frank lavished his considerable energy on his media empire, KP diversified into cattle stations, real estate, property development, engineering, construction, soft drinks, casinos and ski resorts.

Sir Frank died in 1974, leaving a family business valued at $100 million. When KP died on 26 December 2005, his business interests were valued at A$6.7 billion, confirming him as the richest man in Australia and, according to U.S. *Forbes* magazine's annual rich-list, 94th in the world.

Of the media assets inherited through ACP, KP focused on Channel Nine rather than the tabloid newspapers beloved by his father. KP distrusted the print media, and with reason. A Sunday newspaper of a rival media group impugned his reputation with suggestions of money laundering, drug smuggling and complicity in murder, leaked from a government-appointed royal commission. The Federal Government Attorney General eventually repudiated all royal commission's allegations against him, but he never forgot nor forgave the injustice done to his public reputation.

KP's interventions, whether in person or by phone, into Channel Nine program production, were the stuff of legend. A phone call was enough to cancel during broadcast a program incurring his displeasure. According to journalist Les Carlyon:

> He understood television better than anyone ever has in this country. He knew the old-age formula for success in the media, print or broadcasting. He was the richest man in the country—and he knew what taxi drivers and shirt workers were thinking and saying and above all, what they wanted to watch and read. He never looked down on his constituents.

Nothing focused him more than the nexus between television and sport. Whether as a player, spectator or proprietor of a television station with an eye to audience ratings, his commitment was unconditional. Sporting contests were for him the very essence of the human drama. Through sport he had found self-esteem, a release from an ignominy, induced by dyslexia, as the classroom dunce. In a rare interview with the Australian Broadcasting Commission in the early 1970s, he confided:

> I was hopelessly behind everyone else, and became a bit of laughing stock because of it. My method of fighting against that was to devote myself to sport, where I had more ability than most.... I used to play everything. I was never a great natural talent but I worked hard at all the sports I played and I became reasonably competent at all of them. There's no point in being stupid about it—I've got a good ball sense, whether it be from playing polocrosse to tennis, cricket or football, or whatever it is. I lived my life for my sport.

Channel Nine led Australia in filming sporting contests for television audiences. Gambler that he was, KP put money and reputation on the line in 1976 when he took on the close-knit world of international cricket. Rebuffed by the Australian Cricket Board when he sought the television broadcasting rights to Australian cricket, despite offering multiples of what the government-owned broadcasting authority, the Australian Broadcasting Commission, had paid for twenty years, he went to war.

He hired first-class cricketers from all the major cricketing nations and paid them handsomely to stage his own World Series Cricket. He changed the format from five-day test matches to one-day games, played under pressure. His innovations included new dress codes cricket teams; cricket played at night under lights, and in the filming and broadcasting of the sport for television audiences. World Series Cricket ultimately made peace with the international cricketing establishment and was dissolved, but the innovations pioneered by World Series Cricket continue to this day.

KP took up polo in 1986. The first the former Australian 10-goaler Sinclair Hill knew about it was a 3 A.M. phone call from London. It was KP declaring his intention to take up polo with Hill, whom he knew, teaching him the game. Hill asked KP whether he was drunk or off his head, and privately doubted that KP was fit enough, recalling how, on a visit to Ellerston, they had ridden from the homestead at walking pace, with KP gasping for breath and insisting, three gates out, that they turn back.

But KP was immovable. He was calling from a hospital, he explained, where he was recovering from an operation for suspected cancer. He weighed 238 pounds. His doctors had told him he must take up a strenuous, regular exercise to lose weight and relieve pressure on his heart. He wanted a combative sport, and decided on polo.

Hill flew to London to find Packer had discharged himself from the hospital. They attended tournaments at Windsor Park and Cowdray Park, and Hill introduced him to the good and the great of English polo. Courtesy of Prince Charles, whom Hill had coached, they called at Buckingham Palace to try the prince's wooden horse.

Back in Sydney under Hill's tutelage, KP started at dawn each day with stick-and-ball practice in Centennial Park. He installed one wooden horse in his harborside home and another at his beachhouse overlooking the Pacific. On weekends they would fly to Ellerston, a 20,000-acre cattle station inherited from KP's father, 250 miles north of Sydney. With stockmen and staff of a fledgling polo stables, practice chukkers were played on the Ellerston airstrip.

KP's commitment was at first tentative. If he felt too tired he would leave the field. Hill might order him back to the game and he would go, though with no great enthusiasm. Yet within 18 months he had succumbed to polo's siren call, fired by the idea of creating a world polo center at Ellerston. Two thousand acres were cordoned off for the Ellerston Polo Club. Hillsides were removed and levelled for seven polo fields; dams were built and sprinklers installed to water fields; a nearby brick factory was bought to expedite building a stables for 200 polo ponies, a clubhouse, 40 bungalows for guest players and their families and amenities for such sports as golf, tennis, squash, swimming, go-kart racing and a high-tech gym.

Hill's most enduring contribution to KP's polo career was to commend him to Jim Gilmore. Thirty-seven at the time, Gilmore hailed from one of Australia's foremost polo centers, Queensland's Darling Downs. Born into a small-holder farming family in the Darling Downs, Queensland, arguably Australia's strongest polo district, Gilmore had paid his way in polo "making" and trading in polo ponies, not to mention winning tournaments with his brother Stuart. KP hired him, his first and only polo manager, a partnership made in heaven.

KP's ill health, which dogged him to his end, came into dramatic focus in 1990 when he suffered a near fatal heart attack on the Warwick Farm Racecourse polo ground during the Australian Open. Ambulance officers in attendance, fortuitously equipped with a defibrillator, restored his heartbeat after eight minutes and he was whisked off by helicopter to one of Sydney's leading hospitals.

Summoned to his beside the following morning, Gilmore would recall their meeting as the most emotional moment of his life. "Jeez, KP," he started, "I thought you were gone yesterday, I thought you were f-----!" "No way, son," the big man replied as they shook hands. "Not yet, we still haven't won that f------ [British Open] Gold Cup."

Only 50 of the 900 ambulances in New South Wales (N.S.W.) were equipped with defibrillators, an electric heart-starting device. The N.S.W. premier accepted KP's proposal that if the state government installed them in half its ambulance fleet, KP would pay for the other half. Henceforth they were called Packer-Whackers.

Gilmore remains at Ellerston to this day, organizing teams and strings of ponies for tournaments at home and away. After an absence of seven years, in 2006 he despatched an Ellerston team, including Jamie Packer together with Gonzalo Pieres's sons, Facundo and Gonzalito—both ten-goalers, to play the English high-goal season. He also manages the Ellerston breeding program involving 60 mares. Ellerston-bred polo ponies surplus to its own requirements are exported all over the world, not least to mount the Ellerstina team for Argentina's high-goal tournaments.

No profile of KP could do him justice without mention of the fascination he exercised on the Australian imagination. Witness the disparate public figures among the 1,800 who attended his state-funded memorial service at the Sydney Opera House seven weeks after his death: prime ministers, past and present, Hollywood actors, sporting champions and officials of every stripe—not least the Australian cricket team, socialites, billionaires and school choirs conscripted to sing the national anthem and its World Cricket Series counterpart, "C'mon, Aussie, C'mon."

"The Big Fella" in Ellerston White's colors (courtesy Mike Roberts).

Like Sir Frank before him KP inspired fear and loathing, awe, admiration and affection. His passion for sport and gambling, his blunt turn of phrase, his disdain for the arts and the world of ideas endeared him to "ordinary" Australians, while alienating him from many of the so-called hattering class, his shortcomings compounded by his success and, indeed, pride, in minimizing his taxable income.

Of the acres of newsprint published after KP's death reflecting on his life and its significance to Australia, two passages impress me as distilling the essence of the man. Commissioned by the ACP-owned magazine *The Bulletin* to contribute his thoughts to a commemorative issue following KP's death, Les Carlyon (quoted previously) wrote:

> Packer was big and fleshy and direct of speech. He bustled and barged and teased. His wit was waggish and he didn't try to be Delphic. He had an idiom that was all his own. If you wrote down what he said, the dialogue would be sprinkled with italics.... When he was feeling good Kerry made John Wayne's screen characters seem wishy-washy. He was quick to detect humbug and even better at declaiming, in three or four words, that he had done so.

For the *Sydney Morning Herald*, John Huxley characterized him as "an outsize example of that public figure beloved by obituarists, a man of contradiction: brutal but charming, loud but shy, powerful but vulnerable, greedy but generous, hurtful but dryly humorous, omnipotent but lonely."

Neither journalist was employed by KP's media group.

Mike Rattray: Player, Promoter and Environmentalist

by Susan Reeve

To paraphrase Charles de Gaulle's famous assertion, "Je suis La France," when it comes to Mike Rattray the South African polo community would have no hesitation in saying "He is Polo." His contribution to the administration of the sport in that country has resulted, quite simply, in putting South Africa on the world polo map.

Michael Loring Peter Rattray was born in Durban in 1932. His family had been in South Africa for many generations. His great grandfather, William Clark, had emigrated from England in 1840 and lived on a 50-acre farm called Camp Hill—beyond the Westridge Tennis Stadium in Durban—that is now known as William Clark Gardens. He was a renowned wagon-maker in Durban, and Camp Hill was so called because it was the first overnight stop for the ox wagons traveling from Durban to Johannesburg.

William Clark and his wife had four daughters, only the youngest of whom, Ethel, married. She met Major Peter Miller Rattray, who had come to South Africa in the late 19th century. He joined the 1st Scottish Horse Regiment and fought with them in the Boer War, winning a D.S.O.[1] in Moedwill in the Western Transvaal. Maj. Rattray served with the regiment in Bulawayo and in the First World War. Eight days before the armistice his leg was badly shot up and he walked with crutches for the remainder of his life, until he died of malaria at 72, in Kwambonambi.

Peter and Ethel had three sons: Loring, Sylvester—known as "Pud"—and Colin. Craig Rattray, Pud's son, played polo for South Africa for many years. Loring, Mike's father, was born in 1903, grew up in Zululand and worked on Natal Estates in the sugar plantations. William Campbell, head of Natal Estates, used to invite staff to MalaMala Property in the Eastern Transvaal to shoot for a week in winter and this was where Loring was introduced to the Kruger Park bushveld. In 1936 Loring moved to Kwambonambi to join his father on the sugar and timber farms. He was responsible for introducing the giant pulp milling operation SAICCOR to South Africa from Italy.

Loring leased MalaMala Property, which was bought in 1964 by Mike, who took full control of the property in 1976 when his father died.

Mike's polo career started when he was a 14-year-old Michaelhouse scholar[2] under the watchful eye of Barbara McKenzie—then playing off a handicap of 4 herself—at Lion's River. His father, Loring, had founded the Kwambonambi Polo Club where Mike played most of his club polo.

After school Mike farmed in Mkuze using his Piper aircraft to fly south to Kwambonambi—commonly known as Kwambo—to play. The only facility available at Mkuze for "stick and ball" practice was a roughly mowed grass airstrip with long bushveld grass on either side. He had an old pony that he rode up and down the airstrip for twenty minutes every day. As Mike recalls it:

> Whenever I miss-hit the ball into the long grass (often) I had to dismount to find it. The interesting thing is that, following my first summer "off season" on the airstrip, my handicap rose from 4 to 6 obviously because the threat of the long-grass punishment encouraged accuracy![3]

He first represented Zululand in the Junior Inter-Provincial in 1963 and from 1966–1970 he was the automatic choice for the number 1 position for Natal. In 1969, playing off his peak of 6-goals, Mike was selected for South Africa and played against David Stirling's Uruguayan side.

Mike reminisces further:

> Perhaps the most exciting match I ever played in was after relocated from Mkuze to Durban and joined the Shongweni Club. At that time the minimum senior team handicap previously permitted to play in the South African Championships was 16 but, in that particular year, there were only seven entries above 16. Shongweni's team, at 14, was the highest entry in the Junior division and I had been looking forward to playing my first tournament for my new club. However, the powers that be decided that the Senior division must have eight teams and they elevated Shongweni to this section. Lion's River Club, at 22 handicap, were the highest and they were offered to select who they would prefer to play in the first round of the knock-out tournament. They joyously selected Shongweni. We rode very nervously onto the ground and then all proceeded to play well above our individual handicaps and won by two goals. Remember that this was championship play and we never received any goals!
>
> The next day we had to meet my old team Kwambonambi—it was a fierce contest!!! They were off 18 goals and, again, we won but this time just by one goal. Now for the final against the mighty Underberg with the Watson brothers, Jim & Kit. The ball was bowled in, we picked it up and scored in the first half minute. Regrettably, six chukkas later the score was 10–1 and we returned back to earth!!!!!
>
> The most awful chukka I ever played in was at Kwambonambi at a club practice. Good friend John Taylor and I rode each other hard over the ball and I turned quickly, but no sign

Mike Rattray's vision and foresight in polo administration put South African polo on the world map (courtesy Susan Reeve).

of John. His horse had died of a heart attack and had fallen over John, breaking his neck. He died a few days later without regaining consciousness. Very, very sad indeed.[4]

Not long after his first appearance on the South African team Mike sustained an injury to his left hand and this reduced his riding ability. However, he continued for many years playing at a lower and more social, although often no less competitive, level.

Apart from his sugar, timber and cattle ranching, Mike has many other interests, chiefly Big Five[4] wildlife management and breeding thoroughbred racehorses. He has given generously of his time to both interests. For 14 years he served as a trustee of the South African National Parks Board and was also chairman of the Sabi Sand Game Reserve. Within the racing community, Mike was chairman of the Durban Turf Club. He has significant success on the racetrack, having bred two "Horses of the Year" and enjoyed a couple of wins in Dubai. At present he stands Western Winter, the current champion thoroughbred stallion in South Africa.

Michael Rattray owns the world-renowned MalaMala Game Reserve, which borders the Kruger National Park, and Mashatu Game Reserve in Botswana.

Ranking at the top of all these interests, undoubtedly all marvelous, is his love of the game of polo. In his words:

> I have found polo to be a game, played mostly in wonderful company whilst making lifelong friends from countries all over the globe. The old amateur polo atmosphere is regrettably on the wane but everything else in the world is changing and so, to survive, polo has to also accommodate and adapt. Nevertheless it is still the greatest sport in the world. Winston Churchill is reputed to have described polo as a game played hard by sometimes loud-mouthed gentlemen on the far side of a very large ground ... and this is probably true which is why, unless it is in the 30–40 goal bracket, it may not be the greatest spectator sport, but it remains the greatest game to play.[6]

A respected player certainly, but it is in the field of administration that Mike has made such an enormous contribution. Thanks to his foresight and vision the annual international tours made their way onto the South African polo calendar. After the Uruguayan tour he and his good friend, the late Dave Kimber, went to Argentina in 1969 to try and entice the legendary Juancarlitos Harriott to come to South Africa. This trip was unsuccessful but we all know Mike well enough to know that he does not give up easily. He heard through the grapevine that Harriott was desperately keen to shoot a lion. Say no more. The bait was laid and Harriott was in South Africa in 1970 for a tour that truly put polo on the map there. Harriott was to come back, with his friend Horacio Araya, who had also been a loyal supporter of South African polo, for a further two tours.

A happy footnote, for the lions at least, is that an unexpected noise frightened the two male lions Harriott was stalking just as he was about to pull the trigger, could this have come from a carefully camouflaged and hidden Jotham, Mike's loyal groom? "Joti," as he was fondly known in the polo fraternity, has since died so the story remains unconfirmed.

Mike served on the executive committee of the South African Polo Association, including three terms of office as president, for a period spanning 25 years. During this time teams from virtually every polo-playing country in the world have toured South Africa, forging friendships and contacts with hundreds of players and dozens of polo associations. Without exception, Mike and his wife, Norma, have hosted these teams every year at the MalaMala Game Reserve, which has proved to be such a highlight of the tours.

Long-running sponsorships from companies of the stature of BMW and use of the International Polo Series as events for corporate entertainment have raised the profile of the game to an extraordinary level, given that, out of the country's population of nearly 60 million, there are only 450 players. When Mike finally retired from polo administration in 1989, he was unanimously elected Honorary Life President, a position he still holds to this day. The South African polo community salutes Mike for everything he has done, and continues to do, for polo.

Notes

1. The Distinguished Service Order, created in 1886, is a British military decoration for bravery that ranks second only to the Victoria Cross.
2. Michaelhouse was founded in 1896 and is one of the finest independent senior boarding schools for boys. It is situated in the rolling green hills of the KwaZulu Natal Midlands area, near Balgowan.
3. Personal communication from Michael Rattray, April 2005.
4. *Ibid.*
5. The "Big Five" has become a familiar catchphrase in the lingo of game reserve tourism. It consists of lion, elephant, buffalo, leopard and rhinocerous.
6. Rattray, April 2005.

Marcos Uranga: A Vision Splendid

by Horace A. Laffaye

The game of polo is an international sport. There is no one who has surpassed Marcos Uranga's contribution in consolidating the widely different associations representing more than 70 countries into a cohesive, well-structured worldwide organization. The Federation of International Polo is the crown jewel of his achievements.

Marcos Alberto Uranga was born in Buenos Aires on 13 December 1936, of Basque stock. He was the second son of Carlos Uranga and Susana Rey de Uranga. The Urangas had emigrated to Argentina from Spain in the early 19th century and settled in the littoral province of Santa Fe. By dint of hard work, typical of the Basque race, they were able to acquire large tracts of land. In 1857 Marcos's great-great-grandfather, Ignacio Uranga, and his wife, Nicolasa Montaner, purchased nearly two hundred square miles of fertile land. They named the estancia "San Nicolás."[1] A manor house was built, along the architectural lines dictated by an environment still exposed to Indian raids: half dwelling and half fort, with all the characteristics of a defensive outpost, tempered by the charm and elegance of a prosperous family abode. San Nicolás became the center of civilization in the area: post office, stagecoach stop, a place to meet to hear the news and to trade. Eventually, a small town grew nearby, and even before the railway came by it was known as Uranga. It still is. In 1912, Italian colonists, who eventually reached 150 families, were brought to work the land.

It is against this background of the landed aristocracy of Argentina that Marcos grew up. He attended Belgrano Day School, that bastion of English solidity and scholarship in Buenos Aires, where he became quite proficient at rugby football, reaching first division rank playing for Belgrano Athletic Club, and later on being nominated for the Pumas, Argentina's national team.[2] At the time, polo for Marcos was just a family pastime. It had been so since the early 1910s, when the name Uranga first appears in the scarce newspaper reports.[3] Cousins Eduardo and Carlos Uranga quickly gained recognition as up-and-coming players in Santa Fe province. Eduardo was the better player, 5-goals at his peak, but Carlos Domingo Uranga (1887–1960) obtained international recognition. Carlos was a member of the 1922 Argentine Polo Federation delegation of eight players that swept championships in England and America, a tour that placed Argentina on the world's polo map. Marcos's father was a well-respected figure in Argentine sporting circles. Straight as a ramrod, he carried the quiet, dignified demeanor of a gentleman. As a player, he was rated at 4-goals and was a reserve on the celebrated Santa Paula team that carried the Pacific Coast Open and the U.S. Open championships in successive years, 1930 at Midwick and Meadow Brook in 1931. Carlos was elected vice president of the Argentine Polo Association and was one of the umpires in the 1932 Cup of the Americas. As a note of trivia, Carlos Uranga scored the first goal ever at Palermo, polo's cathedral, in its inaugural match on 27 October 1928.

Marcos began polo tutored by his progenitor at the family estancia. Now on his own, he began serious polo near Bell Ville and Villa María, Córdoba Province, before moving his string to Pergamino and playing the season at Buenos Aires. Marcos became polo captain of the Jockey Club, a quintessential institution in Buenos Aires, once reckoned as the richest club in the world. Rated at 5-goals, playing horses of his own breeding along with others that he acquired, he developed into a quick and accurate number 1, playing his best polo in an attacking fashion. Marcos always enjoyed the most playing on teams with higher handicapped players. His major wins in Argentina include the first World Championship of Polo Clubs, the Juan Lavalle, Presidente, and Independencia Cups.

A major event in Marcos's life happened during a tournament at Ascochinga, Córdoba. There he met Silvia Rueda, from the well-known polo family. (Romance between members of polo families is quite frequent in Argentina.) They were married within a year. Seven children followed. Valeria, the eldest, obtained a B.A. from Pepperdine; Marcos Jr. is a 6-goal player; Delfín, a graduate of the University of California at Santa Barbara, took the 1992 World Championship in Santiago de Chile; Paula is married to 10-goaler Alberto "Pepe" Heguy; Diego, is a lawyer and plays off a 3-goal handicap; Mariano, a 6-goal professional player, represented Argentina in the World Championship in Australia, and Juan, the youngest, now plays off a 3-goal handicap.

Marcos Uranga's life revolves around his closely knit family. He is very proud of their achievements and intellectual growth. In his travels around the world—by his own count he has played polo in over 30 countries—he never fails to adjust his itinerary to visit with his children. Professionally, Marcos graduated from university with a C.P.A. degree, which he put to good use in the world of finance and banking. He was named director of the Banco de la Nación Argentina, which is the national bank and has over 25,000 employees. His expertise in rural matters was recognized by his appointment to the governing body of the Sociedad Rural Argentina and as second in command at the Ministry of Agriculture.

The family estancia, San Nicolás, is now run by Marcos and Ignacio Uranga. It is a modern rural establishment, specializing in seed production. Genetic selection and hybridization of Morgan maize, sorghum, and sunflowers has been in place since 1982. Over 50,000 pounds of seed are produced daily. The fifth generation of Urangas keeps on working hard and developing and improving the family homestead. In typical Argentine fashion, the personnel to fill the estancia's increasingly technical positions is mainly recruited from professional family members. There are many of those—Ignacio Uranga alone has eight sons. He raised them on his own when his wife was killed in an automobile accident; the children's ages ranged from a baby to a 10-year-old. Needless to say, the polo ground still sees plenty of use, actually so much that Marcos had to curtail the number of essentially practice games because they "distracted" both hands and family members from their allotted tasks.

His ideas on the game follow along classic lines. He strongly believes that the prospective polo player must first learn how to ride; he must be comfortable on the saddle before he can be taught how to hit the ball. Marcos feels that it is virtually impossible to teach a tyro both skills at once. Uranga is convinced of the advantages of having a coach on the sidelines, someone who can analyze the flow of the game, its hills and valleys, from a vantage point, away from the struggle on the ground. In his opinion, an important aspect of the coach's job is the proper assignment of the horses, matching the ponies to the team's needs and players' characteristics. For instance, a very fast horse, but perhaps somewhat difficult to handle and usually played by the number 3, should be given to the number 1, so as to take advantage of its speed on a breakaway.

On the modern game, Marcos feels that team players should have all the skills needed to play all positions; there are continuous rotations in the game, and the concept of a purely defensive back, for example, is quite obsolete. Winning the throw-ins has become all-important because of the current emphasis on possession of the ball.

As to the future of the game, Marcos envisions only tremendous growth worldwide, based upon his experience in positions of leadership within the Federation of International Polo since its creation.

Marcos served, as his father did before him, as vice president of the Argentine Polo Association. When the incumbent president, Jorge Torres Zavaleta, completed his term, Marcos Uranga was the unanimous choice to be the next association president for a period of four years, from 1983 until 1987. His successor was Francisco Dorignac, who currently is serving a second term. Marcos considers main accomplishments to be the financial support provided to the provincial clubs in a time of great economic distress, the development of training programs for umpires, and planting the seeds for the eventual organization of an international entity encompassing all the polo-playing nations.[4]

The first International Polo Tournament for Clubs took place in Buenos Aires in the autumn of 1978. It was a seminal event, conceived by the fertile brain of Marcos Uranga. Although invitations were extended to all polo clubs, only representatives from South America participated in this unique tournament. There were five teams from Brazil, two each from Chile, Colombia and Uruguay, and one from Peru. Twenty-four teams answered the call. In order to be eligible to enter the tournament, each Argentine club had to provide mounts for one of the visiting teams, although some Brazilians brought their own ponies, perhaps to increase their chances of success. This event has been known ever since as the "Mundialito" because that year Argentina was also the host for the soccer World Cup, the "Mundial." The tournament was a double competition, in the sense that it was played simultaneously on handicap and on the flat. Of course, with the Argentine penchant for nicknames, one tournament was the Little Mundial and the other became the Big Mundial, or "Mundialazo." In the final match, Jockey Club, the host club, took the honors, and appropriately enough, Marcos Uranga was at number 1. His teammates were brother-in-law Rodrigo Rueda, Juan Pedro "Pierrou" Gassiebayle and Juan Lalor. The Argentine club Rancho El Tata took the Handicap tournament and the Colombian squad Macondo received recognition as the best foreign team.[5]

The World Championship of Clubs resulted in an undisputed success. Later on, it was improved when two players from the local clubs formed a team with two foreign players, the reason being that the best horseflesh was then shared with the visiting players.

The good feeling and camaraderie shown during the tournament awakened in Marcos's mind the thought of expanding the concept into a competition among countries. Thus the idea of a world federation of polo took root.

Therefore, in December 1982 the Argentine Polo Association following Marcos Uranga's leadership, invited all the national associations to a meeting for the purpose of creating an international body which would promote international competitions, obtain recognition from the Olympic Committee, unify the rules of the game, further develop the game of polo, and support the breeding of polo ponies. The meeting was held at the Jockey Club in Buenos Aires and was attended by representatives from 12 countries. At the end of the meeting, the following resolutions were taken:

1. To create the Federation of International Polo.
2. To adopt the bylaws as presented by Dr. Jorge O'Farrell.
3. To elect the following officers:
   President: Marcos Uranga (Argentina)
   Vice president: Luis Valdez y Colón de Carbajal (Spain)
   Treasurer: Paul de Ganay (France)
   Secretary: Carlos Palacios (Peru)
4. To organize a Junior Cup of the Americas (The Jack Nelson Cup) between teams representing Argentina and the United States, for players under 25.
5. To have a second general meeting in April 1983.[6]

By electing Uranga to the presidency, the assembly recognized the crucial role played by Marcos in bringing this important initiative to fruition. One of the key points of the federation's success has been the World Championship. Marcos felt very strongly that it was imperative that a competition open to all countries be staged immediately, or at least as soon as possible. The result was the World Championship played in Buenos Aires in 1987, when Argentina took the gold medal, Mexico the silver and Brazil the bronze. It is now competed every three years in different host countries. Germany, Chile, Switzerland, America, Australia and France have each organized the tournament.[7] Limited to teams of up to 14-goal handicaps, formed by players rated between 1 and 5 goals individually, the 2008 World Cup hosted by Mexico will be the eighth edition of this unique tournament. The reason for the handicap limits is to level the field, allowing each nation to compete on equal terms. Approximately 25 countries participate, divided into four zones: 1. North and Central America 2. South America 3. Europe and 4. Asia, Africa and Australasia.

What Marcos thought was an impossible dream has been a reality for two decades. The Federation of International Polo is recognized by the International Olympic Committee as the organization representing the sport of polo worldwide, and the one responsible for putting the game back in its rightful place as an Olympic sport, as it was in 1900, 1908, 1920, 1924 and 1936.

Another of Marcos's initiatives was to organize many Ambassadors Cups around the world, in order to make it more attractive to the national delegates to attend meetings. The first one took place at the Palm Beach Polo Club in 1988, organized by George Haas and Allan Scherer.

In 1995, his seminal work completed, President Marcos Uranga handed over the reins of the federation to his close friend Glen Holden, from California and the Santa Barbara Polo Club.

The strong points of polo today are the superlative ponies and the professional dedication of the players. "My son Mariano spends the whole day at the stables," he said. "Many of the top professionals have full time 'pilots,' four-to seven-goal handicap players whose main task is to school the ponies which have shown some faults, and to progressively bring along top prospects for high-goal polo, playing them in medium handicap tournaments. The players today have an exceptional knowledge of the horses, not only their own, but also of those played by their top adversaries. They even try to figure out which ponies the opposing team will play in each chukker, so they can match pony strengths."[8]

Marcos has not slowed down at all. He and Silvia travel extensively throughout the world, attending just about every F.I.P. Ambassadors' meeting, one of the most recent being held in

March 2006 in Patiala, India, which a long time ago boasted a superior team sponsored by the Maharaja of Patiala, the subject of a well-known and often reproduced caricature in *Vanity Fair*.[9]

His current endeavor is to unify the laws of the game. Currently, there are four different codes: the Hurlingham, the Argentine, the American and the Federation rules. Although basically similar, the important differences, especially in the areas of penalties and the manner of ending each chukker, are confusing to both players and umpires, never mind to the spectators. The issue was addressed at the F.I.P. meeting at Aiken, South Carolina, in September 2006. Marcos feels that significant progress is being made towards having a single set of rules and that within two or three years there will be a unified set of laws in the game of polo.

Uranga plays the role of senior statesman in a most admirable manner. In 2005 he was honored with a Life Membership by the Hurlingham Polo Association. Polite, correct, measured, Marcos is endowed with the social graces that make him respected near and far in the world of polo. With the unconditional support of the charming Silvia, they were for years the first couple of polo, welcomed with open arms everywhere. To use his own words, Marcos Uranga accomplished an impossible dream: the unification of all the polo associations of the world into an entity that now numbers over 70 countries. What a legacy!

Notes

1. According to Pedro Capdevila, the term "estancia" first appeared in the Spanish language in 1514 when Pedro de Ibáñez de Ibarra and Rodrigo de Albuquerque were allotted large tracts of land on the island Hispaniola, now the Dominican Republic and Haiti. At the time it was understood that estancias were dedicated to raising cattle and they were rather large, because the smaller allocations were called "caballerías." The word estancia derives from estar, "to be," not in the Cartesian sense (*cogito, ergo sum*) but in the meaning of location. The word "station" used in Australia and New Zealand has the same connotation. In the United States the equivalent is "ranch," from the Spanish rancho. "Rancho" in Argentina signifies a hut, the usual dwelling of a gaucho.

2. Belgrano is a residential neighborhood in Buenos Aires, named after Manuel Belgrano (1776–1820), patriot and creator of the national flag. Large numbers of British residents built their homes in Belgrano. Hence the schools located in the area: English High School, founded in 1880, and Belgrano Day School, in 1912. Belgrano Girls School, adjacent to E.H.S., merged with its neighbor, as did St. Catherine's with B.D.S., with which it shared a back wall, known to the students as "the weeping wall." Belgrano was the second polo club founded in Argentina; it became dormant around 1900. Belgrano Athletic Club, founded by British residents in 1896, had a superior sporting history, with national championships in soccer, rugby, cricket, bowls, and tennis. As a mark of the strong British influence, until the 1940s the club's minutes were written in English.

3. *The Standard*, September 1912.

4. Interview with Marcos Uranga, March 20, 2006.

5 *Centauros*, Issue 131, June 1978.

6. Delegates attending the meeting included:
   Argentina: Carlos de la Serna, Jorge O'Farrell and Marcos Uranga
   Chile: Patricio Vidal
   Colombia: N. Piedrahita and Camilo J. Sáenz
   France: Paul de Ganay
   Germany: Dirk Baumgartner
   Italy: Carlo Pianzola
   Mexico: N. Gómez Terrazas
   Nigeria: Cameron Chisholm
   Peru: Carlos Palacios
   Spain: Luis Valdez y Colón de Carbajal
   United States: George Haas
   Zimbabwe: Horacio Araya

7. The venues and results of the F.I.P. World Championships are as follows:

Year	*Place*	*Gold*	*Silver*	*Bronze*
1987	Buenos Aires	Argentina	Mexico	Brazil
1989	Berlin	U.S.A.	England	Argentina
1992	Santiago	Argentina	Chile	England
1995	St. Moritz	Brazil	Argentina	Mexico
1998	Santa Barbara	Argentina	Brazil	England
2001	Melbourne	Brazil	Australia	England
2004	Chantilly	Brazil	England	Chile

8. Interview with Marcos Uranga, March 20, 2006.

9. Rajendra Singh Bahadur, Maharaja of Patiala (1872–1900), took the 1899 Indian Open Championship with his own team.

Claire Tomlinson: "The most influential lady player"

by Yolanda Carslaw

She became one of polo's few true masters of the number one position and the first woman in the world to rise to five-goals; she swept away the rule forbidding women in British high-goal and became the first to compete on equal terms with men at the top tier. She is viewed by Argentines as "one of them" and spends more time on a horse than many professional players.

But Claire Tomlinson is more than simply the most influential lady player the world has ever known. With her unswerving determination, exceptional understanding of the horse and sheer love of the game she has become a pioneering coach, a champion for the young and the biggest breeder of polo ponies in Britain.

Claire Janet Lucas was born on Valentine's Day in 1944, the third child of Arthur and Ethel Lucas. She was, she says, an afterthought—her brother, John, was already 14, and her sister, Pat, 18 months his junior.

Arthur Lucas was instrumental in reviving polo in England after the Second World War—having been introduced to the sport by Johnny Traill—and he taught scores of young players at his home in Hertfordshire. Arthur, Ethel, John and Pat all played, in 1951 they won the Holden White Cup as a family at Cowdray Park. John rose to six goals, becoming one of England's best players of the era, winning the Gold, Queen's and Challenge Cups in 1967. John's sons, James and Will, played for England from the late 1980s.

The family bought Woolmers Park, a magnificent estate 25 miles north of London. The novelist Barbara Cartland also wanted the property, but Arthur laid siege to the estate agent, who felt caught between two buyers. The agent tried to escape by a back door but Arthur collared him and closed the deal. He quickly set up Hertfordshire Polo Club in 1949, laying two grounds, and adding a third later.

Claire remembers being surrounded by polo as a child. "Everybody used to come for tea after games, and the pepper, salt and cutlery turned into goalposts and players in the postgame discussions," says Claire. "I watched matches with my mother and the other wives, who were pretty knowledgeable. We saw the best players, at home and elsewhere. Understandably I learnt about the game from a very early age."

The young Claire was immersed in riding, too. She became a show rider for Joan Middleton—Miss Midd, as she was known—competing on some of the top ponies of the day, and also learned with the showing legend Sybil Smith. "It was a full-time thing," says Claire. "On the way home we stopped at gymkhanas to earn pocket money."

She hunted with the Enfield Chace, of which her father was chairman, and competed across the disciplines with the Enfield Chace Hunt branch of the Pony Club. Arthur's head man, Bob Rudkin, who introduced scores of children to polo, taught Claire, too, and she also rode with the Indian player Prem Singh, who was based at Woolmers Park.

Arthur took Woolmers Park teams to Rome, Madrid, Biarritz, Dublin and Deauville, where they won the Gold Cup in 1948 and 1953. Claire would stay with players' families rather than in grand hotels with her parents, and was already displaying an independent, adventurous spirit.

"At Deauville the horses passed our guesthouse between the stables and the beach," recalls Claire. "I used to creep out and ride the ponies in the sea."

Claire went to Stormont School in Potters Bar, then boarded at Sibton Park in Kent, along with her pony. She took O-levels at Wycombe Abbey, Buckinghamshire, playing sports such as tennis, lacrosse and fencing, and excelling in maths and sciences. But her subjects were not well taught at A-level there, and Claire wanted to go to Oxbridge, so she moved to Millfield.

The famously sporty school in Somerset offers riding and polo but Claire pursued fencing, and—showing the same determination that was to take her so far in polo—was picked for the national junior team, competing in France, Holland and Hungary.

Claire went up to Oxford in 1963, to Somerville College, and she credits Millfield's founder and headmaster with her choice of subject. "I initially applied to study physics," she says. "But Jack Meyer—an inspiring man—questioned whether I really wanted to sit in a lab all day, and suggested agricultural economics instead."

She soon earned a squash blue and was short-listed for the Olympic fencing team. But she withdrew before training got under way in earnest. "We were always beaten in early rounds internationally and I missed team games," she says, adding with a smile, "and anyway, by then I was getting interested in polo."

Claire first played as a teenager. "One day we were having tea when someone galloped up and asked me to substitute," says Claire. "I enjoyed it."

In her first year, the university polo team captain, Jeremy Taylor, implored her to join because he was short of players. "I refused, saying my parents didn't think polo was a girl's game—by that, I mean they didn't push me to play," she says. "But he said he knew I could ride, and that they needed me. I said he'd have to ring my father, as I didn't want to beg for ponies."

Arthur—who also hosted Cambridge players at his club—supported the Oxford players generously, although, characteristically, he never gave them anything on a plate. "We'd organize puppy shows and dances to raise money for horses, and only then would he lend us one, too," says Claire. More players joined, including Simon Tomlinson, who arrived at Oxford in Claire's second year. In the summer break the student players would spend a month or so at Woolmers Park.

Simon had grown up in Devon and had his first taste of polo on Abbotsham Cliffs on an Exmoor pony, then, while at school at Christ's Hospital, Sussex, he visited Cowdray. He learned at Sandhurst, spending, he says, one entire winter on the wooden horse with Lord Mountbatten's book, *An Introduction to Polo*, propped against the horse's ears.

In 1966, as the H.P.A. roundup recalls, "Oxford beat Cambridge ... with two records—they were captained by a lady, Miss Claire Lucas, and they won by 7–0." She earned a half-blue.

Claire had always longed to go to Argentina. Her brother, John, had first been in 1957, with his wife, Anne, and Claire had longstanding invitations from her father's friends such as Carlos de la Serna, Oscar Olmos, Alfredo Goti, Norberto Fernández Moreno, Pacho Martínez Sobrado and Jorge Marín Moreno.

When Claire graduated, Arthur agreed to pay half her airfare if she got a job, and she quickly found one, doing fertilizer research in Buenos Aires for a British firm. She confidently assured her interviewer in London that speaking Spanish would be no problem. As soon as she knew she had the job, she taught herself doggedly from books, helped by her fluent French—perfected in Paris on a cookery course. Within months she conversed like an Argentine.

In September 1966 Arthur and Ethel, who had never been to Argentina, traveled to Buenos Aires with Claire and Caroline Tomlinson, Simon's sister, who had a job teaching English in Buenos Aires. The pair shared a flat in Avenida Callao.

That same September the H.P.A. sent an England squad—Sinclair Hill, Paul Withers, Patrick Kemple, Ronnie Ferguson, the Marquess of Waterford and Lord Patrick Beresford—to Buenos Aires to play in a 30-goal tournament. John, by then a five-goaler, traveled to Argentina, too, to find ponies for the following season's high-goal, which he was due to play with Enrique Zorrilla, Celestino Garrós and Jorge Marín Moreno as Woolmers Park.

John enlisted his sister's help in this task and so began the first of Claire's horse-hunting forays to farms countrywide that continue to this day. That winter she spent many weekends with the Marín Morenos at Pergamino, where she became great friends with Jorge, one of the greatest number one players of the era and an exceptional teacher. "I really learnt how to play number one from Jorge," says Claire.

She also stayed with the Garrós family at Coronel Suárez, where she first played 25-goal practices while trying horses to buy for the high-goal. This did not faze her in the slightest: "I played a lot, and everybody lent horses generously. I thought: 'This is fantastic!' and found 25-goal relatively easy because everything happened as you'd expect."

By March 1967, her fertilizer project completed, she and John had gathered 25 ponies. Claire arranged to fly them to England—something that had been done only a few times. The journey, in a Super Constellation propeller plane, was epic. After a delayed departure, several parties and little sleep, the girls hoped they could rely on the grooms to feed and check the horses. But Claire recalls, "I don't think they [the grooms] had been in a plane before and most dived underneath something and wouldn't come out."

They refuelled in Recife (Brazil), then Salt Island (Cape Verde). "We were starving, so the pilot radioed ahead to ask for food," says Claire. "On landing, policemen climbed on board and led us outside to a banquet."

Landing in Las Palmas on the Canary Islands the plane burst a tire, and, as there was no spare, Claire was told to unload the horses. But she knew if their feet touched island soil, they would be forbidden to enter England, because of African Horse Sickness. After further inspection of the tires, the Argentine pilot agreed to risk continuing. Then the plane's navigation system was struck by lightning. "The pilot asked if I knew what the coast of England looked like," says Claire. Thankfully the radio still worked, and at Gatwick fire engines lined the runway.

Woolmers Park swept the high-goal board in 1967. As the 1968 *H.P.A. Yearbook* recorded, "The outstanding high-goal team of the year was Mr John Lucas's Woolmers Park side, the first team to win all three of our main high-goal tournaments, the Queen's Cup, the Cowdray Park Gold Cup and the Cowdray Park Challenge Cup. John Lucas had collected an exceptionally fine string of ponies from Argentina...."

That summer Claire played medium-goal alongside her brother at Cowdray, and also substituted in his high-goal team in Deauville. John went to six-goals and Claire was promoted to two, as was Lavinia Roberts; the two became the first British women to rise above one-goal.

(Other postwar lady players included Daphne Lakin and Judy Forwood, but neither exceeded one-goal.)

That winter Hanut Singh, then aged 67, asked Claire to work for him in Argentina, using her Argentine-Spanish and excellent contacts to help him buy horses. "Hanut would inspect every horse in-hand and watch it move," recalls Claire. "I'd ride the ones he liked — up to 25 — then we'd discuss them. After lunch he would choose some for me to play, then anything he liked he would play, too. I learnt so much, and his analysis was so astute."

In 1968 Claire married Simon Tomlinson at Hertingfordbury Church near Woolmers Park. Simon was serving with the 5th Royal Inniskilling Dragoon Guards, based at Blackpool. "I was intending not to play after we were married, but Simon said I had to so I could school his ponies," she says. They rented a cottage near Cheshire Polo Club and played the 1969 season there, both off two-goals.

They played as Los Locos, a name born after Claire and Simon invited Santiago Gaztambide Senior to join their eight-goal side. Santiago was known as El Loco (the mad one), and with Simon's similar reputation on the field, and Claire's maiden name, Los Locos stuck, and adopted the red and green colors of Woolmers Park.

In 1970 Simon was posted to Germany. By the time he left the army in 1972 to work as a chartered surveyor, they had settled in Fairford, choosing Gloucestershire over Sussex because the hunting was better and they had more friends in the area.

They became friends with Héctor Barrantes and Eduardo Moore, who were based with Mark Vestey at Foxcote. "Héctor and I were horse fanatics, and we talked horses all the time," she says. Claire continued to travel to Argentina, often staying at Eduardo Moore's farm Nueva Escocia, near Carlos Casares, 300 kilometers west of Buenos Aires.

Jorge MacDonough remembers vetting horses for Claire in the early 1970s:

> I first met Claire — Clarita as we call her — when Eddie Moore asked me to vet some horses near Cordoba. It took me a day and half to get there by train. Eddie, Claire and a few others insisted I go back with them in their four-seater plane. We squeezed six people in.
>
> After that I often met Claire at Eddie's place. Normally she was the only lady, but she was like another one of us— like an Argentine player or a groom. It was strange for a lady to join in asados, play polo and speak such good Argentine — not Spanish. Speaking the language was the only way to talk to gauchos, and buy horses— and she drove a hard bargain."

Claire always returned from these trips with horses for Los Locos or for friends. At this time she also played tournaments at Hurlingham, where it was almost unheard of for a woman to play. In the countryside, she says, it had never felt like a big deal.

In 1978, when Claire was three goals and Los Locos had won a clutch of low- and medium-goal trophies, including the County Cup at Cirencester in 1972 and 1977, she and Simon decided to move to high-goal. The H.P.A. rulebook stipulated that high-goal players needed to be at least one-goal, but women could not play high-goal.

Her initial request was turned down: "The press were on to me, because women were making a big hoo-ha about equality at that time. My father was an H.P.A. steward, and I didn't want to tackle them head-on, so I went to see Lord Cowdray. He told me players— especially foreign players— didn't like the idea. I said I'd played 25-goal at Hurlingham and nobody complained, and that I was safer than several one-goalers in high-goal. He asked me to prove players didn't mind."

Claire persevered, collecting signatures from everyone — nearly — who had played in the 1978 Gold Cup and Goodwood Week. She presented the petition to the stewards, who relented.

In 1979 an 18-goal Los Locos, with Claire (three-goals) at one, Simon (four-goals) at two, Juni Crotto at three and David Gemmell (a Gloucestershire neighbor whom the Tomlinsons knew from Germany), at back stormed into their first high-goal season by winning the Queen's

Cup, beating Galen Weston's Roundwood Park. Los Locos met the same opponents in the final of the Warwickshire Cup but lost by half a goal.

Paul Withers, who played back for Cowdray, recalls:

> Los Locos were much more successful than anyone thought they would be. Whoever played back would soon discover Claire was a bloody nuisance, and anyone who made the mistake of taking it easy on her was made to look rather silly. She is the best woman player I've ever seen: her speed and anticipation were brilliant.
>
> She played a genuine number one, so you couldn't leave her, and that stopped me playing more of a part in the game. Claire always lay deep, waiting for these monster passes from Juni Crotto, who chain-smoked and drank like a fish but could hit the ball for miles. They were all utterly determined and Simon was a lunatic. If he thought it was his line, he'd ride it, so there was a danger factor too.

Jorge MacDonough, who played for Foxcote in 1979, remembers being beaten by Los Locos in the semifinal of the Queen's Cup. "It was the first time I had played against a lady," he recalls. "She was fast and well positioned; she played number one very well and her horsemanship couldn't have been better. That was the key—she had to rely on the power of the horse and not on her own power. She is the only woman I know who could really compete with men."

In 1981, after Sam Vestey gave up high-goal, he offered Héctor Barrantes, mounted, to Los Locos for the following season. Horacio Araya was to complete the team, but the Falklands War intervened and Argentines did not play in Britain again until 1989.

A historic moment in British polo captured by photographer Mike Roberts: Queen Elizabeth II presents the Queen's Cup to Mrs. Claire Tomlinson. It was Claire's first high-goal tournament win (courtesy Mike Roberts).

In 1986 Los Locos played with Frenchman Stéphane Macaire and the American Gene Fortugno, winning the Cowdray Park Challenge and County Cups. Claire played number three, and was promoted to five-goals. "I was quite surprised, but I think I went up partly because they saw I could play in the middle of the game," she says.

The H.P.A. discussed selecting Claire for the England team on Cartier International Day. After all, in 1987 she was in the top 15 British players and, more significantly, was probably the most skilled and experienced in the number one position. She says the idea was taken no further because she was female—and, she adds, "That slightly annoyed me, as I would have liked to have played for England."

Claire maintains the limitation for women in polo comes down to strength in terms of moving the stick about and changing position, rather than hitting power:

> You need strength—especially in the trunk and the forearms—to do several things at once, quickly, such as changing sides with your stick. We're a bit slower in this respect. Also, a lot of girl players are quite rigid in their hips and don't move out of the saddle in the same way as men.

Claire has done more fitness training as the years have passed: she swims, goes to a local gym and stretches.

And what about women's polo? "Generally women don't hit the ball far enough to open the game up so it can be scrappy," she says. "But women's polo has its purpose, and is improving all the time."

After a decade in high-goal the Tomlinsons returned to medium-goal. Around the same time their children—Emma, Luke and Mark—were learning polo in Pony Club, and the Beaufort Polo Club, which Claire and Simon founded in 1989, was taking off.

In 1977 the family had moved to Down Farm near Tetbury, then a dairy but from 1929 to 1939 the home of the Beaufort Polo Club. Humphrey Guinness, a former member, showed them where the old grounds had been, among the dry-stone walls. The property's beautifully symmetrical 40-box stable yard was still intact, albeit inhabited by calves.

Simon and Claire put in a ground and practiced at home, opening their gates to the local Pony Club from the early 1980s. They set up the new Beaufort when nearby Cirencester closed to new members because it was full. As it expanded, the Beaufort caused a stir among the "old guard," who felt the new club might be trying to compete, which, says Claire emphatically, it was not. Now, in 2006, it has 148 playing members, 250 social members and six grounds. The family's only major setback has been a fire that destroyed their farmhouse in 1996.

Beaufort has a thriving low-goal calendar, but also hosts the high-goal Evolution Test Match and the Argentine Club Cup, a 22–28-goal all-professional fixture. Other important trophies include the Duke of Beaufort's Cup (15–18-goal), the Arthur Lucas Cup (12–15-goal) and the Prince of Wales' Cup (8–12-goal).

Claire meanwhile has become one of the world's top coaches. In 1993, with Hugh Dawnay, she instigated and set up a coaching system for the H.P.A. from scratch, which has had a profound effect on how players are taught. She is admired for her ability to instruct across the spectrum, working with leading professionals as effectively as novices. She is one of six official H.P.A. team coaches, and regularly coaches British squads at F.I.P. championships as well as holding sessions for the H.P.A. Junior Development Squad at Down Farm.

David Morley, another official team coach, says, "Claire excels both in teaching—giving people skills, and coaching—showing people how to develop their skills to the most effective use. Her strengths lie in her great enthusiasm, knowledge and experience, as well as her directness. She inspires respect, having done so well in the sport—and that doesn't need to be qualified by adding 'as a woman,' because she's done well by all standards."

Peter Sidebottom, a friend and neighbor of the Tomlinsons, has firsthand experience of Claire's teaching, as she persuaded him to take up the game in his forties. "It was so exciting, learning something new at that age," says Peter. "Claire has an instinctive feel for people as well as an incredible natural ability for teaching—but she doesn't take any prisoners. I think she could teach higher mathematics or quantum theory; the subject matter is almost irrelevant."

Peter's son, Harry, who, sadly, has since died, learned both riding and polo with Claire as a member of the Beaufort Hunt branch of the Pony Club. "Claire overcame both my son's nervousness and his terror of being shown up by his sister," adds Peter. "Learning polo literally changed his life because it got him riding and gave him something in sport that he was good at."

Every Sunday morning, year-round, Pony Club children play and learn at the Beaufort, and the sport is positively flourishing at the Beaufort Hunt branch, largely thanks to Claire's input. Schoolchildren (from Marlborough, Westonbirt, Beaudesert and St. Mary's Calne) and university students play at Down Farm, too. Claire also founded County Polo, a system geared to recreational players, often those who have started riding and playing later in life. She has brought the game to a wider audience in other ways, for example, teaching a bicycle courier from Manchester for the television program *Faking It* in 2004.

Down Farm has become a home away from home for various young foreign and British players. Milo Fernández Araujo (from Argentina), David Stirling (from Uruguay), Robert Cudmore (from Australia) and, more recently, Juni Crotto's son, Jacinto, spent their first years in England there, while British players who have been "through the system" include Jason Dixon, Antony Fanshawe, Alastair Archibald, Tim Stakemire and Robert Thame.

A recent picture of Claire and Simon Tomlinson at Beaufort Polo Club in Gloucestershire (courtesy Mike Roberts).

Milo Fernández Araujo was at Beaufort for seven seasons. "Claire treated me like a son—she's very warm, more like an Argentine than an Englishwoman—and now I feel part of the family," he says. "She spends more time on a horse than most professionals—I've never seen anybody ride as much. On the field she's always in the right position. You lifted your head and there she was, and she nearly always scored."

In 2006, the Tomlinsons kept 80 of their own horses at Down Farm, including young stock, and rented 90 boxes to other owners. Claire started breeding polo ponies in the 1970s. Her father had always done so, putting a small thoroughbred stallion to his best mares, including a number of John's 1967 contingent. Claire's parents had always been extremely supportive; Arthur would do a lot of the breaking-in in the early days and most of the ponies that took his daughter to five-goals were from the Lucas breed, broken and trained by Claire. For instance, Cabesita, a mare Arthur Lucas bought from the Moores (and jokingly named "little head," because it had a large head) was the dam of one of Claire's favorite ponies, Nelly, which she played (in a mane, because Nelly also hunted) when she was five-goals.

Now, Down Farm stands two Argentine stallions, Chess and Hector, who came from Héctor Barrantes and are respectively by Top Secret and Sequito, dozens of whose progeny play in the Argentine Open. Several of Luke and Mark's top ponies are homebred out of Claire's best playing mares.

Her daughter Emma, an equine vet, set up an embryo transfer center at Down Farm in 2003, which has become one of only two major centers practicing the technique in Britain. The Tomlinsons' own embryo progeny will start chukkas in 2007. The family has begun breeding in Argentina, too, at La Bonita, their farm on the pampas near the town of 25 de Mayo.

"Breeding our own horses has helped Mark and me enormously," says Luke Tomlinson. "To have that backing has been a big leg-up. My parents playing high-goal, and having good players at home, helped us, as have connections in Argentina."

But Luke and Mark have worked hard, too, in just as focused a fashion as their mother. They won the Cowdray Park Gold Cup together in 2003, and in 2005 they became the first British players in the Argentine Open for 25 years.

Meanwhile, Claire's childhood home has undergone a renaissance. Ethel Lucas sold Woolmers Park in the late 1990s—ensuring it went to a family, not a developer—and she died the day the transaction was completed. The property's new owners—spurred by its history and encouraged by the vendors—revived the polo club there, and now Woolmers Park is thriving again.

Part V

The Great Contemporaries

Introduction

Watching Cambiaso go towards goal is like watching a fox approach a chicken coop.
Guards Polo Club, 1999 Year Book

Polo is most appropriately known as the king of games and the game of kings—there is an often photographed tablet bearing such an inscription by the roadside near Gilgit—and there have been few periods in its history without the patronage and participation of nobility.

Queen Victoria's eldest son, Edward, Prince of Wales, demonstrated interest in the game as a spectator. Two of his sons, the Duke of York—later George V—and the Duke of Clarence, visited Argentina in 1881 and left a tangible mark of their spectacular visit. Two specimens of *Cupressus lambertiana* were planted in front of estancia Negrete's main dwelling, of which one still stands, near a fading plaque commemorating the event. Traditionally, Negrete is the site of the first polo game in Argentina, played on 30 August 1876. There is, however, strong evidence that polo began at Caballito (little horse), a Buenos Aires neighborhood, and in January 1876 *The Standard* published a notice of three polo matches at Henry Wilson's estancia La Buena Suerte.

King George VI played polo; however, lawn tennis was his game, for he was good enough to play at Wimbledon and reach the quarter-finals. His elder brother David, successively Prince of Wales, King Edward VIII, and Duke of Windsor, was an enthusiastic player, enjoying the game both at home and during his numerous tours abroad.

After the Second World War, Prince Philip of Edinburgh took the game up at the behest of his uncle, Lord Mountbatten, who coached him. A 5-goal handicap player, Prince Philip's enthusiasm and support contributed significantly to the renewed popularity of polo in England. He founded what is now the Guards Club and serves as Patron of the Hurlingham Polo Association.

H.M. Queen Elizabeth II is a frequent spectator at polo events and carefully followed the polo careers of her husband, her eldest son, and now follows that of her grandchildren, the Princes William and Harry Wales. In 1960, she presented the Queen's Cup, one of the three main tournaments in Britain.

Royal patronage was not limited to Britain. That sporting monarch, Alfonso XIII of Spain, was a 5-goal handicap player; his private grounds were at Casa de Campo, near Madrid. He was a connoisseur of fine automobiles, and a successful Hispano-Suiza sports car, the Alfonso model, was named after him. A soccer enthusiast, King Alfonso gave the original Madrid Football Club the honorific title Real. Through his British-born Queen, Victoria Eugenie of Battenberg, Alfonso XIII was a constant figure in the London polo season — he was Colonel-in-Chief of the 16th Lancers— until the Spanish events in 1931 cost him the throne. He remained a frequent presence in Britain until his death in exile ten years later.

Many of the "royal" clubs abroad provide evidence of patronage and there are clubs like Real Polo Club de Barcelona, Puerta de Hierro, Pahang and Brunei to show that foreign kings have favored the game.

Though not royalty, but certainly on top of the heap in his endeavors, U.S. President Theodore Roosevelt was an enthusiastic polo player at Oyster Bay Polo Club in Long Island. Incidentally, T.R. is one of only three polo players who have been recipients of the Nobel Prize. The others are Sir Winston Churchill, winner of the Inter-Regimental Tournament in India, also a familiar face in the London polo season until the 1920s, and an Argentine biochemist, Dr. Luis Leloir, who played at Hurlingham off a 2-goal handicap.

Following Juan Carlos Harriott and Francisco Dorignac's retirement from high-goal polo a brand new generation changed the face of the game. The young players, who had been boys in the halcyon days of Santa Ana and Coronel Suárez, immediately made themselves felt. Many were the bearers of distinguished names in Argentine polo: Araya, Heguy, Merlos, Novillo Astrada, to mention just a few. They were part of the strong family ties typical of the game in that country. The Argentine Open has been played on 115 occasions; of those, 73 have been taken by teams that included brothers, and sometimes fathers. Adding six more with father-son combinations, four with brothers-in-law, and two more with fathers-and sons-in-law, there are 85 family champion teams.

The last final (2006) for the Argentine Open followed the trend: La Aguada presented the four Novillo Astrada brothers; La Dolfina, brothers-in-law Cambiaso and Castagnola.

In these days, when international polo at top level is restricted to club teams, with the notable exception of the annual match for the Coronation Cup, it is pleasant to note that Eduardo, Ignacio and Marcos Heguy accomplished what their progenitors failed to do, namely, put the family name on Cowdray's Gold Cup roll of champions, long after their grandfather had done.

The wide world of polo is fittingly portrayed in this final section. The heir apparent to the throne of England is followed by a great-grandson of a Basque immigrant; a smiling cowboy born in Oklahoma is next to the captain of England; and two ultimate professionals stand with the planet's current best player. They are vivid images of what contemporary polo is all about.

H.R.H. The Prince of Wales remains the most recognized polo player worldwide. Alberto Pedro Heguy exemplifies Number 1 play at its best, while Julian Hipwood personified British polo for over two decades, as Joe Barry did in his country. Both Heguy and Hipwood are still playing the game with the same intensity and commitment as they exhibited in their prime. Guillermo Gracida, the perfectionist (Santiago Alvarez once said that when the trailers leave La Herradura, Memo knows the tire pressure in every wheel) and Gonzalo Pieres, player, breeder and entrepreneur, precede Adolfito Cambiaso, whose reputation developed quite early when word spread around polo circles that there was a kid from Cañuelas who was alarmingly good.

H.R.H. The Prince of Wales: The Prince of Polo

by Nigel à Brassard

There are many great family dynasties in polo but possibly the most famous and active in playing the sport from the beginning of the modern game and continuing until today is that of the British Royal Family. Their contribution to the game has been to bring immense attention, interest and glamour to the sport across the globe.

The reasons for the inclusion of the Prince of Wales in this book are his own polo achievements and his role as a representative of his family's association with the sport. Lord Patrick Beresford described the Prince as "an inspiration to other players and spectators, becoming the sport's main bastion, not only in this country, but worldwide, on the retirement of his father H.R.H. Prince Philip."[1] The Prince was a talented player, such that in 1980 Lt. Col. Alec Harper wrote in the Hurlingham Polo Association Yearbook: "The Prince of Wales is now one of the best backs in the country—his anticipation has improved vastly."[2] In 1988 Lt. Col. Harper wrote: "Prince Charles is certainly a contender for the 'Leading Amateur' title."[3] The Prince reached a handicap of four-goals, ranking him comfortably in the top twenty best British players. This is no mean feat for someone with a schedule which prevented him from dedicating himself to the hours of practice needed to excel in any sport. During 2005, for example, the Prince undertook more than 500 official engagements, including over 100 overseas; this was in addition to his responsibilities as patron or president of around 370 organizations and charities. The Prince inherited his family's love of polo and has passed on this enthusiasm to his two sons, Prince William and Prince Harry, who are both showing promise in the sport and playing as much as their military careers allow. The Prince has raised very large amounts of money for charity through his polo playing and a match in which he was to play, no matter where in the world, guaranteed a huge crowd of spectators, press photographers and journalists. Michael Butler said after a game played at Oak Brook Polo Club, "We had over 6,000 spectators for the 1986 Prince of Wales Cup in which Prince Charles played. He's a true polo superstar; there's no question his presence hypes polo's popularity tremendously."[4] Any polo player today will almost invariably be asked by people, "Have you ever played with the Prince of Wales?" Such is his fame and iconic status in the sport.

The Royal Family's contribution to the game cannot be overestimated, as their involvement as players and spectators has done so much to popularize polo. On 6 June 1874 the first polo match was played at the Hurlingham Club, London, between the Royal Horse Guards and the 1st Life Guards. *The Field* magazine commented, "Popular as the game of polo has become, on no previous occasion had such an immense number of the fashionable world assembled for the ostensible purpose of witnessing the game."[5] *The Field* said that much of the excitement was as a consequence of the presence of the then Prince of Wales (later King Edward VII) and a Royal party among the spectators. Over 100 years later John Lloyd, in *The Pimm's Book of Polo,* wrote: "When Prince Charles is due to play anywhere, then things become positively frantic.... Local socialites fight for the chance to appear alongside the Prince.... Such popular appeal does polo no harm and increases the game's charisma."[6] The Royal Family's contribution in more recent times includes that of Lord Mountbatten, who devised and patented a head (R.N.P.A.) for a polo stick; in 1931 wrote *An Introduction to Polo* under the pseudonym "Marco"—still the definitive textbook written on polo; and, as chairman of the Hurlingham Rules Committee in the 1930s, did much to help the coordination of the rules of polo around the world. Prince Philip did much to popularize polo in the 1950s and 1960s and one of his lasting legacies will be his role as a founder of the Household Division Polo Club in 1955 (which in 1969 changed its name to the Guards Polo Club). He achieved a 5-goal handicap and was ranked equal third on the H.P.A. list of leading British players, and his team won numerous major tournaments including the Gold Cup on three occasions. H.M. The Queen has taken an active interest as a spectator and also in breeding polo ponies. At times during the 1980s Prince Charles was entirely mounted on "homebred" ponies. The Queen has presented the Coronation Cup on the H.P.A. International Day and her presence has contributed to the huge popularity and success of this annual event.

The Prince's interest in polo started as a child, watching his father, and was encouraged by his great-uncle Lord Mountbatten. During his school holidays in 1963, the Prince started practicing on a wooden horse and having stick and ball sessions on San Quinina, a pony which had been given to him by his father. This was the start of his love for the game and its horses. The late Lord Cowdray gave the young Prince a pony called Sombra and in the foreword to *Polo at Cowdray,* the Prince wrote: "I will remember his (Lord Cowdray's) particular kindness in giving me one of his old and experienced polo ponies when I first started playing the game. She was a kind of *Maltese Cat* and one of the best teachers you could have."[7]

The Prince started playing practice chukkas and on 6 August 1965 he played in his first competitive match in public in the Chairman's Cup at Smith's Lawn. The Prince's team, Rangers, beat Blacknest and the Prince scored two goals. *Horse and Hound* reported that the Prince had inherited "his father's good eye for the ball and from his mother he has acquired her sensitive hands."[8] While at Cambridge the Prince gained a half-blue for representing and captaining the university in the annual varsity polo match against Oxford University. From 1973 onwards the Prince (by then a 3-goal player) played in the British high-goal season (22-goal handicap), first as a member of Mark Vestey's Foxcote team. Later he played high- and medium-goal for a variety of teams, including Sam Vestey's Stowell Park, Bucket Hill, the Golden Eagles with Sinclair Hill, Guy Wildenstein's Les Diables Bleu, Geoffrey Kent's Windsor Park, Anthony Embiricos's Tramontana and Galen Weston's Maple Leafs. The Prince's handicap was increased to 4-goals in 1980, which he maintained until the end of the 1991 season. While the Prince has mainly played in the back position, he said, "I'd rather play at No. 2 actually because you are more in the thick of it. But I couldn't play at No. 2 in high-goal because I'm simply not good enough or quick enough. But I don't like the idea of being confined forever to Back, so I try to play No. 2 in medium-goal."[9]

The Prince's skill as a polo player is above all because he is "a consummate horseman" (in the words of Michael Clayton, former editor of *Horse and Hound*)[10] and is a fearless sports-

Prince Charles riding hard for Les Diables Bleu at Cowdray Park (courtesy Museum of Polo and Hall of Fame).

man. He has shown his horsemanship in a range of disciplines, including cross-country riding, team chasing and, during the early 1980s, as a jockey on both the flat and over the jumps. His former racing trainer, Nicholas Gaslee, said the Prince had not been credited over the years for his racing achievement: "To come in the top four in his first three races is a record any professional jockey would be proud of, and that is despite his many other commitments at that time."[11]

Writing in the foreword to *Polo: The Galloping Game*, the Prince noted, "Polo players must learn to value their ponies and respect them for their instinctive knowledge of the game. In my opinion, the close bond which develops between polo pony and its rider is one of the great attractions of the game."[12] Commenting on his ponies, Prince Charles said, "The best I ever played was Lula, given to me by Anthony Embiricos. Before there had been two outstanding individuals, both bred by The Queen, namely Pan's Folly and Happiness." (Pan's Folly was awarded the best playing pony in the International in 1985.) The Prince continued: "Of course I have been very lucky with the people who trained horses for me, notably Tony Devcich from New Zealand, Raúl Correa from Argentina and Austin Clarke from Ireland." Lord Patrick Beresford, writing about Prince Charles and the Duke of Edinburgh, said, "They were tactically sound, fearless, hit all the shots clean and hard, were tough competitors, but took no rancour from the field. Both invariably went down to the pony lines after their matches to thank their ponies and grooms."[13] The Prince has remarked on how lucky he was, "with the grooms who worked with me, starting with Roger Oliver and Pam Donoghue in the Mews at Windsor Castle and continuing right through until the moment of my retirement."[14]

In 1971 a match was organized at Cowdray between England and the U.S.A. for the Coronation Cup. In 1972 the venue was moved to the Guards Polo Club and featured a second match in which Prince Charles (by then a 2-goal player) represented Young England against Young America. Prince Charles has played in the supporting match on a further sixteen occasions against international teams including those from Brazil, Canada, France and Spain. Since 1977 the second game has been played for the Silver Jubilee Cup and in recent years Prince Harry has played for the Prince of Wales' team. This fixture has grown to become the world's largest one-day polo event, with a crowd of 30,000.

The Prince of Wales has said he loves polo because of the pleasure and excitement that it has given to him and because of its good sportsmanship. He told Ami Shinitzky (former editor of the American magazine *Polo*): "I look forward to a game of polo more than anything else. It really is extraordinary—it's awful, it's addictive. The problem is that it's like a drug, only better for you."[15] Polo has played an important role in the Prince's life and combines his affection for horses, his love of physically challenging activities and the opportunity that participation in the game provides to shed his formal persona. The Prince has generally preferred sports and pastimes which rely on individual efforts and abilities, including flying, fishing, game-shooting, waterskiing, scuba diving, wind surfing, skiing and parachuting, a list which explains why some members of the press dubbed him "Action Man."

However, the combination of the horse activity and the team game is what the Prince loves about polo. He said: "As a physical contest, polo provides a refreshing break from even the most absorbing of sedentary occupations." The Prince believes that, like his love of drawing and painting, polo is relaxing because of the concentration involved. The Prince has also described polo as "my one great extravagance." Over the years many courtiers, the press and, if it is to be believed, members of his family, have suggested that the Prince should retire from the sport. His response was "I will go on [playing] as long as I bounce when I fall off." The Prince was always a highly competitive player, but while, as noted by John Lloyd, he was "what the English like to call a 'good loser,' there is little doubt he prefers to win."[16] Prince Charles told *Polo* magazine that he used to take losing more badly; he said, "Old Sinclair Hill used to get me really wound up, and if I lost it took me 20 to 25 minutes to get over it. I didn't really want to talk to anybody. But nowadays, I find that half the fun is taking part. I'd far rather play the game and lose if necessary than not have a game at all."[17]

In the Prince's polo career it is difficult to determine specific highlights, but, clearly, being in Les Diables Bleu team that won the Queen's Cup and the Davidoff Trophy (subsidiary of the Gold Cup) in 1986 and being three times a finalist in the Cowdray Park Gold Cup (1982, 1985 and 1987) would rank as highpoints in any player's career. Prince Charles wrote about playing in the Gold Cup in the foreword to *Polo at Cowdray* in 1992 and one can sense a note of frustration: "I have been trying to win it [the Gold Cup] for the past 14 years.... This particular prize has eluded me!" One thing that everybody who played with the Prince is convinced of is that he would have been able to achieve a higher handicap if he had been able to spend more time practicing and playing. Sinclair Hill said, "Prince Charles is fearless.... [I]n two years I can turn him into a six handicap player and ... captain of the England team."[18] The Prince, with characteristic modesty, said that people were kind to say that he could have achieved a higher rating and admitted, "It would have been nice for my pride to have had a higher handicap and, of course, I longed to be a better player as it makes the game infinitely more enjoyable." But, he acknowledged, "I'm not a naturally aggressive person really, so I'm not as aggressive on the polo field as perhaps I should be if I wanted to be really good. And

I'm not tough enough with my riding. The awful thing is I tend to make friends of my ponies, which is rather an English thing to do. They tend to become more pets if you're not careful. If you don't do that, you're more inclined to get the most out of the game. I know I could be more aggressive, more fired up." The Prince said about high-goal polo: "Everybody marks each other so much better ... and from that point of view it's much easier—as long as you've got the ponies. I mean, if you're 2-goals and you've got high-class ponies, it makes a helluva difference. If you're 2-goals with medium-goal ponies, I wouldn't entertain it because then you are in danger. You never keep up. That's why a few years ago when I started getting better ponies they made a *fantastic* difference. If I get really high-class ponies I can go up a goal or more because you can get there. If you're always flogging, you never quite get there, you're pulling up and then your opponent is gone. It's desperate!"[19]

The Prince has played polo in many countries around the world, including Australia, Brazil, Brunei, France, Ghana, India, Jamaica, Kenya, Malta, and the U.S.A. He has played with many of the world's greatest players, many of whom are profiled in this book. The Prince has been tutored in the game by some of the greatest coaches in the world. his father and great uncle included, but also Sinclair Hill and Memo Gracida. The Prince has said that Sinclair Hill is "a marvelous man to whom I owe a great deal for giving me a different outlook on polo." He continued:

> He was wonderful. He was a real inspiration. He's got an absolute genius for encouraging young players and for explaining the game in a very comprehensible way. He explained it to me in a way somehow nobody else had ever done: suddenly I started to see it from a different point of view. He made me *think* about the game much more carefully and tactically. He made an enormous difference to my outlook and actual ability. He'd really encourage me from the stands, and he'd come down at halftime and at the end of the game. He'd tell me I was being a bloody fool this way and I did *really well* there. And in the end, I wanted to play for *him*. You know I was keen to impress Sinclair and that's what every player needs, I think.

Memo Gracida said about the Prince: "He was one of the best teammates I ever had, because he played team polo. He was unselfish, always putting the team first, always taking full responsibility for his position. He was a very strong back with very accurate hitting, very consistent and rarely missing the ball. He followed every advice or instruction given, which gave me great confidence as a coach and team captain."[20]

In the early 1990s the Prince, after a series of injuries, gave up playing competitive polo. These injuries included being thrown from his horse and kicked during a match, which left a two inch scar on his cheek; suffering from life threatening heat exhaustion after a match in Florida; in June 1990 falling from his pony during a match at Cirencester Park breaking his arm in two places; and in 2001, being knocked unconscious while playing with his sons in the final of the Meadow Trophy at Cirencester Park when his pony slipped and came down heavily. In addition, the famous Australian physiotherapist, Sarah Key, warned that a serious degenerative disc problem could cause his back to lock; she commented in passing that "Prince Charles had a higher pain threshold than anyone I have ever treated."[21]

Having decided to bow out of competitive polo, the Prince concentrated his playing on exhibition games. These sponsored matches included generous donations to charity and it is estimated that in the last ten years of his playing career the Prince was responsible for raising in excess of US$15 million. John Lloyd wrote how the Prince allowed his involvement in the game to make money in a discreet way for charity and remarks that "it is typical that he uses even the time he takes for recreational activity to good ends."[22]

Some of the last games the Prince played were with one or both of his sons in the Highgrove team, which had much success, including winning the Meadow Trophy and Buck's Club Challenge. The obvious enjoyment and ribaldry between father and sons were clear to see for all spectators of these games. The Prince played much of his polo over the last few years at Cirencester Park, partly because of its proximity to Highgrove, but also because, as he said, "Cirencester Park has a very special atmosphere and it is a particular privilege to be able to play polo in such glorious surroundings. But one of the best features of Cirencester is that it still has the unique charm of a proper *country* polo club. It is understated, unpretentious, delightfully relaxed and wonderfully rural. I love it there."[23]

The Prince's last match was for the Ronnie Wallace Memorial Trophy played on Ivy Lodge at Cirencester Park on 30 July 2005. Prince Harry was in the same team as his father, playing against a team from the State of Virginia (U.S.A.). The match was played in aid of the Hunt Staff Benefit Society. At the time no one thought this was to be his last match; in fact, Robert ffrench-Blake — the Prince's polo manager — said, "My impression after his last match at the end of July, although nothing specifically was said, was that he had every intention of playing next season."[24]

In November 2005, just days after his fifty-seventh birthday, it was announced from Clarence House that the Prince would be retiring from polo. A spokesman for the Prince said that, after a series of injuries over the years, the Prince had felt that the time was right "to bow out gracefully but regretfully." Prince Charles commented on the announcement: "Of course I shall miss it terribly, particularly since recently I have so enjoyed playing with my sons. It has been one of the best means I know of forgetting the pressures and complications of life. It's the intense concentration that is, funnily enough, what makes it so relaxing. Nevertheless, I thought it better to call a halt when I was still playing reasonably well."

As Lord Patrick Beresford wrote, "However greatly Prince Charles may miss polo, even more greatly polo will miss him. For forty-two years he has been an integral part of the game, an example to us all, both on the field and off, of good manners, enthusiasm, sportsmanship and care for his ponies."[25] Christopher Hanbury (chairman of the H.P.A.) remarked, "The Prince has done a huge amount to raise the profile of polo and has been truly good for the sport in every way, both at home and abroad."[26]

Notes

1. Lord Patrick Beresford, *Guards Polo Club Year Book* (Windsor, 2005), 22.
2. *Hurlingham Polo Association 1980 Year Book* (Ambersham: H.P.A., 1981).
3. *Hurlingham Polo Association 1988 Year Book*: (Ambersham: H.P.A., 1989).
4. Michael Butler, in *The Pimm's Book of Polo*, John Lloyd, editor (London: Stanley Paul, 1989), 184.
5. *The Field*, London, 1878.
6. John Lloyd, in *The Pimm's Book of Polo*, John Lloyd, editor (London: Stanley Paul, 1989) 122.
7. Derek Russell-Stoneham, and Roger Chatterton-Newman, *Polo at Cowdray* (London: P.I.B., 1992), *v*.
8. *Horse and Hound*, 14 August 1969.
9. Ami Shinitzki, *Polo* (Gaithersburgh, October 1989), 36.
10. Michael Clayton, *Prince Charles, Horseman* (London: Stanley Paul, 1987).
11. Nicholas Gaslee, quoted on H.R.H. The Prince of Wales' official Internet Website, www.princeofwales.gov.uk
12. Tony Rees, *Polo: The Galloping Game* (Cochrane, Alberta: Western Heritage Centre Society, 2000), v.
13. Lord Patrick Beresford, *Guards Polo Club Year Book* (Windsor: p.p., 2006), 22.
14. Prince Charles, *Guards Polo Club Year Book* (Windsor, p.p., 2006), p. 23.
15. Shinitzki, p. 36
16. Lloyd, 120.
17. Shinitzki, 35.
18. Sinclair Hill, *Polo* (Dallas, January/February 1998), 55.
19. Shinitzky, 36.
20. Guillermo Gracida, *Hurlingham* (London, Winter 2006), 27.
21. Sarah Kay, *Guards Polo Club Year Book* (Windsor: p.p., 2006), 23.

22. Lloyd, 122.
23. Prince Charles, in *A Century of Polo*, Herbert Spencer, editor (World Polo Associates, 1994), vii.
24. Robert ffrench-Blake, *Hurlingham* Winter 2006), 26–27.
25 Lord Patrick Beresford, *Guards Polo Club Year Book* (Windsor; p.p., 2006), 23.
26. Christopher Hanbury, *Hurlingham* (Winter 2006), 27.

Alberto Pedro Heguy: Basque Blood — Passion and Verve

by Horace A. Laffaye

The Heguys are of French-Basque stock. The family patriarch, Bautista Heguy, purchased large tracts of land in what then was the territory of La Pampa. Bautista fathered ten children, of which three, Ramón, Antonio and Juan Bautista, became part of the band of enthusiasts who on 10 January 1932 founded Chapaleufú, the first polo club in La Pampa. The first committee was established at a meeting which took place in the offices of Heguy, Pezzali & Co., grain and cattle merchants. Juan Bautista was elected treasurer. The club's name means "Muddy Creek" in Araucarian language. Oddly enough, there is nothing geographical bearing such a feature in the area, but it was the district's official name. The initial club's colors were white, red and black vertical stripes, the latter being thinner. After some time, the shirt was changed to white with a red star and red collar. Antonio Heguy, an agronomist, participated in the first match played by the novice club, against Trenque Lauquen. Later on, he captained club teams that took the National Handicap Tournament for the Copa República Argentina in 1948 and 1953, which included his nephew Luis María, nicknamed Lucho. Lucho Heguy was a good number 1, rated at 5-goals and always superbly mounted. However, polo-pony breeding was his passion; the celebrated Malapata and Marsellesa were two of his best known products. Chapaleufú again won the National Handicap title in 1960, 1973, 1988 and 1994; at least one Heguy family member has been on every team. The club also took the World Cup in Chicago, with a team that included Juan José Alberdi, Alberto Pedro Heguy, Gonzalo Tanoira and Alfredo Harriott. It was a formidable 38-goal combination.

Antonio's base in Buenos Aires was Los Indios, which had been founded in 1923 as one of the criollo polo clubs. Its colors are white with a black hoop. When Indios-Chapaleufú was formed in the 1980s, the younger Heguy generation adopted the hoop, but in the red color, to adorn the now famous shirt. It was a team from Los Indios, skippered by Antonio Heguy and completed with his Chapaleufú teammates Pablo Nagore and Juan Echeverz Sr., that joined Dr. Jorge Marín Moreno—a frequent visitor in England—to take Cowdray Park's inaugural Gold Cup in 1956. Only once has the Argentine Open Championship been taken by a team uniquely formed by fathers and sons. In 1958, Antonio and Horacio Heguy teamed up with the Juan Carlos Harriotts to accomplish this feat, playing as Coronel Suárez-Indios and adding to the family's string of records.

The Heguy's estancia had almost 10,000 hectares. It was named Anay Rucá—Araucarian for "Friendly Home." Antonio had three sons and a daughter: Horacio Antonio, Alberto Pedro, Eduardo and Myriam. Tragedy has hit the family hard. Eduardo, a promising 6-goal player, about to receive his agronomy degree, was killed in 1965 in a car crash, at age 22. At the time, he was as good a player as his older siblings were at his age and was seriously considered as a prospective 10-goaler. In his short lifespan, Eduardo Heguy won several tournaments, including the National Handicap Championship. All three brothers won the High School Championship playing for Colegio Champagnat, a Marist school in Buenos Aires. So did Gonzalo, Horacito, Marcos, Alberto "Pepe" and Eduardo "Ruso," members of the next generation, representing the same school as well.

Antonio's only daughter, Myriam, was also killed in a car accident, at a railroad crossing in 1981. Her son, Francisco Bensadón, is now a 9-goal handicap player, who took the 2004 U.S. Open with John Goodman's Isla Carroll team. One of Horacio's infant sons was drowned in a swimming pool, and the world of polo mourned Gonzalo Heguy's death in 2000, following an automobile accident.

Horacio Antonio Heguy (1936–1998) graduated from the School of Agronomy and Veterinary at the University of Buenos Aires. He took 19 Argentine Open Championships—20 if you take into account his replacement for Celestino Garrós during the final match in 1980—ten Hurlingham Open Championships and four Cup of the Americas. His ponies, Solito and

Colegio Champagnat, the 1954 High School's Tournament champions (left to right): Alberto Pedro Heguy (age 13), Horacio Heguy (18), Francisco Dorignac (16) and Gastón Dorignac (14). All four players reached a 10-goal handicap and represented Argentina in international play. As a group, they accumulated 43 Argentine Open individual trophies (courtesy Museum of Polo and Hall of Fame).

Yarará, were awarded the Lady Susan Townley Cup for Best Playing Pony in the Argentine Open.[1] In England, Horacio took the Midhurst Town Cup. Together with Alberto Pedro, they were known as the "Heguy Express" for their unrelenting speed on the polo ground. At times Horacio defied gravity in leaning out of his mount to hit the ball, a style of play that, when imitated by less talented players, led to falls and injuries.

Alberto Pedro had a hidden admiration for his older brother. "I could not compete with him. If he studied agronomy, I had to study veterinary. He played full-blast polo; I tried to learn skills and tactics to improve my limitations, which he lacked; he was just too good," Alberto once said. In regard to ponies, Horacio was pragmatic. If a prospect was unsuitable, he would discard it without a blink. On the other hand, Alberto Pedro would try to persevere with a pony due to its blood line or just because it had a nice stamp.

Once, Alberto complained that Horacio was much better mounted. Horacio answered, "I am a 10 and it is very difficult to keep that rating. Your ponies are fine for your 8-goals." Time went by and both were 10-goal players; Horacio was lowered to 9-goals, still with the better picks. Alberto Pedro complained again and this time the answer was, "I must get back to 10 and that is not easy." In his brother's own words, Horacio lived and played polo like a road roller. Discussing tactics, Alberto asked him to pass the ball in a certain way; Horacio answered, "I win the ball and hit it forward. You find it where it goes, don't ask for more than that." So simple, so visceral.

The 1973 season was not a good one for Horacio; things were just not going his way. Alberto suggested placing his brother at number 1, but Juancarlitos Harriott thought that Horacio would feel hurt. Harriott would rather lose the Open than upset Horacio, and his brother Alfredito agreed. That year Coronel Suárez lost the Open to Santa Ana, but everyone on the team was happy. Perhaps the title, having been so often won, appeared less worth taking. To give an idea of how important Horacio Heguy was to the team, from 1958 until 1980, he failed to take the Abierto at Palermo only in 1960 and 1973. Horacio was unable to play in 1971 because he developed hepatitis.

Horacio Heguy married Nora Amadeo y Videla, from the polo-playing family in Coronel Suárez, and they had five sons; in 1991 Bautista, Gonzalo, Horacio Segundo and Marcos became the first four-brother team to win the Argentine Open. They added three more wins, in 1992, 1993, and 1995.[2] Of Indios-Chapaleufú I, it has been said that Horacito was the brain, Gonzalo the soul, Bautista the scorer and Marcos the engine. It is small wonder that Bautista Heguy, with that ancestry and such talented brothers and cousins, should become a player of great distinction.

Alberto Pedro Heguy, this profile's subject, also married into a Coronel Suárez polo family, in his case Silvia Molinari. They had four polo-playing sons, three of whom achieved prominence in the game, playing off 10-goals. The eldest, Eduardo, known as "Ruso," was born in 1966. He is the winner of four Argentine Open Championships and two Hurlingham Open Championships. In England, he took Cowdray Park's Gold Cup and the Prince of Wales Trophy. Eduardo also captained the Argentine team that won the Coronation Cup at Windsor Park. In America he won the Gold Cup and the C.V. Whitney Cup. In his time, "Ruso" Heguy was the best back in the world.

Alberto Heguy was born in 1967. "Pepe" as he is known, won the Argentine and Hurlingham Open Championships four times each. In England he took the Queen's Cup, the Silver Jubilee Cup and the Prince of Wales Trophy. In the U.S., Pepe took the C.V. Whitney Cup. He is married to Paula, Marcos Uranga's daughter.

The third son, Tomás, born in 1969, played polo as well, reaching a 4-goal handicap, a respectable rating that pales in comparison with his siblings and cousins. However, an accident in his early career convinced him that his future was not in high-goal polo and he decided to pursue a master in business administration degree, graduating eventually from Stanford University in California.

Ignacio, the inimitable "Nachi," was born in 1973. He is the winner of four Argentine Open Championships, the Hurlingham Open and the National Handicap Championship. In England he won the Cowdray Park Gold Cup and in the U.S. the Gold Cup.

Alberto Pedro Heguy, the third child and second son of Antonio Heguy and Myriam Gouaillard, was born on 26 January 1941. He was educated at Colegio Champagnat, the school that was a cradle of polo champions. Alberto then entered Universidad de Buenos, earning his veterinary degree in March 1964. It should have been December 1963, the end of the academic year in the Southern hemisphere, but the game of polo got in the way. In his own words:

> I had to sit for seven final exams and it was the time of my first Abierto. The first four went by fairly easy, but on a Saturday morning I had the two most difficult: Clinical and Obstetrics. The next day we had the final match against Santa Ana. I passed both and that afternoon we played a practice game at Hurlingham. My proud parents told everybody that I had done well in the toughest exams. But Juan Carlos Harriott Senior looked at me with a less than friendly expression. For him, it was a distraction from the task at hand. How could I do such a thing on the final's eve? On the next day we beat Santa Ana in extra chukker. I scored the winning goal.
>
> I was very tired after the game and I failed the last exam, Rural Administration. So I had to take it again in March.[3]

The 1963 Open Championship at Palermo was the first of 17 Argentine Open titles and 14 Hurlingham Club Championship crowns. Alberto went on to participate in 28 consecutive Argentine Open Championships, from 1963 to 1991, representing Coronel Suárez and Indios-Chapaleufú, a record still standing, as well as being the only player to appear in all four team positions.

His sporting resume includes two wins in the Cup of the Americas, at home and in the United States, the World Cup at Oak Brook and the National Handicap Tournament. His ponies Rosa, Titina, Ceniza and Purita won the Lady Susan Townley Cup. When asked about his favorite pony, Alberto Pedro's rugged face softens, and with a smile, he murmurs, "La Purita...."

When Prince Philip visited Argentina during the 1966 International Polo Season, the subject of the Falkland Islands—Islas Malvinas, in Argentina—came up. At a party after the Hurlingham Open, in a festive mood the Duke of Edinburgh quipped, "I'll exchange the islands for the Heguys." Alberto and Horacio plus Daniel González were his teammates on the Windsor Park team which reached the finals of the Hurlingham Open. They were narrowly defeated 9–8 by the Argentine National 30-goal team, which included Alfredo Harriott, Gastón Dorignac, Juancarlitos Harriott and Gonzalo Tanoira.

That year Alberto Pedro Heguy was selected to represent Argentina in the Cup of the Americas. Bad luck intervened when, shortly after the final game of the Argentine Open had started, Alberto broke his wrist. Replaced by the American Dr. William Linfoot, Alberto had to watch the series from the sidelines. Thirteen years were to pass by before he realized his dream of wearing the light blue and white national colors.

Chris Ashton, Australian player, journalist and historian, was impressed with Alberto Pedro's "breadth of vision and sharp intelligence."[4] Heguy's alert mind is evident in a coauthored treatise on biomechanics, injuries and strategy in high-goal polo,[5] and an instructional video, "*Polo—How to Reach 10.*"

He was deeply concerned about his country at a time of political instability and social turmoil. Never afraid to voice his opinion, he ran for governor of La Pampa, and also for National Congressman. He failed to gain a majority in both instances.

Extremely quick, he was as good a number 1 as a number 2, but Alberto Pedro brought a new dimension to the number 1 position play. While up to this time the traditional play achieved

From La Pampa to Chicago. Chapaleufú, winners of the World Cup at Oak Brook in 1977. Right to left: Juan José Alberdi, Alberto Pedro Heguy, Gonzalo Tanoira, Alfredo Harriott, at the time, a 38-goal combination (courtesy Museum of Polo and Hall of Fame).

by a long line of outstanding Argentine number ones—including Arturo Kenny, Alfredo Harrington, Luis Duggan and Juan Cavanagh—had confined themselves to stay up in front of the play, mark the opposing back, and when given the chance run for goal; Heguy became an all-around worker, rotating here, defending there and attacking at the first available opportunity. A tireless player, he was relentless in shadowing the back; however, it was his speed towards goal that characterized his play in the spectators' eyes. But he was much more than that. In the "Heguy Express," Alberto and Horacio, as forwards, were an integral part of the best team ever, just as Juancarlitos and Alfredo Harriott were bringing up the rear.

Their thirst for scoring goals was insatiable. At a match against La Espadaña, Alberto returned to the lineup in midfield after scoring a goal, and heard a shout behind him: "Watch out, Alberto! We haven't won yet!" The score was 14–1. Gonzalo Tanoira, the classy 10-goaler who played for and against Coronel Suárez, once said:

> If they could win by 100 goals they would never be satisfied with 99. They wanted 100. To me, this is a fundamental attribute for any player. Such desperation to win, such hunger for glory; it was fabulous.[6]

When questioned as to why they kept pouring on the goals in an already decided match, the brothers answered that they considered it disrespectful to the spectators and the opposing team to let up.

A criticism has been voiced that the Heguy brothers, especially Alberto, had many chances to score goals but also missed many. In the first match for the Cup of the Americas, Alberto took eight shots at goal; he scored in every single attempt.

A biographical sketch of any member of the Heguy family cannot be considered complete without mentioning Tito Lezcano. In 1947, at age 16, Héctor Antonio Lezcano, nicknamed Tito, started to work for Antonio Heguy at Anay Rucá, remaining there until the present time. Antonio, as are his children and grandchildren, was fastidious about the care and training of his polo ponies. Tito was Antonio's groom until his boss retired; he traveled to England when the elder Heguy took the Gold Cup at Cowdray Park. Lezcano also groomed for Horacio and Alberto in the High Schools Championships and stayed with Horacio until he in turn retired in 1980. Then Tito started working with the next Heguy generation. He decided to quit in 1990; Horacio Senior asked him to remain and Tito relented, grooming for Marcos Heguy.

Alberto Pedro Heguy vouches for Lezcano's absolute dedication to and knowledge of the team's ponies:

> When my nephews were in the 1986 final I went to the pony lines and Tito told me: "If we don't win today, we never will. I have the horses at peak condition. Never better than today. I woke up at 3 A.M., and sip some mates. I woke up the boys and told them: Marsellesa and Malapata, leave then in the boxes because they are fine. Those over there, three laps; the other ones, just two laps." The proof came when Marcos ran away to score the winning goal when La Espadaña's mares were exhausted.[7]

That goal scored by Marcos Heguy, riding Marsellesa, taking the ball near his own goalposts and running the length of the field avoiding adversaries, has earned its place in Palermo's lore as "the goal." It put a dent in La Espadaña's run of six Open titles in seven years.

Tito Lezcano is retired now, but his occasional presence in the pony lines is still acknowledged with respect for his professional achievement and loyalty to the family. Another of the Heguys' grooms with a long tenure is Víctor Mensi. Víctor groomed for Luis María Heguy, Antonio's nephew, for eleven years and then for Alberto Pedro for thirty years.

When asked about polo's current activity, Alberto Pedro is quite forthright:

> Nowdays if a team is winning by two goals they will hit the ball off the field to waste clock-time. That never happened when we played. Far too many fouls are called today. One team will score 10 goals from penalties, the other eight. I think polo has become too subject to the rules book. In our time, the players were also umpires. Gonzalo Tanoira umpired, and even though he seldom blew the whistle, he was Gonzalo Tanoira. When Gastón Dorignac was an umpire, he was Gastón Dorignac.... We respected the umpires, because they exuded authority, and the matches came out fine. Today everything is a foul. Players exaggerate the fouls, and make the ambulance drive onto the field four times a match. Now more fouls are whistled and there are more accidents. I have tremendous respect for the current game and players. They are phenomenal; and yet sometimes it is a terrible spectacle, because the umpires blow the whistle 45 times. One tallies the fouls: one team had 25, the other 18. In fact, when the umpires do not blow the whistle that often, players do not "manufacture" fouls because they know the whistle will not sound. Part of the current strategy is to try to get a foul blown on the opponent and maybe you will win the game.[8]

Alberto Pedro Heguy has had a distinguished trajectory both as a polo player and as a human being. True to his Basque heritage, he has played the game with passion and verve, always giving his best. At age 66, Alberto still enjoys breeding and training ponies at his estancia in Intendente Alvear, La Pampa. Just a year ago, he was selected to play for the Civilians team against the Military team in the annual classic for the Springbok Trophy.[9] Playing in the number 3 position, he led his team to victory. In 2007, he still carries a 6-goal handicap.

When his last appearance in an Argentine Open Championship was completed in 1991 and Alberto Pedro Heguy rode off the field, a tear or two running down his face, the entire crowd rose spontaneously to honor him with a standing ovation. Old timers thought it was the most emotional tribute given to a player at Palermo, polo's cathedral.

It is appropriate to close this essay with Chico Barry's words after the 1979 Cup of the Americas: "Alberto Heguy is the best number one in the world."[10]

Notes

1. The Lady Susan Townley Cup was presented in 1908 by Sir Walter Townley (1863–1945), British Minister to Argentina. Lady Susan (1868–1953) was a polo-pony breeder, owner of the stallion Don Mike, and wrote *My Chinese Notebook*, a record of her time at the British Legation in Shanghai.

2. In 2003 La Aguada, with Javier, Eduardo Jr., Miguel and Ignacio Novillo Astrada, became the second all-brothers team to take the Argentine Open.

3. Federico Chaine, *Los Heguy: Pura Sangre de Polo* (Buenos Aires: Imprenta de los Buenos Ayres, 2001), 66.

4. Interview with Alberto Pedro Heguy, December 2005. Personal communication from Chris Ashton.

5. Alberto Pedro Heguy, and Daniel Martínes Páez: *Biomecánica, estrategia, preparación competitiva y lesions del polo de alto handicap argentino* (Buenos Aires: Fundación de Polo y Entrenamiento Integral, 1994).

6. Chaine, 113.

7. *Ibid.*, 218.

8. Interview with Alejandra Ocampo; *PoloLine*, November 2003.

9. The Springbok Trophy was presented by the South African Polo Association in 1934. It is a stylized bronze springbok — South Africa sporting teams' emblem — sculpted by Mary Ann Stainbank, a Durban artist.

10. *Polo* July/August 1979 10.

Julian Hipwood: A Living Polo Legend

by Sarah Eakin

Young autograph hunters are lining up at the Gold Cup finals at Cowdray Park—a new generation of heroes has arrived for the adolescent polo enthusiasts, names like Gonzalito Pieres and Javier Novillo Astrada. Suggestions for pursuing signatures from other top players in the crowd and not on the playing field are met with blank faces—well they're not in the finals, are they? Then Julian Hipwood is spotted among the crowd. "Julian Hipwood? Now that would be cool...."

Dressed in a panama with a stylish silk tie and pocket handkerchief, the man who never wears a baseball cap, much less a "beanie" is a picture of sartorial elegance. Julian, though far from fashionably hip, has nevertheless stood the test of time as a polo icon. He has also succeeded where others have failed in transcending the polo worlds on either side of the Atlantic. The former England captain is known in the U.K. for his polo prowess, having led England in the Coronation Cup for 20 years and reached a nine-goal handicap (along with his younger brother, Howard) and therefore raised the bar for English players in modern times. In the U.S. he is known as a coach and a professional player, still competing and still competitive in a seemingly timeless fashion.

Julian Brian Hipwood grew up in Pakistan but was born, on 23 June 1946, in the Gloucestershire town of Minchinhampton. He has a younger brother, Howard, and a sister, Marilyn. His father, Brian, was in the Royal Air Force and Julian's childhood had little to do with horses and much to do with machines. When his father came back from his overseas placement to England to live permanently he set up shop in the corner of a field—a garage business that saw his son employed to renew brake pads, pump gas and tinker with engines. "It was an ordinary house and an ordinary garage," said Julian. "I'd put on my grease monkey suit and go to work."

The polo connection came through Julian's maternal grandfather with the distinguished name of Reginald Brice. He owned a riding school and played polocrosse but changed direction as polo came into style, and he began providing horses for the nearby Cirencester Agricultural College—a breeding ground for young players, among whom, Julian recalls, was a young Australian student, Sinclair Hill.

As a child Julian looked forward to his father's leave, which they spent with his grandfather and grandmother Janet. Their English country farmers' lifestyle taught Julian to milk cows before school, and left him with a fond memory of his grandfather presenting a plucked goose to each of the local villagers at Christmas. These flashbacks are a far cry from the dust, mountains and Tonga pony-pulled rickshaws that he recalls from a childhood spent running around constantly shoeless—by choice—in Pakistan.

From the age of three Julian rode, and he was gradually inducted into Pony Club polo where his life took a monumental turn when he met and played alongside the legendary Hanut Singh. When the Pakistan-India war and a call to duty in 1965 took a player—a cavalry officer—out of the Hanut's team, he told his teammates: "I've found a boy who's playing bumble puppy polo," using the Pakistani expression for a form of snake-killing low-goal. "We need to bring him in to play in some good polo."

Hanut became a mentor for Julian as Julian learned the ropes as part of Eric Moller's Jersey Lillies team. Playing in the low-goal team he remembers Hanut inflicting a strict regime of wooden horse practice and stick and balling without ever being allowed to break into a canter.

"It was an extraordinary start in polo," said Julian. "I try to pass on some of the things I learned then to those who ask my advice." Counseling comes naturally to Julian, who has coached several high goal teams and players. "He's one of the greatest strategists in the game," said Terry Hanlon, the voice of Cowdray Park polo for many years, who switches from microphone to mallet for fun. Even after playing with him for over twenty years, Hanlon admits to being mesmerized by Julian's talents. "When I played with him I was like his dog" said Hanlon. "Whatever he said to do, I did without question. He rarely spoke after a match and he never praised me except once. After one match, he simply told me that I'd played well. I've never forgotten that moment."

Julian inspires respect on and off the field. It was on the field that he earned the love of his wife, Patricia. They met—as tradition dictates—treading-in at Cowdray Park. She came from a hunting, dressage and show jumping background and had a distinguished career as a journalist working as fashion editor for *Harper's, Queen* and as American correspondent for *Interiors Magazine*. Both having been married before, they have four children between them, and a long and happy marriage; they now live in Palm Beach and commute across the Atlantic.

Although Julian has played in the States for many years—in Saratoga for the past 10 and for many years in Florida, where, among other notable achievements, he won the World Cup five times at Palm Beach Polo and Country Club—across the pond he is best remembered as England's polo captain. As such he became a figurehead of the sport and transcended the barrier somewhat from polo player to celebrity. He was asked to appear on a talk show once where he was dismayed to find the presenter breaking pre-live show promises and quickly bringing up the subject of the Royals. It was an invitation to indiscretion not welcomed by Julian, who learned a lesson that day and has since taken care where the press are concerned, but not where his opinions are strong and he feels that the future of polo is at stake. "I don't have a problem speaking out," he said. "I love the game of polo and I don't really mind what happens as long as it's for the good of the sport." Such driven sentiments have not always paid off.

For several years he ran a column in *Horse and Hound* and later in *Polo* magazine, raising questions about umpiring, unsportsmanlike behavior and other often taboo issues that were discussed behind closed doors but not necessarily aired in public. A particularly sharp criticism of professional umpires produced a year when, he says, "I don't think I won a game." Ironic when he considers that "I'm a lot quieter on the field than I used to be." Regardless of the fallout, Julian continues to speak out. "I have an interest in putting polo right," he said. "But sometimes there are too many people who have their own agendas and not necessarily

The 1979 Coronation Cup (left to right): Paul Withers, Julian Hipwood, Prince Charles, John Horswell, Howard Hipwood. They defeated Mexico at Windsor Park (courtesy Museum of Polo and Hall of Fame).

the best interests of polo at heart." *Way to go*, some might say. *What does that old codger know about it?* he accepts is also a possible reaction from others.

The same could apply to his growing role as a high-goal coach. "The style of play has changed," he confirmed. "The ball control of the young guys that play today is incredible. I wish I could do what they do with the ball." Some things never change. "Sometimes messing with the ball is not the right play. I point out that you can't travel faster than the ball and sometimes they say 'I never thought about that' but it's so simple really." Proof that you're never too young, or in Julian's case too old, to learn new tricks. "I do smile sometimes," he said. "When I get on the field and I try something that I've seen Miguel Novillo Astrada or Pablo MacDonough do ... and it works. But age doesn't matter really. There is nothing like getting to a man quickly and shutting him down before he can get clever with the ball."

It was this "take no prisoners" approach that inspired victory for England in the International match against North America in 1988 at Guards Polo Club in Royal Windsor Great Park. Played to a crowd of 25,000 spectators and the Queen herself, the atmosphere on the hallowed turf of Smith's Lawn was enflamed by the partisan commentary of Hanlon. England was down by six goals at halftime against the Americans. Hanlon said that Hipwood was more than a little driven by a heckler in the crowd: "Some ex-public schoolboy [private school boy] in the crowd said 'Oh come on England' in a very snooty and denigrating voice. Julian went ballistic. In my commentary, I treated every goal England scored as if it was itself a victory and the crowd responded, inspiring the team to play out of their skins and England ran out winners by 8 goals to seven. I like to think I played a part but Julian was the real factor. Stuart Mackenzie, who was umpiring, said it was the greatest comeback he'd ever seen." Julian remembers the day above many of the other International games. "Hats were thrown in the air," he said. "The crowd went wild."

It may have been one of his best memories and as Julian says, "I have plenty to think back on when I'm old." He's not there yet. An enthusiasm for riding horses has kept him fit and active and while he may not "work out" often, he rarely puts his feet up. "I like to be doing something," he said, "and would rather go and ride a young horse than, say, play golf, which doesn't appeal to me. Too much time spent sitting in the cart...." He still spends plenty of time sitting in the saddle and will dabble with the odd green horse, though he confesses that he did not see himself as a "horse trainer" and tended to leave that to others. He knows what he likes in a prospect, though: "nice looking, good shoulder, good eye, nice across the front, great rear end, put together well, a horse that has agility and is light and that carries its head in the right place.... I hate upside down necks, though I have had a couple like that." One criterion that is a deal breaker for Hipwood is the temperament. "If they don't have that then it doesn't matter how good they are," he says. In reflecting on this comment it becomes interesting to note that the majority of horses on his list of favorites are geldings rather than mares, including Everest, Able, Naranjo, Sauce and Muffin, the latter seeming to have lasted as long as he has. When there have been so many to choose from, what would make some horses so special? "They looked after me on the polo field," he said. "They had power and speed and they would ride sort of 'proud.' They turn on the switch."

In addition to Julian's horses, foremost in his mind when he reaches the age of reflection may be his early days when he looked more likely to take the path of a professional soccer player, taking the field for Bristol Rovers' second team at the tender age of 16. He remains a soccer enthusiast—a passion he shared with his father—and he is a loyal Manchester United fan. Somehow the panama and the pocket handkerchief seem more fitting in the polo setting, and Julian was quick to see his niche on his first polo trip abroad, riding in a Bentley convertible with Gaje Singh to play in Normandy, France, where they spent the night at a local chateau. "It was at that point that I realized what polo was really all about," he said. Today he wears his sport well. Hanlon called on him at the Gold Cup finals: "We have here Julian Hipwood," he boomed. "What do you think, Julian?" A spokesman for the sport he always will be and a man not afraid to speak up for as long as polo matters to him as it does now.

His fireside memories will doubtless also include his wins in the Gold Cup for the British Open Championship, his two appearances in the Argentine Open finals and his long list of victories in both the U.S. and England. In the course of his career he played polo in 22 countries and made his mark on the hallowed turf of Palermo playing with his peers Alfredo Goti, Gonzalo Pieres, Gonzalo Tanoira, Héctor Barrantes, Eduardo Moore and Taio Novillo Astrada. To put his time at the top in perspective, in 1979 his handicap was raised in Argentina from eight to nine, while Gonzalo Pieres moved from seven to eight. Heady days, and a reminder that Julian's career spans more than one crop of players.

The next generation may have arrived but the Hipwood era is not yet over. "It surprises me," he says in his distinguished, calm and English-charm filled voice, "but I was asked to give some of my old jodhpurs and mallets to the pony club. I didn't think the young players would be interested in having them...."

Harold Barry: "A galloping oak with the soul of a poet"

by Horace A. Laffaye

Born in Ponca City, Oklahoma, on 19 August 1943, Harold Andrew "Joe" Barry was a major figure in American and international polo, a savvy horseman and a leader on the field of play. Most who knew him will remember Joe for his warmth, his outgoing optimism, his integrity and his sense of fairness.

Through three generations the Barry family has been a towering presence in American polo. The four children of Andrew Paul and Nora Barry all played polo. Claude was a delegate and Circuit Governor for the U.S.P.A.[1] Claude's son Dwight played at Texas A & M University; regrettably, his polo career was cut short when he was killed in World War II. The second son, Paul Weldon "Bill" Barry—recently inducted into Polo's Hall of Fame—reached a 7-goal rating. The third son, Roy Lawson, also played off a handicap of 7-goals, and his son, Roy Matthews—another 9-goaler and Hall of Fame member—represented the U.S. in the Cup of the Americas in Buenos Aires in 1966 and 1979, and also won the Avila Camacho Cup against Mexico and the Coronation Cup in England, plus three U.S. Open Championships and the Gold and Silver Cups. In turn, "Little Roy's" son, Roy Robert "Bobby," was a finalist in the U.S. Open and currently is one of the best umpires on the polo circuit.

The fourth son, Harold Leon, nicknamed "Chico" ("little" in Spanish) because he was the last born, took the Coronation Cup three times and the U.S. Open on seven occasions; in the banner year 1970, he was on the Tulsa-Greenhill championship team with his son Joe. In spite of his heavy weight, Chico Barry was an excellent horseman and a long hitter who played for the United States in two Cups of the Americas, in 1966 and 1969. He is also enshrined in the Hall of Fame. Thus, we have the Barry family's contribution to American polo.

Harold Andrew Barry was universally known as "Joe," perhaps to distinguish him from his equally illustrious father, to the extent that when Joe traveled to Argentina with the American team he was listed in the official program as Joseph Barry.[2]

With his sister, Betty Sue, he grew up in Truscott, Texas. The town lacked a high school so the siblings went by bus to Crowell High School, some 25 miles away. Football was Joe's game at the time, and he played offensive guard and defensive end. His performance was good enough to merit offers of scholarships to the U.S. Military Academy at West Point and Texas Christian and Texas Technical universities. But his ambition was to be a veterinarian, so he paid his own way at West Texas State. Later on, Joe earned a master's degree in animal nutrition at New Mexico University.

By then he was already playing polo professionally in order to meet the financial burden presented by his college education. A born horseman, he perfected his skill under his father's tutelage. Shortly after college, he met his future wife, Sharon, who at the time was working for 7-goal patron Robert Beveridge. They married in 1972 and enjoyed a happy and fulfilling life together.

Joe Barry quickly developed into a star of the first magnitude on the American polo firmament. He was one of the happy band of polo pals that revived the game after the doldrums of the late fifties and the early sixties. Joe, his cousin Roy and Lester "Red" Armour, Bart Evans, William "Corky" Linfoot (Dr. William Linfoot's son), Charles Smith and Tommy Wayman monopolized the high-goal scene. In the bargain, they all became lifelong friends. Red Armour reminisced:

> It was a special time. The most special time. Those were the good years for me and Tommy and Joe and Bart. If we weren't on the same team in the finals of a tournament, we were on opposite sides lining up against each other. We lived together, we traveled together, we even dined together every night.[3]

First international appearance for Joe Barry: The Coronation Cup in 1971. Left to right: Chico and Joe Barry, Dr. William Linfoot, Hawaiian Ronnie Tongg (courtesy Museum of Polo and Hall of Fame).

Joe Barry took the first of his six U.S. Open Championships with the Midland team in 1968. Two years later he won again with Jim Sharp's Tulsa-Greenhill on a team that included his father. Further wins were with Milwaukee in 1974 and 1975, and with Retama in 1977 and 1979. Other successes included the 12-Goal and three 20-Goal (now called the Silver Cup) tournaments, two Butler National Handicaps, three Gold Cups and two North American Cups.

England saw his first international appearance on a team that took the Coronation and Midhurst Town Cups in 1971. Hawaiian Ronnie Tongg, Dr. William Linfoot, and Chico and Joe Barry represented America at the revival of Great Britain's premier international trophy, which had been languishing 18 long years within the confines of a silver cabinet. Joe was also a member of the American team on the Avila Camacho Cup against Mexico in 1981. He toured Australia with Steve Gose's Retama team; they were winners of the Morton Cup.

Other international appearances occurred during the short-lived America Cup, sponsored by Peter Brant at the Greenwich Polo Club from 1987 to 1989. This unofficial competition pitted high-goal teams from Argentina and the United States, providing fans in the northeast with the sweet taste of the game played at a lofty level of achievement.

Another milestone in Joe's career occurred when his USA-Texas team (Bart Evans, Tommy Wayman, Red Armour and Barry) took the 1979 World Cup at Palm Beach, defeating in an extra-chukker, sudden-death final a Coronel Suárez team that included Horacio Araya, Ernesto Trotz, Juan Carlos Harriott Jr. and Celestino Garrós. This victory raised expectations for a good show in the Cup of the Americas against the Argentines at Palermo later that year.

Alas, it was not to be. Facing Coronel Suárez, a 40-goal team at the peak of its career selected *in toto* to wear the light blue and white of Argentina, the United States went down in two matches. Supported by the generous financial aid provided by Steven Gose and coached by Chico Barry, the team nominated to make the long southward journey included the USA-Texas team's members, with the addition of Joel Baker, Roy Barry Jr. and Charles Smith, Cecil Smith's son. After being selected, Bart Evans bowed out and Corky Linfoot was named to take his place.

After trying many different combinations, Chico Barry selected the foursome that had defeated Harriott and company at Palm Beach Polo seven months earlier, with only one substitution: Charles Smith played at number 1 instead of Bart Evans. Early on, the team was entered in the Indios-Tortugas Open, the first tournament of Argentina's Triple Crown of polo, and was vanquished. At the Hurlingham Open, a team formed by Corky Linfoot, Memo Gracida, Red Armour and Joe Barry lost to Los Cóndores by five goals. The Americans had played well in practice games against local high-goal teams; however, observers noted that in tournament play the Argentine teams seemed to ratchet up a notch their intensity and game velocity. The visitors were paying the price of playing for years at 26-goal level. When matched with opponents at levels of 30-goals and up, speed, both mental and physical, made a huge difference.

Conversely, there was some concern among the Argentine ranks. The anointed Coronel Suárez team was defeated by Mar del Plata in the Indios-Tortugas Open by 13 goals to 8, one of their worst losses ever. At the Hurlingham Club Open final, Coronel Suárez had a desperate struggle against Mar del Plata throughout the entire game, finally emerging victorious 14–13 in extra chukker. Coupled with Coronel Suárez's apparent vulnerability, and the improved performance of the American team in faster practice matches, there was some reason for optimism on the part of the visitors.

All tickets to the series had been sold weeks in advance, to the delight of the Asociación Argentina de Polo's treasurer, and some 20,000 spectators crowded "polo's cathedral" at Palermo for the first game. Argentina showed its 40-goal wonder: the brothers Alberto and Horacio Heguy up front, the brothers Juan Carlos and Alfredo Harriott in the defense. As was its wont,

Joe Barry watching the ball go harmlessly over the back line. Stowell Park's Mark Vestey and Chico Barry follow the play (courtesy Museum of Polo and Hall of Fame).

the Argentines came off the gate running: 3–0 in the first period, 5–0 in the second; 10–1 in the third; 11–2 before the break. The final score was 18–6 in favor of the defending champions.[4]

The crowd left the stadium happy about the result, but also with the negative feeling of having watched a game in which the final result was never in doubt. The second game being postponed for one week because of springtime rains, the American contingent took stock of the situation. It was rumored that a video of the game was carefully analyzed and then consigned to the flames. Some mounts were purchased and the lineup was altered considerably. After much debate, Armour, Wayman, Joe Barry and Roy Barry played in that order. The team performed much better than in the first match, but it was not enough. An early goal by Armour put the American team ahead and close to the end of the second chukker they were leading 3–2. But Alberto Heguy scored the equalizer and in the decisive third period the hosts ran away, marking five goals against nil for the U.S. During the rest of the game, Argentina scored ten goals, the U.S. eight, practically an even match. But it was too late to recuperate from the third chukker debacle. After the game the press was in almost unanimous agreement that Joe Barry and Tommy Wayman had been the steadiest performers on a disappointing American squad. Some commentators pointed out that Joe Barry, an orthodox back, had played out of position at Number 3.[5]

There was much recrimination after the series was over. Ami Shinitzky, *Polo* magazine's editor, who had flown down to Buenos Aires to watch the games, wrote a scathing editorial under the title "Who Was Minding the Store?"[6] Shinitzky pointed out that, after a promising beginning with an abundance of first-rate resources and great expenditure of effort, many things were poorly managed. Ami reported that the lineup changed a few times shortly before the first match and there was discord among the delegation members. The U.S.P.A. took only a supporting role. Shinitzky concluded:

> And so the USPA out of misplaced courtesy, or whatever reason, left the final responsibility to Gose, who certainly cared but never intended to run the show in the first place and left it to Barry, who came to coach but not to manage. Here, then, they were in B.A.—seven of our finest players, 50 good horses, veterinarians, farriers, grooms, families, assorted equipment, gracious hosts and our hopes. And there was no one in charge.[7]

No less candid was Steve Gose when interviewed for the same publication:

> Gose: My biggest disappointment was not so much that the U.S. lost, because I had a feeling we'd be beaten, but that the team lacked a oneness of purpose.
> Polo: Why do you feel that was the case?
> Gose: It was due to two or three players who, in my opinion, are spoiled brats.[8]

Things were better in the next year's series at Retama, Texas, facing once more the Heguy and Harriott brothers. One of the perceived weaknesses on the American team had been the number 1 position. With the up-and-coming Memo Gracida filling that spot, the American team, with Wayman, Armour, and Barry, again in his usual position at back, acquitted itself well, still being defeated in two close games. Before the series started, the pundits expected that Argentina would win comfortably. Win they did, but not comfortably.

For a horseman such as Joe Barry, a great source of satisfaction was the award to his pony, Moonshine, of the 1971 Hartman Trophy, given to the best playing pony in the U.S. Open. Although not a thoroughbred, Moonshine possessed excellent qualities to become a top polo pony candidate: a balanced conformation and quiet disposition.

Also played by Joe, Steve Gose's gray gelding, Alabama, was twice awarded the Hartman Trophy, in 1977 and 1979. Alabama was foaled in 1971 in the state for which Joe named him. He was by Ask the Fare out of Victory Spree. Alabama raced under the name Ask the Victory and at age four was purchased by Chico Barry. Joe's father had an eye for a horse, and he quickly noticed that he had spotted an outstanding specimen. Chico liked Alabama's conformation and disposition; after working him at the ranch, he was ready for polo.

Joe Barry said of Alabama:

> He has the right mind for the game. The horse has a beautiful mouth and is very athletic. It was the first time I asked him for more than one period of polo in a game [the World Cup final] but when it comes to that kind of polo you go with the best you've got. He came through for me. I played him in the fourth [chukker] and then came back on him in the overtime period. If there was going to be a chance for a penalty shot I wanted to be on him.[9]

When Joe was asked by Barbara MacKnight to compare Alabama to Moonshine, Barry was explicit:

> Their attitudes toward the game are the same, but I guess I would have to say that because Moonshine wasn't a thoroughbred he could never go quite as hard or as long as Alabama can. Alabama gives it all to you every time you go to the field.[10]

Opposite top: **The symbiotic relationship between man and horse is exemplified in this picture of Joe Barry and Alabama at the 1979 World Cup, Palm Beach (courtesy Gwen Rizzo, Polo Players Edition).** ***Bottom:*** **Raw power: Joe Barry about to hit an off-side forehand shot. Jim McGinley is in pursuit; umpire Red Armour surveys the scene (courtesy Museum of Polo and Hall of Fame).**

Joe Barry was given the Hugo Dalmar Trophy, which is presented to the player who best exemplifies the sportsmanship characteristics inherent to the game of polo.[11] Also, he was inducted into the Polo Hall of Fame in 1999. Following retirement from high-goal polo, Barry became a highly respected coach, helping Tim Gannon's Outback and John Goodman's Isla Carroll take U.S. Open Championships in 1996 and 1997, among many other high-goal trophies.

As a player, Joe will be long remembered as a tremendously powerful hitter, sometimes scoring goals with a free hit from the center of the field. However, his backhanders were just as powerful. Tommy Wayman once said, "His backshots would go as far as most guys' forward shots." It was not brute force; it was timing and style. A classical back if ever there was one, Joe was variously labeled as the master of swing, the greatest hitter in American polo, and the ultimate back of the modern era. The fact that he was never given the 10-goal rating he so richly deserved has mystified many keen observers of the game.

The back-to-back defeats to Argentina in the Cup of the Americas ushered in a change in American polo. A faster game, with more short, accurate passes became the norm rather than the exception. For a player who had made his livelihood on the polo ground as a huge hitter, Joe Barry modified his thinking to the new fashion rather promptly and efficiently. By the time that he decided to quit high-goal polo in the early nineties, he was still at the top of the game, as a player and as a thinker. The latter quality served him well in his new career as a successful coach.

Joe Barry was an institution in American polo. Ten-goaler Owen Rinehart once mentioned that Joe was the most-liked person in polo. Joe's father, Chico Barry, hit the spot when he stated, "Joe can make you smile on your worst day." Admired and respected, Joe cut an easily distinguished figure on the polo field. One of the few players not to wear knee-guards, he handled his pony with the easy touch of a youth spent on horseback.

Many other memories of Joe Barry will persist, including his self-effacing modesty, his never-failing good humor, his gentlemanly ways and, above all, his personal example on the field. Joe placed a certain stamp of friendly excellence on everything he did. His citation in the Hall of Fame reads:

> In the tradition of the Barry excellence, Harold "Joe" Barry, a galloping oak with the soul of a poet, took his place in the forefront of American polo. An impenetrable Back at 9-goals, no one could hit a longer ball or provide a more reliable presence. Soft spoken off the field and ever the gentleman on the field, polo has no better role model than Joe. A horseman practically from birth, his talents with them are renowned—a chip off the old block.[12]

The end for Joe came swiftly and unexpectedly. On 18 May 2002, after working out his ponies, Joe Barry repaired to his pickup truck for a cup of coffee. A massive heart attack ended his life. He was a young 58-year-old. His funeral service at the Methodist church in Seguin, Texas—the same house of worship where Joe and Sharon had tied the knot thirty years before—congregated representatives from all aspects of American polo. They had come to pay their respects to the man who, more than any other, symbolized American polo in his time.

To commemorate the man and his many achievements, the United States Polo Association instituted the Joe Barry Memorial Trophy, a 22-goal tournament that traditionally signals the opening of Florida's high-goal polo season. Sharon Barry is always there to present the trophies.

Notes

1. Retama Polo Club Program, printed by the Club, n.d.
2. Asociación Argentina de Polo, *Libro Anual* (Buenos Aires: A.A. de Polo, 1980).
3. Eric O'Keefe, "Joe Barry," *Polo Players Edition.* (June 2002), 24.

4. Horacio A. Laffaye, *El Polo Internacional Argentino* (Buenos Aires; Edición del Autor, 1989), 244–245.
5. *Buenos Aires, El Gráfico*. December 1979.
6. *Polo* (January/February 1980), 45.
7. *Ibid.*, p. 15.
8. *Polo* (March 1980), 4–5.
9. Barbara J. MacKnight, "*Alabama Repeats Hartman Trophy Honors.*" *Polo* (September 1979), 16.
10. *Ibid.*
11. Hugo Dalmar Jr. (1927–1976) was a player from Oak Brook who took the U.S. Open in 1971 and 1973. He was chairman of the U.S.P.A. in 1975 and 1976.
12. Polo Museum and Hall of Fame, West Palm Beach, Florida.

Gonzalo Pieres: Superstar and Entrepreneur

by Horace A. Laffaye

On Sunday, 16 November 2003, the number one field at Palermo was the scene of one of the most memorable games ever played on that hallowed grounds. While the record book coldly states that Ellerstina defeated Indios-Chapaleufú II by 14 goals to 13 in the opening game of the Argentine Open Championship's Zone B, the afterglow went much farther. Never mind that a 30-goal team had vanquished a 37-goal team. Forget about a 17-year-old schoolboy making his debut at Palermo. Discard the fact that the gifted teenager was the game's high scorer, with nine tallies. The big story was Gonzalo Pieres Senior's return to high-goal polo.

Ellerstina, with the four cousins Matías and Pablo MacDonough and Gonzalito and Facundo Pieres, had lost Matías's services for one game because of cumulative yellow cards. Into the breach stepped 47-year-old Gonzalo Pieres wearing his customary number 3 blue and white jersey. Once more, the old master had come out of self-proclaimed retirement to direct Ellerstina's victory. Facundo explained after the game: "It's impressive how my game improves playing with Papá. It is so much easier. He is not flashy, but he delivers.... It's a dream; my debut at Palermo, winning the match, and with my father."[1]

Gonzalo's game plan stressed speed. He correctly assumed that if the game's pace slowed down, Indios-Chapaleufú would exploit the situation to its advantage. Based upon Ellerstina's formidable pony string, at opportune moments he sent Pablo MacDonough up the field in his cousins' support, while he kept a close watch on the back door. It worked beautifully. The American player Mike Azzaro, playing at number 2 for Indios-Chapaleufú, commented after the game: "Our horses were a little slower than theirs, and Ellerstina scored three or four goals just by outrunning us."[2]

When the game was over, Gonzalo Pieres, overwhelmed by the situation, cried. So did his two young sons and his wife, Cecilia. Later, Gonzalo said, "Emotionally, it was the most important game of my life."

At age 50, Gonzalo Pieres is the prototype of the immensely successful professional polo player. Worldwide, the dominant figure of the 1980s and 1990s was Gonzalo Pieres. As a 10-goal handicap player, Gonzalo was considered the best number 3 in Argentina, the United States and Great Britain. His teams La Espadaña, White Birch, Ellerston and Ellerstina took practically all the high-goal tournaments. Only the U.S. Open Championship escaped his grasp. As a professional player, he changed the approach to high-goal polo from essentially a paid player to a total overseer of the polo operation: selection of the pony string, stabling, grooms, team selection and tactics. As a breeder, Pieres started, with the help of his friends Héctor and Susie Barrantes, an enterprise that became a model establishment. Ellerstina S.A., which was backed by the late Kerry Packer, is currently a top producer of high quality polo ponies, and perhaps the best. It is not only a polo team; having purchased part of the late Barrantes' estancia El Pucará, Ellerstina increased its own properties in Trenque Lauquen and Córdoba, and added dairy farm production to the breeding operation.

In 2005, Ellerstina's team, again with Pieres's sons Facundo and Gonzalo and nephews Matías and Pablo MacDonough, came within a whisker of capturing Argentina's Triple Crown. Today, Gonzalo is obsessed with perfection as regards the breeding of horses suitable for polo.

In an interview with José María Azumendi, the president of the Argentine Polo Ponies Breeders Association, Gonzalo expounded upon his ideas on polo-pony breeding:

> Ninety percent of all births are from embryo transplants. This implies an increase in investment; therefore, you have an increase in cost; and that translates into us becoming much more concentrated on making fewer mistakes because otherwise you go bankrupt. It fosters expenditure but increases possibilities. Through transplant you get three to four embryos a year from each mare, which allows us to try out the dams much more thoroughly, and in some cases it is convenient to let them off playing the Opens because then they will be much more useful to us as mothers. Before, this was not possible, for the simple reason that you either played them or kept them as brood mares. The second change that is already becoming apparent is the increase in value of these mares.
>
> More money is paid out for a good dam than for a good player. I begin with a search for action, rather than type. My weak point today is that I have too many bloodlines open. In the last years I had ten sires, which tells me that for the moment it is the dams that are dominant, because out of ten sires, nine give me good products. That is something that I must attribute to the dams. We used to wean them systematically at six months. Now, the latest we wean them is at six months, and in several cases we already begin at four months. In all cases we are breaking them in at the age of two, but we are going to try a change: we want to break not less than fifty percent by age three.
>
> Azumendi:
>
> Why are horses changed during each chukker?
>
> Pieres:
>
> I ponder this and think that it is a step forward: many of today's horses are on a level or are better than the best horses of other times. Logic indicates that it is better to distribute the fourteen minutes that you are going to play a horse over an hour-and-a-half match, as opposed to doing what we used to do, which was to play two chukkers running seven minutes each. This habit has changed as a result of the change of rhythm of polo nowadays. Before, polo was more classical, and that way of playing was less tiring to the horse: this is in no way related to the training but to the system of playing. Nowadays the speed changes are constant and that is what wears out the horse most. Quite likely the horses will bear up for seven minutes on the field, but it is very likely that in that case we are exposing them to injury more easily than in the past.
>
> Azumendi:
>
> Does a great horse play in any position?
>
> Pieres:
>
> In our organization, any horse can normally perform in any position. The idea is that systematically, no horse should play at Palermo or in the Cámara de Diputados tournament before age six.[3]

As a breeder and player, Gonzalo has achieved great success. The celebrated Luna, by Top Secret in Guach Acha, bred by Héctor and Susie Barrantes at El Pucará, was given the Lady Susan Townley Cup in 1989 and 1990, and the Breeder's Association Cup in 1987 and 1990. A beautiful mare, Luna was painted in oil by Adriana Zaefferer. Cachamay, another Gonzalo pony, won the 1985 Lady Townley Cup, as well as Lechuza in 1986 and 1987 and Pastora in 1994.

Always well-mounted, Pieres benefited from the Barrantes' expertise in the breeding, selection and training of polo ponies. He also gives credit to Juan José Boote, a 7-goal player and direct descendant of the Gibsons, Scottish settlers who founded a polo club, Tuyú, as far back as 1895.

Gonzalo Pieres was born on 22 December 1955, the youngest of the four polo-player sons of Alvaro César "Bary" Pieres and Inés Garrahan, both prominent surnames in Argentine polo. There are also two daughters, Rosario and Mercedes. Alvaro César (recurrent family names) Pieres was the patriarch. "Papá César" was one of the founding members of Tortugas Country Club — now one of the most important clubs— in 1927; he was also a breeder of note because his stallion Datilero was the sire of a successful and much sought-after blood line of polo ponies. His sons Alvaro "Bary" and Augusto played polo at Los Ranchos— another old club currently owned by the Llorente family — with Bary eventually becoming a top umpire. By his marriage to Inés Garrahan, who was the next youngest of eight siblings, Alvaro Pieres joined

A youthful Gonzalo Pieres gives a hand lifting the Coronation Cup. Left to right: H.M. Queen Elizabeth II; cousins Héctor Crotto, Alex Garrahan and Gonzalo Pieres; Agustín Aguero (courtesy Museum of Polo and Hall of Fame).

La Espadaña, a club located in Abbott, Buenos Aires Province. Their four boys became deeply involved in the game and achieved a significant victory when, as a team, they took the Jockey Club Open tournament. The eldest, another Alvaro César, received his D.V.M. from the University of Buenos Aires, and was a 7-goal player who took the Coronation Cup and Cowdray Park's Gold Cup in England. However, it was his professional work as a veterinarian that gained his compatriots' admiration. His tireless work during the epidemic that affected the Argentine pony string during the 1980 Cup of the Americas at San Antonio significantly contributed to the eventual success of the enterprise.

The second son, Pablo, commonly known as Paul, also a 7-goaler, took the Gold and World Cups in Palm Beach with White Birch. Alfonso Tomás, the third son, reached the 10-goal plateau; he and his younger sibling Gonzalo, Ernesto Trotz and Carlos Gracida completely dominated the high-goal tournaments from 1984 to 1990. More about La Espadaña anon.

Like many Argentine polo players, Gonzalo cut his teeth in the High Schools Tournaments. On a team with his brother Alfonso, they took the championships twice, representing Colegio San Agustín. Then Eduardo "Gordo" Moore was quick to spot his talent, and after some coaching of Gonzalo at estancia Nueva Escocia, took him to England to play with the Vestey organization. Under the aegis of Moore and Héctor Barrantes—another "Gordo"—Pieres made a splash in British polo. In 1975, Gonzalo—age 19—was selected to play for South America versus England for the Coronation Cup on a team that included Juan José Díaz Alberdi and his mentors Barrantes and Moore. It was the first of four consecutive Coronation Cup triumphs for Pieres, who went on to take the Cup again in 1981 and never was on a losing side for this annual match.

His record in Cowdray Park's Gold Cup is equally impressive. The charming village of Midhurst, tucked in the Sussex Downs, saw Pieres take the Gold Cup in 1979 with Songhai, in 1981 with Falcons and in 1995 and 1998 with Ellerston White. He also added wins in the Midhurst Town Cup and the Cowdray Park Challenge Cup, the Club's oldest trophy, dating back to 1911. Replicas of the Queen's Cup, the Warwickshire Cup and the Prince Philip Trophy are ensconced some place in Gonzalo's trophy cabinets. Other significant victories in Europe include the Gold Cup at Deauville with Brattas, Songhai-Chopendoz, Berengueville and Ellerston.

The summer months in the southern hemisphere coincide with the U.S. high-goal season. Along with Héctor Barrantes, Gonzalo and his three brothers played at White Birch Farms, Peter Brant's polo establishment in Greenwich, Connecticut. Gonzalo Pieres became White Birch's most valuable member, so much so that *Polo* magazine once wrote: "As Gonzalo Pieres goes, so goes White Birch." Indeed they went. A total of ten Gold Cups, six of those in seven years, plus several World Cups at Palm Beach and thrice the short-lived Americas Cup at Greenwich, between high-goal American and Argentine teams. Although the latter was an international competition between top teams—38-goals—from each country, both the U.S.P.A. and the A.A. de Polo refused to recognize Peter Brant's creation. The inescapable fact remains that White Birch was the dominant team in America during the 1980s. However, the big prize, the U.S. Open Championship, escaped White Birch's grasp until 2005.

The first Gold Cup win was in 1983, when three Pieres brothers, Paul, Alfonso and Gonzalo, joined patron Peter Brant's team. Through the following years, the team had to bring in new players because their handicaps kept on going up. The only constants were Peter Brant and Gonzalo. Mariano Aguerre, Julio Arellano, Jeff Blake, Juan Bollini, Juan José Boote, Adolfo Cambiaso, Guillermo "Sapo" Caset, Mark Egloff, Federico Escobar, Alex Farrell, Dana Fortugno, John Hensley, Eugene "Tiger" Kneece, Todd Offen and Del Carroll Walton were at the time up-and-coming players who moved on after their apprenticeship at White Birch. Occasionally, established players such as Lucas Criado, Bautista Heguy and Ernesto Trotz would add extra punch to the squad.[4] Behind the scenes, but nevertheless being an indispensable part of the scene were the Masters of the Horse for Peter Brant: first Héctor Barrantes, and, after Barrante's untimely death, Nick Manifold, a scion of the celebrated polo family from Victoria, Australia.

Another extraordinary figure in the White Birch organization was the inimitable Tommy Glynn, a Harvard educated 4-goal player and superb horseman, who started Peter Brant on his way into polo at Ox Ridge and Fairfield County Hunt clubs. "Mr. Polo's" contributions to the game were recognized posthumously with the Iglehart Award by the Polo Hall of Fame. The polo-pony string assembled by Brant was, and continues to be, just about the finest in North America.

An unusual situation took place in 1995. Gonzalo Pieres, by then riding Kerry Packer's golden chariot, took the Gold Cup wearing Ellerston white and black colors. It was a good team — Red Armour, Bautista Heguy, Pieres and Joe Wayne Barry. They defeated White Birch 13–12 in the final match.

Just as Barrantes and Moore had nurtured Pieres in the 1970s, Gonzalo and Barrantes brought to the United States another future star, 10-goaler Mariano Aguerre. Born into a 25 de Mayo, Buenos Aires Province, polo family — his father, Martín, and older brother, also Martín — played at El Rincón, where Mariano's rise to high-handicap was meteoric. When he was playing off a 3-goal handicap at Greenwich, Gonzalo Pieres told the author, "He's going to be a 10-goal player." At the time, Marianito was considered one of several "ringers" notorious in the White Birch organization. The prescient Gonzalo was correct in his forecast; what he could not imagine at the time was that Mariano would marry his daughter, Tatiana. Mariano Aguerre succeeded his father-in-law as White Birch's lynchpin, as well as taking six Argentine Open Championships with Ellerstina, Indios-Chapaleufú and La Dolfina, to this date.

Gonzalo's high-goal career in Argentina began with Eduardo Moore's Nueva Escocia team and then with Mar del Plata, Gonzalo Tanoira's concoction. In an era dominated by Coronel Suárez and Santa Ana, Mar del Plata was the "third team." Based on the brothers Jorge and Gonzalo Tanoira, and usually with Alfredo "Negro" Goti at back, Mar del Plata tried several other players in their quest to break Coronel Suárez's hegemony. Among them, were Juan José Alberdi, Alberto Goti, Julian Hipwood and Diego Ruiz Guiñazú. They achieved significant success: the Hurlingham Open in 1970 and 1980, as well as five Tortugas Open championship and twice finalists in the Argentine Open. The 1980 and 1981 teams had Alfonso Pieres, Gonzalo Pieres, Gonzalo Tanoira and Alfredo Goti.

Enter La Espadaña. The club's origins date back to 1937, when, encouraged by Carlos "Bunny" Land and Tomás Rooney, the Buchanan and Garrahan brothers started polo at estancia New Home. The first success was taking the Copa Anchorena, now the Tortugas Open; many others followed. A team — Carlos "Laddie" Buchanan, Juan Reynal, Juan "Buddy" Ross and Luis Garrahan — traveled to England in 1951 and played a three-match series against a Hurlingham team in the Coronation Cup's revival after the war. The same team won the Roehampton Cup. In Argentina, La Espadaña was quite successful in medium-handicap (18–25 goals at the time) and occasionally in high-goal polo. Old-timers still remember vividly the scare they gave the American team Bostwick Field in an early round of the 1950 Argentine Open. A 22-goal team — Carlos Debaisieux, Tommy Garrahan, Héctor "Boy" Zavalía and Louie Garrahan — took on the 31-goal Bostwick Field — Pete Bostwick, Peter Perkins, George Oliver and Lewis Smith — down to the wire, losing 11–9. For comparison, in the finals the mighty Venado Tuerto defeated Bostwick Field 14–8. During the game, the author's father was sitting next to the Argentine Polo Association treasurer, who was torn between his obvious sympathy for the local team and the financial disaster that might happen if the expected final match lacked an American presence. The poor man probably had a nightmarish vision of what had happened the previous year, when an unheralded La Concepción had eliminated Meadow Brook in the Open's second round.

The next generation took La Espadaña to the very top. Carlos Gracida, Alfonso Pieres, Gonzalo Pieres and Ernesto Trotz played together and quickly became the team to beat. An injury to Juan Martin Zavaleta—he lost some precious front teeth—necessitated his emergency replacement by Gracida. La Espadaña took its first Open, defeating in the final, 14–8, Indios-Chapaleufú, with Horacio Sr., Gonzalo, Horacito and Alberto Pedro Heguy.

The 1985 Open Championship did not take place because of an equine infectious disease outbreak. The tournament took place the following May; once more, La Espadaña walked away the winners, this time with Mexican Antonio "Chamaco" Herrera at number 1. In November, Indios-Chapaleufú I, now with Marcos, Gonzalo and Horacito Heguy, and Alex Garrahan, won the title 13–12 thanks to Marcos Heguy's "The Goal" (see A.P. Heguy's profile). Before the game, Cora "China" Garrahan, Alex's mother and La Espadaña's most rabid fan, was asked which team she would root for. Her answer was: "For my own blood."[5]

This defeat was the only hiccup for La Espadaña in the Abierto from 1984 until the team dissolved after the 1990 season. Years later, Carlos Gracida was asked about this 40-goal team. "It was a time in which all four of us peaked as players and teammates. We couldn't do anything wrong," he reminisced.[6]

It was indeed a great team, the first 40-goal team in Argentina since Coronel Suárez. The record speaks for itself: six Argentine Open Championships in seven years, three Hurlingham Opens in a row, and two Tortugas Open Tournaments. They also changed the face of polo, when they obtained sponsorship from the industrial firm Topper: the first steps towards professionalism in Argentine polo. They also broke with tradition when they discarded La Espadaña's traditional green shirt—all the founders were Irish-Argentine—and adopted a green and white jersey in halves. Following some initial failures, Alfonso Pieres believed the original one was "bad luck."[7]

Following La Espadaña's 40-goal machine breakup, Gonzalo Pieres began his lasting association with Kerry Packer, which became enormously profitable to both parties. Packer, a resolute Australian with a reputation for winning at all costs, had quickly recognized in Pieres the individual he needed to help achieve his ambitions.

Packer's Ellerston team impact upon the English polo scene was enormous. His two teams, Ellerston White and Ellerston Black, were the dominant force during the 1990s. The harvest included three Gold Cups, five Queen's Cups, three Warwickshire Cups, two Prince of Wales Trophies, the Silver Jubilee Cup and the Prince Philip Trophy. Gonzalo Pieres was on eleven of those fifteen winning teams. Add to the total three Argentine Open Championships, three Gold Cups at Deauville, and the Gold Cup in America.

Gonzalo Pieres became Kerry Packer's chief man in Argentina when Packer purchased part of Peter Brant's White Birch property near Pilar. It then became known as Ellerstina, the wearers of the now celebrated dark blue and white shirt. Gonzalo then assembled a top team: Adolfo Cambiaso, Mariano Aguerre, himself at pivot, and Cristián Laprida. They took the Tortugas Open and reached the final of the Open at Palermo. Two years later, superbly mounted and with Carlos Gracida at back, they ended Indios-Chapaleufú Is (that of the four Heguy brothers) three-year winning run in the Argentine Open. In the process, they also took the Tortugas and Hurlingham Open Championships, thus gaining the mythical triple crown, the first one since Coronel Suárez in 1975.[8] Next year, 1995, Ellerstina won the triple crown's first two legs, only to have Indios-Chapaleufú I return the favor at Palermo. After a one-year parenthesis enjoyed by Indios-Chapaleufú II, Ellerstina returned to the fore in 1997 and 1998, with Cambiaso's pal, Lolo Castagnola, at back. The team closed this period in 1999 when they won Hurlingham's Open.

Ellerstina, the 1994 Triple Crown winners (left to right): Carlos Gracida, Gonzalo Pieres, Mariano Aguerre, Adolfo Cambiaso, one of the many teams Gonzalo Pieres led to success (courtesy Museum of Polo and Hall of Fame).

Then came "the split." Gonzalo had been grooming his eldest son, Gonzalito, with great expectations. The gifted youngster already had shown his form as a player—father and son had taken Deauville's Gold Cup on an Ellerston team—and was in England ready to participate in the polo season on a team with Adolfo Cambiaso. As described in Cambiaso's profile, Adolfito elected to replace Gonzalito on the Geebung team. Still in Argentina, Gonzalo made a clean sweep of Cambiaso's people within the Ellerstina organization, and proceeded to nurture a new team. The result was a new Ellerstina, that of the cousins—via the Garrahan connection—Pieres and MacDonough.

The team gradually matured under Gonzalo's eye. The match described in the opening paragraphs was just one step in a superb team's development. Then Gonzalo added a masterful touch: he asked Memo Gracida to coach the team. In 2005, under Gracida's careful guidance, the cousins four took the Tortugas and Hurlingham Open Championships and became the odds-on favorites to win the Argentine Open. In one of the most thrilling-ever contests seen at Palermo, La Dolfina, with Adolfito Cambiaso, Lucas Monteverde, Mariano Aguerre and Lolo Castagnola, defeated Ellerstina 20–19 in the ninth chukker—a match for the ages, one of those games which it is sad to see one team lose.

Gonzalo is married to Cecilia Fernández Piola. They had known each other since childhood, and after a six-month courtship they married. They have five children: Tatiana, 26; Gonzalo, 23; Facundo, 20; Nicolás, 15; and Cecilia, 14. Tatiana, married to Mariano Aguerre, has two girls, Sofía and Lola. "Gonza" is married to María Rapetti. All the youngsters attended Moorlands School; therefore, it is not surprising that Moorlands has won the High Schools Championship several times. Like father, like sons.

The inevitable educational disruption caused by the wandering life of a contemporary polo player was pragmatically solved by Cecilia: every year they took a teacher to Stedham, near Cowdray Park.

When asked about her father as an individual, Tatiana could not hide her genuine affection. "As a person, he is exemplary. I admire him," she said in a recent interview.[9] "He is a family man, devoted to his children." A 6-handicap player at golf, Gonzalo enjoys asados and assiduously plays truco, a card game popular in Argentina. Tatiana adds, "When someone would tell him he was the best player in the world, he just laughed. He never let it go to his head."

Asked to describe her younger brothers, she simply said, "Gonza is very tame. He never seems to be upset. Quite level-headed." As to Facundo she said, "As a person, Facu is like sunshine. But he can get hot under the collar."

Tatiana herself runs Ellerstina's Gold and Silver Cups tournaments every year. Gonzalo had organized the original Seniors tournament in Argentina with his friend and neighbor, the late Gonzalo Tanoira. It was originally designed for older players, in which foreign patrons also participated. When Gonzalo Pieres realized the tremendous interest demonstrated by the visitors from overseas in playing polo in Argentina, he launched the Gold Cup in 1999. This was followed by the Silver and Bronze Cups, for lower handicap teams. In 2005 there were 36 teams in the different tournaments; 22-goals for the Gold, 14-goals for the Silver and 10-goals for the Bronze. The logistics involved in organizing an average of eight daily matches fell upon Tatiana's shoulders. She came through with flying colors.

Back in the 1970s, Gonzalo Pieres had won the Jockey Club Open on a team with his three brothers. In September 2006, Gonzalo added another leaf to his triumphal garland when he again took the Jockey Club Open — a 28- to 40-goal tournament — this time with his three sons, Gonzalito, Facundo, and newcomer Nicolás, still a schoolboy rated at 4-goals. At age 51, Gonzalo Pieres keeps on demonstrating his ability to come out of retirement and perform at top level.

Ellerstina Costa Rica is another of Gonzalo's enterprises. A large polo-oriented development, it offers several polo grounds located at different levels, all with magnificent seaviews. A talented polo player, breeder and coach, Gonzalo Pieres has demonstrated a knack for the business deal as part of his preeminent role in the game during the last thirty years. Gonzalo once said — in a rare display of self-aggrandizement — "There was polo before Pieres and polo after Pieres." With the passage of time, he came to realize how exaggerated his statement was, and perhaps he wished he could take it back. But there is a grain of truth in it.

Notes

1. *La Nación*, 17 December 2003, pp. 1–4.
2. *Ibid.*
3. Interview with José María Azumendi, president of the Argentine Polo Pony Breeders Association, in *AACCP Year Book* (Buenos Aires, 2005).
4. *U.S. Polo Association Year Book* (Lexington, Kentucky), 2006.
5. Personal communication from Esther Cora Cardonell de Garrahan.
6. Interview with Carlos Gracida. Wellington, March 2004.
7. Personal communication from Alfonso Pieres.

8. The Triple Crown winners are:

   1972 Coronel Suárez
   1973 Santa Ana
   1974 Coronel Suárez
   1975 Coronel Suárez
   1994 Ellerstina
   2003 La Aguada

9. Interview with Tatiana Pieres de Aguerre, 7 July 2006.

Guillermo Gracida Jr.: The Field General

by Nigel à Brassard

All the great polo trophies of the world have the name Gracida engraved on them. The U.S. Open polo trophy has Memo Gracida's name engraved on it sixteen times, more times than anybody else; in second position with nine wins is Memo's brother, Carlos. Memo has been described as "the winningest player in the history of the game." With the U.S. Open, Argentine Open, British Open, Australian Open, C.V. Whitney Cup, U.S.P.A. Silver Cup, America's Cup, Avila Camacho Cup, Queen's Cup and Coronation Cup in his bag, is there anything left that he has not won? But it is not only the trophies; he has also been named the U.S. Open Most Valuable Player on seven occasions and is an unprecedented six-time winner of *Polo* magazine's Player of the Year Award.

Guillermo "Memo" Gracida Jr. was born into the game as part of Mexico's leading polo family. His father, Guillermo "Memo" Gracida Sr., won the U.S. Open in 1946 playing on a Mexican team with his brothers, Gabriel, Alejandro and José (the only time the U.S. Open has been won by a band of brothers). The legacy of that team has left an indelible imprint on Memo, his brother, Carlos, and cousins, Rubén and Roberto. The young Memo, born in Mexico City in 1956, soon started playing polo on a local three-quarter sized practice field surrounded by wire netting and affectionately known as "la Luna" because of its far from level surface. "It was rough, bouncy and dry," recalls Memo. "We used to play with a rubber ball slightly smaller than a soccer ball. The games were all family affairs and were two against two." Memo credits his parents for his success in polo and believes that he got his work ethic from his father and his stamina from his mother. By 1976 Memo, playing with his father as part of the Mexico team, beat the United States in Houston to win the Avila Camacho Cup, the first time that Mexico had won since the tournament's inception in 1941. Memo recalls with tears in his eyes how his father would tell him and Carlos when they were young boys about playing in Meadow Brook and Palermo and some of the great players he had played with and watched. He told tales of the Mexican team, financed by the Mexican president, that played in Cuba, the U.S. and Argentina. Memo remembers his father telling him how he went to New York and saw the American military polo setup. His father recalled that "he had never seen so many oats in his life and the Mexicans over-fed their horses and they became furious lunatics;

after that he learned never to feed horses too much." Memo added, "These stories were what any kid likes; they were fairy tales. My father was a quiet person who loved horses. He gave me and Carlos dreams. These are dreams which we are still living out today." As a fourteen-year-old Memo went to watch the U.S. Open in Chicago and vowed to himself that one day he would play in that tournament and hopefully win it. He says, "Can you imagine my delight when a few years later I went back to the U.S. and in my first attempt was part of the team that won the U.S. Open."

In 1976 Memo left his veterinary studies at Mexico City's Universidad Nacional Autónoma de México and moved to America to continue his polo career. His entry onto the American polo scene was explosive, and within a year he was part of the 1977 U.S. Open winning team, Retama. His patron, Steve Gose, who had been instrumental in getting him to move to San Antonio, Texas, described Memo thus: "You only had to watch him once to know he was going to be someone great." By 1982 Memo arrived at what he describes as his greatest achievement when his polo handicap was raised to 10-goals in both Argentina and the United States. The 1982 and 1983 seasons must be his *annus mirabilis,* when he captured the U.S. Open with Retama, the Argentine Open with Santa Ana and the British Open with Falcons. In addition he has held on to his 10-goal rating longer than anyone in the game today.

In 1997 Memo Gracida was elected into the Polo Hall of Fame and to this day remains the only player so honored while still actively competing. His induction announcement refers to him as "level-headed, focused and ten-goals from head to toe; in his path the record book crumbled. East or west and across the Atlantic, he has been the one to beat, the benchmark for all who seek polo immortality." Memo has the distinction of being the only player ever to win the U.S. Open in six consecutive years. There are few comparables in any other sport. The equivalent has not been matched by Michael Jordan, Joe Montana or Tiger Woods. In their heyday the New York Yankees have won only four straight World Series titles. But Memo's career has lasted well beyond that of others; he won his most recent U.S. Open title at the age of 46.

What makes Memo stand out as a polo player is echoed in everything one reads or hears about him: "the quintessential number three," a "superb horseman," "five star field general" and an "inspiration to his teammates." With Memo, it is not the flashes of outstanding, breathtaking brilliance, but rather a consistent and classical style of play. A contemporary of his described this style as more like a chess game where a lot of thought goes into tactics rather than a more opportunistic approach. David Jamison describes Memo's style of play as being "simple but effective, allowing the rest of the team to follow his lead." In 1998 this writer had the privilege to play with Memo at number 3, in his signature yellow helmet, H.R.H. the Prince of Wales at back and Andrew Willans at number 2 in the Asprey Cup at Cirencester. Apart from the pleasure and privilege of playing with one of polo's greats, I was struck by Memo's overall approach, which I think is best described as "team polo."

In many ways he is a classic "natural" polo player, unlike the style of Adolfo Cambiaso, who is more unorthodox and unpredictable. Memo describes polo as having moved on from just being a good athlete. "Nowadays being a great player is just one aspect to your career. You have to be your own agent, trainer and adviser and handle your own P.R., be a diplomat, take care of banking matters, look after your own legal affairs, as well as keep your skills sharp." Memo believes that the most important quality for a good polo player is good horsemanship. Of all the players who have been ranked at 10-goals he believes there are only five who stand out as exceptional horsemen. These are players who can make their top horses perform even better. He put on this list Lewis Lacey—a player he never had the opportunity to see play but whose horsemanship was legendary. Of the players he has watched he lists Cecil Smith, Juan Carlos Harriott, his brother, Carlos, and Bautista Heguy.

Memo remembers fondly his mare Sasha, which he regards as his best horse ever, a pony that he bought and made but is best remembered because "I thought her heart was bigger." Sasha was awarded the Willis L. Hartman Trophy for Best Playing Pony in the U.S. Open in 1997. Another of Memo's ponies, Kalliman, won the Hartman Trophy in 1987 and again in 1989. Kalliman was a horse bought by George Oliver from Bob Tate in Sheridan, Wyoming. Memo remembers that Kalliman "was bought as a 3-year-old and he was 16 hands, big by polo standards. He was an outstanding athlete that played the Americas Championship 40-goal tournament as his first competitive polo. That was totally unusual for any equine athlete." Not surprisingly, Kalliman was inducted into the Polo Hall of Fame. He passed away at the age of 28 on the Oliver's Chester Bar Ranch in North Carolina. During the last years his best friend was another retired polo pony, Mr. Polo. In looking for a good pony Memo rates "conformation, stamina, speed, intellect, handiness and ability to learn, but by far the most important factor is temperament."

Every player who has played with or against Memo or watched him in action speaks of his dedication to the game. He is meticulous in his preparation for tournaments. Based on the adage that games are won both on and off the field of play, Memo is renowned for doing everything possible to prepare for a game. Memo describes the prematch preparation as the work "in the barn." In addition to working continuously to keep the horses in perfect condition, Memo likes the team to practice as much as possible ahead of big tournaments. Nothing is to be left to chance and he believes moves need to be practiced and practiced. A common comment about Memo is that he brought professionalism to the game, but as Memo himself says, "This is not just referring to monetary reward but encompasses everything from training, preparation, a programmed structure from grooms, players, horses, facilities and playing fields." Memo remembers that when he started playing there was "no role similar to that of the current professional polo player. At that time a player would be invited to play for a team and many of his expenses might be picked up by the team patron and the player might make some money from selling some of his horses." But Memo felt he wanted something more. He wanted polo to be regarded as a serious sport: "It needed a work ethic, a dedication, a love of horses and a passion for the game." Memo remembers that while playing for Les Diables Bleu he introduced total color coordination for the team, with matching shirts, saddle cloths and bandages. Also, instead of one groom per player, Memo believed each player needed two or three grooms as the thoroughbreds needed greater care, attention and training. It is this all-encompassing approach which results in his reputation as a true professional and percentage player. David Jamison describes Memo's pre-match preparation as "the most professional I have seen. The day before a match Memo would give us a team talk; on the day of the game Memo would arrive well before kick-off. He would go through our horse list and then tell each of us about the player we were supposed to be marking." These characteristics put him ahead of his time, when even today some teams have little or no practice ahead of tournaments.

Clearly Memo learned a lot from the six years he spent playing for Steve Gose when he first moved to America. Gose, a successful oilman, applied a commercial approach to polo that was almost as important as the game itself. Gose and Gracida were constantly buying green horses and bringing them on and bringing in new players and over the months and years integrating them into the team. This was not a program that could be achieved solely during the polo season; this was an all-year-round process, involving grooms, vets and all the other staff involved in the polo machinery. This was polo as a business, no longer as just an enjoyable summer pastime. These lessons Memo has applied to teams that he has played on and managed. Alex Ebeid, patron of the Falcons polo team, commented on Memo thus: "He is already a legend in the polo world and will go down in polo history as such. While he was a member of the Falcon's team, he was undoubtedly the heart of the team that won all the major tournaments in England and at Deauville." Ebeid remembers that "During May of that year it rained almost every day; even during torrential downpours Memo would insist on my schooling six horses, inspiring a discipline of iron." Ebeid refers to Memo's ability to help younger players come into the game and states: "When we won the Gold Cup, Andrew Hine's handicap was moved from one to three, thanks to Memo's guidance and tuition." Guy Wildenstein, patron of Les Diables Bleu team sees Memo's legacy this way:

> I remember talking with Hanut Singh [the legendary Indian polo player] about what made the greatest players better, different, the best. Singh said they not only used horses, they rode them. They not only played on a team; they organized them. And their games were not only based on instinct, they had a scientific approach as well. I've seen all the great Argentines, and I've seen many of the great Americans. Memo surpasses all of them. He is the only one I've known who has been able to take over everything—the organization, the logistics—everything.[1]

But by Memo's own admission it took a while for him to develop the management style that has become his trademark. He is quoted as saying, "At first I wanted to take charge of everything. It was too much by myself and when I got on the polo field my play fell off. By helping everyone else on their game I was neglecting my own." He felt that there were times when he did not "make the crucial plays or the critical points." He knew that for all his organizational skills, his patron would also expect brilliance on the playing field. Memo remembers: "I was going crazy, going from one season to another trying to organize, trying to manage and trying to do it all. When I got to the polo field my game was off." He was to remedy this by delegating.

In 1994 Memo appointed Rege Ludwig to coach the Aspen team—the eventual winners of the U.S. Open. This was an innovation in polo. "Rege helped with coaching on penalty tak-

Memo Gracida as a successful coach. Ellerstina, with Facundo Pieres, Pablo MacDonough, Gonzalito Pieres and Matías MacDonough, took the first two tournaments of the 2005 Triple Crown, only to be defeated in the last one by a single goal (courtesy Museum of Polo and Hall of Fame).

ing, he helped the patron and he was a fifth member of the team when we were playing," recalls Memo. He thinks that being a polo coach is a demanding job; it requires "planning, analysis, practice and sports psychology," and he likens it to carrying out a chemical experiment where "you have to get all the ingredients right."

Memo's legacy to polo will not end when he eventually decides to retire from active playing. For instance, he has already overseen the development of his son, Julio (currently ranked at 5-goals). In addition he has since 1999 organized, with Glen Holden, the erstwhile president of the Federation of International Polo, a program called the "10-Goal Experience." This is a program aimed at helping under-19-year-old polo prodigies. Memo watches high-goal polo matches with the young players while providing a running commentary explaining why the 10-goalers made the moves they had and what they might have done. The invaluable experience of one of polo's all time greats is thus being passed on to future generations of polo players.

Memo attributes his success in polo to the focus that he has applied to the game from the beginning. He says that his goal has always been to reach the highest rank with a strong will to win and a discipline at all times working on improvement. He describes how every day he would feel he had to improve on something—hitting the ball, horsemanship, his string of horses. Memo's first American patron described his disciplined approach and continual striving for self-improvement as potentially problematic because, "If it had been up to Memo he would've practiced 24 hours a day and run all my best horses into the ground." Alex Ebeid says: "Memo has a rare kind of determination, concentration and willpower that has made him an exceptional and formidable player."

Memo is best known for playing in the pivotal number 3 role but when I spoke to him he told me that his favorite position is number 1. He regards the number 1 role as the most important and exciting, but also the most difficult as it involves getting right the critical balance between offensive and defensive. Memo is well known for his relationship with his patrons, and he regards each of the other three team members as being integral to the team's success. He believes that success for a team is when every player is able to play his best and to this end Memo is known to give 110 percent effort in advice and support to his teammates. David Jamison described Memo's influence on his patrons as "preparing them well, so that they performed higher than their ranking."

It is no surprise that in recognition of Memo's reputation as a tactical player and as a great field captain he finds himself increasingly called upon to help coach other teams. This is a relatively new aspect in polo and one which is becoming more widespread. Having a player who knows the game watch from the sidelines and give pep and tactical talks to the team before the match and between chukkers is becoming commonplace. Most recently Memo has been coaching the Ellerstina team and he comments, "It has been a very successful experience from the point of view of immediate results and also adaptation and communication between the players and me. It has been very rewarding to see the progress made by combining my experience, knowledge of the game and approach with the talent, desire and commitment of the players. The most exciting part is that the team has not yet reached their full potential." Not surprising when you consider how this is used in just about every other sport.

I asked Memo where he thought polo was going. Memo says that since he first started playing people have talked about "all professional" polo, but he thinks that the involvement of patrons is not going to change. He sees them as critical and integral to the sport. While the televising of polo and the new camera technology allow you to see some of the intricacies of the game that a spectator may miss from the sidelines, he does not believe that polo is a sport with mass appeal. He believes that advances will be made in polo if teams have a greater consistency of composition. From the team's point of view they will play better and better if they stick together as a team for longer than the typical 6–8 week period of the season, be it in England or America or wherever. But also Memo believes that there will be greater spectator interest if the team composition is more constant. He cites the success and popularity of some of the Argentinean teams where some of the players have been together for twenty years or more. Memo thinks that team identification is critical in terms of team name, players and colors.

The teams on which Memo has played over the years reads like a roll call of the greatest polo teams of the late 20th and early 21st centuries. They include: Steve Gose's Retama, Guy Wildenstein's Les Diables Bleu, Galen Weston's Maple Leafs, Alex Ebeid's Falcons, Tim Gannon's Outback Steakhouse and John Goodman's Isla Carroll. While he maintained his 10-goal handicap, Memo believes that with each passing year he has gotten better and better at running or, better yet, managing a team.

Joe Barry, one of Memo's Retama teammates, is quoted as saying, "We worked hard every time. That's why we were successful. And I think this attitude and desire is one of Memo's greatest assets." Steve Gose, the Retama patron, puts it even more succinctly: "Memo is like his dad. Neither was afraid of hard work." All agree that if Memo had not made a life in polo, he would have been a success in whatever field he chose. "Without question he would have made top rank in the military," said Guy Wildenstein. "With all that brilliance and thoroughness he would have been an outstanding college professor," said Ambassador Glen Holden. Galen Weston said about Memo, "I'd be happy just as long as he was in any business that didn't end up competing with my own." In the same way Memo's father and uncles competed for Mexico in the 1946 U.S. Open, Memo, his brother, Carlos, and cousins, Rubén and Roberto, competed for Mexico in the 2003 Coronation Cup.

Memo wearing Mokarow Farms shirt. Isla Carroll Polo Club, near Palm Beach, 2006 (courtesy PoloLine, Sebastián Amaya).

Memo regards the victory at Palermo in 1982 as his fondest memory. This was the tournament that gave him the most satisfaction and helped him achieve the greatest reward for a polo player — the 10-goal handicap. Palermo remains his favorite ground — a ground where "you know what men are made of" — not only because it is the biggest stadium and has the tradition but also because of its surface, which is quite the best in the world, and the wooden balls which he believes give a different dimension to the game as "they are more predictable and give inch-perfect control but also require more accuracy in hitting." He describes playing with the wooden balls as being "like playing golf with a new ball, it feels good when you strike it well, as opposed to the plastic balls which are unpredictable, curve and spin and lose their shape so quickly." But while victory at Palermo is remembered fondly, it was victory in the Camacho Cup in 1976 playing with his father that is his most memorable polo moment. Memo remembers that the Mexicans were regarded as the underdogs and that the American team (fresh from victory in the U.S. Open) appeared to the Mexicans as being like "All the King's Horses and All the King's Men." The overwhelming memories of the match were Memo's realization of how good his father was as a polo player and how good were the Mexican team's horses. He watched as his father, playing on green ponies, showed he was very much a match for the American players. Memo remembers with pride playing with his father, a man who had, in Memo's own words, "always been my hero" and he now understands how much he owes to his father's leadership and the confidence given to him as a young boy.

Another player that made an enormous impression on Memo was Alfredo Harriott; he remembers that playing against Harriott in the Cup of the Americas was one of the most influential factors on his own game. He also remembers Harriott as a super athlete in possession of an uncanny discipline. Memo recalls with surprise how Harriott marked him out of the game "so that I was not free to make a single play." He had never before seen such "discipline and single-mindedness."

Memo regards Franky Dorignac as "one of the most admired and respected players of all time and he was without a doubt one of the most influential people in my career." Memo credits the Dorignac family for introducing him to Palermo and high-goal polo in Argentina. It is no surprise that Memo's son was christened Julio Francisco Gracida, with the choice of his middle name reflecting the appreciation and respect that he had for the Dorignac family.

Another player who was to have a great influence on Memo was his father-in-law, George Oliver. Memo credits him as the person who "taught me the importance of managing, producing and preserving champion horses. He was the most experienced horseman in the whole sense of the word." Memo regrets he never had the chance to play with his father-in-law but remembers that "my father and George played and won together the U.S. Open Championship in 1961 with the Milwaukee polo team." Also, as Memo recounts with great affection, it was because of the relationship between his father and George Oliver that he met Mimi Oliver after his very first game in Boca Raton; they were married soon afterwards.

Looking back over his polo career, Memo describes how polo has changed during those thirty-plus years. When he started, classic polo involved players hitting their backhands, constantly passing the ball to teammates, a style of polo which Memo's patron, Guy Wildenstein, described as "treating the polo ball as a hot potato." Memo characterizes the current style as being more about individuals keeping the ball, with other players blocking the opponents to provide space to the more talented players. This style of polo has brought with it pressures and greater demands on the horses, as sometimes a player might take the ball down the full length of the pitch, which has meant that more and more thoroughbreds are playing.

Memo describes some of the current top ranked players as "magicians with a level of ball control that I never dreamed about." In a reflective mood, Memo feels that the current style is not necessarily for the better: "It's not so much fun to play and not so good for the players or the ponies." He believes that the next evolution of the game will be "when the current individualistic style starts to incorporate the classic form of team play." If Memo is correct, polo spectators will have many treats in store over the coming years and without a doubt there will be members of the Gracida dynasty who will be at the center of these changes.

Note

1. *Polo* (Dallas, October/November 1997), 82.

Adolfo Cambiaso: "There is a kid from Cañuelas...."

by Sebastián Amaya

Adolfo Cambiaso is considered the world's best polo player. He was born on 15 April 1975 in Cañuelas, a town some 60 miles from Buenos Aires. His father, also named Adolfo, established La Martina Polo Ranch in 1983 in nearby Vicente Casares, Buenos Aires Province, within the estancia Los Lagartos, owned by the family of his wife, Martina Estrada.

Adolfito Cambiaso was raised in a sporting environment. His father was a 4-goal handicap player, while his stepbrothers Salvador and Marcial Socas took first steps as professional polo players as instructors at La Martina, one of the earliest and most important polo academies in Argentina.

Young Adolfito enjoyed country life but also traveled around the globe with his parents, becoming quite adept at skiing and surfing. It was obvious from an early age that he was endowed with an unusual aptitude for all sports and games. Gradually, riding became his main pursuit, first on ponies, then on the polo school's horses. Anselmo "Tibu" González, who was in charge of the stables at La Martina, eventually became Adolfito's legendary groom and organizer for many years.

Among the frequent visitors to the fledging school run by Adolfo Senior were the Fiorito brothers and an individual that would play a fundamental role in Adolfito's personal and professional life: Bartolomé "Lolo" Castagnola.

From the very beginning, Lolo and Adolfito became inseparable friends. Bartolomé Castagnola's father, "El Chalo" to his close friends, was a neighboring landowner, who always wanted his son to play polo. He also became close to Adolfito and the two friends played and won just about every tournament they entered, from low-handicap trophies to the Copa Cámara de Diputados (24–28 goals). Playing for La Martina were Adolfito—age 15—with Lolo, Sebastián Merlos and Tomás Fernández Llorente.

By then, the polo community was in awe about the skill of the kid from Cañuelas. With limited resources regarding pony power in the initial tournaments, Adolfito used the polo school's ponies, by and large of low quality. He was able to win tourneys by sheer determination and uncommon ability. One of his favorite ponies was Lobo, the only pony to share his ascent from 0-goal to the lofty 10-goal handicap.

Shortly thereafter, Ernesto Trotz, La Espadaña's back, took him to play the 1991 Palm Beach season. This was his first invitation to play away from home, at age 15 and sporting a 4-goal handicap. After the first practice game, the U.S.P.A. handicappers raised his rating to 6-goals. Following his taking the Gold Cup that same season, his handicap went up a notch to seven, and the following year, when Adolfito again took the Gold Cup, this time on a team with Carlos Gracida, he was raised to 9-goals. At this point he became the youngest player in polo's history to reach 10-goals, as a 17-year-old, surpassing the immortal Tommy Hitchcock's record.

Ernesto Trotz, a 10-goal player with six Argentine Open Championships to his credit, recently said about Adolfito:

> One of the outstanding traits in Adolfo's character is his quickness in absorbing technical concepts that other players take years to learn. He was a quiet youngster, who was perfectly aware of his limitations, and continuously wanted to learn the whys and whens of every theory, rule or tactic, both on and off the field, as far as playing and organizational structure.[1]

In 1991, Adolfito took the Cowdray Park Gold Cup in England, playing for Tramontana, once again with Carlos Gracida, defeating the powerful Kerry Packer's Ellerston squad with Alfonso and Gonzalo Pieres. In turn, two years later Packer, the top patron in the game, contracted Adolfito to play for Ellerston White. The outcome was that Ellerston took its first Gold Cup.

Too young and immature to realize his impact upon the game, but tremendously gifted in his ability on the field, Adolfito was recruited by the best organizations at the time, such as White Birch and Ellerston. He learned much, and became experienced at organizing the complex system of a modern polo setup. Most of what he learned was gleaned from Gonzalo Pieres, professional polo's master.

When La Espadaña's team broke up in 1991, Gonzalo Pieres—with Packer's unstinted support—created Ellerstina. Teams including Mariano Aguerre, Carlos Gracida, Gonzalo Pieres, Cambiaso and Castagnola proceeded to take Argentina's major championships between 1992 and 1998, including the Triple Crown in 1994. During this period, Adolfito played in the United States and England, before returning to Argentina to participate in the high-goal season at year's end.

Cambiaso now had improved his own polo string, which included one of the best horses he has owned. Colibrí, winner of the Lady Susan Townley Cup awarded to the Best Playing Pony in the Argentine Open, was given the prize in 1997 and 1998. Colibrí played his last game in the final match of the 2001 Argentine Open at age 19. He is now out to pasture at the estancia in Cañuelas. This small polo pony had fantastic speed over short distances and was extremely easy to play, which made him Adolfo's battle-horse, especially in the dying moments of the final chukker, fundamental moments to define the game's outcome.

In 1999 Adolfo joined forces with Tim Gannon, one of the few patrons that he considers a personal friend. Together, they took the first of three consecutive U.S. Open Championships. Gannon's Outback teams included his son Chris, his friend Phil Heatley, Jeff Blake, Lolo Castagnola, Santiago Chavanne, Brazilian Fábio Diniz, and Sunny Hale, the first woman to take the United States Open.

Side-by-side with his pal, Lolo Castagnola — who would become his brother-in-law as the result of Lolo's relationship with Camila Cambiaso—Adolfito decided in May 2000 to split with Pieres and start his own polo organization. It was a bitter parting of the ways, because contracts with sponsors had already been signed.

Adolfo Cambiaso was then contracted by Australian patron Rick Stowe to play for his Geebung with Gonzalo Pieres Jr. Instead, Adolfo decided to hire Bautista Heguy, which made Geebung the top team in England, taking the Queen's Cup at Guards Polo Club and Cowdray's Gold Cup.

Meanwhile, his personal life became settled with his marriage to top Argentine model Maria Vázquez, who had been his girlfriend for several years.

At this point in his career, Adolfo considered that he had reached professional maturity and decided to break his association with Gonzalo Pieres to start the La Dolfina team. The North American patron Tim Gannon was a great help at this difficult time, because he lent Adolfo his best ponies to allow him to get on with his new organization. For the Argentine season, Lolo and Adolfito joined forces with brothers Sebastián and Juan Ignacio Merlos to form a high-handicap combination. They took the Hurlingham Open, a feat they would achieve three years in a row.

In 2001 Cambiaso took his third consecutive U.S. Open Championship for Outback, this time with Chris Gannon, Fábio Diniz and Santiago Chavanne, another player raised in Cañuelas. In the final match they defeated Orchard Hill by 14 to 12.

That same year in England an outbreak of horse sickness forced the cancellation of the Queen's Cup because the Guards Club suspended all equine activities on its premises. Cambiaso had signed a contract—still in force—with Ali Albwardi, the Dubai's team patron. They took the Indian Empire Shield and Cowdray Park's Gold Cup. In Argentina, after taking Hurlingham's Open, they lost in extra chukker the Open at Palermo against Indios Chapaleufú I, in one of the most exciting final games in recent times.

In 2002, Adolfo started the year in Palm Beach under contract with a new sponsor, Erich Koch, owner of the Jedi team, playing in the U.S. Open. The following year this patron of Austrian origin assembled a group with Cambiaso and seven other professional players, with the sole purpose of playing practice games during the Palm Beach season on his excellent private polo grounds. That year in England his only win was in the Prince of Wales Trophy with Dubai. In Argentina he again won the Hurlingham Open, beating Indios Chapaleufú II in the decisive game. Against this team they would take their first Argentine Open at Palermo by 21–16 in one of the most controversial finals in the tournament's history, when both Eduardo and Ignacio Heguy were sent off.

In 2003 Adolfo played for Dubai with Lolo Castagnola, taking the Queen's Cup and losing in the semifinals of the Gold Cup against the eventual winners, Hildon. In Argentina, this was the year of La Aguada's Triple Crown, this team defeated La Dolfina in the finals of Tortugas and Palermo. After the 2003 season, the team split up. The Merlos brothers joined their younger sibling Agustín, while Adolfito and Lolo went through a transition year with Mexican Carlos Gracida and Santiago Chavanne. 2004 in England was Azzurra's year, when Dubai lost the Cowdray Park Gold Cup final in an excellent game.

The year 2005 was the last year with Jedi, which opened the door for Cambiaso to compete in the Palm Beach high-handicap season, allowing him to satisfy his yearning to return to the challenge of competition in America. On the European continent he had a glorious year with Dubai, winning the Queen's Cup conclusively against Black Bears. In the semifinals of the Gold Cup he suffered an accident against Emerging and broke his right wrist, but the team won the tournament. However, his injury kept him away from the fields until the middle of September. That same year he was contracted by Russ McCall to play the U.S.P.A. Gold Cup in Aiken but he participated in only one game because he had to return to Argentina, where his stepbrother, Salvador Socas, had suffered a very serious accident playing a practice game on his property in Cañuelas.

After Salvador's recovery, it took Adolfito two tournaments (Abiertos de Tortugas and Hurlingham) to find enough motivation to begin one of the best strings of victories in his career. His new team was a conjunction between his friend from the old Ellerstina team, Mariano Aguerre, and through Lolo Castagnola's efforts, another great friend, Lucas Monteverde. The new La Dolfina won the Argentine Open with an outstanding performance by Adolfo facing Ellerstina, the most potent combination at the time because his old team had already won the Tortugas and Hurlingham Open Championships and appeared to be unstoppable. The 2005 final found an Adolfo Cambiaso renewed by the favorable recuperation of Salvador Socas and the birth of his first son, Adolfo Jr. (his daughter Mia was born in 2003). Cambiaso's son was born during one of the matches in the Abierto, causing him to abandon play in the fifth chukker, with the scoreboard safely at 18 to 4, to witness his birth.

Once more Adolfo made one of his horses shine in the final game of the Argentine Open. This time it was the turn of Aiken Cura, a stallion that he bought from his half-brother Salvador Socas and that was one of the pillars in his string in the final stages of the year.

In the United States, together with Russ McCall, he began the year 2006 by winning the Ylvisaker Cup (22-goals) and the Hall of Fame Cup (26-goals) for New Bridge. Cambiaso returned to Argentina in March 2006 to participate in the new Polo Tour, a series of tournaments that he developed in partnership with Gonzalo Pieres. He then took the traditional Copa República Argentina and the Copa Belgrano playing for Italian patron Alfio Marchini's Loro Piana squad. His latest success in Argentina was in a new competition, the Abierto de Washington in Córdoba Province, near one of his polo pony breeding operations.

Bound by contract to Russ McCall's New Bridge team. Adolfo played the U.S.P.A. Gold Cup at Aiken, South Carolina, defeating Goose Creek 14–13 in sudden death overtime. Not surprisingly, Cambiaso scored the winning goal. Competing in Aiken prevented Adolfo from participating in the Tortugas Open, the first leg of Argentina's Triple Crown. Then he joined teammates Lucas Monteverde, Mariano Aguerre and Lolo Castagnola to take the Hurlingham Open, thus becoming odds-on favorites to win the Argentine Open at Palermo. This they accomplished, again in extra chukker. It was a bitter victory for Adolfito, because his wonderful stallion Aiken Cura — twice winner of the Lady Susan Townley Cup — was grievously injured.

In 2007 at Palm Beach, Cambiaso has accomplished an outstanding streak. Playing for New Bridge and Crab Orchard, he led New Bridge to victory in the Joe Barry Memorial and the Ylvisaker Cup. With Crab Orchard, he took the Iglehart Cup, the Gold Cup and the U.S. Open Championship. Adolfito's match record for the season was 22–2 and he also was the season's top goal-scorer. As befits a champion, he led Crab Orchard to victory by 15 to 14 goals, after trailing 1–5. Cambiaso scored the winning goal on a breakaway, with 17 seconds remaining in the game. A fitting end to an exceptional season.

As far as his personal character, Adolfo makes a cult of fidelity. Everywhere, he has a group of friends in whom he absolutely trusts and helps to progress with every step they take. That same self-trust is what allows him to define a play and take the whole team on his shoulders in those moments of pressure when most of the other players have trembles in their pulses. Adolfo Cambiaso has the power to exchange one play for another and make the surprise element an obsession. Ever since he participated in his first Argentine Open for Ellerstina, the world of polo has held him up as an idol and main protagonist. Adolfo has learned how to manage the pressure that causes many number ones in their sports to fall on their laurels by forgetting the basic principles that took them to the top. He is an inveterate lover of the good life among friends and family on his estancias in Argentina, where he finds the privacy he needs to return to polo on the field all that polo has given to him.

Note

1. Interview with Ernesto Trotz, May 2006.

Afterword

In the 150-odd years between Captain Edward Hartopp and Adolfo Cambiaso's heydays, a lot of ground has been covered, yet one can still link them with a few common characteristics: appreciation of the horse, an indispensable regard for the companionship in this most wonderful sport, and the basic understanding that polo is a team game, no matter how dominant one player may be.

Modern polo is a sterner examination of a player's skill, but it has robbed the game of some of its charm. Polo can still be, as it always was, exciting, interesting, and at times dangerous; these are engaging qualities. However, the subtlety implicit in John Watson's confection has departed. The goal from the field, which was the game's overwhelming motive, has been replaced by the score as the result of a foul, which is ruinous to exquisite play.

Some of us cringe when we watch 10-goal players tapping the ball at a walk. The search for an infraction to the rules is omnipresent in today's matches. It is true more goals are scored, but most often as the result of penalties. The open, free-flowing game of the recent past has been replaced by the stop-and-go, rotational tactics that not only became boring for the spectators but much harder on the ponies. When one sees two semifinal games in the U.S. Open finished with three-a-side teams, the only conclusion is that there is something wrong with our beloved pastime.

Perhaps polo has never been played better than today. Look at the number of 10-goal handicap players. Gaze at the pony strings. Consider the quality of grounds. Enjoy the view from magnificent stadiums. Marvel at the infrastructure created by many organizations. Read the polo calendar, replete with fixtures from early January to late December, from Australia to Canada, from Hawaii round the world to New Zealand. It is a time of unprecedented growth and a story of success.

And yet, not everything is right and good in the house that Joseph Sherer built. The foundations are still solid but there are concerns; some may even detect signs of rot. The main problem facing polo today is "arranging" games within the league system. Perversely, it usually happens at the highest level. It is easy to detect, quite the opposite to discipline the culprits. We may smile at old books with their insistence on moral values and sportsmanship, but, looking at the modern game dominated by money, some of us occasionally feel nostalgic for the time the game was played mostly for fun. But then, fun in sport is an obsolete word today. Maybe it will be soon rediscovered.

It is an indulgence commonly allowed to the elderly to complain that things are not what they were. However, even young people who believe their favorite team or a particular player are playing better than ever quite often recall old heroes and the successes of teams which they have never seen or barely remember. This happens because all polo supporters believe in a golden age. They are divided among those who think that the golden age is gone forever, those who believe that it is in the future, and those who are certain that the golden age is here and now. As a confirmed optimist, this editor is with those who believe that the best is yet to come.

There is something intrinsically joyful about the principles on which polo is based. Many of us think that anyone who does not find real pleasure in smacking a ball with a stick should have his head examined. Add to that being on horseback and you have the complete package. Polo's charming qualities will remain forever, because it was meant to make us happy. That will shine through everything that is written about it.

About the Contributors

The world of polo is an extreme passion with us. As writers, editors, players, administrators and collectors we are carrying on a continuous love affair with the most elegant of games. In playing we have experienced the challenge of competition, in collecting we relive the great moments of a glorious past, in watching we enjoy the sport's intrinsic beauty and as administrators we strive to give something back to the game.

The editor has been most fortunate to be able to draw upon the talent of some of the world's leading polo writers and journalists, who have created an articulate collection of essays dedicated to portraying outstanding personalities who truly made a difference.

Nigel à Brassard was born in London. After taking a degree in modern history he worked in investment banking in London, Sydney and New York.

Nigel plays polo at Cirencester Park and is patron of the Courtenay and Band of Gypsys polo teams and captain of the Buck's Club polo team. Apart from polo, Nigel enjoys real tennis, cricket and game shooting. He devised and promotes the first all-professional high-goal British polo tournament: the British Polo Championship.

He has written a number of articles about polo and is the author of *A Glorious Victory, A Glorious Defeat* (about the 1921 Westchester Cup matches), *A Posthumous Life: Keats in Rome*, and *Tommy Hitchcock: A Tribute.*

Nigel has an extensive collection of polo books and polo art. He is married to Adele, a charming American from New Orleans; they have two sons and a daughter.

Dennis J. Amato is a banker in New York who has written more than thirty articles related to various sports and sporting art. Among his publications are "Centennial Sentiments: A Hundred Years of Yearbooks" in the 1990 *U.S.P.A. Year Book*; the 1992 *Long Island Forum* monograph, "Long Island Polo: Past and Present"; and the 2004 *Polo Players Edition* magazine piece, "Poloist and Artist: Charles Cary Rumsey." Dennis has one of the world's largest collections of books, magazines, programs and ephemera related to the sport of polo and served as the club historian to the Meadow Brook Polo Club when that organization hosted the U.S. Open on Long Island in 1994 and 1995. He earned his A.B. *magna cum laude* from Boston College, did his M.B.A. studies at the University of Chicago Graduate School of Business and received his M.A. and Ph.D. from the Johns Hopkins University School of Advanced International Studies. He also studied in Rome and Bologna, Italy.

Sebastián Amaya is a third generation Argentine polo player. Both his grandfather and father took the National Handicap Tournament, twenty-three years apart. Sebastián is a four-goal player with wide international experience. He was born in Buenos Aires and received his education at Colegio San Agustín, from kindergarden to graduation from high school. Then he studied systems engineering at the National Technological University and graduated from Mariano Moreno Institute as a program analyst. He has traveled to Italy and the United States as a professional polo player. Amaya founded *PoloLine* in 2003; currently he is owner, webmaster and editor of this leading global provider of polo news, information, photographs and services. Its Website, *PoloLine.com*, is the number one electronic media in the polo community. His newest addition is the pioneer Polo Television via Internet, the latest advance in electronic communication. Sebastián combines his work at *PoloLine* with playing the game around the world; however, not as a professional—quite happily, he says.

Chris Ashton is the son of Phil Ashton, the youngest member of the Ashton brothers team which dominated Australian polo throughout the 1930s. A journalist by profession, Chris turned to polo in 1992 when Sinclair Hill commissioned him to write *Geebung: The Story of Australian Polo* for the Australian Polo Council. Combining polo and travel writing, he has since reported on polo from all over the world, including eyewitness accounts of primitive precursors of the modern game: hill-tribe polo in the Himalayas and "Chase-the-Goat" in northwest China. For some years he contributed to the U.S. *Polo* magazine and the U.S.P.A.'s annual *International Polo Review*. Now settled in Buenos Aires and married to an Argentine, Ana, neé Pisano, he reports for the British magazines *Polo Times* and *Polo Quarterly International* and for the Australian quarterly *Polo, Leisure & Lifestyle*. He recalls the high watermark of his own brief polo career as representing the Dark Blues in the 1968 Oxford-Cambridge game, marking H.R.H. Prince Charles, and scoring the winning goal in extra time.

Yolanda Carslaw grew up within a mile of Cowdray Park and first watched polo from her pram, when her father played in the 1970s. She and her sister followed the game throughout their teenage years as faithful fans of Tramontana.

After studying languages at the University of Bath, she spent several years in Switzerland and Austria as a ski instructor and guide before embarking on a career in journalism via a postgraduate course in London. She landed a job at the weekly magazine *Horse & Hound* chiefly on her polo credentials but within a year was news editor. She won awards in consecutive years, within the publishing giant IPC Media, for most promising new journalist and best news pages.

Yolanda turned freelance in 2005. She is chief polo correspondent for *Horse & Hound* and a regular contributor to *Country Life* and *Polo Times* on polo and other countryside pursuits. She hunts regularly, a pursuit which she took up only as an adult although her parents hunted and her great-grandfather had his own hounds in Gloucestershire (known as MOBH—my own bloody hounds). She also pursues her first passion—skiing—at every opportunity and plays polo for fun at Terry Hanlon's Ambersham Academy.

Roger Chatterton-Newman was born on St. Patrick's Day 1949, a scion of the Chattertons of Ballynamote House, County Cork, an old Anglo-Irish family who had settled in Ireland during the reign of Elizabeth I.

Ireland has influenced several of his books, notably *Brian Boru, King of Ireland* (1983), the first major study of the ninth and tenth century monarch; *Edward Bruce: A Medieval Tragedy* (1992); and the *Murtagh* trilogy of historical adventure stories for children, the first of which was highly commended by the Reading Association of Ireland Awards.

His other works include *A Hampshire Parish* (1976) and *Betwixt Petersfield and Midhurst*

(1992), which trace the history and legends of the corner of the Hampshire-Sussex border country in which he currently lives, and *Polo at Cowdray* (1990), the story of England's premier high-goal polo club.

He was archivist to Cowdray Park Polo Club from 1991 to 2000 and, since 1997, has been editor of *Polo Quarterly International*, the leading polo and lifestyle magazine. He also contributes to various historical journals and periodicals and is at the moment trying to find a publisher for his biography of Thomas Otway, the seventeenth century dramatist and poet.

Sarah Eakin graduated from London University with a degree in Russian and then became polo correspondent to London's *The Independent* newspaper at the age of 24. She went on to be correspondent to *The Daily Telegraph*. She was also a sports writer at Britain's *Southern Daily Echo* and editor-in-chief of *International Polo Review* and the polo editor of *Hurlingham Polo* magazine before, at the age of 30, she met her husband, professional polo player Gary Eakin, in Palm Beach, and married him six months later, moving to the United States. They bought a farm in Aiken, South Carolina, five years ago and have a five-year-old son, James. Sarah remains a freelance writer and public relations consultant.

Horace A. Laffaye was born in Buenos Aires into a polo-playing family. Following his education at Belgrano Day School, English High School and Universidad de Buenos Aires, he completed his surgical training at St. Vincent's Medical Center and the Lahey Clinic in Boston. Dr. Laffaye recently retired from a professorship at Yale University and a departmental chairmanship at Norwalk Hospital after 22 years' tenure. He played polo at El Rincón in Argentina and at Fairfield County Hunt Club in the U.S. His contributions to the game's literature include *El Polo Internacional Argentino*, *Diccionario de Polo*, and *The Polo Encyclopedia*, a standard reference book that a reviewer called "the most scholarly work published on the game." A contributor to polo annuals and magazines in America, Britain and Argentina, he wrote the articles on polo for the *Encyclopedia of World Sport*, the *International Encyclopedia of Women and Sport*, and biographical sketches of Thomas Hitchcock Jr. and Barney Oldfield in *Scribner Encyclopedia of American Lives: Sporting Figures.*

Susan Reeve (neé Collins) carries the best polo blood in her veins, because she is the legendary international player Tommy Pope's granddaughter. Sue was born in Durban, Natal, in 1949, and studied for an arts degree at Durban University, after which she traveled abroad for several years. She started her working life in 1972 as a journalist at the *Natal Daily News*. After having children, she switched to freelance work and then branched into sports administration and sports sponsorships.

Sue was managing editor of the United Cricket Board publications for 17 years and started with the South African Polo Association in 1982; currently she holds the position of executive director. As part of her duties, she has traveled with the representative national team, the Springboks, to international test matches. Sue never played the game but was exposed to it from a very early age through her grandfather.

She is married to Sir Anthony Reeve, a former diplomat and British High Commissioner to South Africa, and has two children, both of whom live in Durban. She and her husband divide their time between Gloucestershire in England and Durban.

Peter J. Rizzo is a graduate of George Washington University. Peter is the executive director of the United States Polo Association and serves as the executive vice president of the board of directors for the Museum of Polo and Hall of Fame in Florida. Peter belongs to a Long Island family with deep roots in the game of polo. His father Joe, uncles Dave and Vincent and cousin

Paul Rizzo were all horsemen and polo players of repute. Peter learned his polo at the legendary Meadow Brook Club. Following service in Southeast Asia with the air force, Rizzo returned to America to become a full-time professional player. In addition to playing more than 40 years of competitive polo, off a 6-goal handicap, Peter was the general manager of the Royal Palm Sports Club for 16 years, the editor and publisher of *Polo* magazine and *Polo Players' Edition* magazine and has served on numerous U.S.P.A. committees, including a stint as chairman of the U.S.P.A. Rules Committee. Peter is married to Gwen, who succeded him as *Polo Players' Edition*'s editor.

Bibliography

à Brassard, Nigel. *A Glorious Victory, A Glorious Defeat.* N.p: private printing, 2001.

Aldrich, Nelson W., Jr. *Tommy Hitchcock: An American Hero.* N.p: Fleet Street, 1984.

Allison, Benjamin R. *The Rockaway Hunting Club.* Brattleboro, VT: Alan S. Browne, 1952.

Amato, Dennis. "A Brief History of Scholastic, Collegiate and Women's Polo in America." New York: unpublished monograph, 1994.

American Sculpture Series. *Herbert Haseltine.* New York: Norton, 1948.

Archetti, Eduardo P. *Masculinities: Football, Polo and the Tango in Argentina.* Oxford: Berg, 1999.

_____. *El potrero, la pista y el ring.* Buenos Aires: Fondo de Cultura Económica, 2001.

Ashton, Chris. *Geebung: The History of Australian Polo.* Sidney: Hamilton Publishing, 1993.

Asociación Argentina de Polo. *Campeonato Argentino Abierto de Polo.* Buenos Aires: private printing, 1993.

_____. *Libro Annual.* Buenos Aires: 1924–1980.

Barry, Paul. *The Rise and Rise of Kerry Packer.* Morebank, NSW: Bantam Books, 1994.

Bent, Newell. *American Polo.* New York: Macmillan, 1929.

Biscotti, M.L. *Paul Brown.* Lanham: Derrydale Press, 2001.

Boadle, Isabel Cárdenas de. *La historia del Hurlingham Club.* Buenos Aires: Ripolli, 1988.

Brooks Brothers. *Polo.* New York: private printing, 1927.

Brown, J. Moray. *Polo.* London: Vinton, 1895.

Brown, Paul. *Ups and Downs.* New York: Scribners, 1936.

Burke's Landed Gentry of Ireland. London: Burke's Peerage Ltd., 1958.

Burke's Peerage and Baronetage. Edited by Charles Mosley. 106th ed. Crans, Switzerland: Burke's Peerage Ltd., 1999.

Calvert, Blair. *Cecil Smith: Mr. Polo.* Midland, Texas: Prentis Publishing, 1990.

Ceballos, Francisco. *El polo en la Argentina.* Buenos Aires: Dirección General de Remonta, 1968.

Chaine, Federico. *Los Heguy.* Buenos Aires: Imprenta de los Buenos Ayres, 2001.

Christophersen, Pedro F. *Teoría y práctica del juego de polo.* Buenos Aires: A.A. de Polo, 1948.

Clayton, Michael. *Prince Charles, Horseman.* London: Stanley Paul Ltd., 1987.

Coaten, A.W., ed. *International Polo.* London: S. B. Vaughn, 1912.

Cumming, E.D., ed. *Squire Osbaldeston: His Autobiography.* London: John Lane, 1926.

Dale, T.F. *Polo at Home and Abroad.* London: London & Counties Press Assoc., 1915.

Devereux, W. B., Jr. *Position and Team Play in Polo.* New York: Brooks Bros., 1914 [*sic*] [1924].

Dorling, T. *The Hurlingham Club.* London: private printing, 1953.

Dunsany, Lord. *My Ireland.* London: Jarrolds, 1937.

Fernández-Gómez, Emilio Manuel. *Argentina: Gesta Británica.* Buenos Aires: Literature of Latin America, 1998.

Fingall, Lady Elizabeth. *Seventy Years Young: Memoirs of Elizabeth, Countess of Fingall.* London: Collins, 1937.

Forbes, W. Cameron. *As to Polo.* N.p: Manila Polo Club, 1923.

Gannon, Jack. *Before the Colours Fade.* London: J.A. Allen, 1976.

Garrahan, María Lía, and Luis Garrahan, eds. *Polo: Abierto Argentino de Palermo.* Buenos Aires: Garrahan Editores, [2005?].

Grace, Peter. *Polo.* New York: Howell, 1991.

Griswold, F. Gray. *The International Polo Cup.* New York: Dutton, 1928.

Halpin, Warren T. *Hoofbeats.* Philadelphia: Lippincott, 1938.

Harrington, Isabel H. de. *Un criollo irlandés.* Buenos Aires: private printing, 1976.

Hatch, Alden, and Foxhall Keene. *Full Tilt.* New York: Derrydale Press, 1938.

Heguy, Alberto Pedro, and Daniel Martínes Páez. *Biomecánica, estrategia, preparación competitiva y lesiones del polo de alto handicap argentino.* Buenos Aires: Fundación de Polo y Entrenamiento Integral, 1994.

Hennessy, Elizabeth. *A History of the Roehampton Club, 1901–2001.* N.p.: private printing, 2001.

Herbert, F.A. "Polo." In *The Encyclopædia of Sport.* Edited by the Earl of Suffolk and F.G. Aflalo. New York: Putnam, 1897.

Holder, Arthur L., ed. *Activities of the British Community in Argentina during the Great War, 1914–1918.* Buenos Aires: *Buenos Aires Herald,* 1920.

Hoyt, Edwin. *The Whitneys: An Informal Portrait, 1635–1975.* New York: Weybright & Talley, 1976.

Indoor Polo Association of the United States of America. *Official Manuals, 1927–1952/1953.* New York: Quigley Publishing, 1927–1952.

James, Lionel. *The History of King Edward's Horse.* London: Sifton, Praed, 1921.

Kelly, Robert F. *The Year Book of the Horse, 1934.* New York: Dodd, Mead, 1935.

Knox, Northrup R. *To B.A. and Back ... Again.* Buffalo: private printing, 1967.

_____. *To B.A. and Back, Once More.* N.p.: private printing, [1970?].

Knox, Seymour H., Jr. *Polo Tales and Other Tales.* N.p: private printing, 1972.

_____. *To B.A. and Back.* Buffalo: private printing, 1933.

Laffaye, Horace A. "Polo." In *Encyclopedia of World Sport.* Edited by David Levinson and Karen Christensen. Santa Barbara and Oxford: ABC-Clio, 1996.

_____. "Polo." In *International Encyclopedia of Women and Sport.* Edited by Karen Christensen, Allen Guttmann and Gertrud Pfister. New York: Macmillan, 2001.

_____. *The Polo Encyclopedia.* Jefferson, NC and London: McFarland & Co., 2004.

_____. *El polo internacional argentino.* Buenos Aires: Edición del Autor, 1988.

_____. "Thomas Hitchcock Jr." In *Scribner Encyclopedia of American Lives: Sporting Figures.* Edited by Arnold Markoe. New York: Charles Scribner's Sons, 2002.

Linfoot, William R. *Linfoot on Polo.* Gaithersburg, MD: Polo Publishers, Inc., 1978.

Little, K.M. *Polo in New Zealand.* Wellington: Whitcomb & Tombs, 1956.

Lorenzo, Ricardo. *Medio siglo de automovilismo argentino.* Buenos Aires: Editorial Atlántida, 1953.

Macnie, J. *Work and Play in the Argentine.* London: T. Werhner, [1924?].

Mallon, Bill. *The 1900 Olympic Games.* Jefferson, NC, and London: McFarland & Co., 1998.

_____, and Ian Buchanan. *The 1908 Olympic Games.* Jefferson, NC, and London: McFarland & Co., 2000.

_____, and Anthony T. Bijkerk. *The 1920 Olympic Games.* Jefferson, NC, and London: McFarland & Co., 2003.

Malone, Dumas, ed. *Dictionary of American Biography.* New York: Charles Scribner's Sons, 1933.

Marco [Lord Mountbatten of Burma]. *An Introduction to Polo.* London: Country Life, 1931.

_____. *An Introduction to Umpiring.* London: R.N.P.A., 1934.

McKenzie, Donald C., and John R. McKenzie. *Polo in South Africa.* Dargle: private printing, 1999.

Milburn, Frank. *Polo: The Emperor of Games.* New York: Alfred A. Knopf, 1994.

Miller, E.D. *Fifty Years of Sport.* New York: Dutton, [1925?].

_____. *Modern Polo.* London: Hurst and Blacklett, 1911.

Miskin, Nigel. *History of Hurlingham.* N.p: private printing, 2000.

Olivera, Eduardo A. *Orígenes de los deportes británicos en el Río de la Plata.* Buenos Aires: Talleres Gráficos Argentinos L.J. Rosso, 1932.

Parga, Alfredo. *Historia deportiva del automovilismo argentino.* Buenos Aires: La Nación, 1995.

Patten, William. *The Book of Sport.* New York: J. F. Taylor & Co., 1901.

Polo Association of America. *Year Book.* New York: private printings, 1890–1923.

Pondé, Eduardo Bautista. *La Argentina Perdedora.* Buenos Aires: Editorial Legasa, 1995.

Rees, Tony. *The Galloping Game.* Cochrane: Western Heritage, 2000.

Rodríguez Egaña, Carlos. *Manual de Polo.* Buenos Aires: Bernard Buttafoco, 1923.

Rossmore, Lord. *Things I Can Tell.* London: Eveleigh Nash, 1937.

Russell-Stoneham, Dereck, and Roger Chatterton-Newman. *Polo at Cowdray.* London: Polo Information Bureau, 1992.

Sáenz Quesada, María. *Estancias: The Great Houses and Ranches of Argentina.* New York: Abbeville Press, 1992.

Sawaya, Jorge. *Guía Argentina de Polo.* Buenos Aires: Open Guide, 1993.

Secretaría de Turismo de la Argentina. *Argentina: Polo and Golf.* Buenos Aires: Editorial Delfos, 1994.

Serval, Antoine, ed. *International Polo Guide.* Paris: International Polo Guide SRL, 2006.

Sessa, Aldo. *Polo Argentino.* Buenos Aires: Sessa Editores, 2001.

Shaw, Elvira Ocampo de. *Hurlingham.* Buenos Aires: Colombo, 1958.

Shinitzki, Ami, and Don Follmer. *The Endless Chukker.* Gaithersburgh, MD: Polo, 1978.

Smith, Harry Worcester. *Life and Sport in Aiken.* New York: Derrydale Press, 1935.
Spencer, Herbert. *A Century of Polo.* N.p: World Polo, 1994.
_____. *Chukka: Polo Around the World.* New York: Drake, 1971.
The Sportsman. *Polo and Coaching.* London: Sports and Sportsmen, [1923?].
St. Quintin, T.A. *Chances of Sports of Sorts.* London: William Blackwood, 1912.
Stephens, Edward M. *My Uncle John: Edward Stephens's Life of J.M. Synge.* Edited by Andrew Carpenter. London: Oxford University Press, 1974.
Stock, Alphons. *International Sport: Polo.* London: Universal Bridge of Trade, [1930?].
Tamplin, J.M.A, and P.E. Abbott. *British Gallantry Awards.* Garden City, N.Y.: Doubleday, 1972.
United States Polo Association: *Year Book.* New York: private printings, 1924–2006.
United States Women's Polo Association: *Yearbook.* With annotations for 1941 by Helen Park Edwards. N.p.: private printings, 1937–1940.
Watson, J.N.P. *Hanut, Prince of Polo Players.* London: The Sportsman's Press, 1995.
_____. *The World of Polo.* Topsfield: Salem, 1986.
Weir, Robert, and J. Moray Brown. *Riding: Polo.* London: Longmans, 1891.
White, Wesley J. *Guide for Polo Umpires.* New York: U.S.P.A., 1929.
Wilson, Hamish. *Polo in New Zealand, 1956–1976.* Auckland: Viking, 1976.
Wingfield, Mary Ann. *Sport and the Artist.* Woodbridge: Antique Collectors, 1988.
Wrensch, Frank A. *Horses in Sport.* New York: William Morrow and Co., 1937.
Ziegler, Philip. *Mountbatten: The Official Biography.* London: Collins, 1985.

Newspapers and Periodicals

Almanach de Gotha. London: Boydell & Brewer, 1999.
Baily's. London. 1869–1915.
Buenos Aires Herald. Buenos Aires, 1878–2006.
Carlow Sentinel. 24 August 1872 and 14 November 1908.
Centauros. Buenos Aires. 1955–1983.
Debrett's Peerage. London. 1910–1994.
Detroit News. Detroit. 1930–1933.
The Field. London. 1869.
El Golfer Argentino. Buenos Aires. 1930–1958.
El Gráfico. Buenos Aires. 1919–2006.
Guards Polo Club Year Book. Windsor. 1998–2005.
Horse and Horseman. New York. 1936–1939.
Morning Post. London. 24 July 1876
La Nación. Buenos Aires. 1924–2006.
New York Times. New York. 1903–1949.
Polo. New York.1927–1936.
Polo. Gaithersburg, MD, and Wellington, Florida. 1972–1996.
Polo Annual for 1914. London: Field & Queen (Horace Cox) Ltd, 1914.
Polo Monthly. London. 1910–1939.
Polo Players Diary for 1910. London: S. B. Vaughn, 1910.
Polo Players' Edition. Wellington, Florida. 1997–2006.
Polo Quarterly International. London. 1992–2006.
Polo Times. North Leigh, Oxfordshire. 1993–2006.
Polo y Campo. Buenos Aires. 1933–1939.
Polo y Equitación. Buenos Aires. 1924–1932.
Racing Through History. Caulfield, Victoria, Australian Racing Museum. Spring 2000.
River Plate Sport and Pastime. Buenos Aires. 1892–1902.
Sidelines. Wellington, Florida. 1981–2006.
Southern Weekly News. 2 August 1947.
Spalding's Polo Guides, 1921 and 1923. New York: American Sports Publishing Co.
Sports Illustrated. Various editions.
The Sportsman. Various editions, 1927–1936.
The Standard. Various editions, 1874–1948.
Who Was Who in America. Vol 1, *1897–1942.* Chicago: Marquis Who's Who, Inc., 1981 (8th Printing).

Index

Profiled names comprising individual chapters are noted in **bold**. Numbers in ***bold italics*** indicate pages with illustrations. Color illustrations between pages 104 and 105 are indicated ***c1*** to ***c8***.